A HISTORY OF BISEXUALITY

IMPROPER ADVANCES: RAPE AND HETEROSEXUAL
CONFLICT IN ONTARIO, 1880–1929
by Karen Dubinsky

A PRESCRIPTION FOR MURDER: THE VICTORIAN
SERIAL KILLINGS OF THOMAS NEILL CREAM
by Angus McLaren

THE LANGUAGE OF SEX: FIVE VOICES FROM NORTH-
ERN FRANCE AROUND 1200
by John W. Baldwin

CROSSING OVER THE LINE: LEGISLATING MORALITY
AND THE MANN ACT
by David J. Langum

SEXUAL NATURE / SEXUAL CULTURE
edited by Paul R. Abramson and Steven D. Pinkerton

LOVE BETWEEN WOMEN: EARLY CHRISTIAN
RESPONSES TO FEMALE HOMOEROTICISM
by Bernadette J. Brooten

THE TRIALS OF MASCULINITY:
POLICING SEXUAL BOUNDARIES, 1870–1930
by Angus McLaren

THE INVENTION OF SODOMY IN CHRISTIAN THEOLOGY
by Mark D. Jordan

SITES OF DESIRE / ECONOMIES OF PLEASURE:
SEXUALITIES IN ASIA AND THE PACIFIC
edited by Lenore Manderson and Margaret Jolly

SEX AND THE GENDER REVOLUTION, VOLUME 1:
HETEROSEXUALITY AND THE THIRD GENDER IN
ENLIGHTENMENT LONDON
by Randolph Trumbach

TAKE THE YOUNG STRANGER BY THE HAND: SAME-SEX
RELATIONS AND THE YMCA
by John Donald Gustav-Wrathall

CITY OF SISTERLY AND BROTHERLY LOVES: LESBIAN
AND GAY PHILADELPHIA, 1945–1972
by Marc Stein

THE POLITICS OF GAY RIGHTS
edited by Craig A. Rimmerman, Kenneth D. Wald,
and Clyde Wilcox

OTTO WEININGER: GENDER, SEXUALITY, AND SELF
IN IMPERIAL VIENNA
by Chandak Sengoopta

SAPPHO IN EARLY MODERN ENGLAND: THE HISTORY
OF A FEMALE SAME-SEX LITERARY EROTICS,
1550–1714
by Harriette Andreadis

THE CHICAGO SERIES ON SEXUALITY,
HISTORY, AND SOCIETY

EDITED BY JOHN C. FOUT

A HISTORY OF BISEXUALITY

STEVEN ANGELIDES

THE UNIVERSITY OF CHICAGO PRESS
CHICAGO AND LONDON

STEVEN ANGELIDES is an Australian Research Council postdoctoral fellow at the Australian National University and an honorary fellow at the Australian Centre, University of Melbourne.

The University of Chicago Press, Chicago 60637
The University of Chicago Press, Ltd., London
© 2001 by The University of Chicago
All rights reserved. Published 2001
Printed in the United States of America
10 09 08 07 06 05 04 03 02 01   1 2 3 4 5

ISBN: 0-226-02089-4 (cloth)
ISBN: 0-226-02090-8 (paper)

Library of Congress Cataloging-in-Publication Data
Angelides, Steven.
  A history of bisexuality / Steven Angelides.
    p. cm. — (The Chicago series on sexuality, history, and society)
  Includes bibliographical references and index.
  ISBN 0-226-02089-4 (cloth : alk. paper) —
  ISBN 0-226-02090-8 (pbk. : alk. paper)
    1. Bisexuality. 2. Homosexuality. 3. Heterosexuality. I. Title. II. Series.
  HQ74.A54 2001
  306.76'5—dc21

00-013141

♾ The paper used in this publication meets the minimum requirements of the American National Standard for Information Sciences—Permanence of Paper for Printed Library Materials, ANSI Z39.48-1992.

FOR ELLA AND CRAIG

CONTENTS

		Acknowledgments	ix
	1	Introducing Bisexuality	1
PART [1] CONSTRUCTING SEXUAL IDENTITY	2	Science and the Invention of (Bi)Sexuality	23
	3	"The Unsolved Figure in the Carpet"	49
	4	The Pink Threat	71
PART [2] DECONSTRUCTING SEXUAL IDENTITY	5	The Repressed Returns	107
	6	Sexuality and Subjection	132
	7	The Queer Intervention	162
	8	Beyond Sexuality	190
		Notes	209
		Bibliography	259
		Index	277

ACKNOWLEDGMENTS

I would like to thank the Department of History at the University of Melbourne, the place where this study began as a doctoral dissertation, as well as the university's Faculty of Arts and School of Graduate Studies. The transition from dissertation to book was aided by a postdoctoral fellowship in the Adelaide Research Centre for Humanities and Social Sciences at the University of Adelaide, a traveling fellowship from the Australian Academy of the Humanities, an honorary associateship in the University of Melbourne's Australian Centre, and the Department of History at the Australian National University. I would also like to thank Henry Abelove, Craig Bird, Marion Campbell, Kate Constable, Joy Damousi, John Fout, Sarah Griggs, Sally Hussey, Wei Leng Kwok, Vera Mackie, Doug Mitchell, Robert Reynolds, and Christina Twomey. Finally, I am extremely grateful to Marion Campbell for her suggestion of the book's eventual title. Although it might seem an obvious choice, I have to say that in my deluded attempts to invent a title that I hoped would capture the book's argument and methodology, *A History of Bisexuality* is one that never once occurred to me. I *am* glad it occurred to Marion.

INTRODUCING BISEXUALITY

In any case bisexuality merges imperceptibly into simple inversion.
—Havelock Ellis 1901

BISEXUALITY—a state that has no existence beyond the word itself—is an out-and-out fraud, involuntarily maintained by some naive homosexuals, and voluntarily perpetrated by some who are not so naive.
—Edmund Bergler 1956

It is my opinion that while the word *bisexual* may have its uses as an adjective . . . it is not only useless but mendacious when used as a noun.
—John Malone 1980

I'm not sure that because there are people who identify as bisexual there is a bisexual identity.
—Eve Kosofsky Sedgwick 1991

Doubts about the veracity of bisexuality as an identity are not new. Variously characterized within dominant discourses of sexuality as, among other things, a form of infantilism or immaturity, a transitional phase, a self-delusion or state of confusion, a personal and political cop-out, a panacea, a superficial fashion trend, a marketing tool, even a lie and a catachresis, the category of bisexuality for over a century has been persistently refused the title of legitimate sexual identity.[1] Yet, as is all too familiar to scholars of sexuality, the same cannot be said with regard to homosexuality. Since its invention as a peculiar human species in late-nineteenth-century scientific discourse, the homosexual as a modern identity has been the object of a rigorous, frenetic, indeed paranoid, discursive essentialization. Far from having doubt cast incessantly upon its veritable existence, the homosexual has been mapped, measured, and monitored in what can only be described as an interminable and insane reiteration of the supposed 'essence' and 'truth' of its being. On a much smaller scale, but with as much scientific zeal, has been the cataloging of myriad other psychosexual 'deviations'. From the perverts invented by nineteenth-century sexology to the seemingly endless list of twentieth-century paraphiliacs, Western science has placed sexuality in a privileged relation to truth with regard to human subjectivity.[2] As Foucault put it: "Between each of us and our sex, the West has placed a never-ending demand for truth: it is up to us to extract the truth of sex, since this truth is beyond its grasp; it is up to sex to tell us our truth, since sex is what holds it in darkness."[3]

Curiously, however, the category of bisexuality seems to have been spared the rigors of this "never-ending demand for truth." Bisexuality continues, in fact, to represent a blind spot in sex research.[4] This apparent oversight by our all-consuming regime of sexuality is particularly puzzling in view not only of the rather long history of research suggestive of the prevalence of bisexual practices in most human cultures, but also of the emergence, in many Western countries within the last two decades, of burgeoning and highly politicized bisexual movements. On the surface this may come as no surprise, given the common association of bisexuality with (self) deception and unreality. Perhaps bisexuality is *unnatural*, without 'essence' after all? Is it the antithesis of truth, an *untruth*? Or is it an imaginary or nonexistent state? And what would it mean to answer in the affirmative to these questions: Would bisexuality therefore be without history, even outside of history? And might this explain why so little ink has been spilled establishing its veracity, historicizing its (lack of) meaning? Opting for this explanatory path is for me, however, wholly unsatisfactory. For one thing, if so little critical attention has been accorded to bisexuality, how can anyone so confidently assume anything about its meaning, let alone arbitrate its 'truthful' existence?

Marjorie Garber's *Vice Versa: Bisexuality and the Eroticism of Everyday Life* is one of the first comprehensive studies of bisexuality to engage some of these questions.[5] In an encyclopedic account of eroticism within a wide range of cultural and literary texts, Garber sets out not just to put bisexuality on the sexual map, but to challenge common assumptions that have long structured its meaning. Her concern is not with theorizing or politicizing bisexuality as the latest identity "now finding its place in the sun" (65–66). Instead, she seeks to inquire into what bisexuality can teach us about sexuality in general. The lesson, according to *Vice Versa*, is that the 'nature' of sexuality cannot be located in the fixed identities of *gay* and *straight*. It is, rather, mobile and mutable: The "nature of sexuality . . . is fluid not fixed, a narrative that changes over time rather than a fixed identity, however complex. The erotic discovery of bisexuality is the fact that it reveals sexuality to be a process of growth, transformation, and surprise, not a stable and knowable state of being" (66).[6] Garber urges us to dispense with the hetero/homosexual opposition as our starting point for understanding sexuality. Why not begin just with the category of sexuality? she asks. Proposing a framework based on the Möbius model, Garber visualizes sexuality in terms of a three-dimensional figure. This kind of "topological space" makes redundant any concept of sexuality as either/or, as "two-versus-one" (30). No longer radically distinct, the categories of heterosexuality and homosexuality flow in and through one another.

Garber goes even further to suggest that, far from being a third sexual identity, bisexuality is a sexuality that "puts into question the very concept of sexual identity in the first place" (15).[7] The logic behind this idea, as I mentioned above, is that she identifies the *nature* of sexuality to be a kind of unpredictable fluidity, uncontainable within the fixity of hetero/homosexuality. However, this unpredictable fluidity, this 'sexuality', is for Garber none other than bisexuality. That is, in constructing her Möbius model, she actually conflates sexuality with bisexuality, and substitutes the notion of 'sexual identity' with that of bisexual eroticism.[8] The concepts of heterosexuality and homosexuality are thus subsumed by a bisexuality she argues "is neither the 'inside' nor the 'outside' but rather that which *creates* both" (526; my emphasis).

Anything but immature, peripatetic, erroneous, illusory, unnatural, bisexuality in this scenario *is* human sexuality itself. By extension, then, bisexuality is coterminous with human 'nature', with 'truth' itself. The effect of Garber's intervention is thus not so much a disruption of what Foucault would call the *scientia sexualis*—the "procedures for telling the truth of sex"[9]—although she certainly wants to deconstruct 'truth' in the form of fixed and oppositional sexual identities. Rather, and working within this regime of truth, Garber effectively inverts the terms of the *scientia sexualis*: the untruth becomes the sole truth. Such a move of reversal is, of course, not without its uses. Like the first part of any deconstructive movement, it is essential to effect a strategic reversal of any binary opposition in question. It is equally important simultaneously to displace the negative term of this opposition from its position of dependency on the positive and to situate the former as the latter's very condition of possibility.[10] This much Garber has done, and the concept of 'sexual identity', and thus the binarism of hetero/homosexuality, may appear on the surface to be momentarily disrupted. Yet it is this very move that leads her to claim bisexuality's status as inherently deconstructive. Bisexuality, proclaims Garber, is but a "sexuality that threatens and challenges the easy binarities of straight and gay" (65). In order to make this claim, however, Garber remains reliant upon the very opposition which underpins that of hetero/homosexuality: (sexual) identity versus (fluid) difference. The only difference is that the hierarchical relationship between the two terms is reversed, *difference* (which in Garber's model is fluid bisexuality) now elevated at the expense of *identity* (hetero/homosexuality). To leave the deconstructive project at this point is a little frustrating, however. In reifying bisexuality *as a sexuality*, Garber has given it a positive ontological or truth content, even if this content is viewed as fluid, uncertain, and in constant flux. Merely inverting bisexuality's status within conventional figurations of sexual identity, Garber redeploys heteronormative logic and thus remains squarely within the terms of the hetero/homosexual opposition she seeks to deconstruct.

At this point it would appear that Garber's reinvocation of an essentializing oppositional logic comes dangerously close to fulfilling the prophesy of which Eve Sedgwick lamented in an internet discussion list only months before the publication of *Vice Versa*. In just such a discussion of bisexuality's politicodeconstructive potential, Sedgwick wrote:

> There are ways in which the political concept of 'bisexuality' seems to offer a *consolidation and completion* of an understanding of sexuality that can be described adquately [sic], for everybody, in terms of gender-of-object-choice . . . as though, once you've added "goes for both same *and* opposite sex" to "goes for same sex" and "goes for opposite sex," you have now covered the entire ground and collected the whole set.[11]

These comments of Sedgwick's rehearse, indeed intensify, the seemingly irresolvable debate as to whether the concept or identity of bisexuality reinforces or ruptures our binary epistemology of sexuality. Both sides of the political divide have received sufficient airing since the mid-1980s.[12] And Sedgwick is certainly not alone with her characterization of what I call the 'impotence' model of bisexuality. Donald Hall, coeditor of a recent collection of essays, *RePresenting Bisexualities*, agrees: "I . . . especially dislike the term 'bisexual'," he says, "for it inescapably encodes binarism" (11). On the basis of this kind of logic Elisabeth Däumer urges us to resist constructing bisexuality as another sexual identity. For, "rather than broadening the spectrum of available sexual identifications," she too argues that it merely "holds in place a binary framework of two basic and diametrically opposed sexual orientations."[13]

On the other hand, however, these claims of bisexuality's political impotence compete with a chorus of theorists and activists who have been arguing that the politicized category of bisexuality represents a fundamental challenge to the gendered structure of hetero/homosexuality. Bisexual theorist Amanda Udis-Kessler, for instance, argues not only that bisexuals "unintentionally" threaten the "meaning systems by which lesbians, gay men and heterosexuals live," but that bisexuality as a category "inevitably" poses "crises of meaning" for our binary epistemology of sexuality.[14] Like Garber, Udis-Kessler figures bisexuality as inherently deconstructive, subversive, revolutionary, and undermining of the binarized logic and structure of gender and (mono)sexuality.[15]

I have never been comfortable with the 'impotence' model of bisexuality and its rather tidy political prognosis. Nor am I satisfied with the opposing, and rather utopic, position that bisexuality is somehow inherently subversive.[16] Aside from the seemingly obvious fact that within Western culture in general the "easy binarities" of which Garber speaks appear anything but under threat, it strikes me as equally premature to discard the category of bisexuality to the scrapheap of theoreticopolitical sterility; especially in view of its long history of critical neglect within discourses of sexuality. In my view, framing the analysis of bisexuality in binary terms represents a false antithesis. It serves to mystify rather than elucidate the complexity of bisexuality's discursive and political intervention in the 1990s and beyond, just as it misrecognizes the ambiguous and contradictory epistemological history of bisexuality itself. So instead of remaining within the terms of this existing political dispute, I would like in this book to refuse its dichotomous framing and subject it to critical examination *by turning to this epistemological history*. Just as our political and theoretical analyses of homosexuality required the historicization of the very concept of *homosexuality*, so too would I suggest that any political and theoretical analysis of bisexuality is impoverished (if not useless) without an adequate account of its historical construction.[17] Yet a sustained and contextualized account of the history of sexuality and bisexuality's place in it is absent not just within the debate, but within our entire archive of historical knowledge.

Bisexual theorist Michael du Plessis has argued recently that in the current climate of sexual theory and politics it is crucial to examine *how* notions of bisexuality and bisexual identity have "come to be unthought, made invisible, trivial, insubstantial, irrelevant."[18] This imperative is the starting point for this book. *A History of Bisexuality* explores the complex conjunction of issues framing the discursive relationships between bisexuality and modern sexual identity, between bisexuality and figurations of human 'nature', and between bisexuality and the construction of sexual 'truth'. The question of how bisexuality and bisexual identity have been erased is, I suggest, inextricably bound up with the broader history of bisexuality as an epistemological category. I will analyze how bisexuality as an epistemological category has functioned both to foreclose the articulation of a bisexual identity and to reproduce the hetero/homosexual opposition.

WRITING A QUEER HISTORY OF (BI)SEXUALITY

As indicated by the subtitle, the project of writing a *queer history of (bi)sexuality* draws heavily on the interlocking fields of gay and lesbian history and queer theory. So what might this form of history writing look like? In order to expound the methodological contours of this approach, it might first be useful to examine how bisexuality has been figured until now within these interlocking disciplinary formations.

Throughout the last two decades or so, the field of gay and lesbian history has expanded rapidly. Histories of sexuality—of homosexuality, and increasingly of heterosexuality—have been and continue to be published at an astonishing rate. Yet, for the most part, bisexuality scarcely figures within this burgeoning historiographical field. At first glance it would appear, then, that bisexuality has said very little, and has very little to say, to this historical archive. However, I would argue that one of the primary reasons for bisexuality's apparent insignificance might be the fact that the defining mark of gay and lesbian history writing has been a methodological reliance on an identity paradigm. Central to this paradigm has been a distinction between sexual behavior and sexual identity. Constructionist historians, cautious of conflating homosexuality and homosexual identity, have found it useful to examine the history of sexuality through this distinction. As a guiding methodology, this has been effective, as Jeffrey Weeks has observed, as a way of distinguishing "between homosexual behaviour, which is universal, and a homosexual identity, which is historically specific."[19]

For reading bisexuality, however, this approach introduces conceptual problems of its own. While homosexual identity is not universalized, a homosexual act is. The problem of identity is thus only deferred and displaced. Neither an act nor a palpable cultural identity—at least until the late 1960s in the case of the latter—bisexuality merely vanishes into the categories of hetero- or homosexuality. The identity paradigm is thereby reified and bisexuality is completely erased from the historical record. Chris Cagle describes this approach as "monosexual gay historiography."[20] Where bisexuality does rate a mention, it is almost always rendered an epistemological and incidental by-product, aftereffect, or definitional outcome of the opposition of hetero/homosexuality. It is therefore not seen as in any way significant to the diachronic construction of this opposition. For instance, as historian George Chauncey has noted in his most recent work, "Even the third category of 'bisexuality' depends for its meaning on its intermediate position on the axis *defined* by those two poles."[21] Erwin Haeberle, in his introduction to the recent anthology *Bisexualities*, reaches a similar but more historically inflected conclusion: the modern concept of bisexuality "did not arise," indeed, *"could not come into existence,"* he argues, until after "the simple opposition" of homo/heterosexuality had been invented.[22]

Within the field of queer theory bisexuality is also figured as rather incidental to the hetero/homosexual structure, this time in terms of synchronic deconstructive analysis. Queer theorists such as Eve Sedgwick, Diana Fuss, and Lee Edelman, among others, have produced many useful studies that serve to work the hetero/homosexual opposition, as Fuss puts it, to the "point of critical exhaustion."[23] Powered by a desire to expose the relational construction of identity, one would expect an analysis of bisexuality —hovering as the category does somewhere around the two poles of hetero/homosexuality—to form a part of this rigorous deconstruction. Yet in spite of occupying an epistemic position *within* this very opposition, the category of bisexuality has been curiously marginalized and erased from the deconstructive field of queer theory. In many ways this appears to mirror the marginalization of bisexuality within gay and lesbian history. On the surface, it seems that one of the reasons for this is the assumption that, as Lee Edelman notes, the hetero/homo binarism is "more effectively reinforced than disrupted by the 'third term' of bisexuality."[24] However, it would seem that this idea functions as a corollary of the historical assumption that bisexuality is a by-product or epistemic aftereffect of homo/heterosexuality. Just as bisexuality is seen to be of little interest or use to the historicizing project, within queer theory the implication of Edelman's claim is that bisexuality is seen to offer little critical leverage in deconstructions of the hetero/homo polarity. But I suggest that there is more structuring this assumption than appears at first sight. It seems to me that the marginalization and erasure of bisexuality within queer theory is not just a theoretical question, just as bisexuality's marginalization and erasure within gay and lesbian history is not just a historical question. These particular figurations of bisexuality are, importantly, symptomatic of the relationship of gay and lesbian history to queer theory. And, as I will demonstrate in this book, such figurations occlude much more than they illuminate.

The queer intervention in critical theory and cultural studies has certainly held out enormous promise in its deconstructive critique of identitarian frameworks. With its emphasis on demystifying the shifting and relational construction of identity categories, and of exposing the rhetorical and ideological functions that these categories serve, queer theory seems aptly situated to strengthen and revitalize the historicizing project of gay/lesbian history. Yet, as Lisa Duggan has suggested, these queer "critiques, applied to lesbian and gay history texts, might produce a fascinating discussion—but so far, they have not." Outlining the "strained relations" between the fields of queer theory and gay/lesbian history, Duggan goes on to argue that the former has too often failed to acknowledge its debt to the latter; while the latter "have largely ignored the critical implications of queer theory for their scholarly practice."[25] The editors of *Radical History Review*'s queer issue mention something similar, detecting a "sense" that the respective methods of gay/lesbian history and queer theory are thought to "exist in sometimes uncomfortable tension." This appears to reflect the fact that "there has been remarkably little dialogue between these two presumably related projects."[26] This strikes me as rather odd. Despite queer theory's overarching desire to deconstruct Identity in all of its forms, both queer theorists and gay and lesbian constructionist historians are indeed united in the quest to denaturalize categories of sexual identity in order to reveal the contingency, the historicity, and the political processes of their production. In spite of this obvious affinity, however, fruitful dialogue between the two fields has not been forthcoming.

Expanding on Duggan's analysis, then, I would suggest that what in part informs the relationship between the two fields is an implicit and unproductive distinction between social constructionism and deconstruction; this, despite the fact that it is history or, more specifically, an understanding of the historical specificity of Identity, that conditions both of these fields. Put another way, deconstructive critique of all kinds presupposes the historicity of identity categories. Historicization and deconstruction ought, therefore, be part of the same process. One might thus expect the two fields to form a mutually enriching historicotheoretical relationship. After all, queer theory's prized deconstruction of sexual identity is reliant upon, and indeed derivative of, constructionist analyses that traced the historical invention of the hetero/homosexual dualism in the first place. So the neglect or "condescension" Duggan points out in queer theory's (lack of) engagement with gay/lesbian history framed squarely around the identity paradigm is all the more puzzling, especially given queer theory's rigorous attempts to dismantle such a paradigm. Yet what appears to have happened is that 'history' has been in some ways bracketed out as the proper object of constructionism, and 'theory' the proper object of deconstruction, with little critical reflection on their complicitous interlacings.[27]

I hasten to point out that a reliance on constructionist history is not a bad thing by any means. Social constructionist history has been, *and is*, an extremely positive development, without which I and the many other scholars in gender and sexuality studies would not be able to do the work we are doing. Constructionist historians have produced many brilliant histories that have been informed by a desire to denaturalize and historicize those categories of sexual identity long assumed to be ahistorical and universal. On the other hand, no historical account is 'complete'; no one work is able to address the many and varied ways of approaching questions of historical method and interpretation. Constructionist history has been concerned primarily with tracing the emergence of homosexual identities, less often with tracing the epistemological processes informing their production. One of the effects of this, as I have mentioned, is that bisexuality has made only a fleeting appearance in the historiography of sexuality. The emphasis on identity and the fact that, as far as we know, bisexuality has been barely (if at all) visible as a palpable cultural identity until recent decades have meant that in constructionist histories bisexuality is mentioned only in passing by a few theorists of sexuality. It has also meant, I will argue, that the identity paradigm, and thus the hetero/homosexual opposition, have been unwittingly reproduced in a queer deconstructive theory derivative of such constructionist historical accounts. This will be examined more fully in chapter 7. My reason for preempting this argument now is not simply to set out the structure of *A History of Bisexuality*, but to reveal one of the primary assumptions of this work: Although queer theorists and lesbian and gay historians have made a relentless assault on essentialist notions of identity, their efforts to denaturalize and deconstruct the hetero/homosexual structure and its concomitant notions of identity have not gone far enough. And it is around the question of bisexuality's relationship to figurations of sexual identity that both queer theory and gay/lesbian history have in some important ways fallen short.

In this book I would like to initiate a productive exchange between the two fields of queer theory and gay/lesbian history. What I am endeavoring to work toward is what I will call a form of *deconstructive history;* or more specifically in this case, a *queer deconstructive history.* I hope to extend the work of gay/lesbian historians by opening up the history of sexuality to queer analysis and to extend the scope of queer theory by opening it up to history. In order to do this I want to situate bisexuality not as *marginal* to discourses of sexuality, as has been the dominant tendency throughout the last 130 years or so, but as *central* to any understanding of the historical construction of binary categories of sexuality.[28] I am not concerned with the historical reclamation of 'bisexuals' in history, although the analysis that follows may have profound implications for that kind of restorative historical project. Nor is it my intention to offer the definitive word on bisexuality or bisexual identity. Indeed, an underlying motivation for this study is to evacuate both the concept of sexuality and our categories of sexual identity (including bisexuality) of any ontological content. In this way I differ from Garber, who would like us to begin our analyses with the category of 'sexuality' rather than the hetero/homosexual opposition. I do not want to begin with the generic category of sexuality any more than I want to begin with the hetero/homosexual opposition. Both, it seems to me, not only naturalize a range of identifications, pleasures, and desires (among other things no doubt) into a reductive ontological entity, but also marginalize and erase *difference* and the fundamental indeterminacy at the heart of what we so uncritically call 'sexuality' or 'sexual orientation'.[29] This caveat notwithstanding, my genealogy may nevertheless provide a useful framework through and against which to explore the fraught issues surrounding sexual definition. With a focus only on Western discourses and theories, I will not be offering a comprehensive account of all that has been written on the subject. Instead, I intend to identify some of the fundamental epistemological tendencies that have structured dominant Western representations of sexuality and identity.

In the wake of the 'performative turn' in critical theory and cultural studies, I too am interested, as Eve Sedgwick has implored, in asking of bisexuality not "'What does it *really* mean?'... but 'What does it *do*?—What does it make happen?—What (in the ways it is being or *could be* used) does it make easier or harder for people of various kinds to accomplish and think?'"[30] The more tangible objective of this study, then, is to employ bisexuality as a heuristic device for rereading and rethinking some of the critical moments in the history, theory and politics of sexuality. A (*queer*) *deconstructive history* is a form of history writing that takes as one of its primary political aims the deconstructive project of problematizing "the very idea of opposition and the notion of identity upon which it depends."[31] Such a project, as Mary Poovey points out, can provide the basis for a "genuinely historical practice" (58). By tracing the important, and heretofore ignored, role of bisexuality in the construction of the hetero/homosexual opposition, I will invert one of the common (mis)readings of bisexuality's epistemological construction. Far from being 'defined' by, or reduced to an aftereffect of, the 'two' poles of the opposition, as Chauncey, Haeberle, Edelman, Fuss and others might have it, I will show how these two poles have in fact been defined in important ways by bisexuality.

This study begins as an attempt to reframe contemporary discussions of (bi)sexual politics and theory by opening them up to a more theoretically self-reflexive history. Here I draw on the work of Michel Foucault, whose methodological innovations have been groundbreaking in reorienting the discipline of history. In particular, my study is informed by his notions of *problematization* and *genealogy*. This refers to the practices by which something is brought into "the play of truth and falsehood" and set up "as an object for the mind."[32] For Foucault the question of present politics is inextricable from the question of history. And, no doubt, questions of politics and history are inextricable from the question of theory. Problematization is a strategic intervention in present politicotheoretical contests through the deployment of an "effective" form of history. As Foucault describes it, "I start with a problem in the terms in which it is currently posed and attempt to establish its genealogy; genealogy means that I conduct the analysis starting from the present situation" (238).

In Foucauldian terminology, I seek to write a genealogy of what Marjorie Garber has called "the bisexual moment."[33] This is a "history of the present" that attempts to problematize contemporary struggles around the question of (bi)sexuality.[34] As a form of *historiographical intervention*, I hope this book will provide a framework oriented toward opening up possibilities for thinking (bi)sexuality more effectively *as history, as theory*, and *as politics*.[35] Thus, the call to inquire, as Sedgwick urges, into what bisexuality *is doing* or *can do* within the "prevailing discourse" of sexuality is not enough without inquiring simultaneously, and more comprehensively, into what bisexuality *has done* within this discourse. Any deconstruction of historically overdetermined identity categories ought to engage rather than presume the history on whose behalf it speaks. And only when we have historicized the conditions of bisexuality's emergence as both epistemological concept and political identity can we begin to clarify some of the complex issues conditioning bisexuality's various and contested meanings and functions.

[|]

"Like all sexualities, 'bisexuality' has a history," declares Jo Eadie, in what might appear at first sight to be a statement of the obvious.[36] Yet as Eadie himself is fully aware, this history has scarcely even begun to be told, even within the nascent "politically and theoretically confident discourse of bisexuality."[37] Eva Cantarella has written on the history of bisexuality in the ancient world.[38] However, there has been no sustained account of the history of bisexuality in the modern West. Garber's *Vice Versa* is less a study of history than an examination of particular instances of bisexuality as they have appeared in a wide range of historical texts. She is not so much concerned with historicizing bisexuality as an epistemological category or identity as she is with invoking bisexuality as a universalizing metaphor for understanding the truth of human sexuality. In this way *Vice Versa* reads more as a theory of sexuality constructed out of history than a history of (bi)sexuality's construction. In a recent article, "Identity/Politics: Historical Sources of the Bisexual Movement," Amanda Udis-Kessler has attempted to begin the task of historicizing bisexuality as a modern political identity.[39] "There are many points where I could begin this story," she says, "but it seems that going back before the late 1960s does not add much to this discussion" (53). For Udis-Kessler the political identity of bisexuality owes its emergence primarily to lesbian feminism in the 1970s. The overriding concern appears to be with the historical documentation of a somewhat autonomous bisexual movement and identity. However, it seems to me that this kind of approach, while important for the groups it is representing, is problematic in at least two crucial ways. First, to use the words of Foucault, it represents "a form of history that . . . [is] secretly, but entirely related to the synthetic activity of the subject."[40] The history of bisexuality is thus construed as the recent unfolding of individual bisexual consciousness. Second, it ignores the much older history of bisexuality as epistemological construct. As I will demonstrate here, however, it is this history that has in large part conditioned and constrained the historically specific emergence of bisexuality as a political identity. Just as important to the discussion of why this identity has emerged when it has is the question of *why it did not emerge earlier*. Construed through an identity paradigm, Udis-Kessler's historical and theoretical framework leaves this crucial relationship unexamined.

Merl Storr takes some productive first steps toward historicizing bisexuality in its mutually constitutive relation to other axes of identification. In a chapter in the recent anthology *The Bisexual Imaginary*, Storr traces the construction of 'sexuality' in relation to 'race' within a few key nineteenth-century sexological texts.[41] Other writers have made cursory mention of bisexuality as it has inhered in discourses of sexuality before Stonewall. For instance, in recent anthologies such as *RePresenting Bisexualities*, *Queer Studies*, and *Bisexuality: A Critical Reader*, it is not uncommon to read references to sexologists, to Freud, or to Kinsey in theoretical discussions of bisexuality. However, such references are couched largely in terms of synchronic analyses of the failed attempts to theorize bisexuality as an identity in its own right. There has been a tendency to presume rather than to explain the theory and history of how and why these attempts have not succeeded. While I do not question the notion that a bisexual identity has been repeatedly refused at the level of theory, I suggest that it is important to provide a clearer historical picture of the discursive processes of bisexual erasure. *Bisexuality: A Critical Reader* does in fact attempt to document the historical production of thought in relation to bisexuality in the late nineteenth and twentieth centuries. In a section entitled "Genealogy of a Sex Concept," chapters are devoted to the works of Havelock Ellis, Sigmund Freud, Wilhelm Fliess, and Alfred Kinsey. However, in offering only extracts of some of the works of these thinkers, these chapters are not historicized analyses of such work—they are merely compartmentalized presentations of certain notions of bisexuality. This reflects the editorial objective of the entire collection, which is, as editor Merl Storr points out, an exploration of the question of "what bisexuality is" (3).

By conducting a genealogy of bisexuality as an epistemological category, this study departs from these existing, 'historical' readings. This is not a social history of the bisexual movement, a history of bisexuality as an autonomous sexual identity, a reading of bisexuality in historical texts of sexuality, or an attempt to determine what bisexuality *is*. This is a genealogical history, a refusal of the search for origins and truth in favor of an analysis of the very production of (sexual) truth. As genealogical analysis, or, perhaps, as performative diagnosis, my interest lies with analyzing the discursive *function* of bisexuality in the historical construction of knowledge about sexuality. What did and what does bisexuality *do* in and for discourses of sexuality? What purpose has it served as a category of thought? How can we use bisexuality to rethink the history, theory, and politics of sexuality? By employing bisexuality as a category of historical and theoretical analysis, I will attempt to link the existing synchronic analyses of bisexuality to a loosely diachronic account of the history of sexuality in general. This, I hope, will reflect Jonathan Dollimore's suggestion of using history to read theory and theory to read history in an effort to offer new perspectives on both.[42]

THEORIZING HISTORY, HISTORICIZING THEORY

Queer theory shares with poststructuralism and deconstruction a profound distrust of identity. Categories of identity are seen to be exclusionary and normative, falsely unifying and universalizing, contingent and illusory. Their construction, moreover, is seen to rest on classical binary logic that fails to do justice to the representation of difference. This form of reason or logic represents identities by way of a dualized structure and relation of otherness: a relation, as Val Plumwood has observed, of "separation and domination inscribed and naturalised in culture and characterised by radical exclusion, distancing and opposition between orders constructed as systematically higher and lower, as inferior and superior."[43] Such accounts of dualistic logic are by now commonplace in feminist philosophy and critical theory, particularly given the widespread influence of poststructuralist and deconstructive theories, which provide useful tools for analyzing the play of difference and the workings of binary logic. As I will demonstrate, such theories are suitably calibrated to analyze the historically specific articulations and transformations of binary classifications.

In splicing queer deconstructive theory and gay/lesbian history, a queer deconstructive history would try to avoid straightforwardly reinscribing this binary logic within its own categories of historical analysis. Therefore, rather than read history through the identity paradigm, I aim instead to read identity, as Joan Scott suggests, as a historical and "discursive event."[44] This involves an analysis of the discursive processes that enable binary notions of sexual identity themselves to be produced and reproduced over time. In other words, my queer deconstructive history is not a history of the social construction of sexual identities, but a history that traces the epistemic logic and discursive operations within and through which these identities were relationally produced within psychomedical discourse. My genealogy is a historicotheoretical intervention somewhere at the threshold between queer theory and gay/lesbian history, rather than a substitute for constructionist history. Diana Fuss has suggested that "identity always contains the specter of non-identity within it," that "identity is always purchased at the price of the exclusion of the Other, the repression or repudiation of non-identity."[45] Taking this deconstructive insight as a point of departure, this study represents an attempt to reread the history of sexual identity through the very specter of nonidentity. That the category of bisexuality has occupied this position suggests that it provides a useful analytic lens through which to undertake this task. Where Foucault's genealogy sought to historicize the *scientia sexualis* and its production of sexuality and sexual identities, my genealogy aims to go inside the *scientia sexualis* in order to examine how this production of sexuality and sexual identity was made possible through an incessant repudiation of the Other, of nonidentity, of bisexuality. By situating bisexuality at the center of our historical analysis a new and important dimension is added to our understanding of the history of sexuality and to the relationality of identity, and thus in turn, to our deconstructions of binary sexual identity.

In *A History of Bisexuality*, I propose that it is necessary to rethink the methodological foundation of the disciplines of both queer theory and gay/lesbian history. The hetero/homosexual dyad can no longer be employed prima facie as an axiomatic departure point.[46] For, as I will demonstrate in what follows, this is no simple dyadic structure. Rather, it is, or perhaps more accurately, *it has functioned,* as a triadic structure in modern representations of sexuality. What I will thus be proposing is that within Western discourses of sexuality, defined as they have been by classical logic, bisexuality as an epistemological category is part of the *logical or axiomatic structure* of the hetero/homosexual dualism—even if only as this structure's internally repudiated other. To claim this is to claim that bisexuality as a concept cannot be said to postdate those of homo- or heterosexuality. Whether explicitly defined or not at the moment of homo- and heterosexuality's scientific invention, the notion of a dual sexuality, let us call it bisexuality, is without doubt a logical or axiomatic component of such a dualistic structure. Being *either* heterosexual *or* homosexual implies the conceptual possibility of being *both* heterosexual *and* homosexual. Even where the 'law of the excluded middle' might prevail, it can only prevail to the extent that it repudiates the possibility of a dual sexuality, or the third term of bisexuality. Yet such an act of repudiation can take place only by acknowledging in the first instance the conceptual existence of that which is being repudiated. This suggests to me that the concept of bisexuality as a dual sexuality (both/and instead of either/or), as the conjunction of hetero- and homosexuality, or as the epistemological threshold between the two, must emerge as a logical and conceptual possibility *at precisely the same moment* at which hetero- and homosexuality emerged as dualized identities. Of course, it is widely known that the concept of homosexuality was invented before that of heterosexuality.[47] But what I am trying to suggest is that within the binary epistemology of sexuality the *conceptual* possibility of both heterosexuality and bisexuality as modes of sexuality emerged at the moment of homosexuality's invention, despite the fact that these terms were not explicitly named and defined until some years later.[48] I am not suggesting that what I am referring to as "bisexuality" is literally equivalent to the conjunction of hetero- and homosexuality, and that it thus has some positive epistemological content; only that this conjunction is a logical presumption of the hetero/homosexual structure. This theoretical claim will be put to the test of history in chapter 2 and then theoretically elaborated upon in chapter 8. For now, suffice it to note that whether or not this conceptual possibility I am referring to can be identified as "bisexuality" is beside the point. What I am trying to tease out is the logical paradox structuring bisexuality's marginalization and erasure from both queer theory and gay/ lesbian history.

Identifying bisexuality not simply as a pivotal player, but as the third term that structures the hetero/homosexual opposition, also demands a reformulation of an important queer poststructuralist insight. Where queer theory posits the mutually constituting nature of hetero- and homosexuality (i.e., the one term requiring the other for its self-definition), my analysis posits instead a trinary relationship. Within our modern epistemology of sexuality, any figuration of homo- or heterosexuality *necessarily* entails— wittingly or unwittingly (and as my genealogy will show, it is usually the latter)—a figuration of bisexuality. In other words, to invoke and define any one of the terms hetero-, homo-, or bisexuality is to invoke and define the others by default. Each requires the other two for its self-definition. The effect of this logical, or axiomatic, structure is such that shifts in any one of the terms hetero-, bi-, or homosexuality require and engender shifts in the others.[49] If such a proposition is to stand the test of historical analysis, it just might, at the very least, further the interminable project of deconstructing our inherited sexual identity categories and dispossessing 'sexuality' of any positive ontological content.

TRAJECTORY OF THE TEXT

This book is divided into two parts. The central theme unifying parts 1 and 2 is the argument that, historically, bisexuality represents a blind spot in hegemonic discourses of sexuality. Bisexuality has functioned as the structural Other to figurations of sexual identity and has represented the very uncertainty of the hetero/homosexual division. I will provide historical and theoretical support for the idea that, to use Michael du Plessis's words, a theoretical engagement with bisexuality has been continually postponed, "*never to interrupt the present moment.*"[50] That is to say, a particular temporal framing of sexuality has cast bisexuality in the past or future but never *in the present tense*.[51] Part 1 is entitled "Constructing Sexual Identity" and explores some of the critical moments in the production and reproduction of the hetero/homosexual opposition within dominant psychomedical discourses from the mid-1800s to the late 1960s. Far from being marginal to this process, I will suggest that the category of bisexuality played a pivotal role in constructing and maintaining this oppositional framework. My argument is that the elision of bisexuality from the present tense has been one of the primary discursive strategies employed in an effort to avoid a collapse of sexual boundaries—*a crisis of sexual identity*.

In chapter 2 I trace the emergence in the second half of the nineteenth century of what I have called *the economy of (hetero)sexuality*. This refers to the invention of the category of 'sexuality' in general, and the opposition of hetero/homosexuality in particular. I suggest that this new ontological framework can only be understood in the context of profound shifts in the categories of gender. I will argue that the category of bisexuality was central to the structure and coherent maintenance of this new discursive economy. However, I will demonstrate that bisexuality also simultaneously subverted the oppositional categories of man and woman, heterosexual and homosexual. As a result, it was erased in the present tense and remained a necessary blind spot in sexological thinking.

Chapter 3 offers a detailed examination of one of the most influential theorists of sexuality, Sigmund Freud. Freud's extensive oeuvre served to expand and reinforce the emerging economy of (hetero)sexuality. Bisexuality was the centerpiece of his psychoanalytic account of gender and sexuality. However, not unlike its effect in sexological discourse, bisexuality was also a concept that profoundly undermined the identificatory categories of masculine, feminine, heterosexual, and homosexual. I will argue that, in order to ensure the viability of the Oedipus complex, bisexuality was not only a necessary mystery, its articulation in the present tense was an impossibility. Chapter 4 traces a fundamental shift in the theorization of sexuality within psychoanalytic discourse. The radical implications of bisexuality led to a determined effort to secure the troubled boundaries of the hetero/homosexual division. I will suggest that a two-pronged discursive strategy was employed in this task. First bisexuality was repudiated as a scientific anachronism, and second homosexuality was pathologized, the latter made possible by the former. I will argue that this discursive shift was the effect of another crisis: the crisis of (hetero)sexual identity.

Part 2 is entitled "Deconstructing Sexual Identity." In this section I examine some of the significant theoretical and political attempts to contest the hetero/homosexual opposition. Chapters 5 and 7 detail two such attempts as they have been articulated through the movements of gay liberation and queer. Both of these movements have sought in different ways to incite, rather than to avert, a crisis of sexual identity. Chapter 6 examines the emergence of social construction theory, primarily Foucauldian, as a significant theoretical force shaping postliberationist and queer contestations of sexual identity.

Chapter 5 begins part 2 with an analysis of gay liberation in the early 1970s. Drawing from the movements of antipsychiatry, relativist sociology, cross-cultural anthropology, radical Freudianism, the counterculture, black power, Civil Rights, and women's liberation, gay liberation theorists and activists sought to challenge the economy of (hetero)sexuality and its binary taxonomy of gender and sexuality. The concept of bisexuality was revivified as the appropriate concept for this task. I will argue, however, that despite its political and theoretical redeployment, bisexuality was reduced to a nostalgic and utopic dimension and elided in the present tense of gay liberation also.

Any account of the history, theory, and politics of sexuality would be deficient without a sustained analysis of Foucault's enormous contribution to the field. Chapter 6 begins with a brief account of the emergence of labeling and symbolic interactionist theories before launching into a detailed examination of Foucauldian social constructionism. As we will see, with the shift to antiontological accounts of sexuality, and to constructionist and poststructuralist assaults on essentialist notions of sexual identity, the category of bisexuality was rendered irrelevant, losing its political and theoretical appeal. I will evaluate the utility of Foucauldian theory for deconstructing sexuality in general and the hetero/homosexual opposition in particular, arguing that despite his productive and influential intervention, Foucault's theory is limited for undertaking this task. In addition, however, the function of this chapter is to subject Foucault's work itself to a Foucauldian genealogy. In so doing, I will reposition his work as itself caught up in the very deployment of sexuality he sought to escape. What this has meant for my genealogy of bisexuality is that, although irrelevant to his project, one of the effects of Foucault's intervention and reception has been yet another foreclosure (albeit in very different ways and for very different reasons than those occurring in psychomedical discourses) of any consideration of the category of bisexuality. This will provide the basis in the following two chapters for a reconsideration of bisexuality as a useful and indeed necessary tool of deconstructive analysis.

Chapter 7 traces the recent intervention of queer theory in the project of deconstructing sexual identity. While it would seem that queer theory has developed Foucault's work in important ways, I will argue that in certain problematic ways many queer theorists unwittingly reinscribe binary categories of sexuality. One of the reasons for this is poorly historicized deconstructive frameworks, or, to put it another way, an uncritical reliance on a historiography of sexuality that has ignored the role of bisexuality. I will suggest that in order to further the project of queer deconstruction, a historicotheoretical engagement with the category of bisexuality is essential. For what will become clear in this study is that if the category of bisexuality has been pivotal to the construction of sexuality and of the hetero/homosexual structure, then by corollary, it ought also be pivotal to their deconstruction. Through a rereading of a number of recent genetic studies of homosexuality, chapter 8 will then attempt to demonstrate the value of bisexuality as a critical tool for furthering the (queer) deconstructive project.

PART [1]

CONSTRUCTING SEXUAL IDENTITY

2

SCIENCE AND THE INVENTION OF (BI)SEXUALITY

> The lowest animals are bisexual and the various types of hermaphroditism are more or less complete reversions to the ancestral type.
> —James G. Kiernan 1888

In her enormously influential book, *Epistemology of the Closet*, Eve Kosofsky Sedgwick begins with what may appear to be a rather modest proposition: "Many of the major nodes of thought and knowledge in twentieth-century Western culture as a whole are structured—indeed, fractured—by a chronic, now endemic crisis of homo/heterosexual definition, indicatively *male*, dating from the end of the nineteenth century."[1] This is immediately followed, however, by a much more compelling, generalized, and seemingly audacious claim that, as I will suggest in later chapters, provides a point of theoretical and methodological coherence to the burgeoning field of queer theory. Sedgwick's argument is that "an understanding of virtually any aspect of modern Western culture must be, not merely incomplete, but damaged in its central substance to the degree that it does not incorporate a critical analysis of modern homo/heterosexual definition" (1).

The starting point for this chapter is this very definitional crisis. This is a crisis that is, at its very core, as Sedgwick points out, indicatively male: it is a *crisis of masculine identity*. In the second half of the nineteenth century a new discursive economy for the organization of the sexes and their pleasures was being forged. I call this *the economy of (hetero)sexuality*, the representational creation of two distinct but ineluctably entwined epistemic registers, sex/gender and sexuality. Through a historically strategic alliance, this newly emerging Western economy began at the turn of the century to subsume human subjects under a new and more complex ontological order. There emerged during this period a significant and nascent distinction between sex role (active/passive, masculine/feminine behavior) and sexual object choice. Sexuality was individuated and produced as a somewhat distinct but additional component of individual ontology. To qualify as a human being, therefore, an individual was bestowed not only with a distinct sex and gender, but with a sexuality as well; the latter, if all goes to 'nature's' plan, was presumed to be the consequence of the former. One was thereby conceptualized as both a man *and* either a heterosexual or a homosexual, a woman *and* either a heterosexual or a lesbian.

The historical emergence of these modern categories of sexuality has been mapped and analyzed by historians of sexuality in no small measure.[2] Although my project takes as axiomatic Sedgwick's propositions regarding the necessary centrality of hetero/homosexual definition to Western thought and analysis, I suggest, however, that within the domain of sexual science the coherence of this oppositional axis has been dependent epistemologically on a third term: bisexuality. Bisexuality has played a central role in the individuation of sexuality, in theories of what Gayle Rubin has called "erotic speciation."[3] Indeed, as we will see, historically and epistemologically bisexuality was figured not only as the Other to sexual ontology itself, but as the liminal figure through which, and against which, racial, gender, and sexual identities were invented as distinctly separate species of humankind.

The historiography of sexuality has largely ignored the concept of bisexuality, a protean figure which I will situate as central to any historicotheoretical analysis of sex/gender and sexuality. In borrowing Sedgwick's phraseology, then, this book proposes that the history of modern hetero/homosexual definition itself is profoundly impoverished to the extent that it ignores a critical analysis of the figure of bisexuality.

What I intend to demonstrate in this chapter is that the historically specific epistemological alliance of sex/gender and sexuality is made possible through the category of bisexuality. I will argue that, throughout several decades around the turn of the nineteenth century, psychomedical definitions of sex, gender, and sexuality have sought to attain epistemic consistency through an erasure of bisexuality from the present tense. It must be said that the formation of sexuality within the various societies incorporated under the rubric of 'the West' is not a uniform phenomenon, but one characterized by regional specificities and differing historical trajectories. Despite this, however, at the level of psychomedical theory, which is my primary focus in what follows, the dominant representation of sex, gender, and sexuality followed a rather standard epistemological pattern. My purpose in retracing the seemingly well-trodden path to the beginnings of modern sexuality—to that moment where the fracturing of sex into the binary sex/gender paved a discursive course for the invention of an ontological category of sexuality—is not a project of reclaiming a lost and distinct history of bisexuals or of bisexuality.[4] Rather, as I mentioned in the previous chapter, it is an attempt to situate the category of bisexuality as central to the shifting epistemological structure of sexuality, which seems to me to be an essential foundation for a queer deconstructive historical practice. I consider this deconstructive history to be a form of politicotheoretical activism intended to subvert the efficient reproduction of the binarized formula of modern hetero/homosexual identity by exposing its epistemological mechanics. I hope also that such an approach might offer a corrective to the presentist tendencies within much recent queer studies.[5]

GENDER AND THE CRISIS OF MASCULINE IDENTITY

Any attempt to trace the psychomedical invention of sexuality in Western thought must begin with an analysis of the shifting boundaries of sex and gender during the nineteenth century. For it is in direct relation to the gaps, the contradictions, and the contested representations of these categories that sexuality was to emerge as a salient ontological category to be defined by the *sex* or *gender* of object choice. As a possible theoretical starting point for my historical analysis of the psychomedical representation of sexuality, I would like to begin by considering Luce Irigaray's reflections on the representation of sex within Western thought. For Irigaray, the sociohistorical system of representation, or symbolic order, constitutive of Western culture as a whole is inescapably phallogocentric. Phallogocentrism refers to the conjunction of the Derridean concept of "logocentrism" with the Lacanian concept of the "phallus." It is the representational economy whose binary logic reduces the figure of 'woman' to a relation of parasitic dependence on that of 'man'. As Elizabeth Grosz demonstrates, phallogocentric representations of woman take three forms: as the negation or opposition of man, as similar or equivalent to man, or as the complement to man.[6] Irigaray argues in *This Sex Which Is Not One*, that

> this domination of the philosophic logos stems in large part from its power to *reduce all others to the economy of the Same*. The teleological constructive project it takes on is always a project of diversion, deflection, reduction of the other to the Same. And, in its greatest generality perhaps, from its power to *eradicate the difference between the sexes* in systems that are self-representative of a 'masculine subject'.[7]

In each form of phallogocentric representation, therefore, woman is subject to the law of the Same. Through the process of masculine specula(riza)tion she is not only reduced to the status of inferior simulacrum of man, but in fact rendered no sex at all. She is, in short, unrepresentable in phallogocentric discourse:

> All Western discourse presents a certain isomorphism with the masculine sex: the privilege of unity, form of the self, of the visible, of the specularisable, of the erection (which is the becoming of form). Now this morpho-logic does not correspond to the female sex: there is not 'a' sex. The 'no sex' that has been assigned to the woman can mean that she does not have 'a' sex and that her sex is not visible nor identifiable or representable in a definite form.[8]

According to Irigaray, the unrepresentability of woman is indicative of her place in the symbolic order not as subject, but as object of the phallic economy. She is but the mirror through which masculine identity is constructed and reproduced.[9]

Irigaray's reading of woman as the-sex-which-is-not-one in Western discourse is particularly apposite, as we will see, for analyzing representations of sex and gender in the nineteenth century discourses of science and medicine. Moreover, analyses such as these have led innumerable feminist scholars to suggest that gender ought to be a central analytic category in any illuminating account of social relations in any historical period.[10] However, Irigaray's project extends this feminist principle by suggesting that the category of gender *itself* is phallogocentric. Gender is but "the sameness of phallic identity . . . a mere semblance of difference."[11] Thomas Laqueur's groundbreaking study, *Making Sex: Body and Gender from the Greeks to Freud*, could perhaps be read as a testimony to Irigaray's central thesis. Exploring the cultural production of gender over a period of more than two thousand years, Laqueur describes a decisive shift that took place throughout the eighteenth century. In stark contrast to a one-sex model that had dominated Western thought since the ancient Greeks, the gendered body was increasingly conceived of according to a new two-sex model. Instead of viewing the female body as a similar but inferior version of the male form, where the vagina was "imagined as an interior penis, the labia as foreskin, the uterus as scrotum, and the ovaries as testicles," the new two-sex model of "radical dimorphism" was constructed around an "anatomy and physiology of incommensurability." Laqueur suggests that this model "replaced a metaphysics of hierarchy in the representation of woman in relation to man."[12]

Irigaray might go further in deconstructing the terms of this shift. While radical sexual dimorphism was installed in medical discourses, it was nonetheless a dimorphism of the one, the same, the masculine subject. As we will see, this becomes particularly apparent with the emergence of evolutionary theory in the nineteenth century. The hierarchical ordering of the sexes was retained as the central core of this two-sex model, with man positioned as the authorial referent. Woman was construed in yet another guise of phallocentrism, as the complement of man. As an instance of an Irigarayan "economy of the Same," the two-sex model appears to be the one-sex model reconceived. Laqueur attempts to substantiate his claim by suggesting that the nineteenth-century "doctrine of separate spheres . . . explicitly shattered the notion of a hierarchy of the sexes" (195). However, the development of biology, and in particular evolutionary biology in the middle of the century, effected a conflation of the one-sex and two-sex models into an ever more powerful phallic system. So despite Laqueur's appreciation of the gendered construction of both of these models, this chapter will highlight their epistemological conflation in the nineteenth century. It is certainly not my intention to prove the universal applicability of Irigaray's thesis; in fact I would be very cautious of any such attempt.[13] However, at least with respect to dominant theories of sexuality, I hope to provide some significant instances of historical support for her more general theoretical claims, while in some ways refining Laqueur's periodization.[14] This will become clearer as we trace the role of bisexuality in the scientific construction of sex and gender.

The notion of 'masculine identity' that I am using should be distinguished from a univocal understanding of masculinity or from supposed expressions or representations of masculinity. There is no singular, transparent, and bounded definition of masculinity in contemporary cultures and societies any more than there has been throughout earlier cultures and societies. Just as masculinity's meanings are pliable and mutable, so too are they divided and contested. There are always competing ideals of masculinity. Following recent scholarly practice, then, it would appear far more appropriate to speak of 'masculinities', at least when referring to the manifestation of multiple, coexisting representations of gender. However, in borrowing from Irigaray and other feminist analyses, when I speak of 'masculine identity' I am not alluding to specific articulations or representations of masculinity, but to a kind of general epistemological organizing system—or as Homi Bhabha puts it, "an apparatus of cultural difference"[15]—which in fact makes possible particular articulations and representations of masculinity in the first place.[16] This phallogocentric epistemological system, or economy, is less an object than a *process* of relationships which produces social and discursive differences (meaning) against an authorial referent that is artificially figured as a sameness, an abiding presence, *a masculine principle*, albeit an often presumed and seemingly unspecified one. This means that, for the most part, masculinity achieves social and discursive meanings through a series of hierarchical relations to subordinated others, including other masculinities.[17]

That the representation of women's bodies has functioned to shore up phallocentric sameness, or masculine identity, as Irigaray reminds us, is nowhere more apparent than in Victorian discourses of science. As Cynthia Russett has pointed out, increasingly, as the century progressed, "the proper study of mankind was woman."[18] The unmarked sameness of masculine identity was grafted onto the emerging empirical sciences that were endlessly preoccupied with human biological typologies. Here, 'man's' differences had to be marked and classified. This was coincident with a time of enormous contestation of the patriarchal norms of gender, when the boundaries of masculine identity were coming under significant attack. In fact, as numerous feminist historians have argued, movements for racial and sexual equality were fundamental to the reactionary scientific construction of humanity.[19] At stake was a white, middle-class, imperialistic, and patriarchal social hierarchy.

Throughout much of Western Europe and North America in the mid-nineteenth century, cracks began to appear in the patriarchal order of gender. The rise of industrial capitalism and the consolidation of the hegemonic middle classes engendered an expansion of leisure time for bourgeois women. This led to the expansion and formation of women's associations in the pursuit of religious and charity work. Inspired by the evangelical revival and by the French Revolution and the Enlightenment principles of reason and equality, such philanthropic women's groups and organizations were centrally concerned with social and moral reform. Pivotal to this development was the influential religious notion of female moral superiority. Middle-class women worked to help the impoverished, carried out missionary work to convert prostitutes to evangelical Protestantism and Catholicism (while simultaneously attacking the double standard of sexual morality), and were active in temperance and antislavery movements. They also began challenging conventional gender roles in their efforts to campaign for legal, political, and social liberties: for equal rights to education, mothers' custody of children, and ownership of property, as well as greater employment opportunities and female suffrage. The idea that marriage was a woman's sole vocation came under attack and was often identified as a primary factor in rendering her socially and economically dependent on men. Women were demanding the right to self-determination.[20] Woman, as Helen Taylor declared in 1872, "claims the right to belong to herself, as a self-contained individual existence . . . in short her right to live up to the full measure of her capacities to reach up to the highest and most useful standard she can attain."[21]

In Western Europe and North America, masculine middle-class anxieties surfaced around the challenges such reform movements posed to a social order structured hierarchically around differences of race, nation, class, and gender. Like many areas of society, medical and scientific knowledge reflected, and indeed was a conduit for, the expression of many of these volatile social anxieties surrounding the meaning of human difference. As we are about to see, some of the most influential men of science explicitly responded to calls for female emancipation and social reform through their theories. What emerged was a discourse that Cynthia Russett has described as a discourse of "sexual science." Drawing on 'nature' to establish scientific evidence for the innate biological differences between the sexes, races and often classes, one common objective of these theories was to defend and justify existing social hierarchies and social sex roles. This is not to suggest that anxieties about race and gender necessarily reflected a conscious and deliberate racist and antifeminist reaction by scientists (although it is not to rule this out either). What my reading will be suggesting, however, is that scientific theories were constituted through a phallocentric economy of the Same.[22] At issue, then, was not simply the Woman Question, or the question of race. In a decidedly male-dominated profession,[23] what was also at issue was the authorial referent of sexual science itself: masculine identity. And as we shall see, this was a phallocentric discourse of scientific racism within which bisexuality served an important epistemological function.

The publication of Charles Darwin's *On the Origin of Species* in 1859 effectively canonized evolutionary thinking, leaving few spheres of Western thought untouched. Through the concept of natural selection, Darwin posited that all species were not the fixed product of God, but linked to one another on a constantly evolving chain of being.[24] The Darwinian revolution laid the groundwork for the construction of a new racialized order of gender and, ultimately, for a modern science of sexuality. After reading John Stuart Mill's essay, "The Subjection of Women," where Mill had argued that the subordination of the female sex was a hindrance to social improvement and that such a state of inequality "ought to be replaced by a principle of perfect equality," Darwin replied that "Mill could learn some things from physical science." "It is in the struggle for existence and (especially) for the possession of women that men acquire their vigor and courage."[25]

This view was to form the basis of Darwin's theory of sexual selection elaborated in his 1871 publication, *The Descent of Man, and Selection in Relation to Sex*.[26] The fundamental thesis was that sexual selection as a central component of the evolution of all species resulted in a greater differentiation of the sexes proportional to the level of evolution. This was the "principle of sexual dimorphism." There were inherent differences between the sexes, with men enjoying higher mental faculties. Any attempt to contradict this, Darwin suggested, need only draw up a list of "the most eminent men and women" in a number of fields, and they "would not bear comparison."[27] In fact, Darwin suspected that "a sort of sexual selection has been the most powerful means of changing the races of man."[28] The pervasive domain of social Darwinism was thus used to justify the social position of women and blacks.

Other Victorian scientists, many following Darwin's lead, responded to feminist challenges in a more explicitly antifeminist fashion. Despite some qualification, British sociologist Herbert Spencer lamented the movement for emancipation. "While in some directions the emancipation of women has to be carried further," commented Spencer, "we may suspect that in other directions their claims have already been pushed beyond the normal limits."[29] Evolutionist George J. Romanes declared that "whether we like it or not, the woman's movement is upon us; and what we have now to do is to guide the flood into what seem likely to prove the most beneficial channels" (21). These channels were of course women's prescribed social roles of reproduction and motherhood. The reinforcement of the separate spheres was to be seen, as zoologist and evolutionist Edward Drinker Cope argued, "not [as] the product of human law or of man's 'tyranny,' but . . . the flower of her evolution, the product of nature's forces" (25). "If women comprehended all that is contained in the domestic sphere, they would ask no other," Herbert Spencer declares in frustration, "they would seek no higher function" (15). Many scientists were therefore led to claim that education and too much mental stimulation would jeopardize woman's prescribed role, robbing her of the necessary energies for reproduction. To be confined to the reproductive domestic sphere, women were to function as mere objects in the continuing process of masculinist evolution. Within scientific discourse, then, men were represented as the subjects of this economy, the great creators of civilization. Woman was to nature as man was to culture.

The consensus among Victorian scientists was that woman was at a lower stage of evolutionary development than man, closer to the child, and even to the 'savage' (usually Negro). To biologist Grant Allen, woman was "not even half the race at present, but rather a part of it told specially off for the continuance of the species. . . . She is the sex sacrificed to reproductive necessities."[30] In fact, woman, like the Negro, was an evolutionary irregularity, the arrested product of a premature and precocious development. This "earlier arrest of individual evolution" was explained by Spencer as an anomalous yet necessary effect of the conservation and channeling of energy away from physical and mental development toward reproduction. Far from being the 'weaker sex', women were in fact 'weaker' men, arrested men. Indeed, as one Harry Campbell dubbed her, woman was "Undeveloped Man."[31]

The flowering of physical anthropology worked to link women to blacks as less evolved than white men through the comparative analysis and measurement of anatomical, physiological, and cranial differences.[32] Women resembled children in stature and blacks in cranial measurement; and of course blacks resembled children and apes. E. Huschke, the German anthropologist, asserted in 1854 that "the Negro brain possesses a spinal cord of the type found in children and women and, beyond this, approaches the type found in higher apes."[33] Natural historian Carl Vogt, to take another example (and one cited approvingly by Darwin), observed that "it is a remarkable circumstance, that the difference between the sexes, as regards cranial cavity, increases with the development of the race, so that the male European excels much more the female, than the negro the negress."[34] Women, 'sacrificed' to the reproductive function, were nearer to the lower black races in cranial capacity and thus intelligence, not to mention myriad other disadvantageous traits. "The grown up Negro partakes, as regards his intellectual faculties, of the nature of the child, the female, and the senile white," Vogt insisted.[35] As Russett makes clear, for anthropologists, gender and race were not two distinct sets of issues, but interdependent components of the same issue.[36] In fact, for one group, the National American Woman Suffrage Association, the antifeminist rhetorical comparison of women and blacks was so potent that it withdrew from the movement for Negro rights in spite of its early association with the cause of abolitionism.[37]

In the context of the Darwinian revolution in the second half of the century, it is certainly apparent that race and gender became mutually constituting structures, one unthinkable without the other. Racial difference was largely constructed, as Sander Gilman has demonstrated, "on the sexual difference of the black," generally, the black female body.[38] So not only was the 'Hottentot' the representative of blackness, typical of a race with an 'apelike' sexual appetite, but it was the female Hottentot, characterized by 'primitive' genitalia and buttocks, that provided both the antithetical figure for black/white difference and the mirror through which a bourgeois masculine identity was predicated.[39]

The genitalia of black women were described by comparative anatomists through metaphors of excess. Overdeveloped clitorises were thought to be the norm among black women, positioning them closer to the penises of men than their white counterparts. So too with their sexual appetite, which was considered masculine and 'apelike' in its voracity. The underlying assumption was that black races were less sexually differentiated and less evolved than the superior white races; they were closer, that is, to the primitive ancestry of humanity. In Flower and Murie's account of the Bushwoman, for example, they noted "the remarkable development of the labia minora," supporting their claims with eye witness accounts that described the genitalia as "appendages."[40] Sexual excess was equated with masculinity. As Siobhan Somerville puts it, "sexual ambiguity delineated the boundaries of race" (252).

The concept of bisexuality was fundamental to this racialized evolutionary framework of gender. It functioned as a liminal concept, the explanatory pathway to *both* human sameness and human difference. As an epistemological category, bisexuality stemmed from the discovery of the hermaphroditic ascidians by the Russian embryologist Aleksandr Kovalevsky in 1866.[41] Appropriating the finding as confirmation for his theory of evolution, Darwin thus located primordial hermaphroditism as the missing link in the descent of man from invertebrate organisms. This was established in conjunction with the finding in the field of comparative anatomy that "the sexual organs of even 'the higher vertebrata are, in their early condition, hermaphrodite'."[42] Embryological studies thus identified various stages of human development from a state of hermaphroditism, or bisexuality, wherein the embryo displayed both sets of sexual organs before the atrophy of one of them after the third month of development.[43] "It has long been known," affirmed Darwin in *The Descent of Man* in 1871 "that in the vertebrate kingdom one sex bears rudiments of various accessory parts, appertaining to the reproductive system, which properly belong to the opposite sex; and it has now been ascertained that at a very early embryonic period both sexes possess true male and female glands. Hence some remote progenitor of the whole vertebrate kingdom appears to have been hermaphrodite or androgynous" (525). In this framework, therefore, both blacks and women were represented as 'undeveloped men', closer to our bisexual ancestors. The association was strengthened by the recapitulation theory developed by German Darwinian Ernst Haeckel in 1866. This 'biogenetic law' was a central organizing principle of nineteenth-century evolutionary thought. In addition to unifying a heterogeneous range of disciplinary theories such as atavism, degeneration, and arrested development, it served also to reaffirm the dominant equation of women with blacks as primitive evolutionary entities. The principal tenet of recapitulation theory—whereby "ontogeny recapitulates phylogeny"—is that in the development from fetus to adulthood, each human organism *recapitulates* the complete life history of the species. In other words, with individual human growth seen to parallel evolutionary development, the progression to fully evolved adulthood dictates that each individual pass through each evolutionary phase of human development, from our hermaphroditic or bisexual ancestors to mature homo sapiens. Darwinian theorists such as Edward Drinker Cope and Stanley Hall alleged, therefore, that boys on their way to becoming men passed through (and left behind) a "'woman stage' of character," a "feminized stage of psychic development."[44] In the fields of teratology and medicine, living human hermaphrodites were also held up as biological evidence of the theory of human bisexual inheritance.[45] As the nineteenth-century British surgeon Lawson Tait noted, "We must accept Darwin's theory of the descent of man. This acceptance at once becomes the explanation of the occasional occurrence of bisexual vertebrates, and consequently of true hermaphroditism in human individuals. Conversely, the occurrence of such malformations may be offered as one amongst the many proofs which are being accumulated from every quarter in favor of Darwin's theory."[46]

In this phallocentric economy of (evolutionary) sameness, then, bisexuality provided the metonymic link between men, women, blacks, and our hermaphroditic ancestors. The universal starting point for all human development, and thus human differentiation, was embryological bisexuality. As children, men passed through physical and psychical stages of bisexuality until maturity, until *(hu)manhood*. Women and blacks, on the other hand, remained children, undeveloped men; or to Irigaray's terms, *sexes which were not ones*. This meant that each of them was therefore a (hu)man that was not one. For it was in the evolutionary process of becoming (hu)man that one was to transcend the physical and psychical animal ancestry of primordial bisexuality. In the Darwinian chain of being, this was an upward movement out of the domain of nature and into that of culture; an evolutionary progression from sexual ambiguity to sexual distinction. Only the prototypical Western bourgeois male, however, had successfully completed this transition from (bisexual) *nature* to (sexually differentiated) *culture*, divesting himself of his animal heritage. In fact, *man* was synonymous with the totality of culture, or 'civilization' itself. Nature, on the other hand, was that unruly, animalistic (black), and feminine sphere to be dominated, subdued, and controlled, that over and against which 'civilized' Western society was instituted. There is clearly only one sex, one citizen, one (hu)man, in this framework: a male 'one' against which everything else is measured as an anomalous arrest or developmental failure. Bisexuality was therefore installed as both the figure of (hu)man sameness and the figure of (hu)man difference. It was employed as a rhetorical concept to explain and justify, in scientific terms, the social order in which women and blacks (and not to mention those of 'ambiguous' sex) were rendered not only subaltern, but subhuman.

GENDER INVERSION AND THE REPRODUCTIVE PARADIGM

Despite the marginalization of the concept of sexual selection among biologists in the nineteenth century, the legacy of the Darwinian revolution was the omnipresent instantiation of what Gilbert Herdt has called the "reproductive paradigm." Premised on "the principle of sexual dimorphism," this paradigm shift in the nineteenth century thoroughly inflected all domains of Western thought.[47] Principally, it proffered a biological and thus 'natural' legitimation of the sexual (and racial) division of labor. This worked to install a normative heteroteleology as the necessary prototype for human evolution. Men were thus sanctioned as the cultural producers, women the reproducers. This was not simply a socially desired model ensuring the highest form of individual and cultural development. Rather, it was an essential and inevitable biological model driven by the procreative sex instinct. Of course, men were responsible for sexual selection and the concept of sexual instinct was largely their preserve. Women, it was commonly believed, were the asexual nurturers, the passive recipients and vessels of the male sex instinct.[48] To deviate from this reproductive division of labor, therefore, was to work against the gendered and racialized bifurcation of 'nature', a move considered both counter(re)productive and evolutionarily retrograde.[49]

Darwin had suggested that, when removed from the state of nature, the reproductive system of animals is that component of physiology most prone to variation. This was a theme that occupied the texts of the early sexologists.[50] The underlying anxiety built into evolutionary models was that 'abnormal' cultural practices could pervert the human race. Victorian evolutionary theory was thus informed by the conceptual dyad of human progress and human decay. On one side was the notion of the natural flowering of natural/sexual selection to produce the most evolved races and, on the other, the psychiatric concept of degeneration and evolutionary regression.[51] This prevailing model, constituted within a matrix of middle-class values, was framed within a social context of economic decline and increasing urbanization, class conflict, and massive immigration.[52] Moreover, it was the (reproductive) model through which typologies of human perversion and biological variation were established. For by the second half of the nineteenth century, somatic theories of human difference were hegemonic. The variable body itself was seen to produce differences of class, race, gender, sexuality, and so on.

In defining the sexes according to evolutionary imperatives, the principle of sexual dimorphism constructed the category of sex, or gender, in functional terms. An individual's role was her sex. In other words, there was no sex/gender distinction, which was to develop later and to gain explicit representation through the efforts of sexology. Rather, an individual's secondary sexual characteristics issued directly from her genital and reproductive anatomy. However, in many parts of the Western world, the second half of the nineteenth century brought with it a new generation of economically independent and educated women, the New Women, who represented a significant challenge to the bourgeois social order and to the naturalized reproductive sexual division of labor.[53] In addition to this, dandyism and the decadentism of the male aesthetes—of whom Oscar Wilde was the most notable representative—stood in stark contrast to the category of the middle-class male.[54] Naturalized sex roles were being challenged and this led to a fracturing of the category of sex. Anatomy could no longer guarantee the development of appropriately matched secondary sexual characteristics and behavioral roles. Nor could science contain the diversification of these characteristics and roles within their neatly bounded categories of sex. It is important to underline the point that such challenges to conventional notions of gender occurred in the context of significant changes in material relations between the genders. The forces of modernization and urbanization altered the organization of men's and women's work, domestic economies, and family wage structures, as well as reshaping familial relations and boundaries demarcating public and private spheres. This was, without doubt, a time of "sexual anarchy," a time when definitions of masculinity and femininity were put into serious question.[55] The balance of power within and between the genders was under attack, and bourgeois masculinity suffered a profound crisis of legitimation. It is in this context that I suggest we situate the emergence of a scientific category of the third sex and, thus, the sex/gender distinction.[56]

In line with Randolph Trumbach, and as a correction to the gender-blind work of Foucault, I would argue that the emergence of the scientific category of the congenital third sex, or gender (the homosexual), is inextricable from the crisis of gender, or *sexual anarchy*, that is characteristic of the late nineteenth century. The third sex provided, to borrow Trumbach's words regarding the role of the transvestite around 1700, a "wall that guaranteed the permanent, lifelong separation of the majority of men and women, in societies where their relative equality must have been a perpetual danger to patriarchy."[57] Sexual transgression was subject to a discourse concerned less with sexual acts and their effects than with sexual identities and their causes. In the process of providing "itself with a body to be cared for, protected, cultivated, and preserved from many dangers and contacts, to be isolated from others so that it would retain its differential value,"[58] as Foucault describes it, middle-class phallocentric discourses transformed effeminate men and masculine women—against which they were defending and defining themselves—into the erotic species of sexual inverts who became known as the third sex.

The German alienist (psychiatrist) Richard von Krafft-Ebing (1840–1902), credited as the founder of modern sexual pathology, was in large part responsible for the scientific proliferation of the category of the congenital third sex.[59] Influenced by the published writings of Karl Heinrich Ulrichs, a lawyer and self-professed 'urning' (third sex, or homosexual), Krafft-Ebing initiated the shift from viewing homosexual activity as the sinful transgression of the theological doctrine of natural law to viewing it as the manifestation of an individual medical illness.[60] The homosexual third sex was the effect of a form of congenital degeneration whereby the *vita sexualis*, or procreative sex instinct, was thought to be inverted. Subscribing to the work of the French psychiatrist Benedict Morel, Krafft-Ebing thought such sexual pathologies to be hereditarily transmitted via a "tainted" relative who had suffered from environmentally induced diseases of the central nervous system such as syphilis, alcoholism, and mental illness. Certain congenitally tainted individuals were thus born with an "antipathic sexual instinct":

> The essential feature of this strange manifestation of the sexual life is the want of sexual sensibility for the opposite sex, even to the extent of horror, while sexual inclination and impulse toward the same sex are present.... Feeling, thought, will, and the whole character, in cases of the complete development

of the anomaly, correspond with the peculiar sexual instinct, but not with the sex which the individual represents anatomically and physiologically. This abnormal mode of feeling may not infrequently be recognized in the manner, dress and calling of the individuals, who may go so far as to yield to an impulse to don the distinctive clothing corresponding with the *sexual role* in which they feel themselves to be.[61]

For Krafft-Ebing, as for Ulrichs and Carl Westphal before him, the congenital homosexual suffered from a complete inversion of gender role, one aspect of which was the procreative sex instinct.[62] In other words, as George Chauncey has demonstrated, an inversion of the sex instinct was equivalent to an inversion of the total sex role.[63] Sexual object choice was thus a secondary effect of sex role inversion. Ulrichs came close to this point, argued Krafft-Ebing, "when he [spoke] of a female mind in a male body."[64] Similarly, George Beard wrote of gender inversion, that when "the sex is perverted, they [the third sex] hate the opposite sex and love their own; men become women and women men, in their tastes, conduct, character, feelings and behavior."[65]

Clearly, the third sex functioned as a protective interface ensuring a safe distance between the sexes, a catchment zone for the anomalies of gender-transgressive behavior. To this end, the invert served to protect and delimit the boundaries of bourgeois masculinity, not only "transforming sodomites into nonmasculine men who could not endanger the virility of 'normal' men," but also transforming female sex role transgressors into mannish lesbians.[66] As Carroll Smith-Rosenberg points out, for example, "Krafft-Ebing's lesbians seemed to desire male privileges and power as ardently as, perhaps more ardently than, they sexually desired women."[67]

With the challenge to naturalized sex roles and the instantiation of a third sex, the normative category of sex was fractured, effectively producing a sex/gender distinction. Antipathic sexual instinct was not yet fully transformed into a specifically object-directed drive independent of reproductive sex. Instead, it was the inverted product of neuropathic degeneration. In other words, sexuality as a distinct and supplemental register in the matrix of human ontology had yet to be established. Not until the turn of the century would the emphasis shift from one's active or passive, masculine or feminine sex role, to sexual object choice. It is thus important to recognize a conceptual distinction between sex instinct and sexuality, sexual inversion and homosexuality. I will argue that central to the epistemological configuration of sexuality as a distinct register was a developmentally based model of evolutionary theory and, more specifically, the biogenetic concept of bisexuality. Interestingly, as we have seen, this was the very model employed to stabilize the phallocentric register of gender.

FROM GENDER INVERSION TO (BI)SEXUALITY

Arnold Davidson has argued that sexuality as a concept distinct from sex, or gender, is the product of the late-nineteenth-century style of psychiatric reasoning. "Our experience of sexuality," he suggests, "was born at the same time that perversion emerged as the kind of deviation by which sexuality was ceaselessly threatened." Furthermore, "our medical concept of perversion did not exist prior to the mid-nineteenth century but also that there were no perverts before the existence of this concept."[68] By "pervert," Davidson is speaking of a distinct type of person labeled as such not as a consequence of particular moral and ethical choices, but as a consequence of an ontologized identity. I would like to expand on this analysis by suggesting that the shift in medical theory from sex to sexuality, from sexual inversion to sexual object choice, was made possible, *at an epistemological level,* by bisexuality. That is to say, the discursive construction of erotic speciation was brought into epistemic alignment with the doctrine of gendered speciation and was subject to a developmental evolutionary paradigm. At the center of this paradigm was the concept of embryological bisexuality. In fact, bisexuality was positioned at the threshold of the process of speciation itself, serving as the theoretical link between sex/gender and sexuality. Therefore, the individuation of sexuality, to refine Davidson's argument, was an even later effect of the displacing of psychiatric degeneration theory. Before the adoption of the biogenetic model, sexuality, as conceived in discourses of psychiatry, was still tied explicitly to sex role inversion, the degenerate outcome of the chaotic pressures of Western industrializing societies. The notion of separate biological species of sexuality—as opposed to a single-gendered species whose sex instinct was normal or inverted—did not become universal scientific lore until the final years of the nineteenth century.

From about 1897 Havelock Ellis and other sexologists began to delineate more specifically the domain of sexuality as separate yet inextricably interlaced with the register of gender. Sexual object choice proved to be the decisive factor. Despite this shift of emphasis, it is important to remember that the phallocentric notion of sex—the one, the same, the masculine sex—is inscribed at the very heart of the emergent concept of sexuality.[69] Perhaps as a result of the diversification of gender roles and behavior, it became increasingly difficult to maintain the equation of homosexuality with complete gender inversion.[70] Despite his (and other sexologists') difficulty in extending this principle to lesbians, Ellis acknowledged that male homosexuality was not to be conflated with effeminacy or transvestism. For Ellis, that was but a "vulgar error which confuses the typical invert with the painted and petticoated creatures who appear in police-courts from time to time."[71] Homosexual individuals could exhibit what he termed "masculine diathesis," which is to say that "although their affections are directed towards men, they themselves feel as men, not as women, towards the objects of their affections." In short, the homosexual can remain "masculine in his non-sexual habits."[72]

The representations of female homosexuality within sexology at this time continued to equate lesbianism with sex role inversion, and thus with masculinity.[73] "The chief characteristic of the sexually inverted woman is a certain degree of masculinity," declared Ellis:

> The brusque, energetic movements, the attitude of the arms, the direct speech, the inflexions of the voice, the masculine straightforwardness and sense of honour . . . a certain general coarseness of physical texture . . . a comparative absence of soft connective tissue, so that the inverted woman may give an unfeminine impression to the sense of touch . . . [often] a very decidedly masculine type of larynx . . . [and] also a dislike and sometimes incapacity for needlework and other domestic occupations, while there is often some capacity for athletics.[74]

The reason that lesbians continued to be represented for some time as a third sex and as mannish was perhaps because, unlike male homosexuals, the lesbian or New Woman directly challenged the socioeconomic power relations between the sexes. Women were *actively* demanding the right to those social and economic privileges that men, *both* homosexual and heterosexual, enjoyed. In this way, the emergence of the lesbian and the New Woman posed a much more problematic threat to the symbolic order and to masculine identity and power than did the homosexual. For such women were actively seeking status as speaking subjects, or agents in the patriarchal order. This was nothing short of a direct challenge to the very basis of social functioning. In the words of Alice Jardine, "Women who speak are men and, therefore, threaten the very *humanity* of Man."[75] In addition to this, and in a reparative attempt to defend boundaries of gender, scientific discourse had already constructed woman as biologically inferior and suitable only for reproduction. Clearly, however, this failed to contain the feminist challenge. Homosexual men, on the other hand, certainly called into question the boundaries of masculine identity, but their transgressive behavior did not call into question the division between the sexes—one of the primary organizing principles of society.

Epistemic anxieties over transgressions of gender and the challenge to masculine identity remained central to the understanding of sexual inversion, despite the shift of emphasis in regarding sexuality not as sex role related but primarily as object related. However, this shift coincided with the ascendancy within medical discourse of a Darwinian phylogenetic explanatory model of mental disease and sexual behavior.[76] Employed earlier to biologize the differences between blacks and the sexes within the biological and anthropological sciences, evolutionary recapitulation theory became the hegemonic scientific paradigm in fin-de-siècle Western thought. Somatic theories of human difference were paramount, and a developmental model replaced that of degenerative disease. Havelock Ellis, one of the most significant players in this shift, summarized:

> It was during the second half of the nineteenth century, when a new biological conception, under the inspiration of Darwin, was slowly permeating medicine, that the idea of infantile and youthful "perversion" began to be undermined; on the one hand the new scientific study of sex, started by the pioneering work of Krafft-Ebing at the end of the third quarter of the century, showed how common are such so called "perversions" in early life while, on the other hand, the conception of evolution began to make it clear that we must not apply developed adult standards to undeveloped creatures, what is natural at one stage not necessarily being natural at the previous stage.[77]

As George Chauncey has noted, "medical theory tied men and women's gender characteristics so closely to their respective biological sexes that a somatic explanation had to be found for those people who threatened to contradict the theory by appearing to be one sex while assuming the gender role of the other."[78] The third sexes, or homosexuals, thus could not be accounted for by invoking the earlier theories of degeneration that had stressed childhood sexual precocity, masturbation, and neurosis. For these reflected at best, the influential German sexologist Albert Moll suggested, secondary causes of inversion.[79] Moreover, historical and cross-cultural anthropological studies that highlighted the high incidence of homosexuality in cultures such as ancient Greece, undermined degeneration theories.[80]

Instead, the answer had to be found in the evolutionary theory of biological variation. The essence of this phallocentric paradigm was, as I have outlined, the principle of sexual dimorphism, a principle whose very conditions of intelligibility depended upon the concept of embryological bisexuality. This approach to the study of sexuality was developed influentially in the United States. The incorporation of Darwinian evolutionary thought into American psychology led to the promotion of developmental and adaptational theories of human behavior. These were soon applied to the theory of homosexuality. In 1888, the American alienist James Kiernan spearheaded a revolution in the study of sexual development, a move that was to provide the biological bedrock for all of the major sexological theories around the turn of the century. He achieved this through the theory of bisexuality:

> The original bisexuality of the ancestors of the race, shown in rudimentary female organs of the male, could not fail to occasion functional, if not organic, reversions when mental or physical manifestations were interfered with by the disease or congenital defect.... It seems certain that a femininely functioning brain can occupy a male body, and vice versa. Males are born with female external genitals and vice versa. The lowest animals are bisexual and the various types of hermaphroditism are more or less complete reversions to the ancestral type.[81]

A year later, the physician G. Frank Lydston postulated a similar but more biogenetically progressivist account. He invoked the notion of bisexuality to explain sexual perversion as arrested development or maldevelopment, the severest forms of which approached "the type of fetal development which exists prior to the commencement of sexual differentiation."[82] Just as bisexuality had been invoked to account for women's and blacks' developmental inferiority, here too it served to account for sexual inversion. The argument was that the third sex, or homosexual, was an imperfectly sexually differentiated biological variation.[83] "That mal-development, or arrested development, of the sexual organs should be associated with sexual perversion is not at all surprising," suggested Lydston, "and the more nearly the individual approximates the type of fetal development which exists prior to the commencement of sexual differentiation, the more marked is the aberrance of sexuality."[84] This stands as one of the most significant developments in the history of the economy of (hetero)sexuality. *The very process of speciation—of gender, race, and sexuality—takes place through the figure of bisexuality.* Thus, the more highly evolved the species, the more the individual is divested of a bisexual heritage. Each of these three structurally intertwined axes cannot (and ought not) be thought of apart from the others.

Drawing on this theory of bisexual evolution, the influential French Darwinian, Julien Chevalier, offered an apt summary:

> I believe, on the strength of the facts—that is to say, by the evidence of anatomy, physiology, embryology, and teratology—that the prime character-

istic of man, the least contestable although perhaps the most contested, is his animal nature. It is not repugnant to me in the least to consider ourselves as the most elevated in rank among the animals and to regard ourselves further as the inheritors of the qualities and faults that they have bequeathed to the first indistinct races which served as the transition between them and us. All the more so as . . . I consider that it is from the study of sexual evolution in the animal series that one must demand the key to the problem [of homosexuality].[85]

Chevalier was indeed talking about *man*, heterosexual man as the "most elevated in rank among animals," including, of course, blacks and women. It is only the white Western male who had singularly succeeded in reaching the most advanced stage of human evolution by passing through and leaving well behind the residual effects of bisexuality.

Homosexuality was quickly incorporated into the theory of human evolution through the application of the concept of embryological bisexuality. By 1905 it had gained almost universal acceptance among sexologists.[86] As Havelock Ellis noted in 1897, "Embryologists, physiologists of sex and biologists generally, not only accept the idea of bisexuality, but admit that it probably helps to account for homosexuality. In this way the idea may be said to have passed into current thought."[87] Krafft-Ebing also inserted the bisexual theory of homosexuality into his 1892 revision of his *Psychopathia Sexualis*. Relying on the theories of Kiernan, Lydston, and Chevalier, Krafft-Ebing argued that "monosexuality gradually developed from bisexuality" (365). To explain this, Krafft-Ebing proposed, following Chevalier, that "the individual being must also pass through these grades of evolution; it is originally bisexual, but in the struggle between the male and female elements either one or the other is conquered, and a monosexual being is evolved which corresponds with the type of the present stage of evolution" (366). Homosexuality, for Krafft-Ebing, was thus the archaic residue of primordial bisexuality, the disappearance of which was to be expected at the highest phase of monosexual evolution. "This destruction of antipathic sexuality," he noted, "is at present not yet completed" (366). Albert Moll and Havelock Ellis—the two great sexological figures to succeed Krafft-Ebing—appropriated the bisexual theory of homosexuality.[88] Rejecting the theory of degeneration, which Krafft-Ebing retained in conjunction with the new biogenetic concept of bisexuality, Moll and Ellis explained homosexuality as arrested development. Taking as their departure point Max Dessoir's two-stage theory of human development, they argued that in the first stage the sexual instinct of a child was undifferentiated in relation to sexual object. This was followed, however, by the second stage, wherein the libido becomes exclusively heterosexually directed. The failure to progress to the second stage meant that some individuals "remain in an embryonic state and continue to express homosexual, bisexual, or other inclinations as adults."[89]

The displacing of the psychiatric notion of degeneration was clearly part of a larger shift from sex to sexuality in the second half of the nineteenth century. As Frank Sulloway has noted, in one of the most historically contextualized accounts of the shifting terrain of sexological discourse, that

> as long as sexuality had been looked upon as a homogeneous impulse, a congenital conception of sexual pathology had remained synonymous with hereditary degeneration to an atavistic condition. But when the theories of Clevenger, Kiernan, Chevalier, and others began to separate the healthy sexual instinct into bisexual and other evolutionary components, it finally became possible to recognize sexual perversion as arising from *developmental* disturbances in these normal, component impulses.[90]

So with the sexological appropriation of the biogenetic concept of bisexuality, the procreative sex instinct—construed as a singular force dependent upon gender role—gave way to a biologically differentiated, dualistic, and individualized notion of sexuality. On the Darwinian chain of being, therefore, homosexuals were evolutionary anomalies, indicative of a temporally and spatially distinct and retrograde species. There were thus two distinct and separate species with two separate sex instincts, or sexualities: the homosexual and the heterosexual.

HAVELOCK ELLIS AND THE ALLIANCE OF SEX / GENDER AND SEXUALITY

Before Freud's ascendancy to the position of preeminent theorist of sexuality, the most influential and theoretically comprehensive sexologist within the newly emerging economy of (hetero)sexuality was Havelock Ellis. His work represents the indivisibility of the new alliance of sex/gender and sexuality. A forerunner in theorizing the sex/gender distinction, the conceptual inextricability of the categories sex, gender, and sexuality was usefully captured in the title of his synthesized seven-volume work, *Studies in the Psychology of Sex*. In his first book to deal with issues of sex and gender, Ellis began by investigating the differences between the sexes in order to clarify the hotly debated 'problem of woman'. In *Man and Woman: A Study of Human Secondary Sexual Characters*, Ellis aimed to provide a dispassionate review of current scientific knowledge in the area. "What are our standards of comparison for sexual characters in man or in woman?" he asked in a section entitled "How to Approach the Problem." Echoing not only the nineteenth-century preoccupation with race but also the biogenetic developmental solution to this problem, Ellis reminded readers of the two standards: "The first is constituted by the child and its anatomical and physiological characteristics. The second is constituted by the characters of the ape, the savage, and the aged human creature."[91]

Despite his greater sophistication and sensitivity to the evaluation of scientific constructions of sex difference, Ellis largely reproduced the dominant themes of late nineteenth-century thought. Women were deemed closer to the child and the 'savage', or 'Negro', the product of a greater precocity than men, an arrested form of development. This resulted in their proportional resemblance to children (65). Throughout the text Ellis made innumerable allegorical associations between women and blacks, or the 'lower' races, via the equation of the woman with the child: "The child is naturally, by his organization, nearer to the animal, to the savage, to the criminal, than the adult."[92] The comparative analysis of traits such as eyesight, disvulnerability (quick repair of wounds), and sensitivity to pain revealed a kinship between women and 'savages', 'lower' races.[93] While Ellis was quick to point out that (women's and) blacks' greater resistance to pain "does not seem necessarily related to the evolutionary scale of the race," the kinship between women and blacks was always couched in hierarchical evolutionary terms. Women and blacks were always less 'civilized' or advanced. For instance, he noted that "among the lower animals there is a high degree of disvulnerability. Among savages it is everywhere well marked" (151).

Ellis's account of sex difference and eyesight is particularly illuminating in terms of the rhetorical operations deployed to counter 'civilized' man's greater tendency to suffer serious eye defects. "Taking the evidence as a whole," he noted, "we may conclude that in most, if not all, civilised countries women are more liable to the slight disturbances of eye sight, due to defective accommodation, which are peculiarly associated with civilisation; while men are probably more liable to serious eye-defects." Regarding the association of sight disturbances with civilization, Ellis inserted a rather interesting and revealing footnote: "Animals furnish a confirmation of the association of eye-defects with civilized conditions. Motais . . . stated that having examined the eyes of wild beasts, captured after they had reached adult age, he found them normal; those captured earlier, and still more those born in captivity, were short-sighted" (171 n). In other words, women are closer to animals. With civilization capturing woman at a later stage of adult development than man, she thereby suffered less the disturbances due to "defective accommodation" than man, who was born into the captivity of civilization. After all women "have not wandered so far as they [men] have from the typical life of earth's creatures . . . the embodiments of the restful responsiveness of Nature" (171). More specifically, *women, as well as blacks and children, have not wandered so far as men from primordial and primitive bisexuality.*

Ellis thus appropriated the model of neo-Darwinian biogenetic thinking, of which bisexuality was a central figure, in order to solve the 'problem of sex', which he saw as "the central problem of life." "The question of sex," he declared, "—with the racial questions that rest on it—stands before the coming generation as the chief problem for solution."[94] Bisexuality lay at the heart of this solution. Endorsing the theories of "the latest physiologists of sex," Ellis observed that "we have to admit each sex contains the latent characters of the other or recessive sex. Each sex is latent in the other, and each, as it contains the characters of both sexes (and can transmit those of the recessive sex) is latently hermaphrodite."[95]

Clearly, Ellis had inherited the scientific and social concern of defining the relations between the sexes and the races; a concern that represented, as I have suggested, an epistemic challenge to bourgeois masculine identity. Central to this challenge was the problem of sexual psychology and an adequate scientific explanation for "sexual inversion." With the fracturing of sex and the superimposition of a sex/gender distinction, Ellis attempted in *Man and Woman* to reinforce the threatened epistemological boundaries of gender. And the shift from gender inversion to homosexuality entailed the redefinition of the category of homosexuality. As I have shown, for Ellis homosexuality, or sexual inversion, was "a psychic and somatic development on the basis of a latent bisexuality."[96]

Bisexuality was thus the pivotal epistemic tool employed for containing the crisis of masculine identity informing Havelock Ellis's sexual science. In this evolutionary schema, the path to (hu)manhood necessitates the stripping of race, and (bi)sex. Racialized sexual difference is thereby constructed as the effect of the process of white masculine (self-)evolution, or self-definition, the incomplete achievement of which results in the arrested or maldeveloped species variations of blacks, women, and homosexuals. Despite the introduction of the sex/gender distinction, sexuality was no longer conflated with gender (role), and the evolutionary model dictated that the two were not only mutually implicating but mutually constitutive. This was necessary for the scientific cataloging of individuals seen to be transgressing the boundaries of appropriate (hu)manhood in order to account for those disruptive of the phallocentric hierarchies of race and gender. The category of biological bisexuality provided the conceptual link for the alliance of gender and sexuality, purportedly generating the distinct categories and anomalous variations of sex, gender, and sexuality. Within the heteroteleology of human recapitulation, therefore, an individual was seen to be bestowed with a (bi)sex from which ensued the apposite psychical gender and (hetero)sexuality. Deviations from this standard progressivist and linear process were to fall short of the final goal of (hu)man evolution. This was a shortcoming that indicated the unsuccessful repudiation of bisexuality.

(HU)MAN SPECIATION AND THE (DIS)AVOWAL OF BISEXUALITY

In the scientific economy of (hetero)sexuality bisexuality was figured as the elusive Other in the evolutionary process of (hu)man speciation. On the great sexological chain of being, therefore, the heterosexual male was situated at the top of the hierarchy, representative of *the* human and of culture itself; he was a (hu)man defined negatively against the lower and less-than-(hu)man forms of women, homosexuals, and blacks. How, then, did this formula incorporate those who failed to fit into these exclusive and homogeneous categories?[97] After all, even in his 1897 publication, *Sexual Inversion*, Ellis acknowledged the "person who is organically twisted into a shape that is more fitted for the exercise of the inverted than of the normal sexual impulse, *or else equally fitted for both.*"[98] Was there a bisexual species?

The case of psychosexual hermaphroditism, or psychological bisexuality, had been recognized long before Ellis's intervention into sexology. Ulrichs had identified this species as "uranodionism," but had been unable to account for its existence according to his theory of the bisexual embryo.[99] Krafft-Ebing had discussed "psychical hermaphroditism"; however, he argued that the individual manifesting this condition was primarily homosexual.[100] In both of these cases, the possibility of bisexuality as an ontological category scarcely received any substantive analytic attention. Any taint of homosexual activity was usually enough to effect the subsumption of bisexuality into the categories of homosexuality or pseudohomosexuality.[101] Ellis was contradictory on this score. On the one hand, he claimed that "there would seem to be a broad and simple grouping of all sexually functioning persons into three comprehensive divisions: the heterosexual, the bisexual, and the homosexual."[102] Yet, on the other hand, he affirmed, like Krafft-Ebing, that "most of the bisexual prefer their own sex

... [and that this] would seem to indicate that the bisexual may really be inverts [sic]." "In any case," stated Ellis, "bisexuality merges imperceptibly into simple inversion" (278). Clearly, the existence of individuals exhibiting a "double direction of the sexual instinct" (88) occupied a problematic conceptual space within sexological discourse. How do we account for this resistance to construct the bisexual as a species?

Ellis knew precisely the epistemological dilemma for the discipline of sexology. The elementary classification of individuals into the categories of heterosexual, bisexual, and homosexual, he insisted, "seems however of no practical use ... it is scarcely a scientific classification." Why? "The bisexual group is found to introduce uncertainty and doubt" (88). I argue that this is because bisexuality as a definitive human species would disrupt the very classificatory alliance of sex/gender and sexuality. It threatened to absorb both of these differentiating human registers and dissolve the boundaries of human identity. This would effectively render meaningless the axes of human difference within scientific discourse. Indeed, as I outlined earlier, the stability and coherence of 'civilization' was also rhetorically threatened, as implicit to evolutionary science was the notion that the most highly evolved (male) culture required the transcendence and repudiation of sexual ambiguity and bisexuality. The "possession of a [single sex] is a necessity for our social order," declared two French physicians writing on the problem posed by human hermaphroditism.[103] (In the context of the crisis of gender at this time, we might also read this quotation as unwittingly suggesting that a single sex is a necessity *of* social order.) So despite the scientific fact observed by Ellis that the "concept of latent bisexuality of all males and females cannot fail to be fairly obvious to intelligent observers of the human body," that same concept at once rendered the very category of sex paradoxical.[104] For inherent to the notion of the universality of primordial bisexuality was that other biological fact, accepted by Ellis and many influential scientists, that "there is no such thing as a pure male or female."[105] With the epistemic boundaries of sex, gender, and sexuality spilling over into one another, an irresolvable contradiction lay at the heart of discourses of sexual science: if all individuals are physiologically bisexual to one degree or another, then, as a result, there is no reason to assume that they are not also potentially bisexual in psychological orientation. After all, as Ellis himself pointed out,

> Not only a large proportion of persons who may fairly be considered heterosexual have at some time in their lives experienced a feeling which may be termed sexual toward individuals of their own sex, but a very large proportion

of persons who are definitely and markedly homosexual have had relationships with persons of the opposite sex. The social pressure, urging all persons into the normal sexual channel, suffices to develop such slight germs of heterosexuality as homosexual persons may possess, and so render them bisexual.[106]

CONCLUSION

Within sexological discourse, bisexuality provided the fulcrum that enabled the axes of race, sex/gender, and sexuality to be meaningfully mapped onto the hegemonic paradigm of evolutionary speciation. Concomitantly, bisexuality was that over and against which the various hierarchically ordered human species were defined. Quite simply, bisexuality encompassed the very opposition of sameness/difference necessary for the articulation of a homogeneous (hu)man identity erected around distinctions of race, sex/gender, and sexuality. The coherence, or self-sameness, of the entity of the (hu)man was thereby structurally predicated on a repudiation of a difference internal to itself: that is, bisexuality. The effect of an unsuccessful repudiation, the subhuman forms of woman, black, and homosexual retained archaic elements of the *originary* human bisexuality. (Of course the postembryonic hermaphrodite was a living example of primordial bisexuality.)

The difficulty for sexologists constrained by a linear logic of temporal succession was how to reconcile bisexuality as at one and the same time both a cause and effect, nature and culture, origin and omega, beginning and end. To grant bisexuality the status of species only contradicted this logic of heteroteleology; hence Ellis's reduction of bisexuality to the opacity of "uncertainty and doubt," and the general sexological tendency to disregard what was more easily subsumable under the rubric of homosexuality. Bisexuality was thereby dis/avowed: it was both avowed, as an originary human state, and yet simultaneously disavowed, as a distinct sexual identity. Put another way, 'full bisexuality' was erased from the present tense in order to avert a crisis of meaning for the identities of (white) man, woman, heterosexual, and homosexual.[107] It was relegated to a place and time outside culture, to the sphere of prehistory. In this way bisexuality was a necessary blind spot for a sexological discourse stretched to its epistemic limits.

In the following chapter I will examine the concept of bisexuality in the work of Sigmund Freud. Arguably the most influential theorist of sexuality in the twentieth century, Freud took over this concept and made it the centerpiece of his psychoanalytic theory. I will explore how he used and yet simultaneously refused bisexuality in order to construct a coherent theory of gender and sexuality.

3

"THE UNSOLVED FIGURE
IN THE CARPET"

> But why can't bisexuals go to their own venues, you ask? The answer is of course, that there is no such thing as a bisexual venue: bisexuality is a state of mind, not a sexual practice. No one is bisexual at any given moment: there being only two genders (most of the time) specific sexual desire (as opposed to generalised sexual fantasy) must be directed towards one or the other, even if alternatively. So at the moment of truth, which is usually on Saturday night at about 4 a.m., your self-defined bisexual must decide between King St. and Peel St., and he'd better hurry before all the talent gets taken.
> —Lance Spurr 1995

In this chapter, and by way of mapping certain genealogical links to contemporary representations of bisexuality, I would like to retrace Sigmund Freud's account of the development of gender and sexuality. Freud is positioned as one of the crucial progenitors of the economy of (hetero)sexuality. As I demonstrated in chapter 2, this is an economy constructed through a curious dis/avowal of bisexuality, an erasure of (full) bisexuality from the present tense.[1] That is to say, although sexologists defined bisexuality as a prehistoric, precultural, or infantile state, they simultaneously repudiated any definition of bisexuality as a distinct adult identity. Freud reinforced and expanded this emerging economy, consolidating the monosexual framework of hetero/homosexuality. In contrast to the biologistic models of sexology, however, he strove to formulate a coherent psychological theory of sexuality. Bisexuality was the cornerstone of this theory. But it was a problematic concept, precarious and elusive, and one that carried multiple meanings. Bisexuality conditioned and ultimately constrained Freud's theory of psychosexual development. I will argue that Freud was never able fully to elaborate or formulate his theory of bisexuality—a project he vowed to complete—without endangering the coherence of the Oedipus complex.² As a result, and in similar fashion to the early sexologists, in Freud's work bisexuality was elided from the present tense.

Were it not for the discussion of nightclub venues, the statement of Lance Spurr quoted above could just as easily have been written in the late-Freudian 1930s and post-Freudian 1940s or 1950s.³ His remark incorporates a wide range of assumptions from theorists whose work became formative of the economy of (hetero)sexuality. First, it is presumed that there are only two genders "most of the time." The qualifier "most of the time" is not meant here to signal a pluralization of binary gender; rather, it would be to invoke the notion of a third gender. From the ancient and medieval periods to the writings of nineteenth-century biologists and evolutionists, this third gender was often referred to in somatic terms by the concept androgyne, hermaphrodite, or what Freud termed "true hermaphroditism."⁴ It seems that Spurr is alluding to this use of somatic hermaphroditism, and, I suggest, probably even transsexualism.

Second, Spurr equates sexual desire with gendered desire, betraying obvious epistemic connections with sexologists of the late nineteenth century, such as Krafft-Ebing. Third, in what can only be described as an awkward combination of this conflated sexual/gendered desire with a neo-Freudian concept of fantasy, Spurr makes an unusual distinction between "specific sexual desire" and "generalised sexual fantasy."⁵ And fourth, and most important for this chapter, is the suggestion that "no one is bisexual at any given moment." For according to Spurr, "specific sexual desire . . . must be directed towards one or the other [gender], even if alternatively." Here *alternatively* is operating in two senses. On the one hand is the invocation of 'choice', wherein the choice and experience of one "specific sexual desire" in an encounter involves the rejection of the other gendered desire. On the other hand is the sense of *alternating*, such that in a ménage à trois, for example, the two "specific sexual desires" experienced by one person with two opposite gendered objects cannot be experienced simultaneously, but must succeed each other by turns.

As will become apparent later, it is at this point in Spurr's thought that the resemblances to the Freudian theory of sexual desire are most apparent. John Fletcher puts the point nicely in his succinct appraisal of one of Freud's most renowned dogmas: "'You cannot be what you desire; you cannot desire what you wish to be.'"⁶

BIOMYTHOLOGY AND PRIMORDIAL BISEXUALITY

> In the beginning we were nothing like we are now. For one thing, the race was divided into three, that is to say, besides the two sexes, male and female,

> which we have at present, there was a third which partook of the nature of both, and for which we still have a name, though the creature itself is forgotten. For though "hermaphrodite" is only used nowadays as a term of contempt, there really was a man-woman in those days, a being which was half male and half female.
> —Aristophanes

Before tracing Freud's ideas on gender and sexuality, it is important to map out briefly the historical and intellectual context within which his work was situated. Freud's ideas, like the circuitous path of sexual desire itself, do not follow a smooth and elemental course of linear development. His theories progress as much as they regress, constantly shifting and changing according to the vicissitudes of his personal life, his intellectual environment, and his unconscious and conscious responses to these forces in an effort to provide a seamless and coherent narrative of human psychosexual development.

Freud embarked upon a career in science as a biologist, having studied in the fields of zoology, anatomy, and physiology. Lamarckian and Darwinian evolutionary biology were predominant in the intellectual milieu of the late nineteenth century.[7] Mindful of the force of this evolutionary influence early on in his life, Freud stated in his autobiography that the "theories of Darwin, which were then of topical interest, strongly attracted me, for they held out hopes of an extraordinary advance in our understanding of the world."[8] Among nineteenth-century evolutionists, as we saw in chapter 2, a biological concept of hermaphroditism, appropriated from ancient Greek mythology and rewritten in scientific terms, was understood to be contained in the ancestral lineage of all vertebrate organisms.[9] For Darwin, "some extremely remote progenitor of the whole vertebrate kingdom appears to have been hermaphrodite or androgynous."[10] This presupposition was based on the notion of a human bisexual nature apparent in the coincidence of both sexes' sexual organs until the third month of human embryonic life. As Frank Sulloway points out, primordial hermaphroditism thus became the evolutionist's "missing bisexual link."[11]

Wilhelm Fliess, Freud's most trusted friend and mentor of fifteen years, introduced him to the concept of biological bisexuality[12]—the new axiomatic concept of hegemonic evolutionism.[13] In a letter of reply to Fliess in 1899, Freud declared excitedly: "bisexuality! I am sure you are right about it."[14] And in line with the evolutionary theories of primordial hermaphroditism, Freud proposed that such "long-familiar facts of anatomy lead us to suppose that an originally bisexual physical disposition has, in the course of evolution, become modified into a unisexual one, leaving behind only a few traces of the sex that has become atrophied."[15] In 1917 Freud further revealed a decisive intellectual commitment to evolutionary theories when he affirmed that "Lamarck's theory of evolution coincides with the final outcome of psychoanalytic thinking."[16]

Despite his ponderous academic debt to evolutionary thinking, however, Freud directed his efforts toward a disciplinary secession from the biological and physiological domains. In deference to these fields, but with the desire to establish his intellectual originality and independence, he sought to establish the psychological correlate to evolutionary biology. His ideas about the unconscious, for example, could be invoked in a Lamarckian context and proffered as the psychoanalytic manifestation of the notion of 'necessity'. For Lamarck, according to Freud, 'necessity' was responsible for the production and transfiguration of organisms. When translated through psychoanalysis, 'necessity' could be seen as "the power of unconscious ideas over one's own body." Thus, for Freud, this "would actually supply a psycho-analytic explanation of adaptation; it would put the coping stone on psycho-analysis."[17]

After appropriating concepts from biology, and in particular the concept of bisexuality from Fliess, Freud attempted to transform and distance himself from them in order to claim the independence of psychoanalysis.[18] Nevertheless, initially he was cognizant of his debt to Fliess. "We share like the two beggars, one of whom allotted himself the province of Posen; you take the biological, I the psychological," remarked Freud in 1897.[19] But by 1901, Freud misrecognized the centrality of Fliess's contribution to his thought.[20] In what could only have been a letter of response to Fliess's indignation at such a maneuver, Freud defensively declared that he had "no intention of doing anything but working on *my* contribution to the theory of bisexuality"; for after all "almost everything I know about it comes from you."[21] However, it was regarding this point of intellectual proprietorship that Freud had suffered what Ernest Jones called "a very severe case of amnesia."[22] Freud later confirmed this reading himself, when he recalled the event in which the issue of proprietorship surfaced:

> One day in the summer of 1901 [it was in fact 1900] I remarked to a friend with whom I used at that time to have a lively exchange of scientific ideas: "These problems of the neuroses are only to be solved if we base ourselves wholly and completely on the assumption of the original bisexuality of the individual." To which he replied: "That's what I told you two and a half years ago at Br. [Breslau] when we went for that evening walk. But you wouldn't

hear of it then." It is painful to be requested in this way to surrender one's originality. I could not recall any such conservation or this pronouncement of my friend's.[23]

The issue of originality and appropriation led Fliess to initiate a painful dissolution of the friendship.[24] The whole incident had a distressing and lasting emotional effect on Freud and, in a letter to Fliess in July 1904, he revealed his desire to "avoid the topic of bisexuality as far as possible" in writing *Three Essays on the Theory of Sexuality*.[25]

It is against this backdrop of the Fliess-Freud separation that the unsolved figure of bisexuality within the Freudian corpus must be situated.[26] Bisexuality functioned as an "overpresence." Both avowed and disavowed, absent and present, bisexuality was an "excess," a "surplus," an "overabundance."[27] "Since I have become acquainted with the notion of bisexuality," Freud wrote in *Three Essays*, "I have regarded it as the decisive factor, and without taking bisexuality into account I think it would scarcely be possible to arrive at an understanding of the sexual manifestations that are actually to be observed in men and women."[28]

Bisexuality provided the very substratum of psychoanalysis, but a substratum that sat as a painful and threatening reminder of Freud's original debt to Fliess and his subsequent separation from him.[29] Furthermore, bisexuality, not unlike the evolutionist's "missing bisexual link," served as the dialectical link between the two forces structuring Freud's work: the biological and the psychological. In other words, biological bisexuality was Freud's link to the natural sciences which, as I will demonstrate later, could not be severed easily.[30] We are reminded of his commitment to biology in a letter to Fliess prior to their estrangement, in which he pointed out that he had "no desire at all to leave the psychology hanging in the air with no organic basis."[31] Freud thus could not entirely dis/avow biological bisexuality, for "psycho-analysis has a common basis with biology, in that it presupposes an original bisexuality in human beings (as in animals). But psycho-analysis cannot elucidate the intrinsic nature of what in conventional phraseology is termed 'masculine' and 'feminine': it simply takes over the two concepts and makes them the foundation of its work."[32]

Instead, as Marjorie Garber claims, Freud recast bisexuality through four "mythological tropes" as allegories for the representation of a science of the psychology of human sexuality.[33] Thus, through the conflation of evolutionary biology and ancient mythology, Freud attempted to provide a coherent narrative in order to conceal the unbridgeable gulf between biology and psychoanalysis.[34] Situated within this gulf, or interval, bisexuality functioned as a liminal concept with a double-edged effect. "I have no idea yet why I cannot yet fit it together [the psychological and the organic]," exclaimed Freud early on in his career in a letter to Fliess in 1898.[35] In 1930, Freud was still puzzled. He lamented that the "theory of bisexuality is still surrounded by many obscurities and we cannot but feel it as a serious impediment in psycho-analysis that it has not yet found any link with the theory of the instincts."[36] And upon returning to this great enigma toward the end of his life Freud had still made no ground:

> We are faced here by the great enigma of the biological fact of the duality of the sexes: it is an ultimate fact of our knowledge, it defies every attempt to trace it back to something else. Psycho-analysis has contributed nothing to clearing up this problem, which clearly falls wholly within the province of biology. In mental life we only find reflections of this great antithesis; and their interpretation is made more difficult by the fact, long suspected, that no individual is limited to the modes of reaction of a single sex but always finds some room for those of the opposite one, just as his body bears, alongside of the fully developed organs of one sex, atrophied and often useless rudiments of those of the other. This fact of psychological bisexuality, too, embarrasses all our enquiries into the subject and makes them harder to describe.[37]

The most significant *mythological trope* of all for Freudian theory is the myth of Oedipus. An allegory for the universalized account of human psychosexual development, the Oedipus complex was proffered by Freud as an attempt to develop the concept of bisexuality. Resistant, liminal, and in-between, however, bisexuality could not be defined exhaustively through a dialectical logic of binary opposition. As I will demonstrate, it was both constructive and deconstructive of the psychoanalytic theory of sexuality; as such this necessitated bisexuality's 'nature' to be shrouded in mystery. Bisexuality was the central aporia of Freudian thought.

BISEXUALITY, SEXUAL DIFFERENCE, AND SUBJECT FORMATION

Repression, the "crucial problem," as Freud suggested in 1901, presupposes and inaugurates the unconscious with the arrival of the Oedipus complex. It is "only possible through reaction between two sexual impulses."[38] As one of the central postulates of psychoanalysis,[39] bisexuality was originally accorded a pivotal role in repression. Seizing on the theory from Fliess, it was not until 1914 that Freud published a repudiation of bisexuality's place in repression. "To insist that bisexuality is the motive force leading to repression is to take too narrow a view."[40] However, in a characteristic vacillation, Freud later suggested that in the normal oedipal outcome "it is the attitude proper to the opposite sex which has succumbed to repression."[41] As we will see, Freud's attempt here to avoid sexualizing repression on biological grounds faltered in the face of a biologized concept of bisexuality.[42]

Occupying the psychic zone for the playing out of conflict "between two sexual impulses," the Oedipus complex is firmly grounded on Freud's rather ambiguous concept of bisexuality. Installed as "one of the cornerstones" of psychoanalysis,[43] the Oedipus complex takes its name from Sophocles' play, *Oedipus Rex*, the tragic story of an ancient king who gradually discovers himself to have unknowingly killed an old man who was in fact his father, and to have wed and had children with a woman who is in fact his mother. As punishment, Oedipus blinds himself and deserts his kingdom. Freud's discussion of this ancient tragedy and its effect on his thinking in relation to sexuality first occurred in 1897 in a letter to Fliess: "A single idea of general value dawned on me. I have found, in my own case too, (the phenomenon of) being in love with my mother and jealous of my father, and I now consider it a universal event in early childhood."[44] Although it was not formally articulated by Freud until 1910, the Oedipus complex came to designate a complex of ideas that were considered universally responsible for the psychological distinction between the sexes. Freud's early theory of sexual difference was indubitably heteronormative, believing as he did in a form of constitutional heterosexual desire: "A girl's first affection is for her father and a boy's first childish desires are for his mother."[45] Not until his 1931 paper, "Female Sexuality," did Freud come to the conclusion that "the primary conditions for a choice of object are, of course, the same for all children": that is, the first object choice for both boys and girls is the mother.[46] This led him to reject the earlier idea that sexual development for boys and girls was similar.[47] Having discarded the presumption of primary heterosexual attraction, Freud was now faced with the task of providing a psychic account of normative heterosexuality not based directly on any constitutional given, but nonetheless in line with his concept of bisexuality. The crucial move was the introduction of the 'masculine' castration complex and its 'feminine' analogue, "penis envy."

The Oedipus complex, the triangular relation between mother, father, and child, is the manifestation of psychic conflicts arising from the erotic strivings of the child for his parents and the complex interaction of love and competition among them. During the phallic stage of sexual development wherein the child enjoys the satisfactions of narcissistic masturbation (i.e., a libidinal cathexis for the penis in boys and clitoris in girls), the primary object-cathexis for the mother becomes explicitly sexualized and the child desires to have intercourse with the mother. Here, both male and female children are confronted with the biological reality of the genital contrast between the sexes, and their respective paths of gender and psychosexual development diverge.

The boy identifies at this point with the father. "For a time these two relationships proceed side by side," argues Freud, "until the boy's sexual wishes in regard to his mother become more intense and his father is perceived as an obstacle to them; from this the Oedipus complex originates."[48] Thereafter, the boy wishes to dispense with the father and take up the father's position with the mother; this results in an ambivalent relation to the father. By way of avoiding the shortcomings of his earlier presupposition, which could not have accounted for a homosexual object choice, Freud introduces into the Oedipus complex the concept of bisexuality. The boy thus "also behaves like a girl and displays an affectionate attitude towards his father and a corresponding jealousy and hostility towards his mother."[49] The dissolution of the Oedipus complex is brought about by the threat of castration, itself a product of the perception of the female, "whom (he) regards as being castrated."[50] The boy's erotic strivings for both mother and father entail the threat of castration: reserved only for the father, sexual access to the mother is prohibited by the incest taboo, and this cultural law is protected with the threat of castration as punishment. The passive desire to be the sexual object of the father's love also entails the loss of penis as its precondition.

For the boy, therefore, the Oedipus complex is "smashed to pieces,"[51] because, as Freud proposes: "If the satisfaction of love in the field of the Oedipus complex is to cost the child his penis, a conflict is bound to arise between his narcissistic interest in that part of the body and the libidinal cathexis of his parental objects. In this conflict the first of these forces normally triumphs: the child's ego turns away from the Oedipus complex."[52] As a result, the object-cathexes are abandoned and substituted by identifications. The little boy identifies either with the father through the establishment of the superego—which thereby redirects his sexual desires to other women[53]—or with the mother, usually as a result of a narcissistic and intense fixation. In the case of the latter, such boys would "identify themselves with a woman and take *themselves* as a sexual object."[54]

Until 1924 Freud regarded the Oedipus complex of the girl to be a much simpler route than that of the boy.[55] However, by 1935 he had reversed this idea. Freud put forward the hypothesis that the normative oedipal process for the girl was far more complicated due to the fact of two additional tasks. This was the outcome of his surprising discovery—analogous to the equally surprising "discovery, in another field, of the Minoan-Mycenean civilization behind the civilization of Greece"—of the girl's preoedipal attachment to the mother.[56] While the boy has only to redirect his sexual desires to other women while maintaining the primacy of the phallic genital zone, the girl must not only shift her sexual object from woman to man, but as well she must alter her sexual aim, from active, phallic, 'masculine' clitoridal aims, to passive, vaginal, 'feminine' ones.[57] Here we arrive at the female analogue to castration anxiety: penis envy. Despite Freud's recognition that sexual development for girls and boys took different paths, the overarching framework remained a masculine *economy of the same*.[58] The penis was the decisive factor in both male and female sexuality.

Unlike boys, for whom the Oedipus complex is smashed by the castration complex, for girls the Oedipus complex is made possible by it.[59] Inaugurated through a 'momentous discovery' of that paragon of somatic distinction, "they notice the penis of a brother or playmate, strikingly visible and of large proportions," suggests Freud, and "at once recognize it as the superior counterpart to their own small and inconspicuous organ, and from that time forward fall a victim to envy for the penis."[60] Upon acknowledging the fact of her 'actual' castration, the girl holds her mother accountable and cannot "forgive her for their being thus put at a disadvantage."[61] Her intense object-cathexis for the mother is renounced, and with it, active clitoridal masturbation, in an effort to alleviate her narcissistic wound. Having been refused a penis by the mother, the girl turns her attentions to her father in the hope of gaining a penis. And in a rather slippery and unexamined move, Freud figures that 'normal' feminine development is achieved "if the wish for a penis is replaced by one for a baby, if, that is, a baby takes the place of a penis in accordance with an ancient symbolic equivalence."[62]

The active clitoridal desires are thus replaced with passive feminine ones, and the girl hopes to be impregnated by the father and bear him a child: the symbolic substitute for the lost penis. "Only if her development follows . . . [this] very circuitous . . . path does she reach the final normal female attitude."[63] Two other lines of development may ensue, however: a recoiling from sexuality altogether or a masculinity complex. The latter involves both a denial of her castration in the hope of gaining a penis in the future and an identification with the father.[64]

But what in fact determines the dissolution of the Oedipus complex for both sexes? How are the interdependent axes of identification and desire set up? The incessant conflict of masculine and feminine forces (originary bisexual disposition) in every human being is, for Freud, only ever (incompletely) resolved through the repression of either of these "instinctual impulses."[65] The Oedipus complex is twofold, therefore, consisting in positive and negative outcomes. "At the dissolution of the Oedipus complex," Freud proposes:

> the four trends of which it consists will group themselves in such a way as to produce a father-identification and a mother-identification. The father-identification will preserve the object-relation to the mother which belonged to the positive complex and will at the same time replace the object-relation to the father which belonged to the inverted complex: and the same will be true, *mutatis mutandis*, of the mother-identification.[66]

Bisexuality underpins this more complete, twofold Oedipus complex, but it also complicates the matter for Freud. Bisexuality "makes it so difficult to obtain a clear view of the facts in connection with the earliest object-choices and identifications," let alone "describe them intelligibly." "It may even be," Freud admitted, "that the ambivalence displayed in the relations to the parents should be attributed entirely to bisexuality, and that it is not, as I have represented above, developed out of identification in consequence of rivalry" (33). In a typical maneuver, Freud here attempts to cover all bases and to defer the question of bisexuality's meaning through recourse to the nebulous concepts of 'masculine' and 'feminine': "It would appear, therefore, that in both sexes the relative strength of the masculine and feminine dispositions is what determines whether the outcome of the Oedipus situation shall be an identification with the father or with the mother. This is one of the ways in which bisexuality takes a hand in the subsequent vicissitudes of the Oedipus complex" (33).

Moreover, for Freud, it is precisely the fact of identification that foregrounds desire. In other words, in order to reach the genital stage of development and become a desiring subject, an individual must have first—by passing through the Oedipus complex with its installation of identificatory processes—become a psychically sexed subject. Mikkel Borch-Jacobsen observes of Freud that "identification brings the desiring subject into being, and not the other way around."[67] Yet, Freud's recourse to the masculine and feminine dispositions, themselves reflective of originary bisexuality, suggests that his account of gendered psychosexual development fails to explain identification and desire in this way. In fact, by resorting to bisexuality, Freud contradicts this notion of identification as the anticipatory force of desire. Rather, identification overlays and results in part from *masculine and feminine dispositions*, reflecting "the preponderance in him of one or other of two sexual dispositions."[68] And "we must bear in mind," as

Freud had once suggested, "that some day all our provisional formulations in psychology will have to be based on an organic foundation. It will then probably be seen that it is special chemical substances and processes which achieve the effects of sexuality and the perpetuation of individual life in the life of the species."[69]

While Freud does insist that constitutional factors are not in themselves explanation enough without consideration of accidental ones, his model of oedipal identifications does not and cannot proffer an answer to the question of which identification will become manifest in a child. Indeed, the balancing act between the constitutional and accidental factors makes even more inexplicable Freud's exegesis on identification. "The constitutional factor must await experiences before it can make itself felt," Freud explained in a 1915 addendum to the *Three Essays*, while "the accidental factor must have a constitutional basis in order to come into operation." He then goes on to suggest that "to cover the majority of cases we can picture what has been described as a 'complemental series' in which the diminishing intensity of one factor is balanced by the increasing intensity of the other." Then in typical circularity, and in seeming ignorance of its damaging implications, Freud concedes in the concluding part of the sentence, that *"there is, however, no reason to deny the existence of extreme cases at the two ends of the series."*[70] Apart from the fact that the "majority of cases" is a theoretical presumption gleaned from his work on the perversions and neuroses, his assertion of the existence of extreme cases at either end of the series sits as a peculiar and undermining element of his focus on psychical processes. For if the constitutional factors remain impenetrable to psychoanalysis, and their "'continual mingling and blending'"[71] with accidental or acquired factors is inevitable, then how could Freud measure their intensity in any analytic case? Freud's analytic reconstruction of the sexual history of the patient is only ever that: a Freudian story awaiting biological confirmation. And if he postulates the possibility of an extreme version of constitutional causality, then a subtle form of biological determinism is installed simultaneously. Quite simply, because Freud defers to biology regarding the explication of innate constitution, for all he knows (and does not know) about it, innate constitution may be the decisive or even definitive factor in all forms of sexual life.

At moments of theoretical stalemate, Freud would at times employ biologistic myths under the dubious metaphor of *phylogeny*. An effect of Lamarckian influence, Freud understood phylogeny to be the evolutionary acquisition of prehistoric ancestral features that shape the perception and experience of individuals. A girl may not, due to her familial environment, for example, witness the genitals of a male; however, phylogeny can be exploited as a means of explaining the significance of the penis for both girls and boys through a kind of species memory. "The penis (to follow Ferenczi [1925])," Freud argues, "owes its extraordinary high narcissistic cathexes to its organic significance for the propagation of the species."[72] Indeed, Freud's entire castration complex was situated within a phylogenetic epistemic framework. In the case study of the Wolf Man, he interpreted castration anxiety to be not the result of actual threats that had come from women, but a phylogenetically induced fear of castration by his father: "'Heredity triumphed over accidental experience'."[73] In a discussion of the relationship of the fantasies of neurotic patients to phylogeny, Freud attempted to offer theoretical support for both the repudiation of the early trauma theory and the account of universalized oedipal fantasies:

> I am prepared with an answer which I know will seem daring to you. I believe these *primal phantasies*, as I should like to call them, and no doubt a few others as well, are a phylogenetic endowment. In them the individual reaches beyond his own experience into primaeval experience at points where his own experience has been too rudimentary. It seems to me quite possible that all the things that are told to us to-day in analysis as phantasy—the seduction of children, the inflaming of sexual excitement by observing parental intercourse, the threat of castration (or rather castration itself)—were once real occurrences in the primaeval times of the human family, and that children in their phantasies are simply filling in the gap in individual truth with prehistoric truth. I have repeatedly been led to suspect that the psychology of the neuroses has stored up in it more of the antiquities of human development than any other source.[74]

Freud's paradigm of heteronormative psychosexual determination—constructed from his work on the perversions and homosexuality[75]—can, at the very best, only *describe* rather than explain this process. Psychoanalysis "must rest content with disclosing the psychical mechanisms that resulted in determining the object-choice" he says, "and with *tracing* back the paths from them to the instinctual dispositions. There its work ends, and leaves the rest to biological research."[76] Tracing back the paths from the instinctual dispositions, is, as the quote makes clear, a retrospective and descriptive psychoanalytic task. It cannot with any analytic clarity or certainty provide sufficient reason as to why any other path was not taken. However, the castration complex, which was originally introduced as a way of accounting for sexual difference without recourse to a crude form of biological determinism, was always dangerously connected to biological bisexuality—rather than seen as its psychical reflection of this biological fact as

Freud had planned to construct it. Nevertheless, according to Freud the castration complex, premised on bisexuality, determines a child's identifications, and hence, sexual object choice. Yet ultimately these identificatory determinations remain a mystery to psychoanalysis. For the boy, the "repudiation of femininity [castration anxiety] can be nothing else than a biological fact," the "riddle of sex" itself.[77] And for the girl, penis envy is similarly (un)grounded on hypothetical myth, a presumption we are compelled to accept. Reinforcing this position as precarious and unverifiable, Freud admits that "if you reject this idea as fantastic and regard my belief in the influence of a lack of penis on the configuration of femininity as an *idée fixe*, I am of course defenseless."[78] The elucidation of the mystical masculine and feminine dispositions to which Freud had recourse in order to conceal strategically the arbitrariness of identification, however, remained, as he himself conceded, wholly within the province of biology, not psychoanalysis.

EVOLUTION, IDENTIFICATION, AND BISEXUALITY

As we have seen, Lamarckian and Darwinian evolutionary perspectives profoundly influenced Freudian thought. Indeed, they provided the theoretical matter required to buttress his teleological theories of human psychosexual development. In 1915 Freud included phylogeny under the rubric of "temporal factors" in his *Three Essays*, remarking that the "order in which the various instinctual impulses come into activity seems to be phylogenetically determined."[79] A closer look at the figure of bisexuality also betrays Freud's reliance on a distinctive linear model of evolutionary psychosexual *maturation*. The 'normal' heterosexual child *progresses* along an evolutionary line from an immature and originary bisexual disposition passing through the (racialized) axis of identification to the apposite form of 'civilized', mature, genital sexuality.[80] If she or he so happens to regress as a consequence of the incomplete dissolution of the Oedipus complex (and thus the inadequate repression of bisexuality), the child reverts to the primitive phase of narcissism that precedes the ideal state of 'true' identifications and object relations.[81] Freud suggests this much in a footnote added to the *Three Essays* in 1915, which says that "freedom to range equally over male and female objects—as it is found in *childhood*, in *primitive* states of society and early periods of history, is the original basis from which ... both the normal and inverted types develop."[82] While he goes on to suggest that any restriction of object choice—that is, *both* exclusive homosexuality and heterosexuality—is a "problem that needs elucidating," a palpable heteronormativity nonetheless permeates his model. In short, homosexuality represents an arrested form of development, a fixation at an evolutionary point short of heterosexuality. In contrast, heterosexuality, although a fixation, is not a *developmental* fixation. It is, instead, merely a fixation on one sex.

Within the Freudian schema, bisexuality was not even representable as a form of 'arrested development'. That is, it was not considered a form of sexuality at all. Situated so far back on the evolutionary line, it was no more than the nebulous and archaic residuum of a state of primitivity to be mastered by a race of preeminent heterosexuals at the highest point of evolutionary development. This process of mastery was thought to take place, of course, through the repression of bisexuality required by passage through the Oedipus complex. Any manifestation of these prehistoric roots was nothing short of neurosis, regression, inversion, and even hysteria.[83] Without doubt a Victorian of his times, Freud declared that:

> the overcoming of the Oedipus complex coincides with the most efficient way of mastering the archaic, animal heritage of humanity. It is true that that heritage comprises all the forces that are required for the subsequent cultural development of the individual, but they must first be sorted out and worked over. This archaic heirloom is not fit to be used for the purposes of civilized social life in the form in which it is inherited by the individual.[84]

For Freud, civilization was almost synonymous with heterosexuality. Any residual trace of the atavistic bisexual disposition was a regression to a state of primitivity.

The driving forces of Freud's model of subject formation and psychosexual development were, as I have mentioned above, the axes of identification and desire. Here, however, bisexuality lingered as a slippery and problematical figure, at once making possible and yet confusing his portrayal of gender and sexuality. On the one hand, bisexuality was recognized as a presymbolic or precultural state of infantile potential. It designated a set of desires that were seen to prefigure the ground of mature, adult sexual development while functioning as a residual primitive and evolutionary force necessarily repressed on the way to enculturation, to civilization—indeed, to sexual difference.[85] In this scenario, gender, or sexual difference, is seen to be an eventual product of the bisexual disposition as it confronts the Oedipus complex. On the other hand, bisexuality functioned as a concept, *already* gendered, and composing masculine and feminine identificatory tendencies. For Freud, identification and desire were, while dialectically related concepts, mutually exclusive axes constituting individuals, "the possibility of one always presupposing the repression of the other."[86] Yet within this dialectic of identification and desire, bisexuality highlights the extent to which the one (identification) does not precede the other (desire), but is made possible by it. In other words, bisexuality turns this dialectic inside out. This is precisely because the figure of bisexuality cuts across both of these axes while holding them together, thus confounding any attempt by Freud to ensure their independence: *For to identify is to repress bisexual desire, and to desire is to repress bisexual identity; yet to identify and to desire is to be predisposed bisexually.*

Despite the fact that through the ongoing effects of repression and the conflictual relations of the Oedipus complex Freudian theory upsets (at strategic moments) simple conceptions of temporality and progressivist and teleological models of human development, it is at the same time caught within these frameworks. Freud's narrative of human sexuality follows a path similar to his own intellectual evolution: that is, from biomythology to psychology and back to biology. On the one hand, and at crucial moments of an explanatory impasse regarding his theory of sexuality, Freud reinstalled the concept of bisexuality—whose definitive meaning was thought to reside wholly within the domain of biology—within his account, tracing the paths followed by the "psychical mechanisms" back to the instinctual ones. Yet, as he himself made clear, "psychoanalysis must keep itself free from any hypothesis that is alien to it, whether of anatomical, chemical, or physiological kind, and must operate with purely psychological auxiliary ideas."[87]

On the other hand, Freud's intellectual life began with his studies and his primary interest in biology; from there he struggled to develop an independent science of human psychology as biology's disciplinary counterpart.[88] "I must behave as if I were confronted by psychological factors only," he once declared in a letter to Fliess.[89] This psychoanalytic tenet, however, did nothing to solve the mystery of human sexuality. In fact, Freud's reliance on bisexuality (and thus the "continual mingling and blending" of "inherited and acquired factors"),[90] precluded the possibility of establishing the independence of psychology.

In his preface to *Three Essays*, Freud made a point of emphasizing his analytic independence from biology. He claimed to have abstained deliberately from "introducing any preconceptions" from the field of biology, concerned as he was "to discover how far psychological investigation can throw light upon the biology of the sexual life of man" (131). This was contradicted, however, in his final statement of the same work:

> The unsatisfactory conclusion . . . that emerges from these investigations of the disturbances of sexual life is that we know far too little of the biological

> processes constituting the *essence* of sexuality to be able to construct from our fragmentary information a theory adequate to the understanding alike of normal and of pathological conditions. (243; original emphasis)

This biological *essence* of sexuality is none other than bisexuality. This is the psychoanalytic 'bedrock' of sexuality that Freud appropriated, presupposed, and yet could not elucidate. Freudian psychoanalysis erected an elaborate theory of human psychosexual development upon the oppositional concepts of 'masculinity' and 'femininity' and 'activity' and 'passivity'—indeed, these were the "foundation of its work." However, when attempting to discover the psychical mechanism of sexual development, Freud only found "masculinity vanishing into activity and femininity into passivity, and that does not tell us enough."[91] Freud had traveled the full circle, and his point of departure—bisexuality—was his point of inevitable return.

IDENTIFICATION VERSUS DESIRE?

Juliet Mitchell would without doubt reject the claim that, within the Freudian intellectual trajectory, the bisexuality of the Fliessian-dominated years was the very same concept in its post-1920 articulations. In suggesting that Freud's point of departure was his point of return, I have not intended to imply that the contours of Freud's various articulations of bisexuality represented any theoretical uniformity or continuity. What I am arguing, however, is that despite the shifting, ambiguous, contradictory, and seemingly discontinuous nature of the many meanings associated with bisexuality, it is evident that there is also a definite, but often abstruse, link between them. This link relates to the biological underpinnings of bisexuality. This is the 'bedrock' that acted as a springboard for Freudian psychoanalysis and that continued to exert its uncertain and destabilizing influence on all subsequent Freudian thought.

In *Psychoanalysis and Feminism* Juliet Mitchell labored to re-present Freudian theory to a hostile feminist community that had rejected it as patriarchal mythmaking.[92] Eager to offer an account of Freudian theory useful for feminism, Mitchell repudiated the popular feminist misreading that for Freud "anatomy is destiny."[93] Regarding bisexuality, she commented that "like so many of his revolutionary notions it originated as a hunch, was questioned, cross-questioned, modified, found wanting and finally re-established as an essential concept. In the course of its history it moved from its biological origins to a psychoanalytic meaning. As with 'masculine' and 'feminine', the word remained the same but the significance shifted."[94]

This is a very generous gloss indeed. Bisexuality never moved *from* a biologistic definition *to* a psychoanalytic one. Rather, it always carried its biologistic undercurrent within it, regardless of Freud's desperate attempt to distance himself from, and *repress* his debt both to Fliess and to the subject of biology. Mitchell is correct in pointing out that "the end supersedes the beginnings," but it is a rather lavish claim that "it was a case of coming back at the end of his life to his original hypotheses, and confirming them with a new and different understanding that amounted to a new meaning" (49). Bisexuality certainly had a new meaning at the end of Freud's life, but it was one of a totally overdetermined and contradictory nature.

Mitchell goes on to suggest that the shift in Freud's thinking on bisexuality parallels a shift in his way of reading his analytic cases. "Instead of starting with the baby and following his evolution . . . he has . . . reversed direction . . . [and] presented his reading backwards from the experience of the adult in analysis to the problems of the infant" (51). Such a reversal does not entail the dissolution, or movement away, or *from*, his notion of bisexuality as a "sort of infantile unisex" (51). It merely reflects Freud's desire to formulate, on top of this, a workable and independent psychological complement to the biological foundations of psychoanalysis without simplistic recourse to any form of determinism. How else could he be seen as having made an independent contribution to the science of sexuality? Freud never abandoned, nor could he escape, the biological meaning ascribed to bisexuality. Until his death it remained one of the central postulates of psychoanalysis.[95] In fact, it appears that he wanted desperately to bridge the gulf between bisexuality as biology and bisexuality as psychology. One means for crossing this bridge might be made via the instincts, that "concept on the frontier between the spheres of psychology and biology."[96] However, in 1930 Freud lamented the fact that he had not yet found any link between the theory of psychological bisexuality and the theory of the instincts.[97] This is because, as he had pointed out earlier, "though psychoanalysis endeavours as a rule to develop its theories as independently as possible from those of other sciences, it is nevertheless obliged to seek a basis for the theory of the instincts in biology."[98] Psychological bisexuality therefore "embarrasses all our enquiries into the subject," declared Freud in 1938. The reason for this was that biological bisexuality not only grounded Freud's notion of bisexuality as a psychical reflection, but without it such a reflection would disappear entirely.

Throughout Freud's writings bisexuality had, simultaneously, multiple meanings. No single definition superseded or replaced another. Bisexuality was a term of many different disguises, at once biological *and* psychological.

Marjorie Garber points out that for Freud there were at least three meanings of bisexuality: anatomical bisexuality (traces of atrophied sexual organs of the opposite sex), psychical bisexuality (having psyches of both sexes), and a bisexuality "precarious and divided" and "fluid with regard to both identification and object."[99] Under this third definition, bisexuality was not so much a form of sexuality as a constant destabilizing force with the potential to effect a shift from homosexuality to heterosexuality or vice versa. Quoting from one of the last papers of his life, Garber goes further to argue that Freud introduced a fourth meaning of bisexuality—"something like its modern sense" (204). In "Analysis Terminable and Interminable" Freud rather surprisingly stated that

> It is well known that at all periods there have been, as there still are, people who can take as their sexual objects members of their own sex as well as of the opposite one, without the one trend interfering with the other. We call such people bisexuals, and we accept their existence without feeling much surprise about it. We have come to learn, however, that every human being is bisexual in this sense, and that his libido is distributed, either in a manifest or a latent fashion, over objects of both sexes.[100]

Is Freud here describing what today we would call bisexuality, the ability or desire to take as sexual objects members of both sexes? I suggest that he is not. Recall our earlier discussion concerning the centrality of the Freudian axes of identification and desire for sexual life. The possibility of desiring and identifying with the same (gendered) object is precluded in Freudian thought. As the child cannot wish to take the mother as a sexual object and identify with her simultaneously—and vice versa as regards the child and the father—the adult cannot have a feminine identification and take a female sexual object. Freud delimited in a very specific way the forms sexuality *must* take. As Judith Butler neatly puts it, "There is no homosexuality, and only opposites attract."[101]

In cataloging the various "deviations in respect of the sexual object" in his *Three Essays*, Freud described those whose "sexual objects may equally well be of their own or of the opposite sex" and who lacked "the characteristic of exclusiveness," as "*amphigenic* inverts" (136). He also called these inverts "psychosexual hermaphrodites" (136). In line with his oedipal theory of sexual subject formation, this suggests that such individuals could indeed take both sexes as their sexual objects. To do so, however, requires a shifting identification. A sexed identity can only be attracted to an opposite sexed object. Bisexuality is, as Butler argues, "*the coincidence of two heterosexual desires within a single psyche.*"[102] Furthermore, the simultaneous coincidence of these two desires within the one individual is certainly not a form of adult genital sexuality but, rather, hysteria.[103] Clearly, Freud's model is decidedly monosexual. It seems to me that Freud's use of bisexuality in "Analysis Terminable and Interminable" might perhaps better be read as a grafting or conflation of the first three senses of bisexuality suggested by Garber.

Drawing on Jacqueline Rose's and Juliet Mitchell's discussions of bisexuality, Garber argues that Freud shifted from construing bisexuality as a "biological or developmental stage prior to 'mature' heterosexual desire," to bisexuality as fluid with regard to identification and object.[104] Garber then extends their argument to propose (tentatively) that Freud articulated a fourth kind of bisexuality. I am not so sure Rose and Mitchell would go along with Garber's introduction of a bisexuality of the fourth kind. If, as Freud suggested in the above-mentioned quote from *Three Essays*, every human being is bisexual in the sense of having the potential to distribute their libido over both sexes, then clearly he was referring to his very early notion of bisexuality as innate disposition, as evolutionary endowment. In addition to this, it seems that he was also drawing on his notion of amphigenic inverts who lack, it seems due to a combination of both inherited and accidental factors, the characteristic of exclusiveness. And finally, both of these meanings are inflected by and inextricably entwined with Garber's third meaning, bisexuality as precarious and fluid.

While Freud made no mention in "Analysis Terminable" of the relationship of the kind of bisexual desire he was discussing, it would have meant the total collapse of his entire theory of psychosexual development had he meant Garber's fourth kind;[105] unless of course Garber subscribes to a neo-Freudian notion of bisexuality as the *coincidence of two heterosexual desires in a single psyche*. However, if this were the case, her reading of Freud's quote in "Analysis Terminable" would scarcely represent a different meaning than the third and earlier one she had identified (via Rose). And I would then have to question her construction of the "modern sense" of bisexuality.

With the evolution of Freud's work each new and additional discussion of bisexuality brought with it the complications, contradictions and ambiguities associated with and accumulated through all of the meanings that preceded them. This is amply demonstrated in his posthumously published work, *An Outline of Psycho-Analysis*. As Mitchell quite rightly concludes, bisexuality "ended by being the unsolved crux of the matter—both in theory and practice."[106] In this work Freud came back once again to the notion of psychological bisexuality and its relation to the biological fact of sexual difference. His conclusion was that it "embarrasses all our enquiries into the subject and makes them harder to describe."[107] It would appear that this was because bisexuality was both constructive and de(con)structive of his theory of human psychosexual development. It was the outcome not only of Freud's inability to avoid the biologistic foundations and implications of his earlier thought on bisexuality, but more important, as Butler demonstrates, because bisexuality *always already* presupposes "a heterosexual matrix for desire."[108] In other words, regardless of the challenges Freud posed to some of the assumptions constitutive of the economy of (hetero)sexuality, the entirety of his thought was calibrated through its heteronormative optic. Perhaps in an ironic twist of fate Freud was forced to learn the most difficult of his own teachings on the unconscious: that in some form or another the repressed always returns.

CONCLUSION

In terms of the complexity of human sexuality, Freud, unlike most of his predecessors, certainly offered a far more sophisticated analysis through the incorporation of the forces of repression, the unconscious, and fantasy, all couched within a sociofamilial dynamic. However, he was confronted with the same conundrum that underpinned the work of all the sexologists of the period: the inability, or rather, impossibility, of elucidating the biological bedrock upon which theories of sexuality were grounded.

Despite Freud's divergence from sexological theories of the late nineteenth and early twentieth centuries, it is clear that his theory of psychosexual development consolidated and even expanded the emerging economy of (hetero)sexuality, albeit in a rather oblique direction. In the writings of Krafft-Ebing, the axes of gender and sexuality were conflated to produce the categories of sexual inversion, and for Havelock Ellis these axes were, while somewhat disarticulated, inextricably fused through recourse to a notion of biological determinism with regard to sexual object choice. Freud's work was definitely inflected by many of the presumptions inherent to the work of both Krafft-Ebing and Ellis. However, he sought to go beyond the "psychophysiology" of sexology in establishing a 'true' science of the psychology of sexuality.[109]

Within this project, bisexuality was the 'universal joint' providing the necessary flexibility to support a multiplicity of converging and often inconsistent views. In other words, in Freudian thought bisexuality was, like Proteus himself, a variable and changing figure, whose amenability to contortion worked to ensure narrative continuity. However, dramatized within the theater of oedipality, this enigma of bisexuality did little to challenge the economy of (hetero)sexuality. Bisexuality remained awkwardly biologistic and brought gender and sexuality into a more complicated and contradictory alliance. That is, bisexuality functioned (however precariously and tenuously) as the necessary figure to reproduce heteronormative representations of human sexuality. To this end, Freud constructed bisexuality as only ever a precultural or acultural form of human potentiality. Situated within a regressive space outside civilization and sexed subjectivity, bisexuality was contained within a space inaccessible in the present tense. So despite its purportedly threatening and destabilizing nature, bisexuality was subject to the inevitable forces of repression that served both to inaugurate civilization and to ensure its continued functioning (through the production of nonhysterical gendered subjects). This effectively served to reinforce a model of monosexuality that itself ensured the distinctiveness of the modalities of hetero- and homosexuality. Within such a model, bisexuality is collapsed into either of its oppositional terms.

Society was not the only beneficiary from the repression and mystification of bisexuality. The Oedipus complex itself functioned as a safety mechanism to circumscribe and disavow its de(con)structive power: a power Freud had himself (somewhat unwittingly) unleashed. First, the Oedipus complex was the structure erected onto biological bisexuality in order to claim for psychoanalysis a sense of disciplinary autonomy. However, as a liminal concept bisexuality served both to divide *and* unite (or rather blur) biology and psychology, nature and culture, mind and body. In *Homosexual Desire* Guy Hocquenghem points to this paradox: "If the distinction between biology and psychology thus disappears, it is because [polymorphous] desire knows nothing of the separation between body and mind upon which the personality is founded. Nevertheless, this kind of separation is the very life blood of psychiatry and psychoanalysis as an *institution*."[110] Second, bisexuality made problematic the Freudian distinctions of male/female, masculine/feminine, and heterosexual/homosexual. In this way, the mystification and erasure of bisexuality in the present tense effectively averted an epistemic crisis of identity, or meaning, within the very terms of the Oedipus complex.

Freud's thought has continued to animate academic inquiry, and it is therefore not difficult to recognize its residue in many contemporary representations of sexuality. As Lance Spurr, the gay columnist cited at the outset of this chapter, declared, "No one is bisexual at any given moment." Spurr clarified this assertion by suggesting that a subject's sexual desire can only be distributed "at any given moment" toward either one gender or the other. In other words, while allowing for some degree of change or fluidity, no one is bisexual in the present tense. For Freud the notion of sexual fluidity was revolutionary for his time, subverting sexological understandings of the fixity of sexuality while depathologizing those sexualities that deviated from procreative heterosexuality. For Spurr, however, this residual effect of Freudian psychoanalysis, recast within the contemporary morass of overdetermined representations, is indicative of the hostile response of many homosexuals (at least since gay liberation) to bisexuality. Yet despite the radicalism of Freud's claim to be "opposed to any attempt at separating off homosexuals from the rest of mankind as a group of a special character," he nevertheless reinforced the binary division of sexual identity.[111]

Freud refused the present tense of bisexuality through the instantiation of *the* (psychoanalytic) law of sexuality. This functioned to erase at least two forms of bisexuality from his analytic framework. First, all individuals are precluded, or rather *prohibited*, from experiencing a form of sexual desire that is not determined by the *gender* of object choice. Second, it appears to be a structural impossibility to distribute one's sexual desire over two (or more) gendered objects *simultaneously*.

Following Freud's death in 1939, the crisis of meaning posed by bisexuality for theories of sexual identity was sharpened in psychoanalytic discourse. In the next chapter I will explore how a radically shifting psychoanalytic discourse sought to contain the challenges raised by sexological and Freudian notions of bisexuality.

4

THE PINK THREAT

Nobody can dance at two different weddings at the same time. These so-called bisexuals are really homosexuals with an occasional heterosexual excuse.
—Edmund Bergler 1956

Bisexuality is not in itself an orientation, but simply an indication that a man's or woman's basic homosexuality or heterosexuality is something less than exclusive. It is an index of ambiguity, and not a thing in itself.
—John Malone 1980

From its inception the entire psychomedical tradition was constructed around the site of bisexuality. As I demonstrated in chapters 2 and 3, this figure of bisexuality became a necessary lever for the stabilization of the emergent hetero/homosexual opposition, itself the complex product of a crisis of masculine identity. Within early sexological and Freudian theories of psychosexual development, however, the concept of bisexuality occupied an ambiguous space. For instance, for Havelock Ellis, bisexuality introduced "uncertainty and doubt." In the work of Freud, bisexuality was, on the one hand, "the decisive factor,"[1] the "innate . . . disposition of man,"[2] and therefore the biological bedrock to human psychology. Yet, on the other hand, bisexuality was a hermeneutic blind spot, a speculative concept whose elucidation was, as Freud himself admitted, beyond the bounds of psychoanalytic apprehension. Construed as *precultural*, or prior to the development of (symbolic) gender identification, bisexuality was *that against which* culture was founded and that against which both culture and the unconscious must constantly struggle. According to Freudian theory, then, bisexuality was a double-edged figure: on the verso side, it represented a recurrent force whose appropriate management would ensure the (re)production of culture and individual subjectivity; on the recto side, it was seen as a perpetual and threatening force of cultural and individual destabilization.

In the three decades following Freud's death the concept of bisexuality was almost unilaterally repudiated as a scientific falsehood within the domains of psychoanalysis and psychiatry. In addition to this, homosexuality was refigured as a form of pathology. In this chapter I will suggest that the repudiation of bisexuality and the pathologization of homosexuality go hand in hand. The radical implications of Freud's musings on bisexuality, along with the troubling conclusions of the Kinsey report and other cross-cultural anthropological studies, pointed to a potentially powerful challenge to the assumptions of psychoanalytic discourse. Indeed, it appeared that homosexuality was infiltrating the sphere of normality. I will argue that the discursive representation of bisexuality had to be monitored and regulated vigilantly in order to secure the alterity of homosexuality, and thus the inviolable borders of the hetero/homosexual division. Occupying an unstable position within the economy of (hetero)sexuality, bisexuality was repudiated less on the grounds of scientific error than as the effect of an epistemic *crisis of (hetero)sexual identity*.

The social and political context within which this crisis took place was crucial in shaping Western psychomedical representations of sexuality. Particularly in the 1950s, Cold War hysteria concerning national security pivoted around oppositions such as sameness/difference, inside/outside, familiar/foreign, conformity/dissent, patriotism/subversion, normal/abnormal. Hegemonic discourses clamored to reinforce and safeguard national as well as social, political, and moral boundaries. Sexuality traversed all of these rigidly demarcated oppositional spaces. However, as a discursive entity sexuality gave more than a metaphorical inflection to national, social, political, and moral categories. Sexuality was metonymically linked to them; each was constituted in and through the others. In other words, anxieties around national identity were not simply coincident with the moral panic surrounding homosexuality. As Lynne Segal has noted, homosexuals "were once again scapegoated as moral decadents, and now—with a new twist—as traitors to their country."[3] Like communism, therefore, homosexuality was structurally excluded from figurations of *the nation*. Both represented difference, a disavowed alterity from the purity, stability, and security of the heteronormative nation. The 'red threat', or the figure of the communist, was therefore both metaphorically and metonymically associated with that of the homosexual.

Histories of sexuality have ignored the discursive function of bisexuality during this period. Bisexuality was itself the epistemic border between the heterosexual and the homosexual, the normal and the abnormal, the patriotic citizen and the subversive communist. It seems to me that by situating bisexuality at the center of our historical analysis a new and important dimension is added to our understanding of the history and theory of sexuality. I will argue, therefore, that shifts in the representation of homosexuality —and by negation heterosexuality—are both the cause and effect of shifts in the representation of bisexuality.

FREUD, HOMOSEXUALITY, AND PATHOLOGY

In order to provide a contextualized discussion of the post-Freudian pathologizing of homosexuality and the elision of bisexuality, it is necessary to return to Freud and retrace his ideas on homosexuality. For what was to develop within psychoanalysis after his death in 1939—particularly in the United States, which became the dominant center for psychomedical representations of sexuality—was a homophobic discourse "claiming to stand in the tradition of Freud."[4] Many psychoanalytic theorists, some of whom trained under Freud, set off to stake their claim to the production of the scientific truth of sexuality. In doing so, however, they distorted and selectively appropriated Freud's work to reinforce individual and cultural prejudices of the day.

On 23 September 1939, Freud, crippled by the recurrence of an irremediable form of cancer, and with the aid of his personal friend and doctor, Max Schur, was administered lethal injections of morphine so that he could escape needless suffering.[5] During his life he had wondered about the direction his theories would take: "What will they do with my theory after my death? Will it still resemble my basic thoughts?"[6] Little did he know of the use to which his work was to be put after his death. Freud was indeed revolutionary for his time. Among other things, he directly challenged the notion of normality in regard to gender and sexuality. He introduced the notion of childhood sexuality, which by its nature is *perverse*, but which, he argued, is a universal prerequisite to the development of gender identification. Normality, he held, is but a convoluted and precarious *achievement*. He situated homosexuality at the center of every individual's subjectivity by suggesting that all persons experience homosexual incestuous desires and that those fantasies are housed in the unconscious. And he undermined the moralistic norm that tied sexuality to procreation. Reproductive heterosexuality was no longer the normative site for the manifestation of sexual desires.[7] Not only were Freud's ideas revolutionary for early-twentieth-century Western societies, but it seems that they were also a bit too radical for many of his own psychoanalytic proselytes.

In chapter 3 I proposed that despite Freud's concession that heterosexuality, like homosexuality, was a "problem that needs elucidating," a certain heteronormativity nevertheless informs his account of sexual development.[8] This is not to suggest that Freud was homophobic; far from it. I am merely exposing his bias in favor of heterosexuality, not his hatred or revulsion of homosexuality.[9] It would be later distortions of Freudian theory that, as I will show below, effected a conflation of heteronormativity and homophobia. Freud, it would seem, was in many ways antihomophobic. He held the view that homosexuals were not sick; in his view, they were neither criminal nor immoral. In an interview with a German newspaper in 1903 he issued an emphatic statement of this position: *"Homosexual persons are not sick, but they also do not belong in a court of law!"*[10] Freud supported measures to decriminalize homosexuality in Germany, and he rejected Ernest Jones's position that homosexuals be refused membership in the psychoanalytic profession. In a letter written with Otto Rank, Freud responded to Jones's query as to whether this "would be a safe general maxim to act on": "Your query dear Ernest concerning prospective membership of homosexuals has been considered by us and we disagree with you. In effect we cannot exclude such persons without other sufficient reasons, as we cannot agree with their legal prosecution. We feel that a decision in such cases should depend upon a thorough examination of the other qualities of the candidate."[11] And in the now infamous and oft-quoted "Letter to an American Mother," Freud further reinforced his view on the matter:

> Dear Mrs.———
>
> I gather from your letter that your son is a homosexual. I am most impressed by the fact that you do not mention this term yourself in your information about him. May I question you, why you avoid it? Homosexuality is assuredly no advantage, but it is nothing to be ashamed of, no vice, no degradation, it cannot be classified as an illness; we consider it to be a variation of the sexual function produced by a certain arrest of sexual development. Many highly respected individuals of ancient and modern times have been homosexuals, several of the greatest men among them (Plato, Michelangelo, Leonardo da Vinci, etc.). It is a great injustice to persecute homosexuality as a

crime, and a cruelty too. If you do not believe me, read the books of Havelock Ellis.

By asking me if I can help, you mean, I suppose, if I can abolish homosexuality and make normal heterosexuality take its place. The answer is, in a general way, we cannot promise to achieve it. In a certain number of cases we succeed in developing the blighted germs of heterosexual tendencies which are present in every homosexual, in the majority of cases it is no more possible. It is a question of the quality and the age of the individual. The result of treatment cannot be predicted.

What analysis can do for your son runs in a different line. If he is unhappy, neurotic, torn by conflicts, inhibited in his social life, analysis may bring him harmony, peace of mind, full efficiency whether he remains homosexual or gets changed.[12]

As Henry Abelove has pointed out, Freud maintained an antihomophobic therapeutic integrity by declining to treat homosexuals unless they displayed significant neurotic characteristics.[13] Clearly, this position was in line with his theoretical account of psychosexual development in which 'normality' was but one of many outcomes. Upon entering the triangular Oedipus complex, the child is faced with two sets of competing identifications and desires: that is, at some point in the child's oedipal conflicts, he or she will identify with both parents and take both parents as objects of desire.[14] Not only can the resolution of the Oedipus complex result in twelve possible sexual outcomes due to the various permutations of the dyadic structure of identification/desire, but only one of these is conventionally understood to be 'normal'.[15]

It was not only Freud's concept of bisexuality that was shrouded in ambiguity. To a large extent, and as a result of this abstruse universal disposition, homosexuality was effectively obfuscated. Despite the fact that the roots of sexual object choice and identification were putatively anchored in the oedipal constellation, the biological substance of congenital bisexuality exerted an unidentifiable and often even overriding force over sexual development. This left open the possibility that homosexuality may reside not in the oedipal, but in the *preoedipal* phase. Notwithstanding the fact that Freud's notion of sexuality as both constitutional and acquired was couched in an antihomophobic framework, his psychoanalytic libido theory provided other analysts with the theoretical tools necessary to construct homosexuality as a morbid psychological condition. The effect was to appropriate homosexuality as a "proper object" of psychoanalytic/psychiatric knowledge in order to reproduce this economy of 'scientific' discourse and expand its powers.[16]

THE *PROPER OBJECT* OF PSYCHOANALYSIS

In a period characterized by rigid binary formulations of the relationship of sexuality to gender, Freud was a rare and challenging thinker. Contrary to most of his contemporaries, Freud attempted to think about sexual identification in a somewhat more complex way than the dominant binary logic of noncontradiction would allow.[17] For example, the etiology of sexuality was not simply one of a congenital versus acquired nature, as it was in the case of Krafft-Ebing, Magnus Hirschfeld and Havelock Ellis. "The constitutional factor," Freud argued, "must await experiences before it can make itself felt; the accidental factor must have a constitutional basis in order to come into operation."[18] This position prevented him from laying total claim to the object of homosexuality, deferring to biology for the explication of the organic "*essence* of sexuality" (243). Psychoanalysis was thus situated in a kind of interdisciplinary space, separate from, yet reliant upon the discourse of biology. Freud thus adopted a posture of therapeutic pessimism in relation to the possibility of a psychoanalytic cure for homosexuality. "In general, to undertake to convert a fully developed homosexual into a heterosexual does not offer much more prospect of success than the reverse," he argued, "except that for good practical reasons the latter is never attempted." At best, success—"possible only in specially favourable circumstances"—would involve not cure, but the restoration of a person's "full bisexual functions."[19]

In the 1940s, however, the dominant discourse of psychoanalysis sought to expand its discursive power in two ways: first, via the wholesale appropriation of the object of homosexuality; and second, through a disciplinary secession from biology. As we will see, the proclamation, contra Freud, that a therapeutic cure could be achieved by the psychomedical discipline was both a cause and effect of this process. Among other things, it served to legitimate psychoanalysis and psychiatry as an independent science. As Judith Butler makes clear: "The institution of the 'proper object' takes place, as usual, through a mundane sort of violence. Indeed, we might read moments of methodological founding as pervasively anti-historical acts, beginnings which fabricate their legitimating histories through a retroactive narrative, burying complicity and division in and through the funereal figure of the 'ground'."[20] Along with the death of Freud went those aspects of his theory that threatened to dissolve the once seemingly rigid borders protecting heterosexual identity. The socially reviled and criminalized object of homosexuality occupied a central place in the Freudian account of the psychosexual constitution of all individuals. However, the increasing social legitimization of psychoanalysis and psychiatry provided for a more markedly conservative, heteronormative, and indeed, homophobic psychoanalytic posture.[21] In addition to this, the legitimization of psychoanalytic discourse produced a veritable explosion of interest in the study of homosexuality. Homosexuality was plunged further into what Foucault would call a seething "political economy of truth."[22] The United States provided the fertile site for this profound shift in psychomedical discourse. Mirroring its newly acquired status as economic and military world power, it was not long before the United States also became a geopolitical superpower for the production of sexual truth.

Psychoanalytic discourse became the dominant representational apparatus within this economy of (sexual) truth. Subject to what Foucault would call the discursive triptych of *power/knowledge/truth*, homosexuality became a strategic commodity whose essence had to be exacted and secured as *the proper object of psychomedical knowledge*. Within this epistemic field there emerged a factional 'ideological' struggle powered by a compulsion to speak and master the truth of homosexuality. This frenetic determination to 'discover' truth became the fictitious guise of self-misrecognition. That is, it was a cover for the deep-rooted crisis of (hetero)sexual identity. Crisis management was the necessary process for the reiteration and refiguration of the economy of (hetero)sexuality, a process which, as we are about to see, required the containment of bisexuality.

SANDOR RADO AND THE SEPULCHER FOR FREUDIAN BISEXUALITY

Five years before the death of Freud, Wilhelm Stekel, friend, former pupil, and assistant to Freud, published a book entitled *Bi-Sexual Love*. The Freudian notion of constitutional bisexuality provided the departure point and centerpiece of this book. However, it seems that Stekel attempted to rid the Freudian account of (bi)sexuality of *some* of its heterosexual bias.[23] In deference to his teacher, Stekel stated that "I turn my own conception of homosexuality, formulated, on the basis of psychoanalytic data and as an outgrowth of the teachings of *Freud*" (27). However, moving in a rather unexpected direction, Stekel proposed the idea that *both* homosexuality and heterosexuality are neurotic compromise formations. In other words, homosexual and heterosexual object choice are *symptoms* of neurosis: the inability to master "asocial cravings . . . which society rejects as conflicting with its cultural demands" (43). Without exception, there is no such thing as a monosexual person for Stekel. Bisexuality is the only given 'truth' of human sexuality. "*All persons are bisexual*" (27), he declared: "There is no inborn homosexuality and no inborn heterosexuality. There is only bisexuality. Monosexuality already involves a predisposition to neurosis, in many cases stands for the neurosis proper" (41).

Not surprisingly, Stekel's extension of Freud's concept of bisexuality went largely unacknowledged. Yet, Stekel's work stands as a palpable reminder of the radical potential of Freudian bisexuality. But it was not until Freud's death that the hegemonic psychoanalytic theory of (bi)sexuality shifted direction. One must surely wonder whether it took such an event to induce a substantive challenge to the founding father's work. Unlike Stekel, the analysts who sought to take up where Freud left off had other motives for the direction of psychoanalysis. Sandor Rado was one of the most significant figures in the homophobic development of post-Freudian psychoanalytic theory. Not only is he responsible for the development of an adaptational, or sociological theory of homosexuality, but he also managed simultaneously the repudiation of the concept of bisexuality. As Kenneth Lewes notes, Rado's refutation of bisexuality came just eight months after Freud's death.[24]

Rado's work must be situated in the broader context of a shift away from the classical analytic emphasis on the Oedipus complex. Beginning in the early part of the 1930s, considerable attention was being paid to the oral phase of childhood development.[25] This phase, authored by Freud, and elaborately developed by Melanie Klein in *The Psycho-Analysis of Children*, gradually became the locus for the denouement of the drama of sexual identification.[26] Despite Freud's primary focus on the phallic and genital phases, his work on sexuality pushed consistently in the direction of earlier infantile conditions.[27] As we saw in chapter 3, for example, the opposition between masculinity and femininity was central to Freud's account of identification and sexual object choice. Yet, as he maintained from start to finish, such terms tell us very little, "masculinity vanishing into activity and femininity into passivity."[28] In other words, the preoedipal polarity of activity/passivity developmentally precedes that of masculinity/femininity. Moreover, in beginning analysis not with the baby but with the adult and working backward toward the instincts, it is not surprising to arrive at an interest in the oral stage of development. So, far from being a contradiction to Freudian theory, the emphasis on the oral antecedents to sexual object choice provided a logical theoretical development to his retrospective form of analysis.

Rado was the precursor to the eventual psychoanalytic disciplinary secession from biology and the development of a psychomedical climate of therapeutic optimism. In "A Critical Examination of the Concept of Bisexuality," first published in 1940,[29] Rado rejected completely the notion of biological homosexuality. Instead, he argued for an environmental (adaptational) approach focused exclusively on social relationships. Ironically, however, he (re)installed (hetero)sexuality in a normative biologistic matrix. "It is imperative," he implored, "to supplant the deceptive concept of bisexuality with a psychoanalytic theory based on firmer biological foundations" (149). These foundations lay in the imperative of species survival, wherein the "evolutionary differentiation of the sexes and of sexual behavior originates from reproduction" (186). Despite the fact that in Rado's theory "the genital pleasure function" is "inseparable from the reproductive action system" (146), human beings are not issued with a biological command toward heterosexual object choice at birth.[30] Due to the transformations of mating behavior as a result of 'brain evolution', the inherited pattern has been broken down and become "dependent for its completion upon the animal's individual experience." Hence, to complete the binarized formula, "the cultural pattern enters the picture as a new and powerful determinant" (140). The appropriate cultural institutions and practices therefore furnish the developing individual with the requisite heteronormative morality. Free from the constraints of biological causality, homosexuality can thus safely be controlled and eradicated by the correct form of cultural management: marriage and psychoanalysis.

Rado's construction of an environmental (psychoanalytic) theory of homosexuality was dependent upon the complete rejection of the Freudian concept of bisexuality. First, he dismissed the mythological account of originary hermaphroditism as a "simple solution" predating science and created by a "primitive mind" in accordance with the "primeval, emotional needs of animistic man" (140). Second, he discredited the notion that because humans, like lower animals, derived from a common embryonic origin, they contained rudimentary sexual organs of the opposite sex, which made them bisexual. Rado argued that these scientific speculations were gleaned from "an undeveloped embryonic structure." In this way they were extrapolated incorrectly to fully developed 'man'. Rado identified a common source of confusion regarding biological bisexuality. He suggested that despite the fact that genetic sex differentiation is not enough to predict the (reproductive) sex of the developing zygote due to successive action of genes and endocrine substances, this does not validate the appellation "bisexual." For it does not end there, he suggested:

> Thereafter, one set of primordia develops further while the other degenerates, regresses, or remains in a rudimentary state. In accord with these facts the zy-

> gote as well as the early embryonic stages are no longer referred to as bisexual, but are said, more accurately, to possess bipotentiality of differentiation. Under normal developmental conditions, as differentiation proceeds and one type of reproductive action system grows to completion, the original bipotentiality ceases to have any real significance. (143–44)

The logical conclusion for Rado was that the abandonment of the biological hypothesis of bisexuality required that "the data accumulated by psychoanalysis would have to be reinterpreted" (141–42). So how did he account for the development of homosexuality? Clearly, the environmental "factors that cause the individual to apply aberrant forms of stimulation to his standard genital equipment" (148) had to be explained. Having recast the biological ground of sexuality in terms of the reproductive coupling, Rado reinstalled a reformulated notion of Freudian castration anxiety. It is this fear of castration, he claimed, that obscures the *"true guiding points of inner orientation"* (119; my emphasis);[31] that is, heterosexual "pleasure organization."[32] Castration anxiety is responsible for both male and female homosexuality. Let us first examine the case of male homosexuality. If persistent, the sense of horror at the sight of the little girl's genital mutilation of which he considers himself to be a potential victim "may cause him to avoid the 'wound-like' female organ ever after; or if he salvages some capacity for penetration, he will be forced to perform as if in a hurry to get out of that dangerous place" (196). The boy's fears and resentments, partly repressed according to the familial educational system (the Oedipus complex), turn into self-reproaches. These harm his "inner stature" and set in motion processes of ego repair; or what Rado called "reparative adjustments" (137). An inferior source of pleasure is needed as a means of compensation for the lost, but ever threatening, norm of heterosexuality. Homosexuality thus becomes a secondary formation.

Rado's model of female homosexuality, or the "flight from men," is even more peculiar. At the center of this "reparative pattern" are "the two mutually opposed strivings: the genital masochistic, and the illusory penis." In Rado's account, the attitude 'proper' to the female is precluded due to the "repression of genital masochism." This is an inherent "'female' desire . . . to enjoy the pleasure of her own pain." Menstruation, childbirth, and coitus are all perceived as the threat of excruciating pain. Resisting this masochistic female desire results in the reactively formed opposite, the illusory penis (also called "the masculine attitude"). The homosexual woman, having cathected an illusory organ to protect herself against the very source of sexual danger that is man, experiences the concomitant fear of the exposure of her 'lack'. This is "a modified fear of castration" (94–99). Female homosexuality is thus a neurotic and compensatory disturbance, a secondary formation with which to guard against 'true' female heterosexual (masochistic) pleasure. Lesbian pleasure is pleasure by default. It is a form of gratification that ensures "the successful avoidance of the dangerous man and the 'realising' of the masculinity inaugurated by the illusory penis" (99).

The adaptational model of sexuality propounded by Rado represented the culmination of a significant transfiguration of the Freudian-dominated oedipal theory of psychosexual development. His strategic intervention consolidated and extended the emerging shift toward oral analysis. It is little wonder that psychoanalysis took Freudian theory in this direction at a time of disciplinary legitimization. For to opt for a focus on 'constitutional' factors, or even their combination with acquired ones, would result in a surrendering of epistemic authority over the *object of homosexuality*. Freud, in contrast, used the already legitimated field of biology in order to secure a position of legitimacy for the fledgling discourse of psychoanalysis. Once established and authorized, the appropriation of *the proper object of homosexuality* was an antihistorical maneuver whose effect was to relegate to scientific obsolescence those very precursors inimical to its knowledge/truth claims. For Rado, these precursors were Freudian bisexuality and constitutional homosexuality. Their repudiation was necessary for the founding of a purely psychosociological approach to sexual causation.

Dominant constructions of the evolution of science, such as teleological notions of linear progress toward an ultimate truth of human sexuality, provided the epistemic conditions for the supersession of one form of biological knowledge for another. Teleology was for Rado, "a methodologic principle," viewing the behavior of individuals "in the relation of means to ends" (211–12). Freud was dead, and so too were his 'outdated' ideas of scientific knowledge. They were deemed mythological in their origins, and metaphysical in their implications. "If Freud's discoveries were to bear new fruits by stimulating further scientific inquiry," Rado asserted, "it was necessary to segregate the factual findings of psychoanalysis from its metaphysical elements and to build some other frame of reference that would rest on our established biological knowledge of man and suit our medical needs" (131–32). This *new* and *truthful* frame of reference was, of course, Rado's own.

In sum, Rado, contrary to the belief in (his) scientific progress, was on at least one major account taking a step backward and undoing much of the challenging work achieved by Freud. Freud, in disarticulating the sexual drive from a preordained aim (reproduction) or object (man or woman), had undermined the notion of sexuality as reproductive genitality. Before the development of object relatedness, the sexual drives of the developing infant are attached to the functions for self-preservation. Once detached from this need for nourishment, the sexual pleasures become psychical manifestations for the repetition of the experience of infantile anal and oral pleasures;[33] hence, the introduction of the concept of unconscious fantasy. This radical aspect of Freudian theory was instead replaced by a pre-Freudian sexological insistence on the reproductive sexual norm. This was a kind of heteronormative 'inner compass' thrown out only by the magnetic field of social relationships.[34]

Rado made no attempt to offer a sustained analysis of the (complicitous) relationship between the biological, or the 'natural', and psychological, or the 'cultural', spheres; this was an *interspace* that structured the work of Freud. Instead, in rejecting the concept of biological bisexuality, he then dismissed any consideration of psychological bisexuality. Male and female homosexuality were reduced to the status of defective *pseudo*sexualities.[35] "'Bisexuality' and 'homosexuality' are deceptive concepts," Rado proclaimed, "misleading when applied in medical theory and practice."[36] This refusal to entertain any notion of constitutional homosexuality or bisexuality, was as Kenneth Lewes remarks, "not so much an inference from his argument as it is its motivation."[37] Furthermore, lesbian sexuality was subject to the phallocentric violence sustaining the economy of (hetero)sexuality. It was reduced to a variant of masculinity, either by negation as man's opposite or by similarity as man's inferior version.

Rado effected a hardening of the axes of gender and sexuality, sedimenting their oppositional categories. This served to conceal the contradictions and complicities associated with the workings of gender and sexuality that Freud had so radically revealed. It also enabled Rado to lay the groundwork for the referent of masculine heterosexual identity to be refigured, and the economy of (hetero)sexuality around which it was constructed to be reinforced. The crisis of heterosexual identity was thus a crisis of boundaries. Freud contended that the identity boundaries demarcating heterosexuality from (despised) homosexuality were in a state of constant conflict due to the repetitive effects of bisexuality and the oedipal scenario. Elastic, unstable, and mutually interacting, homosexuality and heterosexuality (through the figure of bisexuality) were under perpetual threat of a collapse into one another. However, this was far too fragile a basis upon which to build a discipline working to secure homosexuality as its proper object. Biological bisexuality had to be exorcised from the sphere of normative heterosexuality. As we are about to see, with this move the foundations for the discourse of homophobic psychoanalysis were irrevocably set in place.

THE PINK THREAT [83]

THE BURIAL OF BISEXUALITY AND
THE RESTORATION OF ORDER

Rado's significant intervention in the 1940s provided the concrete 'scientific' ground for what would later become the hegemonic psychomedical consensus regarding the etiology of sexuality. While many and varied theories debated the specific psychological trajectory the developmental anomaly of homosexuality was thought to take, a nonbiologically essentialist or even antiessentialist posture regarding the etiology of homosexuality became commonplace by the early to mid-1950s.[38] Clearly, after the publication of Rado's critique of the Freudian concept of constitutional bisexuality, and in conjunction with the emergent shift to theories of orality, bisexuality was being slowly displaced as an explanatory principle. In 1943, for instance, Bernard Robbins reflected the emergent emphasis on the theory of orality in accounting for homosexuality. Robbins explicitly attempted to distance himself from the Freudian libido theory (at the center of which was constitutional bisexuality). In fact, the framework of the libido theory, he suggested, was perhaps itself responsible for the conceptual quagmire of psychoanalytic explanations of homosexuality. Homosexuality, he argued, stemmed from a form of sadism. From whence does sadism arise? At pains to avoid resorting to biological bisexuality for its explanation, Robbins preferred to disengage himself from the search for origins, purportedly concerned only with its manifestation in the "dynamics of homosexual marriage." Yet in a footnote he concurred with Erich Fromm, who saw sadism as the probable outcome of "authoritative parental patterns."[39]

Similarly, the *American Journal of Psychoanalysis* ran a report from the 1948 New York Academy of Medicine panel on homosexuality, which also distanced itself from Freudian libido theory and theories of hereditary causation. Implicitly positioning these theories as scientific anachronisms, Charles Hulbeck declared that "*today* we find reason to believe that homosexuality develops from character neurosis . . . brought about by special adverse environmental circumstances existing during early formative years."[40] Reporting from two other panels in 1952 and 1953, Harry Gershman noted more of the same. He argued that what "Freud calls instinctive does not seem to be the case." Homosexuality, he declared, is "not related to underlying biological necessity."[41]

John Poe, a psychiatrist at the University of Arkansas, was less reluctant to engage directly with the problem of bisexuality. Writing in the late

1940s, but not published until 1952, Poe's work established a direct connection to Rado's theoretical approach. Indeed, he adopted Rado's "adaptational view of sexual behavior as a frame of reference."[42] Published in the American journal *Psychoanalytic Review*, Poe's work was typical of the growing trend toward therapeutic optimism regarding the treatment and cure of homosexuality. Interestingly, this sense of confidence typical of the 1950s coincided with a more vehement rejection of biological bisexuality and constitutional theories of sexual deviation. "If one sees homosexuality as an inborn constitutional trait or as a possible development of a bisexual organism therapeutic nihilism must result," declared Poe (32). In other words, constitutional theories had to be rejected in order to lay claim to a scientific diagnosis and treatment of homosexuality. The air of therapeutic optimism was reflected in the title of Poe's article—"The Successful Treatment of a 40-Year Old Passive Homosexual Based on an Adaptational View of Sexual Behavior." However, Poe's therapeutic optimism was less the result of actual therapeutic successes than it was the effect of a broader disciplinary desire to reject Freudian bisexuality and thereby appropriate homosexuality as the proper object of psychomedicine.[43] Lionel Ovesey, a highly influential analyst of the 1950s and 1960s, ironically and unwittingly suggested as much in an article in *Psychiatry*. Identifying Rado as the theoretical instigator of this shift, Ovesey pointed out that "in recent years Freud's concept of homosexuality has been challenged by those workers who discarded the libido theory in favor of a more adaptational approach. *This made possible the reclassification of homosexuality as a neurosis and opened pathways to psychotherapy.*"[44]

The drive to cure or eliminate homosexuality from the social/national body gained momentum in the West during the Cold War. Representations of homosexuality throughout the 1950s clearly reflected and reinforced broader cultural anxieties about national and social security and stability. Relations of gender and sexuality had undergone profound changes as a result of the dislocating forces of the Great Depression and the Second World War. In Britain and North America birth and marriage rates had significantly decreased throughout the depression, and during wartime women entered the workforce in unprecedented numbers. The availability of contraceptives, the increasing sexualization of femininity, and the emphasis on sexuality and pleasure as necessary components to the ideal marriage produced fundamental challenges to prewar constructions of gender and sexuality. In addition to this, with the rise of urban subcultures homosexual visibility and awareness also grew. The publication of the Kinsey report in 1948 served to inflame this growing anxiety.[45] Statistics contested the presumed correlation between conservative morality and actual sexual practices. Instead, the report revealed that the conjugal model of sexual relations was not the only norm, that it was in fact competing with premarital, extramarital, and homosexual sexual practices. Furthermore, cross-cultural and cross-species research, such as Ford and Beach's *Patterns of Sexual Behavior*, reinforced and extended the groundbreaking work of the Kinsey report. In an analysis of seventy-six cultures and various animal species, Ford and Beach concluded that "a biological tendency for inversion of sexual behavior is inherent in most if not all mammals including the human species."[46] The norm of heterosexuality was significantly denaturalized. The terrain of cultural life and sexual morality in the modern West was in a state of radical transformation.[47]

The 1950s saw the emergence of a widespread effort to stabilize social, moral, and political order through the reassertion of hegemonic norms. The model of the stable, nuclear, heterosexual family—the metaphorical exemplar of social and moral stability and purity—became the hallmark of this period. Deemed responsible for the (re)production and socialization of upstanding citizens, the family was simultaneously identified as the institution responsible for the production of social delinquency. With the rise of ego psychology and adaptational psychoanalytic theories such as Rado's, maladjusted individuals or social deviants were no longer seen as constitutionally or biologically anomalous. Instead, they were to be classified as psychologically and developmentally retarded. Within psychomedical discourse, therefore, child rearing and parental relationships came under scrutiny as the principal determinants of individual asociality. More specifically, motherhood and the child's relationship to the mother were considered crucial. It is perhaps no coincidence that motherhood at this time became rigorously promoted and glorified in public discourse. As Lynne Segal notes, "The fixing and freezing of women as mothers, and nothing other than mothers, was central to the vision of the fifties."[48]

Reflecting the anxieties surrounding a perceived shift in sexual morality and social delinquency, psychomedical discourses of homosexual etiology were framed around the mother and the family constellation. Proclaiming a cure for homosexuality, psychoanalysts and psychiatrists positioned themselves as patriotic defenders of the family and the nation, purifying them of the subversive threat of homosexuality. Not unexpectedly, homosexuality became increasingly demonized. Construed largely as a personality disturbance or psychological maladjustment, it was seen as the net effect of problems encountered by the developing child in its relationship to the mother and to family dynamics in general. For example, Melitta Sperling demonstrated to a 1954 panel on perversion that "deviant sexual behavior in children, the probable precursor of later perversions, represented the fulfillment of the unconscious perverse need of the parents, *usually the mothers.*" Sperling argued that these unconscious perverse needs prevented mothers from coping with the manifestation of deviant behavior in their children. The result was that mothers "were responsible for defects in the structure of the child's superego."[49] Furthermore, the psychological disturbance of homosexuality was constructed as a pathological and neurotic symptom, a disorder of the entire ego structure. Represented as psychologically unstable, therefore, the homosexual individual was seen to be easily corruptible and liable to blackmail by communists.[50]

The construction of homosexuality in psychoneurotic terms was a further move away from the classical Freudian position. For Freud, "neurosis, is, so to say, the negative of the perversion." Clearly, this meant that homosexuality could not be a form of neurosis because the neurotic symptom is formed at the "cost of repressed pathological (infantile) sexuality";[51] that is, it is formed at the cost of homosexuality itself. In other words, the homosexual does not repress but rather expresses this form of infantile sexuality. Clearly, Freud's libido theory conflicted with oral and adaptational theories that situated etiology in the sphere of preoedipal object relations. As I have argued in chapter 3, biological bisexuality formed the bedrock of this libido theory. The point of departure for this analytic shift depended, therefore, on its outright rejection.

FROM REPUDIATION TO REPULSION

Edmund Bergler was one of the most significant and extreme denouncers of homosexuality and bisexuality in the history of psychomedical thought. He was indeed an exemplary representative of the climate of Cold War homophobia. Bergler was a psychoanalytic psychiatrist, serving at the Freud Clinic in Vienna and occupying the position of assistant director between 1934 and 1937. Upon moving to the United States he went on to hold a lecturing position at the Psychoanalytic Institute in New York City. Prior to Rado's published refutation of bisexuality, and as early as 1933, Bergler had forged an intimate alliance between the object relations of Melanie Klein and the general oral trend toward the theorization of homosexuality. In her enormously influential work *The Psycho-Analysis of Children*, Klein touched on the issue of homosexuality in relation to paranoia. All homosexual activity, she argued, is the expression of a sadistic impulse springing from the sadistic hatred of the mother's breast and a fear and hatred of the father's "bad" penis.[52] In conjunction with Ludwig Eidelberg in 1933, Bergler bolstered the emerging oral tradition with the publication of an article on "the breast complex."[53] This work was to play an important part in the later theorizing of homosexuality.

In Freudian terms, if one of the meanings of the crisis of heterosexual identity is related to the repressive structure of the law of the incest taboo, with its ever-present and dangerous effect of a returning repression for the individual and society, then in Bergler's world this crisis was *seemingly* something of an altogether different order. It was indeed a potential individual and social crisis surrounding the effects of homosexuality. However, it was not the fear of a return of the repressed homosexual components of bisexuality. Instead it was a case of protecting the "young people who, because of an appalling unavailability of accurate information, erroneously consider their homosexual difficulty to be their final destiny."[54] Cold War anxieties emerging from the perceived laxity in relation to conservative codes of sexual morality were more than evident in Bergler's writing in the 1950s. His putative benevolence and concern was also extended to the broader society—to the wives and families of these young homosexuals who were forced to endure the stigmatizing effects of homosexual association. And all this suffering was because of misinformation and a media conspiracy of silence regarding matters homosexual.

In the closing sentence of the foreword to his *Homosexuality: Disease or Way of Life?* Bergler summed up his feelings on the crisis: "Without being an alarmist, or sounding the alarm, I believe that a serious social problem, so far totally mishandled, exists, and there is an urgent need for public clarification" (10). Clearly, for Bergler, the problem pertained, first, to faulty theories that constructed homosexuality as constitutional and incurable in nature and, second, to the problem of circulating misinformation. In Bergler's view, this was the failure to understand the fact that homosexuality is a remediable condition that could only be controlled and corrected by psychoanalysis. In this text Bergler was not just attempting to ensure the viability of the *proper object* of psychoanalysis. He was, more important, ensuring a critical distance from the exclusions at the heart of heterosexual identity: the abject modalities of homosexuality and bisexuality. I suggest that the social problem, or crisis, of which Bergler spoke was not just a concern with the therapeutic surveillance of homosexuality. It is important to recognize that it was also a concern with the surveillance of heterosexuality and a strengthening and safeguarding of its fragile boundaries.

The publication of Alfred Kinsey's *Sexual Behavior in the Human Male* in

1948 only intensified the sense of crisis for Bergler. Kenneth Lewes, in his historical study of psychoanalytic theories of sexuality, has suggested that upon researching the Kinsey report he discovered to his surprise that it led to no such crisis in the representation of homosexuality within psychoanalysis. The importance for psychoanalysis of Kinsey's enormous sample of fifty-three hundred white American men "is easy to imagine," as Lewes pointed out, given the incredibly small samples of patients that had led to psychoanalytic universalizing theories of human sexuality. Some analysts had justifiably raised concerns that such small samples could be unrepresentative of the human condition.[55] Kinsey's 'startling' statistics, which included a figure of 37 percent of all postadolescent white males having engaged in homosexual activity to the point of 'orgastic discharge', were couched in a theoretical framework that rejected the psychoanalytic distinction between normal and perverse.[56] The report was decidedly antipsychoanalytic, representing a significant potential challenge to the psychoanalytic paradigm.

Lewes goes on to argue, however, that he could have very easily omitted the chapter on "Analytic Responses to the Kinsey Report." "The psychoanalytic theory of homosexuality was, surprisingly, unaffected by it." He suggests that the formal psychoanalytic community in large part ignored the report.[57] Edmund Bergler was either an exception to this observation or else one of the few analysts willing to tackle the report directly. Or perhaps his anxiety about the conflict and fragility inherent in heterosexual identity led to a form of neurosis? Perhaps Bergler's theory of sexuality was the manifestation of an extreme neurotic condition, a condition psychically managed to a greater degree by most analysts of the period? Despite the lack of formal psychoanalytic engagement with the report, as I have already suggested, it nonetheless formed a significant part of the cultural and political context of the United States in the late 1940s and early 1950s. Psychomedical discourses must be analyzed in this broader context. I would argue that even in its apparent absence in much of psychoanalytic discourse, the Kinsey report was a palpable force, indeed, a structuring absence. It certainly led to no major revisions to the dominant theoretical approach to homosexuality. However, the statistical 'findings' and the popular hysteria that surrounded them effected a pronounced reiteration (defense?) of psychoanalytic principles, along with a sense of disciplinary propriety in relation to the object of homosexuality.[58]

For Bergler, the Kinsey report was a direct attack on the discipline of psychoanalysis. Kinsey rejected both the notion of homosexuality as a disease and the concomitant therapeutic belief in its necessary treatment and cure.

It is perhaps little wonder that psychomedical discourses largely rejected the significance of Kinsey's work. As Jacob Arlow pointed out in a report from a 1954 panel on perversion, "all participants demonstrated little use for the findings of Kinsey." This sentiment was based on the claim that "in the interdisciplinary correlations of psychoanalysis with other fields of science so much is borrowed from analysis which in the last instance must supply the criteria for normality."[59] In other words, homosexuality was the proper object of psychoanalysis *in the last instance*. Bergler published a virulent denunciation of the report in an article entitled "The Myth of a New National Disease: Homosexuality and the Kinsey Report."[60] The title immediately signaled a challenge to Kinsey's statistical findings. To accept the statistics is a nonsense, Bergler suggested. Furthermore:

> If these figures are only approximately correct (Kinsey sticks to percentages and does not translate them into actual numbers), then "the homosexual outlet" is *the predominant national disease*, overshadowing in numbers cancer, tuberculosis, heart failure, infantile paralysis. Of course, Kinsey denies that the "homosexual outlet" is a disease in the first place. But psychiatrically, we are dealing with a disease, however you slice it. (86)

Bergler's work alerts us to a purported crisis of twofold significance, the one feeding into the other: on the one hand was the social crisis of misinformation and its damaging effects; and on the other was an impending crisis of national authority. On this second point Bergler almost reached a level of hysteria: "Kinsey's erroneous psychological conclusions pertaining to homosexuality will be politically and propagandistically used against the United States abroad, stigmatizing the nation as a whole in a whisper campaign, especially since there are no comparative statistics available for other countries" (87).[61] Bergler's hostility toward the Kinsey report only exacerbated a sense of crisis surrounding the 'problem of homosexuality'. At the height of homophobic Cold War rhetoric, and as his psychoanalytic career progressed, so too did his vituperative homophobic stance on the issue of homosexuality and bisexuality. Describing homosexuals as 'immature', 'infantile', tending toward 'parasitism', he went so far as to suggest that "every homosexual is a prima donna."[62] In *Homosexuality: Disease or Way of Life?* he even attempted to qualify a palpable homophobic posture by ensuring his 'scientific' impartiality:

> I have received a good many compliments for lectures and publications on this topic. All in all, I have no reason to complain of homosexuals. Still, though I have no bias, if I were asked what kind of person the homosexual it

[sic], I would say: "Homosexuals are essentially disagreeable people, regardless of their pleasant or unpleasant outward manner. True, they are not responsible for their unconscious conflicts. However, these conflicts sap so much of their inner energy that the shell is a mixture of superciliousness, fake aggression, and whimpering. Like all psychic masochists, they are subservient when confronted with a stronger person, merciless when in power, unscrupulous about trampling on a weaker person. The only language their unconscious understands is brute force. What is most discouraging, you seldom find an intact ego (what is popularly called 'a correct person') among them." (26)

The homosexual is implicitly constructed here as a duplicitous figure. With fragile ego boundaries he is worthy only of suspicion, a potential menace to the democratic nation. Do not be fooled, Bergler further declared, if homosexuals try to convince you that they are happy: "This is a convenient blind. There are no happy homosexuals."[63] Homosexuals unconsciously seek disappointment, "as does every adherent to the 'mechanism of orality'" (405). Despite the fact that Bergler grew increasingly more extreme, he was never censured within his own intellectual community. An adherence to the legitimized psychoanalytic model of orality implicitly authorized his views on sexual development. Furthermore, he insisted that psychoanalytic therapy could cure homosexuality; and this only amplified the disciplinary claim on the *proper object*. The post-Freudian research into oral factors responsible for homosexuality provided a claim to 'therapeutic optimism' that "could not have been made a decade ago."[64]

Beginning with the 'discovery' of the so-called breast complex in 1933, along with its theoretical extension to the theory of homosexuality published in his 1944 article "Eight Prerequisites for the Psychoanalytic Treatment of Homosexuality," Bergler provided one of the earliest comprehensive oral theories of homosexuality. The Freudian phallic stage of development as a determinant of homosexuality was obsolete. Bergler argued that the "Oedipal palimpsest is in itself a covering cloak for earlier pre-Oedipal vicissitudes."[65] In deference to the Freudian tradition, Bergler suggested that while Freud acknowledged the oral phase, he was unable to account for its importance in the development of homosexual object choice because at that time it was either overlooked, or more important, 'undiscovered'.[66]

Bergler's theory of homosexuality represented an interesting yet ironic twist on the debate over congenital versus acquired determinants. It was seemingly neither. "It is an unfavorable *unconscious* solution of a conflict that faces *every* child," argued Bergler.[67] This conflictual condition, resulting from the meeting of childhood fantasies of omnipotence with the objective intrusive reality, produces psychic wounds. The intrusions of the mother as she cares for the child expose the illusion of "childhood megalomania," motivating a hatred of the mother and a defensive mistaken belief in her/his autarchy: "'I produce everything I need, and am independent of anyone else'."

The trauma and anger of weaning, and the resultant "disappointing breast or breast substitutes," reflect an indignity to the child's autarchic sense. This effects a libidinal displacement whereby the cathexis of the breast is transferred to the child's own penis through the belief in the substitutive character of the penis as the nutritional organ. The developing homosexual then aspires to a "reduplication" of the omnipotence of the penis, having rejected the breast in its favor. However, uncertain of his new-found status as "breast-barony," the homosexual requires the constant reassurance of this phallic omnipotence. This is achieved by a reduplication enacted by the "sex organ of his partner [through which] he recognises his own."[68] Thus discarded is "the whole disappointing sex: woman." Bergler concludes that "every analysis of homosexuals . . . confirms the fact that behind their frantic chase after the male organ, the disappointing breast is hidden."[69]

The pathos of homosexuality for Bergler rests with the fact that as a defense mechanism against wounded megalomania, the child unconsciously desires and enjoys "psychic masochism, plus."[70] Hence, "homosexuality . . . is a neurotic disease" (13). However, in an ironic homophobic twist, Bergler wants to rescue both society and the parents of homosexuals from any culpability. The behavior of "parents may *contribute* to the child's inner troubles, but cannot *create* them." Rather, "the use or misuse of the raw material" at the disposal of a child "is accomplished by the selective action of the child's unconscious ego" (31). In short, while homosexuality is supposedly neither biologically determined nor produced as a result of the triangular familial (oedipal) relationships, it is nonetheless reinstalled as an individualized phenomenon. This is why I call this discursive tactic of Bergler's homophobic. For he aimed to project the 'disease' of homosexuality onto individual homosexuals, thereby safely expelling it from all things heterosexual.

Bergler did this by going so far as suggesting that even "the mechanism of orality does not make a homosexual":

> What is *specifically* characteristic of the homosexual, is the fact that the narcissistic structure accentuates the mechanism to the nth degree. . . . Precisely because of their narcissistic substructure, the blow caused by incapacity to maintain the infantile fiction of omnipotence, hits the children who become

homosexuals so severely. They recover only partially from the defeat of weaning, and even then only with narcissistic recompense.[71]

Homosexuals thus have projected on them all of the disparaging characteristics rejected by compulsory heterosexual identity: they are fundamentally impotent children whose unconscious mechanisms of defense are defective. Bergler did not, however, attempt to locate the basis for this narcissistic 'incapacity'. If it resides wholly within the individual and cannot be accounted for by a sociological explanation, then we are back to that ambiguous and misleading (Freudian) notion of *constitution*, whose repudiation provided Bergler's point of departure.

"The genesis of female homosexuality," Bergler proposed, "is identical with that of male homosexuality: an unsolved masochistic conflict with the mother of earliest infancy." Unlike the male homosexual, however, the "lesbian" cannot "flee to 'another continent'—man."[72] Acting on the principle of the "'itinerary of the opposite',," the little girl's hatred toward the mother is reactively transformed into "*pseudo*love" by the superego. "This alibi leads straight to Lesbianism" (246). Immediately unclear is why the "lesbian" cannot flee to the continent of man. It seems to me that the reason for this is because the female does not possess the penis and therefore is without an 'appropriate' substitute for the breast. Also unclear is why the penis should be endowed with the power of substitution. In any case, the "prima donna" and the "incipient lesbian" are severe neurotic diseases, defective deviations of normative heterosexuality. What is interesting is that Bergler did not attempt to replace the Freudian norm of biological bisexuality with a scientifically corrected version of biological heterosexuality. It was merely presumed that the development of heterosexual object choice was the 'normal' outcome for the human species. In fact, as Kenneth Lewes suggests, the issue of homosexual perversion for Bergler borders on being an issue of moral corruption.[73]

Bergler's construction of (hetero)sexuality provides a clear illustration of the workings of what Irigaray calls the phallic economy of the same.[74] Female homosexuality is explained according to a framework whose referent is man. In addition to this, homosexual object choice could no longer be seen, as Freud indeed saw it, as an integral force in the psychic structure of human sexuality. Instead, heterosexuality commanded the position of master signifier, of truth transcendent, against which all else was defined. The status of homosexuality was thus the diseased, distorted, and indeed fictitious, simulacrum of the deity of heterosexuality. Therefore, contrary to Bergler's distinction between "real" and "spurious" homosexuality, there was actually no such thing as a homosexual within this economy.[75] A homosexual was no more than a neurotic heterosexual in dire need of therapeutic reorientation.

Clearly, bisexuality had no place whatsoever in this heteronormative order of the same. Existing only as a "flagrant misnomer," it is refused even the honor of a taxonomic title. Bisexuality, that is, figures only as a catachresis: a trope without a referent.[76] In *Homosexuality: Disease or Way of Life?* in a chapter entitled "Does Bisexuality Exist?" Bergler declared precisely this: "BISEXUALITY—a state that has no existence beyond the word itself" (80). This refusal, as I have argued earlier, was a structural necessity, functioning to secure the inviolable boundaries of heterosexuality from any 'perverse' incursion. That is to say that bisexuality is situated in an all too threatening proximity to heterosexuality; indeed, bisexuality partakes of heterosexuality itself. No element of the 'perverse' must contaminate heterosexual purity. However, bisexuality presented a conceptual problem in Bergler's binary schema, dominated as it was by the law of noncontradiction. "Nobody can dance at two weddings at the same time," he said. If they could, Bergler would have had difficulty incorporating a dynamic and shifting psychical organization into a framework based on linear phases of sexual development.

In such a system, dichotomous relations between unconscious forces prevail. There are no in-between states, only positive and negative, pleasure and displeasure, activity and passivity, normality and neurosis, heterosexuality and homosexuality. The first term in each of these pairs is positively defined, the second its negation. The introduction of the third term, bisexuality, complicates Bergler's presumption of the (constitutional?) narcissistic substructure of the unconscious of all homosexuals. The child, it seems, must resolve, *in one way or another*, the traumas of orality in order to enter the world of object relations. This is construed as a fixed mechanism of defense with no possibility of regression and renegotiation (except of course through psychoanalytic transference). In other words, there is no form of ambivalent resolution of the phase of orality. Moreover, despite the fact that there exist multiple forms of perversion, there is only one form of normality in the economy of the same, with no gradations. For heterosexuality, the origin and universal signifier, *is all heterosexuality*. No perversion, or *disease*, can possibly claim any part of its untainted essence. Any suggestion that a person can be alternately or concomitantly homosexual and heterosexual "is as rational," Bergler argued, "as one declaring that a man can at the same time have cancer and perfect health."[77]

Bergler was by no means alone in his rejection of constitutional homosexuality and outright dismissal of the very existence of bisexuality. While he was the most vociferous in his denunciation, he was also the most comprehensive of the early oral theorists in detailing the concepts of homosexuality and bisexuality. In 1959, Abram Kardiner, Aaron Karush, and Lionel Ovesey summarized the prevalent opinion of the hegemonic adaptational and oral schools.[78] In an article in the *Journal of Nervous and Mental Disease* they outlined the thematic departure from Freud. Referencing Rado as an authorizing gesture, Kardiner et al. argued against the "tautological [Freudian] reasoning involved in justifying an aetiological hypothesis [i.e., bisexuality] by citing as evidence its assumed consequences."[79]

Nor was Bergler alone in the representation of homosexuality as a morbid neurotic condition. Such was the pervasive psychoanalytic theme of the entire period from the 1940s to the 1960s.[80] Karen Horney developed the influential concept of homosexual neurosis in her 1937 work, *The Neurotic Personality of Our Time*.[81] Firmly grounded in the hegemonic oral tradition, works such as Horney's spawned a multitudinous array of psychoanalytic theories eager to map the variously disturbed personality structures of homosexuals. Homosexuality was identified during this period as a subsidiary sexual symptom deriving in the last instance from a prior structural ego deficiency. This represented a desexualization of the etiology of psychopathology. In her 1949 review of the literature on homosexuality, Clara Thompson concluded by urging psychoanalysis to "deal primarily with the personality structure, realizing that the symptom is a secondary development from that."[82]

This is precisely the direction taken by discourses of psychoanalysis and psychoanalytic psychiatry. In fact, in 1952 the accumulated efforts of theorists of homosexual neurosis led to the official classification by the American Psychiatric Association of homosexuality as a mental disorder.[83] So despite the apparent extremism of Bergler's paranoiac homophobia, it was par for the course in the 1950s. Homosexuality was, as Gershman declared, "tantamount to psychic illness."[84] To avoid resorting once again to bisexuality, however, this form of psychic illness was to be more explicitly framed as a developmental and adaptational disturbance of gender (the gendered ego).

THE FORMALIZATION OF A DISCIPLINE

In 1962 the publication of *Homosexuality: A Psychoanalytic Study of Male Homosexuals* marked the consolidation of the postwar pathologization of homosexuality.[85] Under the chairmanship of Irving Bieber, this study became the canonical tract for the discipline of psychoanalysis. Indeed,

Bieber himself became *the* expert in the field.[86] *Homosexuality* was the product of nine years of research by seventy-seven members from the Society of Medical Psychoanalysts. Involving clinical and statistical analyses of 206 men (106 homosexual and 100 heterosexual), it was the largest psychoanalytic project ever assembled. Such an impressive body of data could only strengthen scientific legitimacy by providing a much-needed boost to a discipline that, for the most part, had relied on a very small number of case studies for the construction of theories of homosexuality.

It is in this context that we can see the shadow of Kinsey looming even larger perhaps than Kenneth Lewes's historical reading has suggested. Kinsey's enormous sample and impressive statistics were deployed as a direct challenge to psychoanalytic concepts. Critical of these concepts, Kinsey argued that they were problematically framed around the arbitrary distinction between normality and abnormality. Yet this distinction was the outcome of tiny samples of only those individuals who had sought therapy. "To have so limited the study would," Kinsey argued, "have constituted a pre-acceptance of the categories whose reality and existence were under investigation." So he rejected the terms of normality and abnormality, suggesting that they were perhaps inappropriate "in a scientific vocabulary."[87] Begun only four years later, Bieber's study is more than likely an implicit psychoanalytic response and corrective to the challenge effected by the Kinsey report.[88] For psychoanalysis had come under fire increasingly for extrapolating from grossly unrepresentative population samples. *Homosexuality* thus provided the appropriate archive in support of psychoanalytic 'truths' regarding the pathological status of homosexuality.

Bieber offered few fresh insights. Like so many others, he proceeded from the requisite repudiation of Freudian bisexuality. "The bisexual theory as a set of conceptualizations to explain the aetiology of homosexuality is no longer tenable," he argued, "nor is there any existing evidence to support a genetic theory of homosexuality."[89] However, unlike many others, he unhesitatingly and blatantly reinstalled the notion of biological heterosexuality: "We assume that heterosexuality is the *biologic* norm and that unless interfered with all individuals are heterosexual. Homosexuals do not bypass heterosexual developmental phases and all remain potentially heterosexual."[90] In other words, "every homosexual is, in reality, a 'latent' heterosexual" (220). Not unexpectedly, Bieber promoted a sense of therapeutic optimism above and beyond earlier analysts. In fact, he suggested the success rate to be "considerably higher in recent times than formerly, when psychiatrists were imbued with gloomy prognostications about this condition."[91]

The theory of homosexuality propounded by Bieber was a diluted amalgam of adaptational, interpersonal, and even Freudian theory. Like Rado, Bergler, and the other oral theorists before him, Bieber continued to explain homosexuality as a secondary or neurotic symptom. However, where he differed from analysts of the 1950s was in his suggestion that the decisive developmental period was less the oral than the oedipal and postoedipal phases. The oral period was certainly important in the formation of personality and psychopathology, he argued, but it was not marked by sexual processes. Despite this shift of emphasis, Bieber was in fact extending one important theme: the desexualization of homosexual etiology. This, of course, was a necessary by-product of the imperative to reject constitutional bisexuality. Bieber took it one step further, however, in arguing that "heterosexual responsivity" begins with the "onset of the Oedipus complex."[92] Yet it would seem that Bieber had in fact taken two or three steps back. Not only does he deny preoedipal sexuality, but he appears to conflate the axes of gender and sexuality. Deviations from the universal biologic norm of heterosexuality thus become deviations in terms of gender development. This represents a line of continuity with the oral theorists and is curiously reminiscent of mid-nineteenth-century sexology before the emergence of the economy of (hetero)sexuality.

Reflecting postwar concerns about the nuclear family, the central focus of Bieber's research was on motherhood and family relationships. The "homosexual adaptation" was the product of faulty parenting and the "exposure to highly pathologic parent-child relationships and early life situations."[93] According to Bieber, the "'classical' triangular pattern" is therefore "one where the mother is CBI [close-binding intimate] and is dominant and minimizing toward a husband who is a detached father, particularly a hostile-detached one" (172). This constellation he considered in itself gender dysfunctional. It provided the basis for generating profound conflict in the child upon sexual awakening.

With the emergence of the Oedipus complex and heterosexual responsivity, the male child directs his "sexual orientation" toward the mother. The close-binding mother, however, inadvertently promotes homosexuality in the child by interfering with heterosexual development, interfering with the father-son relationship, interfering with peer relations, and interfering with the development of independence. She achieves all of the above through sexual overstimulation, inhibition of heterosexual responsiveness, discouragement of masculine attitudes and behavior, fostering of father-son competitiveness, interfering with boyhood friendships, fostering adult relationships, and encouraging timidity and maternal dependence

(79–82). Paternal rivalry over the mother as sexual object—"perhaps a concomitant of heterosexual orientation"—must also be negotiated and adequately resolved. However, the father provokes feelings of fear, hostility, sexual competitiveness, and rejection in the child. This hampers the child's ability both to "master feelings of rivalry" and "to cope with antagonistic behavior from other males."[94]

Homosexuality for Bieber was thus symptomatic of "irrational fears of heterosexuality," the basis of which is a fear of "attack from a male competitor." Heterosexual encounters are avoided, and the homosexual adapts by "eroticizing objects and attributes he most fears—aggressive males and masculine strength" (973, 971). This homosexual adaptation is nothing but a neurotic compromise necessary to "rehabilitate a damaged sense of masculinity" (971).

Bieber was concerned primarily with male homosexuality. Female homosexuality was little more than an adjusted footnote to a model framed almost entirely around cases of male homosexuality. "The prevailing concepts of the aetiology of lesbianism," he said, "follow the same general line of thought as for male homosexuality" (974). The little girl finds herself in competition with a hostile and jealous mother intent on 'defeminizing' her. The mother does this by "fault finding, rejection, and control" in order to "interfere with an easy, natural relationship between father and daughter." "Homosexually inducive mothers" also interfere with "heterosexual peer relationships," favor sons over daughters, rival "with daughters for males," and induce paternal guilt over sexual feelings for daughters. The father is usually submissive and detached, but this, in part, "is a submissive renunciation demanded by the mother." In short, lesbianism appears to be the product of an inadequate feminine gender identity whose development is hampered by faulty parental relationships and role models. "It is unlikely," argued Bieber, "that an affectionately related mother who encourages her daughter's femininity will produce a lesbian." Regarding the appropriate father figure, Bieber was even more certain of the outcome: "Fathers who are strong figures in the family and who are openly affectionate and masculine with their daughters do not produce lesbians" (974–75).[95]

Bieber aimed to retain homosexuality as the proper object of psychoanalysis by proposing two forms of treating the 'problem'. The psychoanalyst/psychiatrist is indispensable to both: (1) "prophylaxis": prevention of homosexuality by public education and early detection and psychiatric examination; (2) "reconstructive therapy": resolution of irrational fears of heterosexuality and a restoration of masculine gender identity (972–73). In line with the homophobic turn in psychoanalysis, Bieber accepted as an unexamined given the notion of homosexuality as a significant social and national problem.

This was made even more explicit by the influential analyst Charles Socarides. Working from within a more classical psychoanalytic framework, Socarides' writings in the 1960s and early 1970s represent the apotheosis of the post–World War II pathologization of homosexuality. They also signal, however, a growing anxiety around the disciplinary object of homosexuality. Counterdiscourses following in the wake of Kinsey had begun to gain strength and momentum throughout the 1960s, providing the impetus for a burgeoning homophile movement. Theorists such as Ford and Beach, Evelyn Hooker, Thomas Szasz, and Judd Marmor were among those who, like Kinsey, expressed dissatisfaction with psychotherapeutic discourse and its universal pathologization of homosexuals. Despite being somewhat marginal to the psychiatric hegemony, the cumulative efforts of these figures worked nonetheless to challenge many of its fundamental assumptions. They did this by providing empirical research that contested the view of all homosexuals as abnormal and socially and psychologically maladjusted. They also provided the foundations for a radical homosexual movement, as we shall see in the next chapter. Socarides was clearly concerned by this dissenting movement:

> We practice today in the atmosphere of a sweeping sexual revolution. Together with the mainstream heterosexual revolt has come the announcement that a homosexual revolution is also in progress and that homosexuality should be granted total acceptance as a valid form of sexual functioning, different from but equal to heterosexuality. Such acceptance of homosexuality, as being a simple variation of normality, is naive, not to say grounded in ignorance. Equally misleading is the idea that it is merely an aspect of normal development, a transient stage of adolescence, without meaningful sequelae. That we, as physicians, could be persuaded to overlook such tendencies among our young people is a harmful fantasy.[96]

Socarides attempted to reignite and reformulate Cold War hysteria over the subversive threat of homosexuality. Homosexuality was indeed a social and national problem for Socarides, however, it was no longer a threat to national security. Instead, it represented a dangerous threat to national health. Writing in the *Journal of the American Medical Association*, he sounded a public warning: "Homosexuality is a medical disorder which has reached epidemiologic proportions; its frequency of incidence surpasses that of recognized major illnesses in the nation" (1199). Even a statistically "conservative estimate," argued Socarides, showed homosexuality to be in excess of the statistics for heart disease, arthritis, impairment of the spine, and nervous and mental disease (1200). Not surprisingly, responsibility for restoring the health of the nation was again seen to rest squarely and solely with scientifically and medically trained psychiatrists and psychoanalysts. In fact, according to Socarides, anything less than psychotherapeutic expertise may be not only unhelpful, but individually harmful and socially undesirable: "Tampering with his [the homosexual's] psyche by unqualified persons is to be condemned as he may become seriously disorganised if a premature attempt is made to interrupt his homosexual activities. Conversely, an individual, however impelled toward them, who has refrained from homosexual activities may be tragically pushed into them by unwise guidance" (1201). The medicalization of homosexuality functioned as a rhetorical strategy for inciting public and medical concern over the health of the country. Ironically, the high statistical incidence of homosexuality, which antiestablishment critics had calculated in efforts to challenge psychiatric dogma, was implicitly reappropriated and recast by Socarides as a medical pandemic. Inheriting the widespread rejection of bisexuality as a constituent of normal sexuality, Socarides, like many analysts, installed a notion of universal heterosexuality as a normative and ahistorical given. Anything less was therefore a functional malady flying in the face of human evolution.

However, in more classical psychoanalytic style, and in contradistinction to Bieber, Socarides argued that heterosexuality did not issue from a biological directive. "The choice of sexual object is not predetermined by chromosomal tagging. Heterosexual object choice is determined from birth due to cultural and environmental indoctrination." This left him with the presumably difficult task of deflecting arguments—proposed by such thinkers as Kinsey and Ford and Beach—regarding the relativity of cultural norms and values. For if individuals are indoctrinated with culturally specific and relative values, perhaps pathologizing homosexuality is a historically recent and peculiarly anthropocentric and Western phenomenon. Anticipating this critique, Socarides went on to account for the naturalness of heterosexual object choice in terms reminiscent of Sandor Rado. Heterosexuality, he claimed "is supported by universal human concepts of mating and the family unit with the complementariness and contrast between the sexes. It is further determined by 2.5 billion years of human evolution and is a product of sexual differentiation, at first solely based on reproduction but later widened to include sexual gratification" (1201). The development of the male-female coupling is only disrupted, according to Socarides, by "massive childhood fears" (1201). Within this schema heterosexuality is seen to be a functional requirement of "evolution favoring survival."[97] In other words, the survival of the species and the evolutionary advancement of society depend upon the nuclear family. In disturbing this evolutionary process, homosexuality becomes a dangerous medical disease and epidemic that threatens the human species and the nation.

Like Bieber and the oral theorists before him, Socarides effected a marked desexualization of homosexual etiology. This was not merely the corollary to the assumption of a universal heterosexuality. More important, it was a necessary epistemological maneuver that functioned to maintain a critical distance between the species of 'homosexual' and 'heterosexual'. Central to the viability of this process was, of course, the disavowal of bisexuality. In contrast to the Freudian tradition, Socarides no longer saw homosexuality as a form of (bi)*sexual* perversion inherent to all, but a "learned maladaptation arising from faulty *gender* identity in the earliest stages of life."[98] "All male homosexuals suffer, paradoxically," he argued, "from the yearning to be a man, not a woman as commonly assumed" (1201).

In this schema homosexuality is tantamount to gender disorder. It is symptomatic of a deluded attempt at recovering a "forfeited" masculine identity through the identification with those attributes of the sexual partner that the homosexual lacks.[99] "They hope to achieve a shot of masculinity in the homosexual act," argues Socarides. "Like the addict, he must have his 'fix'."[100] In fact, homosexuality is scarcely considered a form of sexuality at all, for as one analyst put it, "it is not sexual satisfaction that is sought but rather a defense against anxiety."[101] Thus, as Harry Gershman argued, homosexuality is the "symbolic expression of a person's inner conflict in sexual language."[102]

Two presumptions made possible this desexualization of homosexuality. First, homosexuality was incorporated within the theory of neurosis. With biological bisexuality extirpated from the theory of perversion, the classical Freudian position on the relationship of perversion and neurosis was reformulated. The two were conflated, and homosexuality was reduced to the status of *pseudo*heterosexuality. Same-sex sexual behavior was no longer reducible to an inherent (bi)*sexual* striving. All homosexuals were thus neurotic but latent heterosexuals, the entity of homosexuality, as Frederick Weiss argued, nothing but "an expression of the total personality, a comprehensive attempt to solve inner conflict."[103] Second, the homosexual individual is seen either to have regressed to or to be arrested at a stage prior to true object relations and adult genital sexuality. For as Weiss summarized, "with no well-defined distinction between subject and object, in homosexuality there is no choice of object (because this would mean being detached from the mother) and no relation (for the same reason)" (74).

PSYCHOLOGICAL BISEXUALITY

Within discourses of ego psychology the substitution of biological bisexuality with universal heterosexuality effectively elided the possibility of a psychological bisexuality. 'Bisexuals' are certainly mentioned in most of the psychoanalytic texts I have been exploring; however, they appear only as manifestations of homosexual neurosis. The appellation 'bisexual' is used only to describe sexual practices, not ego structure. In other words, the theory of homosexual neurosis incorporates those who engage in bisexual sexual practices. For example, Bieber described as bisexual "men who become involved repetitively [in homosexuality]—be it in prisons, during periods of absence from women, out of curiosity presumably, or for kicks." However, such individuals, he argues, "shift to overt homosexuality when under psychological stress."[104] What this means is that any instance of homosexuality disqualifies *during that moment of stress* the heterosexual character structure of the individuals involved. Homosexuality and heterosexuality cannot, therefore, be present simultaneously in an individual ego. There is no possibility of theorizing bisexuality as a distinct character structure without reinstalling homosexuality in the realm of normative sexuality.[105]

The genealogical roots of this mode of thinking can be traced to Freud. As I demonstrated in chapter 3, the possibility of desiring and identifying with the same (gendered) object is precluded in Freudian psychoanalysis. In various forms this principle has influenced each of the psychoanalytic theorizations of sexuality treated in this chapter. This was most explicitly captured by Bergler's statement that "nobody can dance at two weddings at the same time."[106] It is also apparent in the pervasive use of the categories of *pseudo*homosexuality and *pseudo*heterosexuality, and "spurious" and "overt" homosexuality. Each of these categories was constituted through the law of contrariety. Therefore, as long as no individual could at any given moment occupy two opposing camps, psychological bisexuality was to remain a catachresis. For if all bisexuals are either homosexual or heterosexual, and all homosexuals latent heterosexuals, then in order for a state of psychological bisexuality to exist, heterosexuality would no longer be latent at all. Instead, homosexuality, as Freud had argued, would exist somewhere *within* heterosexuality, as one of its structuring elements.

In an apparent twist of sexological and Freudian theories, bisexuality was no longer used as an explanatory principle for homosexuality. Rather, the theory of homosexuality was used to account for the prevalence of bisexual practices and to explain away the notion of psychological bisexuality. In a symposium on homosexuality, George Wiedeman hints at this ambiguous and superficial use of the category of bisexuality within post-Freudian psychoanalytic discourse: "If the word bisexuality is used as a term applicable to individuals who engage in sexual relations with persons of both sexes, we obviously use it as a descriptive and not as an explanatory dynamic concept."[107]

CONCLUSION

In this chapter I have suggested that the repudiation of bisexuality from the scene of post-Freudian psychoanalysis was anything but inconsequential to the history of sexuality. It was a strategic move that conditioned a number of important shifts. First, it enabled psychoanalysis to expropriate homosexuality as its proper object. In this way the essence or truth of the homosexual condition was seen as a privilege conferred *only* on an independent psychoanalytic discipline. Second, it made possible the pathologization of homosexuality. Third, now construed as an adaptational neurotic condition, homosexuality, as Lionel Ovesey put it, was "susceptible to psychoanalysis."[108] That is, homosexuality was subject to therapeutic cure—a move that fed back into and strengthened claims of disciplinary authority and autonomy. Fourth, the expulsion of bisexuality from the psychoanalytic theory of sexuality aimed to reinforce the tenuous discursive boundaries of the hetero/homosexual division.

It would be tempting to turn back onto the psychoanalysts of this period the very theoretical tools that made possible the pathologization of homosexuality and elision of bisexuality. Two Freudian protégés suggested as much in relation to the early psychoanalytic inattention to the concept of bisexuality. "*Their* basic predisposition is precisely what men are least disposed to recognize," argued Stekel.[109] Similarly, Douglas Bryan explained the neglect as being due to "some deep psychological resistance to it even among psycho-analysts."[110] Forgoing the reactive and simplistic pleasure to be gained from this style of analysis, I have been offering a very different interpretation. I have argued that the transformation in psychoanalytic thinking was the product of an *epistemic crisis of (hetero)sexual identity*. This notion of identity crisis is meant to signal a problematization of both an individualistic, or subject-centered, notion of identity crisis *and* a sociocultural one. In other words, the crisis of (hetero)sexual identity was neither simply an individual anxiety over the return of repressed homosexuality, nor was it a therapeutic or moral crisis over the perceived social 'problem' of homosexuality—although it may appear as one or the other or both. Instead, the notion of crisis I have employed is a discursive, or epistemic, one.

The crisis of (hetero)sexual identity was thus a crisis of epistemological boundaries. It was the attempt at regulating and concealing the contradictions inherent in the discursive construction of (hetero)sexual identity.[111]

As I have demonstrated in this chapter and the previous chapter, this crisis was made palpable by Freud's radical theory of the perversions and by the behavioral sociology of Kinsey. For Freud, for instance, "the most important perversion, homosexuality, hardly deserves the name. It comes down to a general disposition to bisexuality. . . . All human beings are capable of making a homosexual object-choice and have in fact made one in their unconscious."[112] From a sociological and anthropological perspective Kinsey and Ford and Beach said much the same, claiming that human beings have the erotic capacity to respond to either sex.[113] With sexuality construed as a potentially shifting object choice or disposition—a *bipotentiality*—the ontological distinction between separate hetero- and homosexual species is increasingly difficult to maintain. In other words, each of these divergent researchers had placed bisexuality, or bisexual potential, on the inside of the category and identity of heterosexuality. As Marjorie Garber notes of the social impact of the Kinsey report, "What may have shocked mainstream America most of all . . . was not the existence of significant numbers of *homosexuals* but rather the overwhelming presence of *bisexuals* and *bisexuality* in American life."[114] The only way for psychoanalysts to circumvent the collapse, into one another, of the boundaries of hetero- and homosexuality was therefore to repudiate both the biological and psychological residue of bisexuality. At the level of biology this was achieved by Sandor Rado. At the level of psychology it was initiated by Freud himself and unapologetically completed by Edmund Bergler and the dominant American form of oral-centered psychoanalysis.[115] Fundamentally a strategy of crisis management, bisexuality was thereby refused a referent and rendered a misnomer. It was elided, or *disavowed*, not only in the present tense, therefore, but in any temporal sense at all.

The concept of bisexuality was by no means dead and buried, however. As we will see in the next chapter, it continued to circulate in a number of forms within anthropological and sociological discourses. It was even revivified in a discourse of post-Freudian psychoanalysis. In the 1970s these strands converged in the radical sexual politics and theory of gay liberation. Chapter 5 turns to an analysis of gay liberation and the place of bisexuality in attempts to counter the psychoanalytic monopoly on sexuality.

PART [2]

DECONSTRUCTING SEXUAL IDENTITY

5

THE REPRESSED RETURNS

> Look out, straights. Here comes the Gay Liberation Front, springing up like warts all over the bland face of Amerika. . . . We are the extrusions of your unconscious mind—your worst fears made flesh.
> —Martha Shelley 1972

The period between World War II and the late 1960s saw the consolidation of the hetero/homosexual opposition. Structural instabilities exposed by Freud were concealed and reframed in an effort to fortify the oppositional boundaries of gender and sexuality. The repudiation of bisexuality thus served a dual purpose: to reinstall heterosexuality as the universal source of individual and cultural reproduction and to remove homosexuality from the sphere of normative relations. This repudiation functioned to naturalize gender and ontologize the homosexual (once again) as a distinct human species—albeit a specifically aberrant psychological species to be eradicated through psychoanalytic 'cure'.

For over two decades post-Freudian psychoanalysts worked hard to rewrite Freudian theory. In struggling to safeguard the cultural distinctions between man and woman, heterosexual and homosexual, it was not enough to ensure a theoretical distance between them by simply removing the bridge of bisexuality. Much more was at stake. The legitimacy and coherence of a psychoanalytic discourse premised on *curing* society of homosexuality itself required the fundamental division between the normal and the pathological. Within such a framework homosexuality could only ever be synonymous with the latter, always already outside the bounds of normality.

Beginning with the work of Alfred Kinsey, however, the distinction between the normal and the pathological was seriously questioned. Despite an apparent hardening of normative sexual categories at the time of its publication and beyond, the Kinsey report provided later researchers and activists with important empirical and theoretical material upon which to mount a major challenge to the hegemony of psychomedical discourses of sexuality. By the late 1960s Western societies witnessed the emergence of not only a powerful antipsychiatry movement, but of "new historical subjects" constituted around the axes of race, gender, and sexuality.[1] Having established distinct social movements serving the interests of their specific identities, these new historical subjects declared "a sort of counter-hegemony to the dominant social and ideological order."[2] Of these movements, it was gay liberation that took as its target the economy of (hetero)sexuality.

In this chapter I have identified the discourses of gay liberation as representative of the next decisive phase in the construction of sexual identities. Drawing from the movements of antipsychiatry, relativist sociology, cross-cultural anthropology, radical Freudianism, the counterculture, and black and women's liberation, gay liberation attempted to deconstruct the economy of (hetero)sexuality and its taxonomy of sexual species. Under assault, therefore, was not just the distinction between the normal and the pathological, but those of masculine and feminine, heterosexual and homosexual. A world without heterosexism was for gay liberation a world without such distinctions. Significantly, bisexuality was revivified as the appropriate deconstructive concept for this challenge. I will argue that despite its theoretical reappearance, bisexuality was elided in the present tense of gay liberation. It was reduced to a utopic dimension that effectively contained the very crisis of sexual identity that gay liberation sought to engender.

AMERICAN GAY LIBERATION AND ANTIPSYCHIATRY

On 24 August 1970, just over a year after the infamous Stonewall riots, the *New York Times* carried an article that detailed "a new mood taking hold among the nation's homosexuals." This new homosexual sentiment was *gay pride*. "In growing numbers," Steven Roberts declared in an article entitled "Homosexuals in Revolt," "they are publicly identifying themselves as homosexuals, taking a measure of pride in that identity and seeking militantly to end what they see as society's persecution of them."[3] In stark contrast to the assimilationist tactics of homophile activists of the 1950s and 1960s, gay liberationists represented a new and unapologetic brand of political activism.[4] Drawing heavily on the revolutionary rhetoric of the New Left, on women's and black liberation, and on antiwar, youth, and hippie groups, gay liberation joined the fray of antiestablishment new social movements intent on challenging dominant social and political structures. As John D'Emilio has remarked, this was a decidedly new "culture of protest" that "contrasted oddly" with the reformist aspirations of homophile organizations.[5]

The social and political contexts within which homophile and liberationist groups were situated were markedly different. Gender codes in dress and behavior had been profoundly challenged through the sexual revolution, the hippie and countercultural movements, and women's liberation. The introduction of the contraceptive pill dissociated sexuality from the imperatives of procreation, and young hippies rejected dominant middle-class values and the ideals of monogamy and the nuclear family. Instead, they experimented with alternative living arrangements and lifestyles, drugs, and sexual promiscuity. The radicalism of the 1960s saw a significant reconceptualization of the sphere of the political and of social relations of power. Hegemonic institutions, social structures, and political and moral values were exposed as serving the interests of primarily white, middle-class, middle-age, heterosexual men.

The institution of psychiatry was increasingly seen as "modern capitalism's ... ultimate weapon of social control against dissidence" and deviance.[6] The marginalization and oppression of women and minorities such as blacks and homosexuals became central concerns in the effort to contest and restructure dominant systems of social and ideological power. With revolutionary fervor reaching dizzying heights in the years surrounding the "nodal year" of 1968,[7] women, blacks, and homosexuals were impelled by the imperative of self-determination.[8] Rejecting the bland face of homogenizing liberalism, the new historical subjects confronted society with a *demand* for social recognition rather than a *plea* for social tolerance or acceptance.

Dennis Altman has argued that gay liberation was "much more the child of the counter-culture than it [was] of the older homophile organizations; it [was] as much the effect of changing mores as their cause."[9] As Bob Milne, a forty-nine-year-old homophile activist in the Mattachine Society remarked, "People my own age have been running scared all their lives. The younger people just won't take anything any more."[10] Or as Michael Brown of the New York chapter of Gay Liberation put it: "The older groups are oriented toward getting accepted by the Establishment, but what the Establishment has to offer is not worth my time. We're not oriented toward acceptance but toward changing every institution in the country—male domination, capitalist exploitation, all the rest of it."[11] The first step toward self-determination was to challenge the psychomedical establishment with its monopoly on the representation of homosexuality. Gay pride and the new homosexual militancy were not simply protests against the pathologization of homosexuality, but part of a broader process of a desire to "decondition ourselves, to undo all that self-contempt" internalized from psychomedical definitions.[12] The experience of homosexuality ought no longer be construed as only a personal, private 'problem' of coming to terms with one's 'affliction'. Rather, for gay liberation it was imbricated in a process both individual and social. As I will discuss later, crucial to such a process were the mutually interlocking strategies of *coming out* and *consciousness-raising*. Internalized self-hatred had to be extirpated through the recognition of the collective experience of homosexual oppression and the redefinition and revalorization of gay identity.

While the genealogy of gay liberation may indeed, as Altman points out, owe more to countercultural forces than to homophile activism, it is important to note other historical preconditions that preceded and informed "the making of a counter culture."[13] In particular, the vociferous gay liberation critique of psychomedical discourses of sexuality was made possible by (and indeed often explicitly grounded in) traditions of antipsychiatry and cultural relativism that began at least as far back as Kinsey. Two fundamental challenges were issued from within these traditions. Not only had the psychiatric distinction between the normal and the pathological been seriously questioned, but the division of humankind into distinct and opposing species of sexuality was regarded by some as psychomedical prejudice.

When Alfred Kinsey professed a profound skepticism of the scientific validity of the categories of 'normal' and 'abnormal' for describing human behavior, he was in fact underscoring their inescapably subjective and thus culturally specific nature. For instance, the term 'abnormal', he suggested, may refer to little more than a form of behavior that transgresses "the socially pretended custom." These were more often than not merely descriptive terms of reference for statistical variations of behavioral frequencies on a continuous curve. "One sometimes suspects," he reminded his readers, that normal and abnormal "are terms which a particular author employs with reference to his own position on that curve."[14]

Second, Kinsey rejected the widespread notion of separate species of sexuality. "We have objected to the use of the terms heterosexual and homosexual when used as nouns which stand for individuals" (657). Moreover, Kinsey noted, "males do not represent two discrete populations, heterosexual and homosexual. The world is not divided into sheep and goats. Not all things are black nor all things white. It is a fundamental of taxonomy that nature rarely deals with discrete categories. Only the human mind invents categories and tries to force facts into separated pigeon-holes" (639). With the aid of cross-cultural and cross-species research, Ford and Beach extended the critique of the separation of species of sexuality:

> When it is realized that 100 per cent of males in certain societies engage in homosexual as well as heterosexual alliances, and when it is understood that many men and women in our own society are equally capable of relations with partners of the same or opposite sex, and finally, when it is recognized that this same situation obtains in many species of subhuman primates, then it should be clear that one cannot classify homosexual and heterosexual tendencies as being mutually exclusive or even opposed to each other.[15]

It is interesting that these antiontologizing gestures paralleled the emerging tendency in post-Freudian psychoanalytic discourse to reject biological theories of homosexuality. Contrary to Kinsey and Ford, however, conservative post-Freudians had to ontologize the homosexual, if not as a distinct biological species then as a distinct psychological species, in order to ensure the mutual exclusivity of the concepts of heterosexuality and homosexuality. As we saw in chapter 4, this effected the subsumption of sexuality within gender, reducing homosexuality to a form of neurotic and pathologic gender disorder. However, with the instantiation of heterosexuality as the universal human norm and the repudiation of bisexuality, psychoanalytic discourse was still unable to circumvent a possible collapsing of homosexuality into heterosexuality. The only option was to reject or to ignore the findings of such researchers and to ride on the tidal wave of public disapprobation of homosexuality.

The work of Evelyn Hooker extended Kinsey's challenge to psychiatry's structuring opposition between the normal and the pathological. As Ronald Bayer has argued, in contrast to Kinsey and Ford—who, while indeed subversive of psychiatric definitions were at the same time outside of their official discourse—Hooker as a practicing psychologist was able to "address directly the issues of greatest importance to clinicians."[16] Using members and friends of the homophile group the Mattachine Society, Hooker published research that clearly contradicted the psychiatric association of homosexuality and pathology. Via widely used and independently assessed psychological tests, this was demonstrated in an article first published in 1957. Having attained a sample of thirty matched pairs of homosexual and heterosexual men who were not involved in psychological or psychiatric counseling, Hooker argued in "The Adjustment of the Male Overt Homosexual" that homosexuality was not synonymous with social maladjustment. "It comes as no surprise that some homosexuals are severely disturbed," declared Hooker. "But," she went on to say:

> what is difficult to accept (for most clinicians) is that some homosexuals *may* be very ordinary individuals, indistinguishable, except in sexual pattern, from ordinary individuals who are heterosexual. Or—and I do not know whether this would be more or less difficult to accept—that some *may* be quite superior individuals, not only devoid of pathology (unless one insists that homosexuality itself is a sign of pathology) but also functioning at a superior level.[17]

Like Kinsey, Hooker also rejected the psychiatric method of extrapolating from a clinical population of homosexuals to homosexuals in general.[18] So it was that such work was to provide a legitimate scientific basis for gay liberation to critique psychomedical knowledge and deconstruct the notion of binary species of sexuality.

Bisexuality as a form of cultural and mammalian potential underpinned the sociological, anthropological, and psychological works of Kinsey, Ford and Beach, and Hooker. While this was a very different notion to the one rejected by Rado and his post-Freudian successors, it nevertheless retained a biological sense, even if only as a biological potential. Recall that within the sexological and Freudian traditions bisexuality was a rudiment of evolutionary development, a vestige of our primitive and animal ancestry prior to civilization and sexual differentiation. The manifestation of homosexuality was either a regression (or 'throwback') to this earlier stage of evolution, or else evidence of the incomplete transition from 'lower' to 'higher' forms of animal development. Bisexuality was therefore the evolutionary "outside" or "alongside" to the highest form of human civilization, situated in a relation of contiguity that exerted a constant pressure on civilization. This relationship thereby helped to define the boundaries of 'civilized' culture and exposed the limits of evolutionary achievement.

However, for Kinsey and Ford and Beach, bisexuality was not related to the evolution of sexually differentiated organs. Instead, it was recast as "an inherited capacity for erotic responsiveness to a wide range of stimuli . . . [an] original, intermediate condition which includes the capacity for both forms of sexual expression."[19] In this schema both heterosexuality and homosexuality represent a "movement away" from this bisexual or polymorphous potential, a movement away that is culturally conditioned, or as Ford and Beach put it, "modified under the impact of experience" (259). Hooker also inherited the notion of a universal bisexual potential. In fact, she cited Ford in order to suggest that homosexuality is not only "within the normal range psychologically," but also "on a biological level."[20] Commenting on the question of biology and homosexual etiology, Hooker replied: "It's probably closer to the truth to think of infants as sexually neutral, with their sexuality shaped by the interaction of dozens of variables. The interaction is so delicate, so complex, that it is impossible to predict the outcome."[21]

Bisexuality does not therefore explain the existence of the identity or species of homosexual, as Freud and the sexologists assumed. After all, the identity of the homosexual is the product of psychiatry and the enforcement of cultural ideologies, the activity of homosexuality the product of the vagaries of human choice, as Kinsey, Ford, and Hooker suggested.[22] Rather, for these researchers *the existence of homosexuality proves the bisexual potential of human beings.*

It is important at this point to register Kinsey's circumspection with respect to the term 'bisexuality', at the very least to justify what may appear on my behalf to be a significant distortion of his views regarding human sexuality. Kinsey made particularly clear the problematic nature of employing a term that he rightly observed had been marked by "considerable confusion."[23] He suggested that "the capacity of an individual to respond erotically to any sort of stimulus, whether it is provided by another person of the same or of the opposite sex, is basic to the species" (660). I have rewritten this as 'bisexuality', or 'bisexual potential'. Kinsey's wish to avoid referring to this notion of sexuality as bisexuality was due to the historical usage of the term, which up to that point had largely implied that "'bisexual' persons have an anatomy or an endocrine system or other sorts of physiologic or psychologic capacities which make them partly male and partly female, or of the two sexes simultaneously" (657).[24]

In the late 1960s and early 1970s the challenge to the psychomedical hegemony initiated by Kinsey, Ford, and Hooker was substantially revivified by figures such as Thomas Szasz, Judd Marmor, and the growing movement of antipsychiatry.[25] The psychiatric oppositions of normal/abnormal and heterosexual/homosexual continued to come under sustained attack.[26] However, antipsychiatry theorists brought this already-damaging critique to an even higher level. Among others, the work of Michel Foucault, R. D. Laing, Erving Goffman, and Thomas Szasz led to a questioning of the legitimacy and epistemological validity of the very discipline of psychiatry itself. Moreover, as Peter Sedgwick has pointed out, the books that generated the notion of psychiatry as modern capitalism's most efficient means of social control also provided the foundations for "a wider social critique."[27]

Of all the antipsychiatry theorists it was Thomas Szasz, himself a professor of psychiatry, who provided the most profound theoretical attack on the epistemic underpinnings of the discipline in a manner explicitly relevant to questions of homosexuality. Furthermore, he issued a damning indictment of the function and power of psychiatry as a social institution. In fact, as Bayer has demonstrated, the publication of his first essay concerning homosexuality in 1965 "coincided with a sharpening of antagonism toward psychiatry on the part of the homophile movement."[28] Szasz's rejection of the social utility of psychiatry laid the groundwork for the emergence of a more militant gay liberation movement that in many ways served as an adjunct of the broader movement of antipsychiatry.

Szasz began by identifying and rigorously deconstructing the primordial concept constitutive of psychiatry. The concept of mental illness, he bemoaned, forms the heart of virtually all contemporary psychiatric theories and practices.[29] Arguing that there is no such thing as mental illness, Szasz declared that its only function is to conceal and "render more palatable the bitter pill of moral conflicts in human relations" (24). While not denying the existence of the "social and psychological occurrences" to which mental illnesses refer, Szasz implored their removal from the category of 'illness'. Instead, like languages, 'mental illnesses' are more properly "the expressions of man's struggle with *the problem of how he should live*" (21; original emphasis). For Szasz this was a problem not of illness, but of social, moral, and ethical concerns. Such an approach left any notion of psychiatric 'cure' as superfluous and outdated.

Szasz revealed his absolute hostility to the social function of psychiatry, rendering it but a discourse of dogmatism: "My contention is that the psychiatric perspective on homosexuality is but a thinly disguised replica of the religious perspective which it displaced, and that efforts to 'treat' this kind of conduct medically are but thinly disguised methods for suppressing it."[30] In describing psychomedical knowledge on homosexuality as mere "medical prejudice" (174), Szasz insisted on deconstructing its discursive function. He did this by revealing the authorial referent with which it was most crucially concerned as not the homosexual at all, but in fact the psychiatrist. Szasz trenchantly asserted that: "Like the inquisitor, the psychiatrist defines, and thereby authenticates, his own existential position by what he opposes—as heresy or illness. In stubbornly insisting that the homosexual is sick, the psychiatrist is merely pleading to be accepted as a physician" (173). The stance of gay liberation clearly owes a good deal of its rhetoric and theoretical critique of psychomedical discourse to the work of antipsychiatrists such as Thomas Szasz. The acceptance of, or at the least, the ambivalence toward psychiatry that was often characteristic of the earlier homophile attitude was nowhere to be found in gay liberation. For the emerging liberation groups, it was not individual, psychological maladjustment that produced the pathology of homosexuality, but the pathology of capitalism that produced a vast array of social problems. The very notion of psychiatric 'therapy' or a psychiatric 'cure' for homosexuals was repulsive to gay liberation. So too was the question of homosexual etiology. As reported in the aforementioned front page article in the *New York Times*, the "inevitable reply to the question is, 'Why are you heterosexual?'"[31]

BISEXUALITY AND THE GLOBALIZATION OF GAY LIBERATION

> The postwar hegemony of the United States, especially among the advanced capitalist nations, as well as among much of the third world, has also had an impact upon the social organization of homosexuality and the development of a political movement.
> —Barry D. Adam 1987

Despite differing historical traditions and regional specificities, gay liberation movements modeled largely on the U.S. model sprang up all over the Western world. Neither "monolithic nor even an entirely coherent social movement," as Annamarie Jagose has observed, national and international gay liberation movements were nonetheless united around several broad discursive themes.[32] This loose correspondence enables us to identify a somewhat global, although often contradictory and heterogeneous, gay liberation theory. Borrowing heavily from contemporaneous new social movements, the model of gay liberation was a mélange of theoretical and political concepts and practices.

The universally adopted gay pride slogan "Gay is good" was the refashioned appropriation of the black liberation slogan "Black is beautiful." The homophile practice of 'coming out' was reworked in order to challenge the conventional liberal political boundaries of public/private and individual/social. Coming out functioned to confront society with what it forcibly represses, while simultaneously challenging the self-oppression of homosexuals themselves. The women's liberation theory of sexism and the practice of consciousness-raising were used to enable the release of a gay revolutionary consciousness. This revolutionary consciousness was infused with antipsychiatry rhetoric. The New Left critique of capitalism as a monolithic oppressor of all marginal groups, along with the concept of repression/oppression, helped to explain the historically disadvantaged position of homosexuals. It also served theoretically to unite them with the socially disenfranchised in the development of a broad-based social critique. The rhetoric of revolution, enmeshed with the radical Freudian concept of liberation, signaled both the means for transforming the repression of modern capitalist societies and the utopian dream of new and harmonious social formations expected to emerge from a refashioned society.

Such themes allow us to identify a loosely coherent and ideologically united global gay liberation movement. As will become evident, contradictions were certainly present within gay liberation theory. However, even these were played out in remarkably similar ways within each of the major national movements. In order to elucidate the position of bisexuality within gay liberation, I have chosen to focus to a greater extent on examples from the North American and Australian movements. While replete with local particularities, these examples typify many of the ideological debates and resultant internal divisions also found in their British counterparts.[33] In fact, Lynne Segal goes so far as to note that "GLF [Gay Liberation Front] in Britain was a perfect replica of GLF in the USA."[34]

Militant "counterpsychiatry" groups were a fundamental feature of all regional gay liberation movements. The aim was to challenge dominant definitions of homosexuality with their attendant claim to therapeutic cure, and to expose the myth of psychomedical objectivity. In the United States this led to a string of confrontational protests at various psychiatric conferences and lectures. Disruptive "zap" actions were initiated by gay liberationists that "were designed to put a halt to discussions considered inimical to their interests."[35] Gay liberationists were not content with reciprocal dialogue with the psychomedical establishment, but with "forcing psychiatrists to recognise that homosexuality can be a happy and satisfying way of life."[36] Speaking at an Australian Forum on Sexual Liberties, Dennis Altman captured the sentiments of gay liberationists when he branded the psychiatric 'treatment' of homosexuality as "a more sophisticated version of beating up 'poofters'."[37] Moreover, attempting to treat or cure individuals of homosexuality was considered a brutal means of repressing a natural component of human sexuality.

Imploring closeted homosexuals to come out and reject psychiatry, American gay liberationists developed the slogan: "Off the couches and into the streets!"[38] Conservative psychiatrists remained steadfast in their opposition to both homosexuality and the gay liberation movement. For example, Lionel Ovesey, in reiterating the by-then-mundane psychiatric axiom, "Homosexuality is a psychiatric or emotional illness," went even further to castigate gay liberationists. "It's possible," he surmised, "that this movement could consolidate the illness in some people, especially among the young who are teetering on the brink."[39] However, gay liberationists would not give up their claim of how to 'treat' the social 'problem' of homosexuality. The problem was reversed, and it was the psychiatrist who was seen as "the greatest obstacle to his patient's health and wellbeing."[40] In response to the attitude of the likes of Ovesey, they sarcastically urged psychiatrists to refer their homosexual 'patients' to gay liberation. They were "convinced that a picket and a dance will do more for the vast majority of homosexuals than two years on the couch."[41] This quickly spread worldwide as gay liberationists in Australia and Britain argued Szasz-style that psychiatrists had become *"the high priests of modern society,"* serving to reinforce the "primitive Judeo-Christian morality."[42] As one activist's banner read (which led him to be arrested for "unseemly words"), "We're not fucked up. We're fucked over."[43]

One of the central principles unifying the globalization of gay liberation and legitimating the attack on psychomedical constructions of homosexuality was the notion of a universalized human nature. Frustrated with the political and ideological dominance of the generic 'man' of Western liberal discourses and democracies, gay liberation theorists proffered a reverse discourse of the generic human. This developed in part out of the confrontation between gay liberation and psychiatry. In order to contest psychomedical constructions of human nature in general, and homosexuality in particular, gay liberationists sought to provide a counterconstruction. Bisexuality was axiomatic to this doctrine.

Revealing a reliance on bisexuality, American gay liberationist Martha Shelley published an article entitled "Gay Is Good" in 1970. Assuming the rhetoric of repression in an address to straight society, she declared that "you cut off your homosexuality—and we cut off our heterosexuality."[44] Similarly, in the globally reproduced "A Gay Manifesto," Carl Wittman described bisexuality as the key to the "complete" individual. He went on to suggest that the realization of this 'wholeness' had been precluded by the *straight*jacketing of binary logic. "The reason so few of us are bisexual," he insisted, "is because society made such a big stink about homosexuality that we got forced into seeing ourselves as either straight or non-straight."[45] Robert Reynolds has traced a similar tendency among Australian gay liberation groups. Until 1972, Reynolds demonstrates, bisexuality commanded a position of privilege within gay liberation theory.[46] The Sydney Gay Liberation Front constructed bisexuality as "probably the ideal condition." The group in Melbourne sounded a more Freudian note in suggesting that "everyone is intrinsically bisexual."[47]

Steven Seidman has argued that gay "liberation theory presupposed a notion of an innate polymorphous, androgynous human nature."[48] Similarly, in her study of the Sydney Gay Liberation Front, Denise Thompson has suggested that Altman's appropriation of Freudian bisexuality became "a popular theoretical catch-all in the early days of gay liberation."[49] Both Thompson and Seidman are referring to the appropriation of the Freudo-Marxian work of Herbert Marcuse, most explicitly carried out by Dennis Altman: "Liberation, as Marcuse has pointed out in another context, will only come with a new morality and revised notion of 'human nature'."[50] This theory of liberation was clearly a form of *sexual* liberation. "Inevitably such a theory will rely heavily on Freud," continued Altman, "and despite the hostility of many of those in the sexual liberation movements to parts of Freudian—and particularly neo-Freudian—thought, these movements are also part of a contemporary revival of Freudian thought, and in particular of its emphasis on the central and paramount role of sexuality in both social and individual life" (72). In conjunction with the individualization and socialization of sexuality, the other crucial aspect of Freudian thought to which Altman referred—and which grounded this understanding of sexuality—was "the essential bisexual nature of our original sex drive" (75). Originally polymorphously perverse and bisexual, Altman argued (via Freud) that homosexuals, and indeed all human beings, have had their polymorphous potential repressed through culturally enforced norms. Instead of insisting that this process of repression was a necessary foundation for the reproduction of 'civilization' (as did Freud), Altman (via Marcuse) argued for its conditional removal in order to liberate or free our authentic bisexual human nature.[51]

That this kind of radical Freudian notion of an innate bisexuality was but one theme within gay liberation theory I do not dispute. However, I do caution against identifying it, as Seidman, Thompson, and others tend to suggest, as the theoretical core of liberation theories of sexuality and human nature.[52] Both Jeffrey Weeks and Altman have pointed out that radical Freudianism was "never particularly popular in the gay movement."[53] I will argue that the kind of bisexual potential outlined by Kinsey, Ford and Beach, and Hooker was in fact a more crucial part of this framework than was the Freudian notion and that it is this meaning of bisexuality that has been obscured largely in histories of gay liberation.[54]

"BISEXUALITY IN BLOOM"

> There is a new vibration to spring this year. While the birds and the bees are striking up their vernal hum, so are the boys and the boys and the girls and the girls. Bisexuality is in bloom.
> —*Newsweek*, 13 May 1974

The same month that *Newsweek* magazine ran a story on bisexuality, *Time* featured a story entitled "The New Bisexuals."[55] For a short period in the early 1970s bisexuality was seen to enjoy the status of radical chic among the cultural avant garde. In 1974 Margaret Mead announced that "the time has come, I think, when we must recognize bisexuality as a normal form of human behavior."[56] Kate Millett sounded a more utopian note when she declared in the same year that bisexuality is "the key, not merely to a new sexuality, but to a new sexual culture."[57] On the other hand, the new bisexual chic had its share of critics. Among them was Charles Socarides, who clearly had not been transformed by the growing mood. "Bisexuality is a disaster for culture and society," he proclaimed vehemently. "They're selling a phoney sexual utopia in which the kingdom of the orgasm will supposedly replace the house of the ego."[58] Manhattan psychoanalyst Natalie Shainess concurred, after having outlined the deleterious effects of bisexuality on children and friendships from the "constant ricocheting from one sex to another." "Is this invitation for anything-goes helping human beings lead more satisfying lives?" she asked rhetorically. "It is not."[59]

This was not the simple manifestation of radical Freudianism.[60] Rather, it was intimately bound up with the countercultural loosening of sexual mores and a blurring of gender distinctions in dress and behavior. It was also implicitly legitimated and influenced by the theoretical tradition framing the works of figures such as Kinsey, Ford and Beach, and Hooker. As far as Kinsey was concerned, the kingdom of the orgasm had indeed already replaced that of the ego. His statistics had revealed that something in the vicinity of 18 percent of white American men had engaged equally in homosexual and heterosexual behavior to the point of orgasm for a period of three years in their adult life. More startling, perhaps, was his claim that 46 percent of the white male population had engaged in both heterosexual and homosexual activities to the point of orgasm throughout their adult lives.[61] Moreover, not only was bisexuality considered a not uncommon form of sexual practice, but sexuality had been recast by all three researchers within a model of social conditioning.

Predicated on the notion of an inherently sexual, yet sexually neutral human subject, this model proclaimed that the form sexuality was to take was not dictated by biological tendencies or universal psychic mechanisms such as the Oedipus complex. Instead, through the process of cultural learning, conditioning, and individual experience, each individual is molded into shapes appropriate to dominant cultural categories and meanings. The counterculture was in many ways influenced by radical Freudianism and the New Left. However, central to the cultural context within which bisexuality was to blossom was this alternative model of sexuality. It played a crucial part in the forging of spaces for the contestation and experimentation of cultural boundaries of gender and sexuality.

Bisexual activist David Lourea reflected upon this experimental countercultural milieu. "With Kinsey and Masters and Johnson," he recalled, "people began to question their sexual assumptions."[62] With a touch of irony he described his experience of the time:

> The late '60s and early '70s were exciting times. During the Sexual Freedom movement, swingers were exploring their sexuality and challenging stereotypes within the context of group sex scenes. In the process, many people began to open up to bisexuality. If you were lying down blindfolded and a number of people were touching you, you couldn't tell whether they were male or female. . . . Oh! A light bulb goes on! Maybe there isn't a difference![63]

It is against this backdrop that we must situate the emergent phenomenon of bisexuality in the early 1970s. In this account bisexuality as radical chic is framed less as a form of explicit political practice than as the playful effect of erotic experimentation. Radical Freudian notions of polymorphous perversity and innate bisexuality certainly influenced some of the rhetoric of gay liberationists.[64] However, this was often accompanied, overshadowed, and even itself inflected by the simultaneous intermingling of something closer to Kinsey and Ford and Beach's very different conceptualization of bisexual potential. Moreover, while sexuality was at times narrativized through notions of repression, this was less often construed in terms of a psychic repression of innate bisexuality. Rather, it was a notion of the social repression or discouragement of the exploration of *bisexual potential*. Missing from the latter was the notion of an unconscious reservoir housing either repressed homosexual or heterosexual desires. In other words, bisexuality was often framed not psychoanalytically, but sociologically.

For example, despite the radical Freudian tone to Carl Wittman's call to "free the homosexual in everyone," one of his primary assumptions was that "nature leaves undefined the object of sexual desire. The gender of that object is socially imposed" or learned.[65] "What we have called sexual 'orientation'," speculated Wittman, "probably just means that we have not yet learned to turn on to the total range of musical expression" (337).[66] I suggest that Wittman is drawing here more from ideas of an inherited sexual neutrality that is conditioned or learned socially than he is from radical Freudianism. While the sexual capacity (*bisexual potential*) of Kinsey and Ford and Beach approximates to Freud's notion of polymorphous perversity, much gay liberation theory such as Wittman's departed from radical Freudianism in its disinterest in psychic repression and the unconscious.

Despite the fact that certain strands of gay liberation discourse politicized the radical Freudian notion of bisexuality, this was by no means the dominant construction of human nature. The general tendency within the discourses of gay liberation was to view bisexuality as not necessarily innate truth, but as did the 'swingers' and Kinsey, Ford and Beach, and Hooker—as an erotic human capacity or potential.[67] Moreover, as Reynolds has pointed out, the emphasis on the Freudian version of bisexuality was not without its critics.[68] In Australia there emerged various "complaints that a 'bisexuality fervour' had ossified into a Gay Liberation 'doctrine'."[69]

Even when the concept of repression was employed with regard to sexuality it was often emptied of its Freudian and psychoanalytic meaning. For example, it was often metaphorized as the *suppression of human potential*, a form of social enforcement or imposition of gender roles and sexual categories. The construction of the category of "humansexual" within gay liberation discourses exemplifies this point. The humansexual was "a person who has sexuality." All sexual categories—heterosexual, homosexual, and bisexual—were deemed artificial impositions, their removal considered, as Melbourne GLF put it, "the first and perhaps most important step in recognising the unity of sexuality."[70] As Jim Anderson of London GLF declared, "the total homosexual is as much a bizarre and strange creature as the total heterosexual."[71] For in typically utopian style, gay liberationists were not content remaining within the confines of the category 'homosexual'. Instead, as Tony Diamond put it, homosexuals were "aspiring to be Gay people."[72] The unity of sexuality was unable to be captured or bound by social categories, and, once freed, would lead one to a 'gay' sexuality where, according to Melbourne GLF, individuals would "experience to the fullest their human, sexual, spiritual and economic potential."[73] The self-designation of 'gay' was for many liberationists not, as Don Clark reiterated, a "restriction" but rather a sexual "capability." It was not a term limited to or defined by homosexuality: "We who are Gay can still love someone of the other gender."[74]

So while the liberated individual was considered "the complete person," this was not the combination of two complementary halves.[75] The complete person was one who was able to fulfill her or his potential outside of, and thus undefined by, a social system of sexual categories. As Allen Young put it in his gay liberation manifesto in 1971, "Children are born sexual."[76]

Often drawing explicitly on the work of Ford, the Melbourne chapter of the American Radicalesbians posited something similar:

> We can't say that sexuality is divided up into homosexuality, bisexuality, heterosexuality. . . . We all have sexuality—of the same order. We all have energy; we direct it, we define it, we use it—for contact with people, with things, with ideas. Our energy has the potential for expression towards anyone of either sex. But the expression does not define the nature of it.[77]

Sexuality was thus a biological capacity that could express itself bisexually outside the constraints of a heterosexist culture. However, as a form of human *potential*, bisexuality could not be defined. "The non-repressed person recognizes his bisexual potential," Altman pointed out, yet this does not mean she or he is "some ideal person midway along the Kinsey behavioural scale."[78] Even in Altman's neo-Freudian schema the notion of innate bisexuality took no fixed ontological form. It was not some static conception of human nature to be freed upon the realization of our bisexual potential. After all, like all liberation movements, gay liberation was premised on "an optimistic view of human nature, above all . . . its mutability."[79] Rather, the universal human bisexual potential was an as-yet-unrecognized utopian ideal whose cultural achievement would dissolve the artificial ontological categories of heterosexual, homosexual, *and* bisexual.[80] "People will still fall in love and form relationships, and these relationships would be homosexual as well as heterosexual," Altman pointed out.[81] In other words, heterosexuality, homosexuality, and bisexuality could at best only describe adjectivally particular sexual practices. They could not, as Kinsey suggested, be used as nouns to refer to species of sexuality.[82] With the freeing up of *bisexuality*, suggested Altman, "What would be different is that the social difference between the two would vanish, and once this happened we would lose the feeling of being limited, of having to choose between an exclusively straight or exclusively gay world."[83] Ironically, Dennis Altman's reliance on Freud's concept of innate bisexuality was in some ways contradictory and incompatible with gay liberation theory. He did reflect the universal belief of gay liberation with regard to the sex roles of masculinity and femininity as artificial categories that "are a first, and central distinction made by society" (83). Furthermore, Altman argued that such sex roles were responsible for norms of heterosexuality and the oppression of homosexuals. However, his claim that liberation from oppressive sex roles required the overcoming of sexual repression in order to "bring to its logical conclusion the Freudian belief in our inherent bisexuality" was made problematic by the very Freudian terms he employed. For, as I demonstrated in chapter 3, both biological and psychological concepts of masculinity and femininity, heterosexual and homosexual were inscribed at the very heart of Freud's concept of innate bisexuality. Moreover, the very concept of innate bisexuality was retroactively installed at the center of the economy of (hetero)sexuality as the *effect* of a crisis of gender. On the one hand, therefore, Altman attempted to construct a notion of bisexuality as a dynamic, undefinable potential, unmoored from gender (sex roles). Yet, on the other hand, the unreconstructed Freudian underpinnings of his thought served to naturalize bisexuality through gender. In his radical Freudian schema, it would seem that the removal of sex roles and the categories of homosexual and heterosexual required the very removal of bisexuality.

As I have argued, however, this was not the only, or even most common, version of bisexuality structuring gay liberation discourse. While the sociological meaning of bisexual potential seemed to be interchangeable with that of Freudian polymorphous perversity, the two diverge when they are situated in their distinct intellectual traditions and theoretical models. Polymorphous perversity was one side of Freud's notion of the human sexual disposition, innate bisexuality the other. Together they formed a very different construction than the sociological sexual disposition. In both cases (i.e., radical Freudianism and sociology), however, bisexuality was framed less as an identity and practice in the present tense than it was a future aspiration or utopian ideal. Indeed, as we shall see, bisexuality in the present tense became a highly problematical issue.

In spite of the different theoretical constructions of bisexuality, the radical Freudian and sociological approaches were united in their desire to set free the energy of human sexuality. For gay liberationists sexuality was "the single most significant part of our existence."[84] Following the groundbreaking work of Kate Millett, gay men and lesbians required, as Altman noted, "a new and broader definition of politics to meet the requirements of our oppression."[85] Stimulated by the women's liberation slogan "the personal is political," gay liberation sought to disrupt the artificial division between the public and private spheres.[86] The realization of the ideal of bisexuality demanded not only the politicization of sexuality, but the polymorphous perversification of the public sphere. Gay liberationists staged 'kiss-ins' and encouraged members to hold hands and show affection in public places. As Guy Hocquenghem put it, the "special characteristic of the homosexual intervention is to make what is private—sexuality's shameful little secret—intervene in public, in social organisation."[87] This eroticizing move was also aimed at deconstructing phallocentric notions of sex and sex roles. Eroticizing all parts of the body and mind represented, as one liberationist described it, this "new liberatory form" she called "'sensuality'":

> It is touching and rubbing and cuddling and fondness. It is holding and rocking and kissing and licking. Its only goal is closeness and pleasure. Smashing the notion of sex, getting away from these concepts so intimately tied up with the penis, helps destroy sex roles. . . . Sensuality is something that can be collective. Sex is private and tense. Sensuality is often spontaneous. Sex is something you want power and territorial rights over. Sex is localized in the pants and limited by that. Sensuality is all over and grows always.[88]

IDENTITY AND THE ENEMIES WITHIN

Before long the gay liberation goal of a polymorphous utopia began to recede from view. As Robert Reynolds has pointed out, "Visions of untrammeled desire did not encourage the discussion of restrictions, boundaries and identification." Yet these are, he suggests, "core political questions" in the quest for reorganizing collective lives.[89] In fact, the problem of identity became *the* fundamental issue that was to shape the direction of gay liberation's future. Internal exigencies required attention as the unity of gay liberation identity fractured on at least two fronts. On one side, the existence of 'nonhomosexuals' within the movement soon began to exert pressure on the very definition of this identity. "There is a strong tendency within the gay liberation movement," observed Altman, "to reject all heterosexuals, to demand a self-affirmation that denies any contact with non-gays."[90] On another side, lesbians became extremely dissatisfied with gay liberation, claiming that it was a microcosm of the broader sexist society. "All men are guilty of sexism until proven innocent," declared a group of lesbians at the International Gay Liberation conference in Edinburgh. This kind of rhetoric resounded worldwide throughout almost all gay liberation movements.[91]

Between these two shifts gay identity was not only fractured by gender, but hardened in its discursive opposition to heterosexuality. As we will see, this functioned effectively to squeeze out both the theory and practice of bisexuality from the present tense of gay liberation.

THE HETEROSEXUAL ELEMENT

In October 1972 the Melbourne Gay Liberation Publications Group published an article that reflected the growing concern over propriety and identity. Entitled "Queens and Dykes Want Gay Lib Back," it debated the issue of nonhomosexuals in the movement. Gay liberation was not "a sorting-out house for all (including homosexuals) for whom the expression of their sexuality presents some problem." This hampered, they argued, the creation of "gay self-understanding, group identity and solidarity in the face of oppression." Clearly, it was felt that heterosexuals could not contribute to a process of understanding a kind of oppression they had not experienced. "To be gay is something only a Gay person knows about."[92] In Britain and the United States, similar concerns had been fracturing gay liberation groups for some time. The issue of 'nonhomosexuals' in the movement came to a head over the purpose and dynamics of consciousness-raising groups. Designed to enable homosexual men and women to develop an awareness of the patterns of gay oppression, consciousness-raising groups sought to foster this through the sharing of the common experiences of its members. Those without such personal experiences were seen to have nothing to offer the groups. Writing in New York's leading gay liberation magazine, *Come Out*, Steve Gavin summed up the growing mood: "The group should be limited at least initially to individuals interested in developing a gay consciousness. Needless to say, straights and 'bisexuals' should never be admitted into a gay consciousness raising group; otherwise, the whole procedure is a sham."[93] This issue became a significant part of the process of refiguring gay identity. Gone was the utopian optimism that had defined a free society in which "everyone will be gay."[94] As Allen Young affirmed, "Gay, in its most far-reaching sense, means not homosexual, but sexually free."[95] In the present tense of gay oppression, however, the most pressing task was the development of a separate movement. "We have a separate movement of gay people because we are fighting for survival," declared Young, "and because that is the only way that we can establish an identity and advance our struggle" (29). Conscious of its pitfalls, Altman also sensed that "separatism as such does seem an inevitable development.... Talk of us being 'human sexuals' too often means ignoring the reality that, whatever we may like, society has defined homosexual persons apart."[96] "We gays want and need autonomy," claimed Young.[97] *Gay Power*, New York's first radical homosexual newspaper had, since 1969, professed separatist principles, its manifesto calling for the development of independent "homosexual ethics and esthetics."[98] Reynolds has usefully identified this shift in gay liberation as the emergence of a "politics of homosexual experience."[99] The emphasis turned to exploring the specificities and uniqueness of the homosexual condition. As Melbourne Gay Liberation put it, this involved a "common core of experiences of its members."[100]

The reconstruction of gay identity was in many important ways the effect of gay liberation's inability to position its discourses outside of the binary structure of Western thought. In revalorizing homosexual identity, gay liberation was unable to circumvent the discursive tendency to construct alterity. Heterosexuality therefore became the monolithic "other" to gay sexuality, and "human sexuals" or liberated bisexuals were deemed a distant dream so long as the sexist structure of society was firmly in place. A growing and reactive attitude of elitism set in as homosexuals constructed themselves as the vanguard for engendering revolutionary change. As Sydney Gay Liberation proclaimed, "By being who we are, we are in fact revolutionary."[101] Thought to have more "successfully thrown off the shackles of 'false consciousness',"[102] homosexuals situated themselves as either partially or even wholly outside of sexist heterosexual institutions. While Wittman conceded that "all men are infected with male chauvinism," he also proclaimed that gay men could "junk it more easily" than straight men as it was "not central to us." Gay men were seen to have "opted out of a system which oppresses women daily."[103] This led many male gay liberationists to the claim of being more progressive and closer to liberation than heterosexuals. The globally reproduced "Gay Liberation Manifesto" stated that "in some ways we are already more advanced than straight people. We are already outside the family and we have already, in part at least, rejected the 'masculine' and 'feminine' roles society has designed for us."[104] Or, as Allen Young asserted, in an even more self-assured tone, "We have already broken with gender programming, so we can more easily move toward equality."[105] Heterosexuality was branded inherently sexist, heterosexual relationships part of a "system which has male supremacy built in" (29).

So while the ideal of bisexuality had faded from view, the path to its utopic dimension was firmly in sight. This was the path of homosexuality, a necessary first stage in the progression to freedom. In other words, this was a utopic "bisexuality which [was] derived from homosexuality."[106] "I believe the homosexual holds the key" to this utopic society, declared Ralph Hall, "let's shape it."[107] Liberation, then, became the privileged task of homosexuals, for "in a society dominated by the sexist culture it is very difficult, if not impossible, for heterosexual men and women to escape their rigid gender-role structuring and the roles of oppressor and oppressed."[108]

The reverse did not seem to apply for homosexuals. To partake of heterosexuality was tantamount to a form of regression. After all, as Guy Hocquenghem claimed, "what is repressed in homosexuals is not the love of woman as a particular sexual object but the entire subject-object system which constitutes an oppression of desire."[109] "Gays will begin to turn on to women," argued Carl Wittman, "when (1) it's something that we do because we want to, and not because we should, and (2) when women's liberation changes the nature of heterosexual relationships."[110] Or in what was perhaps a less naive assessment, Martha Shelley belligerently declared, "We will never go straight until you go gay."[111] Clearly, the suggestion of partaking of heterosexuality was viewed by some as yet another form of oppression. As Paul Foss, Australian gay liberationist, anxiously questioned, "Were we celebrating our homosexuality or were we to inflict the desire to change to something else upon ourselves?"[112]

That bisexuals were seen to partake of heterosexuality made them transgressors not only of this elitist aspect of gay liberation ideology, but also of the boundaries of the newly emerging separatist identity of distinct homosexual experience. In other words, bisexuality would be a viable practice only *after* sex roles and sexual categories had been abolished. The American Gay Revolution Party Women's Caucus summed up the growing attitude to bisexuality in the present tense: "The claim to bisexuality is commonly heard within the movement, and while bisexuality is not physiologically impossible, the term cannot be used to characterize a stable socio-sexual orientation. . . . No heterosexual relationship is free of power politics and other masculine mystifications."[113]

As Bob Martin pointed out in an article entitled, "Gay Power: An Evolutionary Step," the most important first phase of cultural (r)evolution was to emphasize the "bonds between the varied members of our minority and their differences from the exclusive, uptight heterosexuals. Only when this has been accomplished can we then with confidence merge the subculture into a free and mature, bisexual society."[114] Dennis Altman expressed something similar. A universal bisexuality was not the immediate aim, he noted, "contrary to what a lot of people thought." Talk of a utopian bisexual society did not mean that one had to "run straight out and screw a boy or a girl or whatever."[115] In short, many gay liberationists had come to the realization that, as Larry S put it in *Come Out*, "it would be rash to insist on this from where we're standing now."[116]

Like consciousness-raising, the strategy of coming out made particularly palpable the problematic position of bisexuals and of bisexuality. The individual and collective political process of 'coming out' was a strategy aiming to facilitate the overt confrontation of society with homosexuality and homosexual relations. Coming out "is so important to remind everyone you are a homosexual."[117] It was also thought to undermine the easy division between public and private as a necessary phase in the eroticization of social life. Gay liberationists urged all homosexuals to come out of the closet, not only as a liberatory gesture of self-affirmation and self-pride, but as a collective and public declaration. Avoiding this was to play into the hands of the dominant discourse of liberal tolerance, to "adopt the attitudes of their oppressors—even the logic and language of non-gay people."[118] Clearly, however, coming out was problematic for bisexuals within gay liberation. As Brenda Marie Blasingame has noted: "To come out as bisexual in the gay community for many means a loss of support in the face of heterosexism. This fear kept me 'in the closet' as a bisexual, because I was so fearful of losing my community, the gay community, my support system and grounding."[119]

Many bisexuals like Brenda felt compelled to come out as gay in order to avoid the charges of complying with sexism, courting the enemy, and attempting "to escape the greater stigma of homosexuality."[120] Jill Matthews recalled that bisexuality was also often branded a political cop-out. In Verity Burgmann's paraphrasing of Matthews, the concern was that "people could gain the pleasures of gay life but retreat to 'hetero safety' in times of trouble."[121] Despite the desire to deconstruct the public/private distinction, the gay liberation strategy of coming out was dependent on its very terms. This further alienated bisexuals, whose sexuality seemed to question both the easy association of homosexuality with the closet, and the very public/private distinction that made possible the coming out strategy in the first place. Such regulatory conditions for the production of gay identity personally discouraged and structurally occluded an individual from coming out as bisexual.

Even the theory of bisexual utopia was being deferred slowly to the point of erasure in gay liberation. The sociological model of sexual conditioning was all but replacing the increasingly irrelevant radical Freudian doctrine of bisexuality. For example, in *Sydney Gay Liberation Newsletter*, Trevor Wilson urged a rejection of the Freudian "concepts such as repression and innate bisexuality." Instead, he proposed a model of "behaviourism," which viewed all sexual behavior as learned, and the resultant "end products" as the outcome of "different conditioning."[122] As Reynolds has suggested, this ideological shift complemented and reinforced the burgeoning separatist politics of homosexual experience (254).

THE MALE ELEMENT

Transcending the artifice of sex role differentiation was the primary objective of gay liberation. Freeing the unity of human sexuality was thought to be the natural effect of the abolition of the sexist categories of masculinity and femininity. Once these dissolved, so too would the distinctions between heterosexuality and homosexuality. In other words, gender was seen as irrelevant to sexuality, an oppressive constraint on its free expression. However, gender was to prove itself a far more intractable element in the deconstruction of sexuality than originally presumed. The elitist notion of a gay identity as more liberated than its heterosexual counterparts was soon contested. Lesbians exposed this notion not as homosexual privilege, but as male privilege. So while subjugated (masculinist) homosexual knowledge had challenged culturally dominant *hetero*sexism, subjugated lesbian knowledge sprang up to expose (male) *homo*sexism. This engendered a split, and many lesbians chose to leave gay liberation to form radicalesbian and other women-only organizations.

At least as early as August 1970 in parts of the United States, and by mid-1972 in Australia, lesbians began to feel increasingly marginalized from the politics of homosexual experience.[123] Dominated by gay men, the *common core of experiences* thought to bind all homosexuals actually excluded the specificities of lesbian sexuality. Group consciousness-raising was one significant arena through which lesbians experienced their erasure from the masculinist definition of gay identity and the male-dominated nature of gay liberation. Borrowed from the women's movement, consciousness-raising was the method of exploring the "common root of our experiences" in an effort to foster a unified group consciousness, identity, and solidarity.[124] Sessions were developed to raise the level of antisexist consciousness by working to transcend gender roles and stereotypes. However, gender differences in homosexual experience soon became apparent. "I began to feel uneasy about the fact that it was dominated by men," revealed Jocelyn Clarke of Melbourne Gay Liberation: "They were learning to take pride in their homosexuality but they were not learning to question the roles and stereotypes they had taken over from the heterosexual world. Again and again the men assumed that their experience was *the* homosexual experience, the norm. They were not interested in what the women had to say but they found it convenient to have token women in Gay Liberation."[125] The analytic intersection of gender and sexuality led to an ideological merger between gay and women's liberation. "Women's liberation and gay liberation meet in the radicalesbian," was the slogan of many gay women's groups.[126] The radical feminist principle of universal male sexism was adopted and used to challenge gay male claims to transcendence. No longer could gay men lay claim to being *more advanced than straights*. In fact, for the radicalesbians, all men and women could not claim ever to denude themselves fully of 'sexist conditioning'. "As a woman I will never be free," argued Chris Sitka, "will never divest myself of my oppressive sexist conditioning. Neither can any man divest himself of his oppressive status."[127]

Clearly, all hopes of transcending gender were quickly deflated by the radicalesbians. To even allege such an ability was considered "masculine arrogance."[128] Central to radicalesbian discourse was a necessary polarization of gender. Masculinity and the male subject position were seen to be inherently oppressive. "Men as a class oppress women as a class. Men obtain automatic privileges from their maleness."[129] Organizing separately from homosexual men and "living without" them was the logical conclusion to this doctrine.[130] The development of a separate women-only culture was the first prerequisite to liberation. This was a call for total independence from men and masculinist society.[131] Yet, like the male gay liberationists, the radicalesbians constructed themselves as more subversive of gender roles and heterosexuality. Lesbian sexuality was thought to be "logically" dislocated from the "patriarchal society," and hence "freer."[132] The lesbian was "more of a threat to patriarchy than the male homosexual."[133]

The gendering of the politics of homosexual experience effected the total disavowal of bisexuality in the present tense of gay liberation. The virulent critique of maleness meant that the gates to the emergent lesbian separatist culture were slammed shut on the practice of bisexuality. Paradoxically, a utopian belief in bisexual potential was retained. Yet, in contradictory fashion, this was precluded by the belief in the impossibility of divesting oneself of sexist conditioning. In addition to this, many lesbians were suspicious of the theory and practice of bisexuality, concerned that it might mean the "imposition of yet another authoritarian solution: the utopia of bisexuarchy."[134] The Hobart Women's Action Group described bisexuality as a "panacea," which not only deferred immediate political problems, but rendered lesbians nonexistent. "It is as irrelevant as talking about black problems in terms of melting pot theory."[135] Bisexuality was thus cast off to the imaginary and undifferentiated space, or 'no place', of an impossible future ideal.

CONCLUSION

The erasure of bisexuality in the present tense served to foreground a set of paradoxes at the heart of gay liberation. First, the theory of bisexuality or bisexual potential was *avowed* as the basis of a new liberating ontology of sexuality. Yet this potential was located in a utopic space that was a nowhere place. Second, the exclusion of 'nonhomosexuals' from the elite *gay* discourse and identity (and later radical lesbianism) actively *disavowed* bisexuals from gay liberation practice. Third, while the utopian potential of bisexuality was thought to promise a liberation from the oppressive constraints of gender, the very same notion was itself constructed in phallocentric terms.

Within gay liberation discourse, the lesbian woman was rendered the *sex which is not one*,[136] she who *lacks* the requisite organ with which to assume the position of desiring gay subject. With the specificity of (gendered) difference erased, the notion of a universal and undifferentiated bisexuality served to replace the liberal notion of a generic (hu)man. Despite the sociological revisioning of Freudian bisexuality, gay liberation discourse implicitly redoubled the lesbian as a kind of lack or absence. She was not only lacking a penis, and therefore denied entry to the 'common core' of gay liberationist experiences, she was seen also to lack bisexuality. The implication was clear: to be liberated all that lesbians needed was to be fucked by a man.

The radical deconstructivism of gay liberation remained an illusory ideal. Only momentarily disrupted, the economy of (hetero)sexuality emerged triumphant. Not only did the hetero/homosexual opposition petrify, but so too did that between the genders. No longer irrelevant to sexuality as gay liberation had once hoped, gender remained an intractable element in its discursive construction. The axes of gender and sexuality were therefore realigned through the emergence of a nostalgic politics of homosexual experience. That is, the construction of a common homosexual past worked to exclude any notion of a bisexuality in the present tense. This *dis/avowal* of bisexuality contained the very crisis of sexual identity that both attracted and ultimately repelled gay liberation.

It was with the demise of gay liberation that the category of bisexuality slipped out of radical sexual theory and politics. As we will see in chapter 7, it was not until the emergence of 'queer' in the 1990s that bisexuality reemerged in any significant way as a political player. Chapter 6 will explore how the intervention of what has become known as social constructionism, primarily Foucauldian constructionism, has effected a profound shift in the theorization of sexuality. Here, bisexuality has been rendered irrelevant to the project of challenging the hetero/homosexual opposition and initiating a crisis of sexual identity. Despite this, however, it is important to analyze the nature of this theoretical intervention not simply in order to understand bisexuality's fall from grace, but to contextualize the emergence of 'queer' and bisexuality's relation to it. Chapter 6 will also provide the basis for what I will argue is a necessary reconsideration of bisexuality as a tool of deconstructive analysis.

6

SEXUALITY AND SUBJECTION

> Between each of us and our sex, the West has placed a never-ending demand for truth: it is up to us to extract the truth of sex, since this truth is beyond its grasp; it is up to sex to tell us our truth, since sex is what holds it in darkness.
> —Michel Foucault 1980

In chapter 5 we saw how the category of bisexuality, despite its erasure in the present tense, provided the centerpiece of the gay liberationist challenge to the hetero/homosexual structure. In the 1970s and 1980s, however, this category fell out of favor within dominant antihomophobic theories. The development of an academic movement indebted to gay liberation, yet crucially transformative of its central doctrine, was to reorient theorizations of sexuality profoundly. This movement became known as social constructionism. Stephen Epstein has noted that it was during this period that constructionism became "gospel" within antihomophobic academic circles.[1] In fact, it is upon the foundations of this 'gospel' that queer theory has since been built.

This chapter will introduce the contribution of constructionist ideas to contemporary understandings of sexuality. The work of Michel Foucault has been central to this process. However, Foucault is not the sole bearer of constructionist ideas. I will begin by outlining the emergence of some of these ideas in labeling and symbolic interactionist theories before moving on to a more comprehensive analysis of Foucauldian thought. As we will see, with the shift to antiontological accounts of sexuality, and to constructionist and poststructuralist assaults on essentialist notions of sexual identity, the category of bisexuality was rendered irrelevant, losing its political and theoretical appeal. I will evaluate the utility of Foucauldian theory for *deconstructing sexuality in general and the hetero/homosexual opposition in particular*, arguing that despite his productive and influential intervention, Foucault's theory is limited for undertaking this task. This will serve to contextualize bisexuality's fall from grace in radical sexual politics. Additionally, however, and by reframing Foucault's work as itself part of a genealogy of (bi)sexuality, I will argue that his intervention can be seen in crucial ways to be complicitous with the very deployment of sexuality from which he sought to escape. What this means for the discussion here is that, although irrelevant to his project, one of the effects of Foucault's intervention and reception has been yet another foreclosure (albeit in very different ways and for very different reasons than those occurring in psychomedical discourses) of any consideration of the category of bisexuality. My concerns about the limitations of constructionist perspectives will provide the basis in chapters 7 and 8 for a reconsideration of bisexuality as a useful and indeed necessary tool of deconstructive analysis.

As I discussed in chapter 5, Western gay liberation movements were extremely short-lived. Groups in Britain, North America, and Australia had all but disbanded by the early to mid-1970s, their aspirations for broad-based social change vanishing into utopic space. A gendered politics of homosexual experience had replaced the dream of a future society free from the hetero/homosexual structure. This was a presentist politics concerned only with the day-to-day exigencies associated with the separate struggles against lesbian and gay oppression. As Dennis Altman has noted of homosexual politics in the West, the emphasis shifted, for gay men in particular, from "the language of oppression, liberation, and movement to one of discrimination, rights, and community."[2] Assimilation and legitimation became the immediate concerns of a gay community increasingly structured in terms of an *ethnic* minority group.[3] This necessitated the recognition, insertion, and integration of homosexuality as a valid cultural form and lifestyle within hegemonic social structures. The emergent gay community stood in stark contrast, however, to a burgeoning lesbian feminist movement intent on eschewing coalitionist and assimilationist tactics in favor of gender separatism.[4] Adrienne Rich summarized the rationale behind this position in her landmark 1980 essay "Compulsory Heterosexuality and Lesbian Existence." "Lesbians have historically been deprived of a political existence through 'inclusion' as female versions of male homosexuality," she declared. "To equate lesbian existence with male homosexuality because each is stigmatized is to erase female reality once again."[5]

The disadvantaged economic positioning of lesbians (as lesbians and as women) in relation to gay men further underlined the divergent concerns of the two groups. Rich argued that homosexual men enjoy a level of "economic and cultural privilege" relative to all women (239). Moreover, if "all women . . . exist on a lesbian continuum" (240), then it is clear that, for Rich, lesbian feminists have more in common with heterosexual women than they do with homosexual men. It was this kind of reasoning that led Marilyn Frye to conclude that "far from there being a natural affinity between feminist lesbians and the gay civil rights movement, I see their politics as being, in most respects, directly antithetical to each other."[6] Lesbian feminists remained committed to challenging the entwined structures of 'patriarchy' and capitalism. Gay men, on the other hand, were seen as complicit benefactors of these oppressive formations. Vociferous in her rejection of many of the "principles and values" of gay male culture, Frye went further to argue that this culture was "in many central points considerably more congruent than discrepant with . . . [the] phallocracy . . . so hostile to women and to the woman-loving to which lesbians are committed" (130).[7]

The 1960s to 1980s played host to a cultural shift in Western societies that has been described by Altman as the "sexualization of modern society," or the "commercialization of desire."[8] Sex became a product to be bought, sold, and immediately gratified on the ever-expanding markets of consumer capitalism. With a high disposable income, the emergent and newly visible gay man was quickly absorbed into the sexualized economy in the 1970s. David Harvey has identified the early 1970s as emblematic of a decisive shift in the organization and accumulation of capital. Following Harvey, John Frow has described this as the process of "postmodernization," a fundamental tendency of which was a profound "aestheticization of everyday life."[9] The postmodernization of gay culture exemplified this aestheticizing trend. The development of bathhouses, gyms, discos, restaurants, magazines, and all kinds of consumer products and services directed at gay men helped to create a distinct gay image, experience, and lifestyle. This worked to expand and to reinforce the emergent ethnic-like gay identity and community. It also worked to reinforce lesbian feminist claims of gay men's complicity in patriarchal structures. As Altman has argued, "The new homosexual could only emerge in the conditions created by modern capitalism" (93).

For the new gay male consumer, liberation was no longer freedom from repressive sex roles and the artificial categories of hetero- and homosexual, but freedom *as homosexuals* to access the proliferating economy of sex. Ironically, the gay liberation goal articulated by Guy Hocquenghem of making "what is private—sexuality's shameful little secret—intervene in public, in social organisation" was on one level realized.[10] However, the sexualization and aestheticization of society was a far cry from the revolutionary force imagined by gay liberationists. Instead, as sex became further commercialized, the existing social structures were opening up to homosexual men in unprecedented ways. Increasingly, for example, gay men were being targeted as part of an attractive consumer market, and gay businesses were forming economically powerful organizations. For Scott Anderson of the U.S. gay group, the National Association of Business Councils, such organizations were themselves seen to be potentially liberating. He suggested that they "could well become the most potent force for gay liberation in the 1980s . . . [occupying] the best position to influence conservative policymakers through the medium they best understand: dollars." After all, declared a Toronto newspaper, "a buck is a buck. Who the hell cares if the wrist holding it is limp?"[11]

The formation of an ethnic model of identity continued to strengthen the notion of homosexuality as representative of a distinct category of being. Simultaneously, however, constructionist social scientists continued the work of gay liberationists and earlier sociologists and cross-cultural anthropologists in dismantling the categories of hetero- and homosexuality. Labeling theorists and symbolic interactionists, in identifying the social, cultural, historical, and political forces responsible for the construction of sexual categories, saw homosexuality as merely a social role. The primary argument was that individuals transgressive of sexual conventions were socially branded or derogatorily labeled as homosexual. This functioned both to enforce an arbitrary code of morality and to demarcate the normal and the abnormal, the citizen and the criminal. Such a theoretical approach helped formulate what was to become social constructionism. It is to the antecedents of this body of knowledge that I now turn.

LABELING THEORY, SYMBOLIC INTERACTIONISM, AND THE MOBILIZATION OF SOCIAL CONSTRUCTIONISM

Labeling theory and symbolic interactionism emerged in critical opposition to essentialist theories of homosexuality. Indebted to the earlier work of Kinsey, Ford and Beach, and, most directly, the interactionist theories of social deviance, sociologists such as John Gagnon, William Simon, Mary McIntosh, and Kenneth Plummer mobilized a loosely connected tendency that became known as social constructionism. Mary McIntosh has been widely recognized as the precursory mother of this heterogeneous movement.[12] Carole Vance points out, however, that McIntosh's "observations vanished like pebbles in a pond, until they were engaged with by mid-1970s writers, clearly motivated by the questions of feminism and gay liberation." Vance goes on to argue that an "identifiably constructionist approach dates from this period, not before."[13]

I wonder, though, if this move of Vance's is not indicative of what Judith Butler would call a moment of "methodological founding." The birth of social constructionism is read through a process of historical erasure in order to install the constructionist paradigm as the "proper object" of feminist and gay and lesbian studies.[14] But it seems to me that social constructionism has a broader and more diffuse genealogy that problematizes any easy disciplinary division. Constructionist methodologies are the effect of an ensemble of intersecting and interacting disciplinary paradigms and concepts. As I demonstrated in chapters 4 and 5, there were many researchers and theorists critiquing various aspects of essentialist theories of sexuality. In addition to this, sexual labeling theory and interactionism have complex historical lineages. Discursive links can be found as early as the 1920s in critiques of positivist criminology developed by sociologists of deviance, functionalism and the work of Durkheim, interactionism framed around the Chicago school of sociology and George Herbert Mead, conflict theory influenced by Marx and Engels, and the phenomenology of Edmund Husserl and Alfred Schütz.[15]

One of the earliest applications of interactionism to the study of sexuality was carried out by M. H. Kuhn in 1954. In response to the lingering essentialism of the Kinsey Report, Kuhn outlined a constructionist approach long before the apparent advent of social constructionism:

> Sex acts, sexual objects, sexual partners (human or otherwise) like all other objects towards which human beings behave are *social objects*; that is they have meanings because meanings are assigned to them by the groups of which human beings are members for there is nothing in the physiology of man which gives any dependable clue as to what pattern of activity will be followed toward them.... In short, the sexual motives which human beings have are derived from the social roles they play; like all other motives these would not be possible were not the actions physiologically possible, but the physiology does not supply the motive, designate the partners, invest the objects with preformed passion, nor even dictate the objectives to be achieved.[16]

It is this conceptual theme that animated the groundbreaking applications of labeling theory and interactionism to the study of homosexuality. John Gagnon and William Simon spearheaded this approach with the publication of *Sexual Deviance* in 1967, an edited collection of essays by interactionist sociologists. Gagnon began by critiquing the Freudian-inspired models of sexuality as an instinctual energy source located in the individual. Retaining some of the insights of Freud (such as "the unconscious"), he argued that the instinctual model ought to be reconceived as a "transactional information system." This is an interactive model of sexual development rooted in childhood learning through relations with others, primarily the mother. Gagnon argued that in identifying certain behavior as sexual, adults construct the meaning of sexuality and sexual behavior for the infant. By both displacing the instinctual model for a "noninstinctual theoretical model" and rewriting the Freudian seduction theory, he suggested that "it seems more likely that the parents may unknowingly be sexually initiatory to their children." Parents "may [therefore] interpret nonspecific behavior as sexual and respond to it, giving it such a definition to the child."[17] The child thereby begins to accrue "sexual scripts," which are the means by which he or she negotiates future interactions with others.[18]

Gagnon aimed to critique Freudian models in two fundamental ways. First, he rejected the notion that childhood behavioral responses were located in some instinctual reservoir of sexual drives within the human organism. Second, he disputed the reading of sexual meaning in all forms of infantile functions and actions.[19] In other words, as Jeffrey Weeks has observed, it seems that according to Gagnon and Simon "nothing is intrinsically sexual, or rather that anything can be sexualised." As Weeks goes on to point out, however, the construction of the very notion of sexuality is left unexplained.[20]

This problem was inherited in the work of influential interactionist Kenneth Plummer, who drew directly from the work of Gagnon and Simon. "The fundamental axiom of the interactionist approach is simply put," he declared, *"nothing is sexual but naming makes it so. Sexuality is a social construction learnt in interaction with others."*[21] Simultaneously, however, interactionists held a contradictory position: Gagnon and Simon suggested that sexuality was rooted in "biological processes, capacities and even needs"; and Plummer described sexuality as a "biological property." Each subscribed to the view that "the sexual area may be precisely the realm wherein the superordinate position of the socio-cultural over the biological is most complete."[22] Contrary to the theory that sexual meanings are created through social encounters, therefore, the realm of the sexual is here granted a degree of autonomy outside that of the social. Sexuality remains a contradictory and ambiguous concept.

Social categorization was central also to Gagnon and Simon's understanding of sexual deviance. Like sexuality, deviance does not reside *within* the individual but is the effect of interaction *between* individuals. Furthermore, neither sexual nor nonsexual behavior could be labeled intrinsically deviant. Deviancy is thus a subjective concept, a social construct. "A form of behavior becomes deviant when it is defined as violating the norms of some collectivity," wrote Gagnon and Simon in their introduction to *Sexual Deviance*.[23] When applied to homosexuality, the question becomes one of "social structure" and "self-conception" rather than one of "a fixed and seemingly immutable set (or sets) of moral postures" (2–3). In other words, sociologists resisted viewing homosexuality as representative of a distinct type of person. Instead, the analysis focused on the social and subjective processes through which one identifies, or is branded, with the label "homosexual." This view stood in stark contrast to sexologists and psychoanalysts, who had increasingly individualized the phenomenon to the point of psychopathology.

In 1968 Mary McIntosh supplemented this growing body of sociological work with the publication of her highly acclaimed article "The Homosexual Role." Conjoining labeling theory with a historical and cross-cultural analysis, McIntosh traced the emergence of the homosexual role to seventeenth-century England. Like Gagnon and Simon, she argued that the homosexual should be understood as "playing a social role, rather than as having a condition." "The creation of a specialized, despised and punished role of homosexual keeps the bulk of society pure," she noted, "in rather the same way that the similar treatment of some kinds of criminals helps keep the rest of society law-abiding." Furthermore, McIntosh suggested, such labeling works to "segregate the deviants from others" in order to contain the despised practices within a "relatively narrow group."[24]

Recasting 'the problem of homosexuality' in terms of social and moral structures was a crucial and positive move in constructionist discourse. Yet it also had its difficulties. "This approach to deviant behavior makes systematic study extremely difficult," noted Gagnon and Simon, "since it requires going beyond merely describing and categorizing behavior to the task of tracing out the complex processes of societal definition, the emergence of the deviant self-conception by a so-labeled actor, and the contingency-laden career that follows the labeling experience."[25] Much energy was therefore expended on assiduously mapping and analyzing the homosexual role, experience, and label. McIntosh inadvertently hinted at the problems of this approach in her discussion of labeling as a technique of social control. "One might expect social categorizations of this sort to be to some extent self-fulfilling prophecies," she warned. "If the culture defines people as falling into distinct types—black and white, criminal and non-criminal, homosexual and normal—then these types will tend to become polarized, highly differentiated from each other."²⁶ When mapping and analyzing the homosexual experience or self-conception, therefore, interactionists may well have merely represented and reinforced dominant understandings of homosexual difference (deviance). This use of deviance and homosexuality as paradigms of analysis worked to reify the hetero/homosexual distinction even as it tried to challenge it. Here, an analysis of bisexuality was glaringly absent.

Plummer's study *Sexual Stigma* is a case in point. An explicit attempt was made to move away from defining homosexuality as a condition and people as homosexuals. For example, Plummer classified four forms of "homosexual experience": "casual homosexuality," "personalised homosexuality," "homosexuality as situated activity," and "homosexuality as a way of life." The majority of the book was concerned with *homosexuality as a way of life* and its attendant social and individual reactions, as well as with the individual and social processes of becoming homosexual.²⁷ However, bisexual behavior was collapsed into either situated or casual homosexuality (heterosexuality) or else erased when mapping the processes of becoming homosexual. No systematic analysis was made of the specific ways in which bisexuality figured in the construction of the homosexual label and role. Nor was there any discussion of bisexuality as a sexual experience. In short, Plummer left no discursive space for the meaningful existence of bisexuality as a sexual act, sexual identity, or epistemic category in the construction and regulation of the hetero/homosexual opposition.

Symbolic interactionism and social labeling were thus made possible, yet simultaneously constrained, by the emergence of a gay lifestyle and a homogenizing category of homosexual identity. In this way these researchers were restricted by a reliance on the experiences and definitions of hegemonic categories of sexuality. In other words, self-conceptions of homosexuals as a distinct minority were both the cause and effect of the consolidation of a counterhegemonic gay subculture. As reverse formations, gay community and identity were inextricably produced through, and thereby reiterative of, the hegemonic structure of hetero/homosexuality. Stephen Epstein has suggested that such early deconstructive analyses worked at cross-purposes with gay and lesbian communities' focus on elucidating and demarcating the specificities of their respective experiences, lifestyles, and political identities. A "growing tension" has emerged, he claims, between an "essentialist politics" and "constructionist theory."²⁸ He goes on to argue that "while constructionist theorists have preached the gospel that the hetero/homosexual distinction is a social fiction, gays and lesbians, in everyday life and in political action, have been busy hardening the categories" (71).

I argue, however, that labeling and interactionist theorists did not exactly work at cross-purposes with the hardening and essentializing of gay and lesbian categories. Instead, there emerged a tendency to overanalyze *the homosexual role* and thereby reify the hetero/homosexual distinction. In large part this was an understandable outcome of the constructionist desire to debunk essentialist notions of a universal *homosexual species* and to map the conditions of its historical production in hegemonic thought. But it also reflected a damaging inattention to the place of bisexuality in the historical and discursive formation of the homosexual role. The reliance on homogenizing community and identity formations problematically occluded bisexuality from the field of vision. With no highly developed subculture or politicized identity, nor a coherent theory or definition of a bisexual type of person or role upon which to focus, bisexuality was squeezed out of both hegemonic and counterhegemonic discourses.[29] So despite the morally neutral redefinition of homosexuality and the cogent challenge to essentialist discourses of sexuality, the labeling and interactionist work of the late 1960s and 1970s replicated the sexological and psychoanalytic tendency to treat homosexuality as *the* problem to be elucidated.[30] In so doing, the mutually implicating structure of hetero/homosexuality was left somewhat unproblematized. With deviance foregrounded, heterosexuality continued to enjoy its status as unmarked norm, relatively free from analytic scrutiny.[31] Clearly, this analytic imbalance undermined the deconstructive potential or intent of such work. In fact, Mary McIntosh acknowledged this in the 1981 postscript to her article "The Homosexual Role":

> I now think that what needs to be understood is heterosexuality and that you can't understand homosexuality without locating it in sexuality in general.... What I did was take heterosexuality for granted, and so accept the whole deviance paradigm and the idea that what needed to be studied was the deviance, even if you recognized deviance as socially constructed.[32]

Historians also drew heavily on the sociological deviance paradigm. The groundbreaking works of Jeffrey Weeks, Jonathan Katz, John D'Emilio, Randolph Trumbach, Carroll Smith-Rosenberg, and Lillian Faderman spearheaded a constructionist approach to history by tracing the origins and shifting form and meaning of the modern homosexual.[33] Steven Seidman has also suggested that despite the challenge issued to essentialist paradigms, this approach worked to supplement and reinforce a minoritizing view of homosexuality. In other words, such studies "legitimated a model of lesbian and gay subcultures as ethnic-like minorities."[34] In addition to this, I would argue that an overemphasis on the historical construction of homosexuality left heterosexuality, and indeed sexuality in general, without history.[35] So while undermining the notion of homosexuality as an ontological fact, such a challenge was not extended to the categories of heterosexuality in particular and sexuality in general. These retained their status as natural, normal, and universal. Nor were these categories adequately historicized in relation to one another. This, I would suggest, is itself reflected in a marked silence on the question of bisexuality in such histories of homosexuality.

Foucault's intervention in the historiography of sexuality provided an enormously influential alternative to the almost-exclusive focus on the category of the homosexual. In order to challenge homogenizing identity categories, he sought to locate hetero- and homosexuality within the broader problematic of 'sexuality'. In the next section I turn to an examination of Foucault's contribution to the field of sexuality to make clear how Foucault's analysis, albeit in ways quite different from the labeling and interactionist theorists, also made the concept of bisexuality redundant. I assess the usefulness of his model both for historicizing sexuality and for challenging binary notions of sexual identity in contemporary discourse. In order to do this it is important to begin with a detailed exposition of Foucault's radical rereading of sexuality.

THE FOUCAULDIAN INTERVENTION

The intervention of Foucauldian thought inspired a revolutionary transformation in constructionist understandings of the history, theory, and politics of sexuality.[36] First published in France in 1976, Foucault's *La Volonté de savoir* (translated in the West as *The History of Sexuality*) is a book firmly located within the most celebrated poststructuralist phase of his writing.[37] Edward Stein has identified the Foucauldian poststructuralist challenge to sexual essentialism as the force, along with interactionism and labeling theories, that formed the dual origins of social constructionism.[38] The first in a proposed six-volume series on the history of sexuality, Foucault situated historical and contemporary analyses of sexuality in a more rigorous and deep-seated deconstructive framework. This was not simply a linear history of the variegated meaning of sexuality as a cultural and biological entity. Rather, it was a genealogical analysis of the very emergence of sexuality as an object of Western discourse.

The History of Sexuality took as its primary task an analysis of power, knowledge, and subjectivity in the history of the modern West. More accurately translated as "the will to know," it identified sexuality as the privileged site of analysis in the construction of forms of human selfhood. In other words, sexuality has been equated with individual depth and affirmed as the source of human truth. While for the interactionists the *meaning* of sexuality was socially constructed, for Foucault, *sexuality itself* was socially and historically constructed, a mere invention of modern science. It "must not," he implored, "be thought of as a kind of natural given which power tries to hold in check, or as an obscure domain which knowledge tries gradually to uncover."[39] Rather, sexuality as a discursive object has a history, and Foucault aimed to locate this historically contingent phenomenon in relation to shifts in the construction of forms of modern selfhood.

Foucault's *History of Sexuality* is in large part an explicit critique of the history of psychoanalytic discourse and its truth claims regarding sexualized subjectivity. More than this, however, it is a damning indictment of the psychomedical deployment of the notion of sexuality as innate force. According to Foucault, this notion (and thus psychoanalysis) is itself one of the principal forces of human subjection and social control: "The deployment of sexuality has its reasons for being, not in reproducing itself, but in proliferating, innovating, annexing, creating, and penetrating bodies in an increasingly detailed way, and in controlling populations in an increasingly comprehensive way" (107). In other words, the advent of Freudian psychoanalysis did not liberate humanity by helping to resolve for the individual the necessary burden of a Victorian civilization and its repression of human bisexuality. Nor would the gay liberation goal of releasing bisexuality liberate humanity from an oppressive Victorian or familial ethic typical of the 1950s. Instead, these deployments of sexuality propped up a more insidious apparatus of social control, the *scientia sexualis*—that is, "procedures for telling the truth of sex" (58). This scientific apparatus worked to create modern subjects by imposing the illusion of an inner sexual depth and by inventing and cataloging human beings according to myriad species of sexuality. In other words, it is this deployment of sexuality that has produced not only the categories of hetero- and homosexuality, but a notion of sexuality that totalizes individual identity.

HISTORICIZING SEXUALITY

Deconstructing the historical production of sexuality was for Foucault the first crucial step in challenging the subjugating *scientia sexualis*. This entailed a genealogical tracing of the descent of knowledge through which sex was "'put into discourse'" (11). By exposing the historical conditions under which sexuality became an object of discourse and by revealing its normative and illusory nature, Foucault aimed to dislocate and thus to delegitimize conventional historical and political truths in relation to human subjectivity:

> In short, it was a matter of seeing how an 'experience' came to be constituted in modern Western societies, an experience that caused individuals to recognize themselves as subjects of a 'sexuality,' which was accessible to very diverse fields of knowledge and linked to a system of rules and constraints. What I planned, therefore, was a history of the experience of sexuality, where experience is understood as the correlation between fields of knowledge, types of normativity, and forms of subjectivity in a particular culture.[40]

As an irreducibly discursive object, therefore, sexuality cannot be dissociated from social and political relations of power. Foucault sought to historicize sexuality by historicizing power. Not only was sexuality seen to be an "especially dense transfer point for relations of power,"[41] but it was, precisely, a shift in power that conditioned the production of the object of sexuality. This is in stark contrast to the sexological, psychoanalytic, and liberationist models within which power was construed in a relation of exteriority to sexuality, and sexuality as that which "power tries to hold in check" (105).

Foucault traced this transformation of power to the seventeenth and eighteenth centuries. In a section entitled "Right of Death and Power over Life," he described a shift in the organization of power in which the emphasis was placed less on a concern with death than on life. This was characterized as a movement from a sovereign or juridical model of power to a productive or administrative one. "One might say that the ancient right to *take* life or *let* live was replaced by a power to *foster* life or disallow it to the point of death" (138). The emerging power over life—made possible largely through economic and agricultural development—evolved through two "poles." The first centered on "the body as a machine," the maximization of its potentials, its efficient integration into economic structures, its necessary disciplining and docility; the second and later formation centered on "the species body," the analysis, codification, and control of its biological functions (139).[42] This was seen as the "entry of life into history" and "the beginning of an era of 'bio-power'."[43] No longer primarily concerned with staving off death wrought by epidemics and famine, a preoccupation with matters of population and the "control over life" ensued (142).

By the nineteenth century the two "axes" constitutive of biopower coalesced around a concern and preoccupation with sex. It is this conjunction that was pivotal to the emergence of what Foucault called the "entire political technology of life" (145):

> On the one hand it was tied to the disciplines of the body: the harnessing, reintensification, and distribution of forces, the adjustment and economy of energies. On the other hand, it was applied to the regulation of populations, through all the far-reaching effects of its activity. It fitted in both categories at once, giving rise to infinitesimal surveillances, permanent controls, extremely meticulous orderings of space, indeterminate medical or psychological examinations, to an entire micro-power concerned with the body. But it gave rise as well to comprehensive measures, statistical assessments, and interventions aimed at the entire social body or at groups taken as a whole. Sex was a means of access both to the life of the body and the life of the species. It was employed as a standard for the disciplines and as a basis for regulations. (145–46)

Foucault identified the isolation of the "sexual 'instinct'"—itself the effect of the separation of "the medicine of sex from the medicine of the body"—as crucial to the development of both a science of sexual perversion and of a taxonomy of sexual species (117–18). He argued that the practice of Christian confession as a means for extracting and controlling sexual behavior had been recast in scientific terms. This meant that sex was increasingly framed not by "notions of error or sin, excess or transgression, but was placed under the rule of the normal and the pathological" (67). Thus, the doctor or psychiatrist began to replace the priest as the expert qualified to pronounce and heal matters relating to sex. In short, sex in the nineteenth century underwent an extensive process of medicalization.

This process was the effect of a form of power that, as Foucault was to describe it in "The Subject and the Power," functions most effectively through discursive identity categories: "This form of power applies itself to immediate everyday life which categorizes the individual, marks him by his own individuality, attaches him to his own identity, imposes a law of truth on him which he must recognize and which others have to recognize in him. It is a form of power which makes individuals subjects."[44] Itself responsible for "a new *specification of individuals*," this form of (bio)power advanced and multiplied through the tactical delineation of "peripheral sexualities." This allowed Foucault to conclude—in one of his most widely quoted lines—that along with the *speci(e)fication* of zoophiles, gynecomasts, and dyspareunist women (to take but a few examples), the "sodomite had been a temporary aberration; the homosexual was now a species."[45]

The genealogy of power traced by Foucault advanced the social constructionist study of sexuality in at least three important and original ways. First, it mapped the pivotal social and historical conditions through which sexuality itself emerged as a discursive object at the beginning of the nineteenth century. Second, this mapping provided a framework within which to situate the construction of a hetero/homosexual structure that made its first appearance only toward the end of the century. Third, it historicized the very structure and function of modern deviance and social normalization. That is, as Foucault demonstrated, a "normalizing society is the historical outcome of a technology of power centred on life" (144).

PROBLEMATIZING SEXUALITY

Foucault's methodology in The History of Sexuality is decidedly transdisciplinary. This is a practice that Rosi Braidotti has defined as the nomadic crossing of "disciplinary boundaries without concern for the vertical distinctions around which they have been organised."[46] Addressing the interrelatedness of historical, theoretical, and political concerns, the driving force of Foucauldian nomadism was *problematization*. His primary aim, however, was not simply to question or cast doubt upon received histories of sexuality, but to expose (genealogically) a particular form of power whose mode of operation is to construct and regulate historical, theoretical, and political inquiries into sexuality past and present. This "history of the present" enabled Foucault to deconstruct the place of sexuality in the networks of power in Western *normalizing* societies.

Foucault began his inquiry by outlining the accepted history of sexuality in the West. This is the story of the apparent advent of Victorian prudery. Confined to the conjugal bedroom, sex and its discussion were purportedly silenced, the transgression of its normative role repressed. Foucault called this "the repressive hypothesis."[47] In order to problematize the repressive hypothesis and the formations of sexuality it produces, he asked three interrelated and mutually informing questions: a historical, a historicotheoretical, and a historicopolitical question.[48]

The historical question he asks is whether this story of repression was a historical fact. Foucault did not deny that forms of repression occurred. However, his counterhypothesis, gleaned from a detailed historicization of sexuality, suggested that far from a reticence to speak or write about sex and far from a prohibition to speak or write about nonprocreative or perverse sex, what was characteristic of the Victorian period was a determined effort to speak about it *ad infinitum*: "a polymorphous incitement to discourse" (34–35). Of course, this was strictly regulated insofar as the discussion of sex was channeled into scientific and psychomedical discourses.

The historicotheoretical question refers to Foucault's query as to whether power really works in our Western societies primarily by way of repression, interdiction, censorship, and denial. As his genealogy made clear, power is not simply repressive but complexly productive. Foucault was here engaging in more than a critique of the sexological, Freudian, and liberationist traditions and their reliance on this problematic notion of repressive power. He was also offering more than a critique of the corollary proposition that power is in a relation of exteriority to sexuality. More important, he was situating this sexological tradition as itself an effect of biopower. In this way, such a tradition was a central part in the deployment of sexuality within the very unfolding of the *scientia sexualis*. For Foucault this has constituted a "centuries long apparatus of subjection."[49]

Finally, in the third, historicopolitical question, Foucault considered whether there was a rupture between "the age of repression and the critical analysis of repression."[50] Here he was referring to the sexual libertarian discourses championed by Reich, Marcuse, and gay liberation. Rather than viewing these as challenges to the sexual order, Foucault identified such discourses as "a tactical shift and reversal in the great deployment of sexuality" (131). The call for a liberation of a repressed sexuality is merely an essentializing gesture produced by the repressive hypothesis. "The irony of this [antirepressive] deployment," declared Foucault, "is in having us believe that our 'liberation' is in the balance" (159). The objective of relieving the apparent taboos and restrictions on discussing sexuality and perverse sex thus leads only to a further incitement to discourses of sex.

Foucault was therefore pessimistic about emancipation movements that take as their point of departure the category of homosexual. For it is this identity of homosexuality as a *reverse discourse* that was conditioned in advance by the apparatus of sexuality.[51] Foucault considered such defiant responses to pathologizing medical discourses as but "a strategic turnabout of one and the 'same' will to truth." They are akin to saying: "All right, we are what you say we are—by nature, disease, perversion, as you like. Well if that's what we are, let's be it, and if you want to know what we are, we can tell you ourselves better than you can."[52] While recognizing the importance of such "movements of affirmation" in securing the human right to choose one's sexuality, Foucault suggested that "we have to go one step further."[53] "It is not enough to liberate sexuality," he intoned, "we also have to liberate ourselves . . . from the very notion of sexuality."[54]

LIBERATION AND ANTI-IDENTITY

Foucault proclaimed a profound skepticism of the theme of liberation. "Does the expression 'Let us liberate our sexuality' have a meaning?" he asked rhetorically. "Isn't the problem rather to try to decide the practices of freedom through which we could determine what is sexual pleasure and what are our erotic, loving, passionate relationships with others?" (193–94). Distrust notwithstanding, there was a liberatory and perhaps even utopian impulse in the thought of Foucault. I will return to this point later. For now let me suggest simply that this impulse took a decidedly different form from the discourses of sexual liberationism. The difference lay in radically different constructions of power, resistance, and subjectification. It is to a brief discussion of Foucault's reworking of these concepts that I will turn now in order to highlight the revolutionary impact of his thought on the future direction of deconstructive models of sexuality.

Gay liberationists, as I have noted earlier, construed power as a negative and repressive force against which truth, knowledge, and human freedom were opposed. Correspondingly, resistance was seen as a negation of power, power's "outside." Displacing this tendency to bifurcate the spheres of knowledge and power, Foucault instead stressed their interconnectedness. He argued that truth functions in discourse for the production of knowledge and that power enables the production and accumulation of discourses.[55] Both productive and constraining, power is therefore not that *against* which human knowledge and freedom fight, but that *through* which notions of truth and liberation are inevitably articulated. In other words, truth, knowledge, liberation, resistance, and freedom are not external to power but internal to its dynamics.

Foucauldian power is not a centralized force locatable in an institution or individual. Neither is it the negative possession of some individuals imposed onto others. Rather, "power is everywhere, not because it embraces everything, but because it comes from everywhere." It is a "complex strategical situation in a particular society," an "over-all *effect*" of a "multiplicity of force relations." Power is "exercised from innumerable points, in the interplay of nonegalitarian and mobile relations." A liberation *from* power is thus impossible for, according to Foucault, there is no "absolute outside" to power.[56] Resistance is the only means of negotiating power's *omnipresence*. In fact, power and resistance are synchronous. Without resistance one is left with relations of pure force, complete determination. Resistance is but a strategic deployment of power. Freedom is not, therefore, some harmonious state outside of the clutches of power and attained as a result of resistance. Freedom is that which makes possible the exercising of power and resistance.

Foucault's reformulation of power/resistance is inextricable from his understanding of human subject formation. We have already seen how he described the emergence of the modern sexual subject as an effect of biopower. "There are two meanings of the word *subject*," he pointed out, "subject to someone else by control and dependence, and tied to his own identity by a conscience or self-knowledge. Both meanings suggest a form of power which subjugates and makes subject to." I will interrogate the gendering of this subject shortly. For now, it is necessary to follow the contours of his account. The subject who becomes tied to an identity and to the illusion of some inner sexual truth is thereby produced *within* and *through* a network of power relations. Resistance is central here. In other words, while we become *attached* to a sexual identity which imposes on us "a law of truth," it is that identity which simultaneously makes the freedom of human thought and action possible. This process of subjectification is thereby both productive and constraining.[57]

Foucault's distrust of sexual liberation ideologies now becomes clearer: in attaching ourselves to sexual identities we remain caught within "a conscience or self-knowledge" which is the effect of a more profound form of subjection. This is a highly pessimistic account of resistance for which Foucault has been heavily criticized. For while resistance may function to provide moments of relief, it is a form of resistance internal to the very apparatus of sexuality from which he suggests we need liberation. This, as we shall see, is not a liberation *from* power, but an attempt to effect a reorganization *of* relations of power.

So how do we go about liberating ourselves from the very notion of sexuality? Foucault suggested that the most pressing political task revolves around the struggle "against the submission of subjectivity" (213). Instead of rebounding back and forth within the double bind of identity based on modern forms of subjectivity, Foucault advocated a displacement of its very terms:

> Maybe the target nowadays is not to discover what we are, but to refuse what we are. We have to imagine and to build up what we could be to get rid of this kind of political 'double bind,' which is the simultaneous individualization and totalization of modern power structures. . . . We have to promote new forms of subjectivity through the refusal of this kind of individuality which has been imposed on us for several centuries. (216)

Foucault was here suggesting that we need to reframe the relationship of "self with self and the forming of oneself as a subject."[58] For example, this requires a more complex form of resistance to and negotiation of subjectifying practices than reverse discourses seem to allow. Taking as his object the hermetic economy of power/knowledge/subjectivity, Foucault was working toward a reshuffling of its internal relations in order to create new forms of subjectivity. Indeed, his political history of the present was an attempt "to learn to what extent the effort to think one's own history can free thought from what it silently thinks, and so enable it to think differently" (9).

The departure point for this political strategy is a refusal to dwell on the question of sexuality's ontological status. "The rallying point for the counterattack against the deployment of sexuality," Foucault declared, "ought not to be sex-desire, but bodies and pleasures."[59] Here he was attempting to disarticulate the all-too-pervasive Freudian assumption that pleasure is irreducibly sexual. This counterattack entails, he suggested, "much more the *art of life* than a science" of sexuality.[60] It involves creating ourselves as works of art forever in process, not as bearers of truth and static exemplars of fixed forms of being. In place of "the trend of 'always more sex,' and 'always more truth in sex'," Foucault called for a unending process of exploration and the invention of "other forms of pleasures, of relationships, coexistences, attachments, loves, intensities."[61] He was suggesting that challenging this trend would require loosening the grip that regimes of truth have on ethical questions in relation to sexuality.

We ought not, it would seem, pursue pleasure, or rather sexual desire, according to the identities to which we are affixed. Instead, our launching point ought to be pleasure detached from sexual identity, a pleasure in becoming other than what we are. "Liberation movements," lamented Foucault, "have always spoken about desire, and never about pleasure. 'We have to liberate our desire,' they say. No! We have to create new pleasure. And then maybe desire will follow."[62] David Halperin describes this emphasis on self-creation as a "modern form of ascesis."[63] Ascesis is a call to forge new relations of *self with self* "that would make us," Foucault suggested, "work on ourselves and invent (I don't say discover) a manner of being that is still improbable" (78).[64] Unlike gay liberationists, Foucault did not hold out any faith in notions of some glorious revolution that would one day usher in a utopian society free of inequalities. There was no such world for Foucault. Resistance and becoming are open-ended struggles that require one's engagement in forms of "hyper- and pessimistic activism."[65]

Foucault did go some way to clarifying this notion of pessimism when interviewers expressed the concern that pleasure, like desire/identity, might also be a basis for subjugating practices. "Can we be sure that these new pleasures won't be exploited in the way advertising uses the stimulation of pleasure as a means of social control?" asked Bob Gallagher and Alexander Wilson. "We can never be sure," responded Foucault: "In fact, we can always be sure it *will* happen, and that everything that has been created or acquired, any ground that has been gained will, at a certain moment, be used in such a way. That's the way we live, that's the way we struggle, that's the way of human history."[66] The freedom of resistance is thus a form of perpetual revolt.[67] It is an interminable form of political activity directed against the inevitability of identitarian appropriations and the tendency toward stability, fixity, categorization, and thus control.[68]

PROBLEMATIZING FOUCAULT'S HISTORY OF THE PRESENT

Foucault's anti-identitarianism was also the driving force behind his methodological transdisciplinarity. He resisted attempts to circumscribe his intellectual position according to traditional disciplinary boundaries. Allan Megill has described Foucault's attitude to the discipline of history as "one of wariness and contempt."[69] Despite suggesting his own works to be "studies of 'history'," Foucault went on to argue this to be only by virtue of "the domain they deal with and the references they appeal to." "But they are not," he declared, "the work of a 'historian'."[70] After all, as he had once noted sarcastically in a lecture at the University of Vermont, "I am not a professional historian; nobody is perfect."[71]

Foucault's genealogy of sexuality was an example of his attempt to undercut traditional paradigms of historical analysis. He was vociferous in his denunciation of those forms of history writing premised on notions of truth, objectivity, continuity, and unified subjectivity. Such histories are concerned with monolithic structures and monocausal explanations. Instead, Foucault drew on Nietzsche to posit a counterhistory he called "effective history."[72] This is an antimetaphysical history that "deprives the self of the reassuring stability of life and nature." It is a form of history which rejects notions of truth, objectivity, origin, and causality.[73] Effective history is framed instead by notions of rupture, discontinuity, contradiction and perspectivism. Foucault's history of sexuality was purportedly not an explanatory study of why sexuality was constituted as a discursive object. For this would mean invoking notions of causality and truth. Rather, it is an analysis or description of "*how* an 'experience' came to be constituted in modern Western societies, an experience that caused individuals to recognize themselves as subjects of a 'sexuality'."[74] Effective history is also animated by a contemporary political problematic, a desire to challenge the residual effects of the deployment of sexuality upon present day formations.

I argue that it is impossible to dissociate the how and the why of historical and discursive change, and that Foucault's attempts at doing so led to the elaboration of an exclusionary and decontextualized account of the emergence of sexuality as an object of discourse. In light of my findings in chapter 2, and by drawing on the groundbreaking work of feminist, gay/lesbian, and postcolonial theorists, I argue that this was primarily a failure to engage critically the analytics of race and gender. Extending this, however, I contend that Foucault's *most spectacular failure*[75] was an inability to recognize that his account of sexuality was itself conditioned by the very deployment of sexuality from which he (cl)aimed to "stand detached."[76] I suggest that his history of the present is often more obfuscating than elucidating. The economy of (hetero)sexuality's alliance of gender and sexuality is left largely untheorized and, as a result, bisexuality is erased from view. In light of this, Foucault's anti-identitarian political agenda needs to be seriously rethought.

In the introduction to *The Use of Pleasure,* the second volume of *The History of Sexuality,* Foucault reflected on his two-pronged attempt to problematize both the history and the concept of sexuality: "My aim was not to write a history of sexual behaviors and practices, tracing their successive forms, their evolution, and their dissemination; nor was it to analyze the scientific, religious, or philosophical ideas through which these behaviors have been represented" (3). Instead, he aimed to write "a history of [the object of] 'sexuality'" and of how individuals came to recognize themselves as subjects of sexuality (3). To do this, as I have already suggested, Foucault posited an analysis of power not as external to discourse, but as discourse's *modus operandi.* A shift in power and its transformation into bio-power was seen, therefore, to generate the object and subject of sexuality.

Yet, I ask how it is possible to ignore the representations, behaviors, and practices of sexuality without also ignoring a substantial part of the workings and relations of power. For if power operates through discourse, and discourse produces truthful representations and sexual subject positions, and resistance is synchronous with power, then clearly the individual's negotiation of these elements is crucial to any understanding of the history of sexuality. In other words, power, resistance, discourse, and subjectivity are indissociable forces in the production of sexuality. Representations and behaviors are constituted in and through this dynamic. Yet nowhere in Foucault's work do we find an analysis of the ways in which individuals *recognize* themselves as subjects of sexuality. This, despite Foucault's claim that, in the dynamic of power/resistance, "resistance comes first, and resistance remains superior to the forces of the process."[77] Contrary to the claim that "power relations are obliged to change with resistance" (29), sexual subjects in Foucault's account appear to be subjected to a form of power that merely "*imposes* a law of truth on him which he *must* recognize and which others *have* to recognize in him."[78]

Foucault's account of the medicalization of sexuality is deeply problematic in this respect. As I demonstrated in chapter 2, crises around the discursive boundaries of gender and race were pivotal to the construction of sexuality in the nineteenth century. Transgressions of normative social roles and relations were therefore central to scientific representations of gender and sexuality. These shifting relations of power/resistance do not rate a mention in *The History of Sexuality*. As innumerable feminist historians and theorists have made clear, Foucault's account of the emergence of biopower completely erases resistance and ignores its gendered dimension.[79] For Foucault to honor his claim that "*resistance* is . . . the key word in this dynamic"[80] of power would be, as Frances Bartkowski points out, "to include the oppositional practice of women, gays, even children in the history of sexuality."[81]

Foucault's account of the invention of a homosexual species provides a particularly acute example of this erasure. In his schema the homosexual appears to be little more than the product of the gradual unfolding of the *scientia sexualis*. However, a reliance on medical discourses to tell the history of sexuality has left him unable to inquire into forms of agency and resistance that might themselves have been partially responsible for this development. Frederick Silverstolpe and Randolph Trumbach reject the primacy accorded to the medical sciences. They claim that medical discourses were themselves shaped by the self-representations and behaviors of those engaging in homosexuality and cross-dressing. For example, Silverstolpe highlights the fact that as early as the 1860s Karl Ulrichs and Karoly Benkert had written extensively on the innate difference of people who love members of their own sex. Struggling for emancipation, the categories invented to describe this type of person—"uranians" and "homosexualists"—were grounded in self-perceptions. Silverstolpe argues persuasively that "when medical science intervened against the 'sociopolitical' claims of Ulrichs, Benkert and others with their pathology-approach, it can in fact be seen as a reaction *against* the invention of the homosexual category, with all its controversial implications, as well as an effort to *control* and redefine this new category when it was already there."[82] Bartkowski has argued that Foucault has merely reproduced and produced "as history" the phallocentric history of sexuality as told, viewed, and heard from those in the position of power.[83] Clearly, she is criticizing the exclusionary nature of Foucault's account. However, she is also suggesting that power is gendered in a way Foucault failed to recognize. Similarly, Abdul JanMohamed has bemoaned the ethnocentrism structuring *The History of Sexuality*: "The history of 'bourgeois' and 'racialized' sexualities is deployed in a relation of negative specularity. . . . The first can write itself as 'universal' only if it averts its gaze from the second, its dark other."[84] I would like to draw out what is perhaps implicit in the claims of Bartkowski and JanMohamed: namely, that in his reliance on a phallocentric and ethnocentric history, Foucault's genealogy of biopower is *itself* conditioned by the deployment of sexuality from which he claims to stand detached.

In chapter 2 I demonstrated the centrality of power struggles around gender and race to the construction of the nineteenth-century category of sexuality. I argued that the ensuing economy of (hetero)sexuality was the effect of a crisis of white, middle-class, masculine identity. Foucault's account, on the other hand, effects a wholesale effacement of gender and race as constitutive forces in the social and discursive construction of sexuality. This severely damages the theoretical and historical cogency of his genealogy of power. For such erasures can only be enacted by relying on both a homogenous and a disembodied notion of power and a power dislocated from social and material relations. Biopower thus seems to replace the sovereign subject as the universal, monolithic, and causal force in the history of sexuality. Foucault *described* the success of power as "proportional to its ability to hide its own mechanisms."[85] Ironically, it would seem that it succeeded with Foucault as well. Perhaps even for Foucault, power was "tolerable only on the condition that it mask a substantial part of itself" (86): namely, its racial and gendered dimensions and its part in the constitution of his own subjectivity.

The erasure of gender and race renders Foucault's account of the historical formation of modern forms of subjectivity suspect. Recall that the deployment of sexuality is thought to have ushered in these new subjectivities. Indeed, Foucault argued that modern subjectivity is synonymous with sexual subjectivity. Having ignored the shifting racial and gendered power relations central to this formation, however, the deployment of sexuality appears to unfold in large part without history. Lynn Hunt has argued that Foucault "only partially historicizes subjectivity."[86] Suggesting his concept of the individual or the self to be often ahistorical and always gendered as "adult male," Hunt goes even further to invert the terms of Foucault's account. She suggests that it was not the deployment of sexuality that generated the modern self but the modern self that generated the deployment of sexuality. This modern self—described as the separate and self-possessing individual, the "self that owns itself and its own body" (85)—is for Hunt the product of eighteenth-century materialism.[87] As she points out, of course, it was only upper-class, adult—and I would add white—men who enjoyed this privilege.[88]

Women, nonwhites, and children were thus excluded from this form of self-possession. Yet Foucault described the emergence of a singular form of modern sexual subjectivity by relying precisely on this exclusionary and historically specific notion of the self-possessing individual. According to Foucault's account, then, it would seem that modern subjectivity is synonymous with a hegemonic white, bourgeois masculinity. This runs not in opposition to but parallel to the phallocentric logic of sexological and Freudian figurations of sexual subjectivity. Far from standing detached from the deployment of sexuality, Foucault's history of the present is itself conditioned by it. *The History of Sexuality* thus remains complicit in a will to reproduce a hegemonic white, masculinist discourse, power, and identity.

THE ERASURE OF BISEXUALITY

The concept of bisexuality was methodologically foreclosed, if not irrelevant, in Foucault's history of sexuality. Serving for the most part as an epistemological tool of specific scientific discourses, bisexuality, as I demonstrated in chapter 2, was an evolutionary concept pivotal to the theorization of sexuality. Yet, as Foucault has pointed out, he was not concerned with analyzing specific scientific representations. In fact, he had already accounted for the appearance of peripheral sexualities in the nineteenth century by suggesting them to be an extension of a subjectifying form of biopower that began in the seventeenth century. Again, this effaces the very real power struggles that led scientists to invent theories designed to reinforce normative social roles. Nor is Foucault interested in analyzing the various sexological texts responsible for inventing and disseminating the medical notion of a homosexual species. He does point out that the isolation of the "sexual instinct" in the nineteenth century was a decisive phase in the medicalization of sexuality. However, he has little to say to questions of how and why the sexual instinct was discursively isolated. It is merely subsumed as part of the evolutionary unfolding of biopower. Addressing the how and why of the sexual instinct's discursive isolation would require more than a macroanalysis of biopower and the deployment of sexuality, as Foucault had done. Additionally, it would require a microanalysis, that is, an analysis that would delve inside the apparatus of sexuality to analyze its very epistemic configuration.[89]

As my microanalysis has shown, with the advance of science in the nineteenth century, the evolutionary concept of bisexuality was incorporated into the notion of subjectivity as self-possession. Only adult white men were thought to have evolved to the point of owning themselves. They managed to achieve this by supposedly transcending their (bisexual) evolutionary heritage. Women, blacks, homosexuals, and children, however, were further down the evolutionary scale, not fully human because not fully male or not white. Such scientific representations were clearly mobilized against claims to self-possession being made on behalf of women and blacks. This was a crucial part of precisely *how* sexuality was able to emerge as an object of phallocentric discourse. In other words, the history of sexuality cannot be told without an analysis of the ways in which sexual behaviors, perceptions, and representations are at once constituted by and constitutive of relations of power and forms of subjectivity. Contrary to Foucault's claims, therefore, such elements are a crucial part of tracing the history of the object of 'sexuality' and of how individuals came to recognize themselves as subjects of sexuality.

LIBERATION FROM SEXUALITY, LIBERATION FROM GENDER

Although Foucault failed to address the gendered and racialized power relations constitutive of sexuality, he did go some way toward providing an analysis of the epistemological functioning of the category of 'sex' (or what I call gender) within this apparatus.[90] In fact, a multilayered concept of sex was the linchpin of his account of modern forms of subjectivity. The "notion of 'sex'," he suggested, "made it possible to group together, in an artificial unity, anatomical elements, biological functions, conducts, sensations, and pleasures, and it enabled one to make use of this fictitious unity as a causal principle, an omnipresent meaning, a secret to be discovered everywhere: where sex was thus able to function as a unique signifier and as a universal signified."[91] Sex is thus the principal effect and regulatory core serv(ic)ing the deployment of sexuality. For, he wrote, it is

> through sex—in fact, an imaginary point determined by the deployment of sexuality—that each individual has to pass in order to have access to his own intelligibility (seeing that it is both the hidden aspect and the generative principle of meaning), to the whole of his body (since it is a real and threatened part of it, while symbolically constituting the whole), to his identity (since it joins the force of a drive to the singularity of a history). (155–56)

Here Foucault was referring to three interconnected meanings of the way in which the category of sex has structured individuals and societies through

CHAPTER SIX   [156]

the deployment of sexuality. First, as humans we are only intelligible by being inscribed with a coherent sex. Second, this sexed identity is installed as the originary force determining bodily desires and pleasures. Third, sex is the basis for grasping the truth of individual subjectivity. I argued earlier that for Foucault liberation is not the freeing up of a sexuality repressed by a puritanical Western culture. Instead, as he pointed out, it "is the agency of sex that we must break away from" (156). So in liberating ourselves from the deployment of sexuality we are not just *refusing* 'sexuality', but refusing forms of modern subjectivity constituted through the chimera that is sex.

According to this model, identity politics (gay/lesbian and feminist) would seem doomed to failure in the last instance. The "rallying point" for a "counterattack . . . ought not to be *sex-desire*," Foucault argued, but the "multiplicity" of "bodies and pleasures" (157; my emphasis). The argument suggests that in mobilizing around "sex-desire" we would merely remain entrapped by a unifying logic of identity conditioned by the apparatus of sexuality.[92] In short, gay, lesbian, and feminist identities rely problematically on 'sex' for their political point of departure. It is around these claims that Foucault's anti-identitarian political stance faces very difficult problems.[93] Is this to suggest a denial or repudiation of an individual's experiences through which they became a subject? If sex is that through which we must pass in order to be intelligible as humans, does its rejection not render us unintelligible? Is this *modern form of ascesis* the only or even the best practice for challenging the apparatus of sexuality? How does a rejection of sex and sexuality sit with feminist and gay/lesbian theorists who struggle to challenge oppressive discourses structured through such terms? And does Foucault's rejection of the depth model of sexuality and ontology deflect important attention away from the very real individual psychical affects wrought by the apparatus of sexuality?

Clearly, Foucault was not suggesting meaninglessness or unintelligibility to be a desired goal, let alone a possibility. He was suggesting, however, that refusing the terms laid down by the apparatus of sexuality is part of a broader process of reinventing ourselves, our desires, our pleasures, and our relationships in ways not dictated by 'sex'. Of course, with these new meanings will come new discursive formations and new configurations of power. These in turn will congeal into normative and restrictive subject positions, which will also need to be resisted. This is to be expected in Foucault's anti-idealist and pessimistic vision. However, as Judith Butler has cogently demonstrated, a certain utopian tendency does in fact inhere in Foucault's thought. While this is not immediate grounds for its rejection, I suggest that it does reflect deeper problems with Foucault's political history of the present.

Butler has deftly exposed the "emancipatory ideal" structuring *The History of Sexuality* by reading the text against Foucault's introduction to *Herculine Barbin*, the memoirs of a nineteenth-century hermaphrodite.[94] The latter, she claims, contradicts the former. Furthermore, this contradiction is evident as an "unresolved tension" in *The History of Sexuality*.[95] I will not rehearse Butler's well-known arguments here. Suffice it to say that she sees in Foucault's invocation of a 'multiplicity of bodies and pleasures' a trope situated seemingly outside of any power/discourse economy. This, she suggests, is not far from Freud's concept of polymorphous perversity and Marcuse's bisexual Eros. Butler finds confirmation of this contradiction in Foucault's introduction to *Herculine Barbin*. For in *Herculine Barbin* Foucault himself appears to find confirmation of his notion of the liberatory potential of prediscursive bodies and pleasures. In tracing the personal narrative of Herculine, he suggests that "what she evokes in her past is the happy limbo of a non-identity." This is a reference to a time when Barbin occupied a world free from the dictates of 'sex'. For Foucault this "is a world in which grins hung about without the cat."[96] For Butler, Foucault invokes Barbin's state of "happy limbo" as a synecdoche for his political ideal. In other words, he is describing "pleasures that clearly transcend the regulation imposed upon them, and here we see Foucault's sentimental indulgence in the very emancipatory discourse his analysis in *The History of Sexuality* was meant to displace."[97]

I suggest that Foucault was too quick to abandon identity politics. The deployment of sexuality conditioned not simply his trope of 'bodies and pleasures', as Butler has pointed out. So too, I suggest, was his strategy of refusing "what we are," of refusing those identities and modern forms of subjectivity produced through sex. The Foucauldian celebration of nonidentity was just the obverse of identity, the reverse discourse of the apparatus of sexuality. Or to put it differently, the refusal of identity was symptomatic of a utopian desire to step outside power, discourse, history, and subjectivity. Yet Foucault knew only too well the impossibility of this task. How then do we account for this contradiction?

It seems to me that this contradiction reflects a deeper problem with Foucault's account of the emergence of modern subjectivity. Foucault's refusal of identity and subjectivity was predicated on his account of the historical emergence of the modern self. Yet, as I have argued via Hunt, this modern self, parading as the universal Western subject, is merely *a* white, bourgeois, male self.[98] Foucault's discourse, to invoke the words of Irigaray once again, was driven by a phallocentric power which "*reduce*[s] *all others to the economy of the Same.*"99 In refusing modern subjectivity Foucault can be seen, therefore, to be refusing only a specific version, or the dominant fiction, of masculine subjectivity. His anti-identitarian agenda would thus appear to be inapplicable to other forms of subjectivity—in particular, those subjectivities excluded from his history of sexuality. Moreover, this strategy of refusal appears to be premised on a notion of the self-possessing subject of the Enlightenment. And as Christopher Lane has made clear, this desire of Foucault's "to disband an insistence that sexuality is the subject's truth" ignores the very real "*psychical* history and resistance" of individuals as they negotiate desire and identity.100 Perhaps Foucault's strategy said more about Foucault's own subjectivity. Perhaps he was engaging in a kind of self-analysis or self-deconstruction, a refusal of the illusion of self-possession. On the one hand, this might be construed as a laudable, albeit unwitting, feminist project of challenging his own patriarchal subjectivity. On the other hand, however, it would be a form of masculinist naïveté to assume that one can simply refuse one's gendered inscriptions.

In addition to this, the subject of Foucault's idealized political activism seems to simplify and even contradict the dual meaning of the subject he presented in "The Subject and Power." Recall that for Foucault modern power functions by categorizing the individual, attaching him to his own identity and *imposing* a "law of truth on him which he must recognize and which others have to recognize in him."101 How exactly is someone capable of refusing a "kind of individuality" that is in large measure the effect of a seemingly external *imposition*? To answer this it appears that Foucault was forced into a paradoxical position. It seems to me that he merely invoked a reverse subject position conditioned by the construction of the modern self. That is, the ground for such a strategy of refusal is the self-possessing subject, a "self that owns itself and its own body."102 Contradictorily, however, this would appear to be a non-Foucauldian self that *possesses* rather than exercises power, in this case, the power of refusal.

I would argue that identity categories and subjectivities cannot simply be refused except in a utopian and masculinist formulation. For as subjects we are interpellated into discursive structures that inevitably require us to negotiate the forms of individuality through which we must necessarily "pass in order to have access to . . . [our] own intelligibility."103 As Diana Fuss argues:

> It would be difficult, not to say delusionary, to forget the words . . . 'heterosexual' and 'homosexual,' without also losing in this act of willed amnesia the

SEXUALITY AND SUBJECTION   [159]

crucial sense of alterity necessary for constituting any sexed subject, any subject as sexed. The dream of either a common language or no language at all is just that—a dream, a fantasy that ultimately can do little to acknowledge and to legitimate the hitherto repressed differences between and within sexual identities.[104]

Refusing sexual identities amounts to a refusal of one problematic notion of self for another equally problematic one. That is, where Foucault says that we should "work on ourselves and invent (I don't say discover) a manner of being that is still improbable,"[105] I say that he has himself, paradoxically, *already reinvented and rediscovered* the very Enlightenment manner of being from which he seeks to flee.

CONCLUSION

Foucault's work has been groundbreaking in attempts to historicize and to theorize how individuals have been constituted as subjects, or species, of sexuality. It has also been influential in reshaping issues of how best to challenge the restrictive and homogenizing effects of this subjectification. However, as I have attempted to demonstrate in this chapter, Foucault neither adequately deconstructed sexuality, nor analyzed its relationship to gender.[106] In fact, he aimed simply to disengage sexuality and to keep the axes of gender and sexuality problematically distinct. This was in part the outcome of his desire to challenge the psychoanalytic reduction of sexuality to gender. His call to rally around the trope of 'bodies and pleasures' was therefore meant to assist in the extrication of desire and pleasure from the "agency of sex" (what I call gender).[107]

Two interesting points must be made in relation to this theoretical move. First, it recapitulated the phallocentric repudiation of gender characteristic of early gay liberation theory. Second, it provided the theoretical impetus for queer theory's call to disarticulate gender and sexuality. As we will see in the next chapter, unlike queer theory, however, Foucault left the opposition of hetero- and homosexuality relatively free from deconstructive scrutiny. In contrast to queer theory's aims of working this opposition to the "point of critical exhaustion,"[108] Foucault preferred simply to set it aside, to stand detached from it. He was attempting merely to evade, or to *refuse*, the grip of sex and sexuality by constructing a genealogy that was a macroanalysis of the shift in epistemes from the seventeenth to the nineteenth centuries. He sought to historicize the *scientia sexualis* and its production of sexuality and sexual identities. As a deconstructive genealogy, or microanalysis, my work here aims instead to go *inside* the *scientia sexualis* in order to examine how this production of sexuality and sexual identity was made possible through an incessant repudiation of the Other, of nonidentity, of bisexuality. It remains to be seen, however, how effectively queer theory has theorized, or is able to theorize, the relationship of gender and sexuality.[109]

I have argued that this move of Foucault's is a phallocentric one propped up by a historical misunderstanding. "We must not refer a history of sexuality to the agency of sex," Foucault claimed, "but rather show how 'sex' is historically subordinate to sexuality."[110] If my argument is correct, however, the deployment of sexuality did not precede and produce sex. Rather, the notion of sexuality as a distinct component of the self was produced in and through crises around the boundaries of normative sex. This erasure seriously undermines Foucault's anti-identitarian political strategy. For the only way to refuse sex and sexuality and to experience the delights of nonidentity is to assume the masculinist position of self-possessing subject. This does not situate Foucault outside the deployment of sexuality as he would like to think. On the contrary, he remains firmly within its grasp.

The terms of Foucauldian discourse produced and yet ultimately constrained a deconstructive impulse. In other words, Foucault was more a constructionist than a deconstructionist; his rabid antiessentialism was in fact the reverse discourse of essentialism. It is important to keep in mind, however, that constructionist and essentialist positions are partners in a binary conditioned by the deployment of sexuality.[111] Bisexuality stands in a curious relation to the essentialist/constructionist opposition and the axes of gender and sexuality. Historically, it has been framed by both essentialism and constructionism, while mediating essentialist and constructionist theories of gender and sexuality. Yet with the rejection of both the notion of an innate sexuality and the psychoanalytic model of gender identity formation, bisexuality was completely disavowed from social constructionist discourse.[112] This has rendered gender and sexuality as rather autonomous, free floating, and even unconnected axes in the constitution of subjectivity, desire and pleasure.

It is the argument of this book, however, that if bisexuality was indeed central to the epistemic construction of the economy of (hetero)sexuality from the late nineteenth century through to the early 1970s, as I have demonstrated in part 1, then as a corollary it would seem to be central also to its deconstruction.[113] This means that in order to challenge heteronormative structures and discourses it is essential to theorize the mutually structuring relationship of sexuality and gender as it is produced, maintained, and inflected by the figure of bisexuality. This is not a call to reinvoke a notion of innate bisexuality as the truth of sexuality, as attempted by gay liberation. It *is* to suggest, however, that if the boundaries of the hetero/homosexual opposition have been secured by erasing bisexuality in the present tense, then the category of bisexuality must be situated within each and every articulation of this opposition, past and present. Moreover, as the structure of hetero/homosexuality is as culturally pervasive as ever, we cannot, in my view, work toward its deconstruction by any simple strategy of evasion. Our unceasing interpellation into this binary system requires us to engage constantly, and in myriad arenas, with the power relations and internal dynamics that inform and influence its operation. It is worth remembering that our interpellation within this system, and our negotiation of the identity categories thus produced, need not imply the rather structuralist Foucauldian conclusion that resistance is co-opted in advance. One of the crucial insights of *post*structuralist theory is, as Slavoj Žižek points out in his critique of precisely this issue in Foucault's thought, the possibility of an effect, let's say sexual identity, "outgrowing its cause, so that although it emerges as a form of resistance to power and is as such absolutely inherent to it, it can outgrow and explode it."[114]

In the next chapter I will introduce the most recent movement for thinking through identity in order to challenge the binary structure of sexuality. This movement, heavily indebted to Foucauldian social constructionism, is known as 'queer'. We shall see whether queer theory is better positioned to deconstruct the hetero/homosexual opposition and how well it has been able to theorize the negotiation of identity and bisexuality. This will provide the basis for a reconsideration of bisexuality as a useful, indeed necessary, tool of deconstructive analysis; and as perhaps even one of those internal identity effects that just might outgrow its cause, to become, to redeploy Žižek's terms, a force whose excess our binary epistemology of sexuality "is no longer able to master and which thus detonates its unity, its capacity to reproduce itself" (256).

7

THE QUEER INTERVENTION

> Even when coupled with a toleration of minority sexualities, heteronormativity has a totalizing tendency that can only be overcome by actively imagining a necessarily and desirably queer world.
> —Michael Warner 1991

In chapter 6 I traced the emergence of a profound shift in the theorization of sexuality and sexual identity. In contrast to attempts by sexologists, psychoanalysts, and liberationists to extract and construct an essential truth of sexuality, there emerged in the late 1970s and 1980s a counterdiscursive challenge determined to invert the terms of such truth claims. As a result of social constructionist theories, particularly Foucault's, the category of sexuality in general, and hetero- and homosexuality in particular, was identified as contributing to individual and collective oppression. This poses immediate theoretical and practical problems for those involved in the politics of sexuality. Not only are the categories of 'gay' and 'lesbian' emptied of any ontological content, but forms of political mobilization organized under their rubrics have been shown ultimately to feed rather than to contest modes of sexual oppression. Foucault's solution was to retreat from affirmations of identity. He sought to engage a wholesale critique of sexual identity by employing a strategy of anti-identification.

In many parts of the United States, Britain, and Australia, another approach to the problems animating the theory and politics of sexual identity has emerged. Clearly indebted to social constructionist and Foucauldian critiques, yet unwilling to abandon altogether the productive, and indeed inevitable, function of identity, a multifaceted discourse of queer theory has come to prominence in the last few years as a means of negotiating this impasse or double bind of identity.[1] Queer marks a decisive break with both liberationist and ethnic assertions and theorizations of gay and lesbian identity. Despite a resistance to homogenizing metanarratives, one of queer theory's primary principles is the claim that all identities, sexual or otherwise, are only ever constructed relationally. The central paradigm of analysis has been the axis of sexuality in general and the hetero/homosexual opposition in particular. Theorists such as Eve Kosofsky Sedgwick, Diana Fuss, and Lee Edelman, among others, have produced many useful studies that serve to challenge heteronormative constructions of sexuality and work the hetero/homosexual opposition, as Fuss puts it, to the "point of critical exhaustion."[2] Despite an epistemic location *within* this very opposition, however, the category of bisexuality has been curiously marginalized and erased from the deconstructive field of queer theory. It is an analysis of this marginalization and erasure that concerns me in this chapter.

While many bisexual theorists have identified this erasure of bisexuality (e.g., Hemmings, Eadie, James, Young), none has yet provided an adequate explanation of how and why it has occurred.[3] This chapter attempts to do this by subjecting some of the canonical works of queer theory to historical and deconstructive critique. I will argue that the failure to account for bisexuality is the effect of two interrelated factors. First, contrary to stated aims, one of the tendencies of many queer theorists has been to think the two axes of gender and sexuality vertically or hierarchically rather than relationally and obliquely. Second, interrogations of the axes of gender and sexuality have been subsumed within poorly historicized deconstructive frameworks. What this means, I will contend, is that efforts to deconstruct the hetero/homosexual structure have foundered precisely because of a failure to address the history of (bi)sexuality.

INTRODUCING QUEER

What is queer? Who is queer? Why is queer, queer? Any attempt to define queer is immediately problematic, if not essentially paradoxical. In the most basic sense in the realm of sexuality, queer as a noun is slang for a male homosexual. Historically, however, queer has signified more than mere slang. It has functioned within heterosexist and homophobic discourse as a derogatory signifier, as a boundary marker of normality. This relates to a second and more interesting level, where, according to the *Concise Oxford Dictionary*, queer is an adjective denoting that which is "strange, odd, eccentric; of questionable character, shady, suspect."[4] Or in the *Collins Concise English Dictionary*, it signifies something "differing from the normal or usual." In addition to this, queer is also defined as a verb. For instance, in the *Shorter Oxford English Dictionary*, it means "to cheat," "to spoil," and to "put out of order."[5] In other words, queer is something mysterious, enigmatic, unknown, and even troubling. It is the *terra incognita* of Western knowledge; it cannot readily be pinned down, but it is decisively juxtaposed to the safety of the known, the verifiable, the familiar, indeed, the *normal*. Queer is therefore both known—in the sense that it is assigned a *definition*—and unknown—in that the very terms of its meaning suggest duplicity and dubiousness. This is not mere semantic sophistry, but an attempt to illustrate the semantic ambiguity of queer—queer exceeds any unifying definition. Moreover, as I will demonstrate in this chapter, it is this conceptual multiplicity and ambiguity that extends to the level of political and theoretical practices within which queer is being invoked.

In the United States queer *identity* emerged most explicitly out of a younger generation of sex radicals disillusioned with the liberal politics of gay assimilationism and the inadequate response of the American government to the problem of HIV/AIDS.[6] The militant organization Queer Nation formed as an offshoot of ACT UP, taking up the challenge of direct confrontation. Queer's *debut* as a sign of radicalism and nonconformity was, in this context, a revalorized and reanimated substitute for gay or lesbian.[7] However, queer identity has also been crucially informed by feminist and lesbian feminist discourses that developed in the 1980s. Critiques of heterosexuality as a cultural institution and debates about the legitimacy of sadomasochism and butch/femme within feminism significantly reconceptualized monolithic notions of sexuality and sexual oppression. Queer was used by a number of lesbian feminists as a distancing device from the homogenizing politics of radical feminism.[8] It is in the intersection of these two movements that queer can be seen to emerge as an effect of the necessity to forge coalitions across boundaries of gender, race, ethnicity, class, and sexuality.

Queer has since been taken up in myriad ways in the United States, Britain, and Australia. The forms it currently assumes range from queer *essentialism*, queer nationalism, and queer as an individualist erotics of the sublime,[9] to a kind of queer communitarianism that is inclusive of differences, purportedly inclusive of everyone.[10] The one central thread linking the diversity of queer constructions is in the adoption of queer as a sign of pride. In all cases queer is invoked as a rhetorical term, an explicit revalorization of that which has been hitherto denigrated, medicalized, marginalized, and pathologized by Western regimes of sexuality. Or, in less specific and more encompassing fashion, Michael Warner suggests that queer represents a "thorough resistance to regimes of the normal."[11]

I suggest that it might be useful to identify three predominant intersecting and overlapping conceptual layers through which this diversity of queer formations currently circulate. At the first level, queer has been actively seized as the latest fashionable catch-phrase for what might be seen as the somewhat more staid conjunction of 'gay and lesbian'. That is, queer is invoked as style and symbol for homosexuality. Within the second layer, queer functions as an umbrella category for the sexually marginalized. Here it occupies the ground of a highly contested site within the representational politics of sexuality, initiating a formidable challenge to lesbian and gay identity politics. Queer has effected a discursive intervention in the domain of sexuality as a self-consciously constructed and pliable space that houses differences rather than elides them. This seems to represent, as Lisa Duggan has suggested, an analogous conceptual move to that of 'women of color'.[12] The construction and policing of a unitary identity that is threatened by alterity and historicity is eschewed. Instead, queer becomes the site of a kind of radical alterity, a space for the very production and accumulation of differences. Like 'women of color', queer is inclusive and facilitates communication between the sexually marginalized who are united in their opposition to the normalizing practices of Western discourses. Bisexuals, transvestites, transsexuals, and transgendered people who have been ostracized from gay and lesbian communities, and yet who have offered valuable potential strength and support to such communities, now have in their grasp a new discursive position through which to maneuver.

The third layer, and the one that concerns me in this chapter, sees queer function as or in theory: not as a metanarrative or a unified body of knowledge but as a philosophic and self-reflexive force of critique of essentialized notions of gender and sexual identity. In Foucauldian fashion, all identity categories are deemed cultural and discursive fabrications, regulatory ideals. In other words, identity categories are seen to be falsely unifying, totalizing, exclusionary, and normative constructions that serve to deny ambiguity, contradiction, and difference. Queer, in this context, seeks to expose, affirm, and celebrate what identities are forced to deny. It does this in order to enact a profound destabilization of identity as a social organizing principle.

As a theoretical position, then, queer is characterized by a multilayered grid of meaning. Even when it seems to operate as an alternative to 'gay and lesbian', its polyvocality points to a more profound shift in the practices and politics of sexuality. The invocation of queer immediately signals a problematization of sexual identity and identity politics. By this I am not suggesting queer to be always and necessarily a self-conscious challenge to identity. Rather, at the very least, articulations of queer reflect the changing status of identity and attest to the transformative nature of identity concepts. As I have argued elsewhere, it is perhaps the very imbrication of each of these layers that provides much of the productive potential of queer.[13]

POSTMODERNISM, POSTSTRUCTURALISM, AND QUEER THEORY

The Foucauldian and poststructuralist critiques of identity subtend the discursive manifestations of queer and the changing cultural status, or function, of identity.[14] This is indicative of the third, more overtly deconstructive layer of queer and the one upon which I will now focus. Its intersection with the economy of (hetero)sexuality must be understood in the broader cultural context of postmodernism. Postmodern accounts of Western culture highlight a contemporary period characterized by chaos and uncertainty: hypercomputerization, global organization of production, and the commodification of social relations; the development and advances in cyberspace and virtual reality that have transformed conceptions of space and time; the eclipse of modernist epistemologies rooted in linear certainties have been in part replaced by new ways of (un)knowing driven by the logic of (dis)order and chaos; all of these events and actions have led to a significant challenge to hegemonic economies of knowledge production and have produced new modes of being.[15]

Queer innovation is imbricated in this complex and ever-changing set of cultural matrices. In a seemingly orderless, or chaotic amalgam of disparate cultural forms, images, styles, sensibilities, and practices, the positionality of queer appears to be the embodiment of postmodern pastiche, oppositional politics, and elite poststructuralist theory. Truth, inner depth, agency—in short, the embodied modernist sexual *self*—are deemed retrograde concepts hampering the creation of and experimentation with new sensibilities, new subject-positions, new subjectivities. The subject in this locale is an anti-Cartesian queer actor who finds and employs discursive power and mobility through anonymity, imitation, and appropriation.[16]

Despite its recent intellectual emergence, queer theory resists conventional narratives of its own historicity. Origins and utopian end points, causes and effects, are among the binarized concepts challenged by queer's disruption of discursive teleologies. As Annamarie Jagose has made clear, "Queer's contemporary proliferation is enabled, in part, by claims that it has always already significantly structured the anti-homophobic impulse."[17] Jonathan Dollimore's *Sexual Dissidence* provides an exemplary theoretical and historical reading of this kind. While not identifying the term queer in his text, his work bears the mark of the queer refiguration of lesbian and gay studies. Dollimore gestures toward an exposure of the already queer nature of both early modern English forms of cross dressing, and the "transgressive aesthetic" and subversive knowledges produced by "postmodern" thinkers such as Oscar Wilde and Jean Genet.[18]

Queer knowledges and practices effect an assault on unified identity categories and the centered Cartesian self. They do this by inverting, displacing, and perverting the very terms of hegemonic discourse. Gaps and contradictions that exist within and between identities, but that have been sutured closed or denied, are revealed and activated; liminal and fluid subject positions are seized by queer actors and theorists, all in an effort to destabilize hegemonic categories and discursive structures. Dollimore sees these strategies to have been made possible by what he terms "the perverse dynamic." In postmodernist style, the artifice of humanist fictions is exposed through strategies of irony, resistance, subversion, and transgression. Read through Dollimore, then, queer could be a form of "transgressive reinscription." It is the "agency which might intensify those instabilities, turning them against the norms" (33). This enables him to read and to queer history without privileging the categories of homosexual or heterosexual, gay or lesbian. Queer might be seen, therefore, as *both* a historically specific category and a structural force central to normative binary logic.

Judith Butler has been most widely referred to as having theorized this transgressive agency as a useful political strategy of the present. This is undertaken in her groundbreaking book *Gender Trouble*, which is an analysis of the reiteration of gender norms as constitutive of compulsory heterosexuality. In theorizing identity as a signifying practice, a performative effect of a process of repetition, Butler proposes "a set of parodic practices" that might be useful in subversively resignifying the categories of sex, gender, and sexuality.[19] Drag, cross-dressing, and butch/femme role playing are posited as examples of such parodic practices. "*In imitating gender, drag,*" she argues, "*implicitly reveals the imitative structure of gender itself—as well as its contingency*" (137). According to Butler's argument, the institution of heterosexuality—founded as it is on the binarism of gender—is potentially disrupted through her notion of gender parody. Butler's work thus lends support to my reading of Dollimore's implicit use of queer as a force active in England in the early years of the modern period and in the postmodern period.

Despite Butler's overwhelming methodological influence on queer critiques and analyses of identity, it is Eve Kosofsky Sedgwick who has, in my mind, provided the centralized *epistemological* focus for the burgeoning field of queer theory itself. Unlike Butler, whose challenge to the coherence of hetero- and homosexual identities proceeds through gender, Sedgwick instead shifts and narrows the focus to the hetero/homosexual opposition itself. In what appears now to be an unshakeable queer dictum, she argues that "an understanding of virtually any aspect of modern Western culture must be, not merely incomplete, but damaged in its central substance to the degree that it does not incorporate a critical analysis of modern homo/heterosexual definition."[20] The hetero/homosexual binary has thus become the central paradigm of analysis for queer deconstructive models. This has been opened up, in large part, by Foucault's exposure of sexuality as *the* structuring principle of modernist subjectivity. In contrast to the constructionist project of mapping and explaining the modern homosexual (to the exclusion of the heterosexual), the Foucauldian and poststructuralist inspired queer theory attempts, as Steven Seidman points out, to shift the focus toward an interrogation of "heterosexuality as a social and political organizing principle."[21] Instead of reifying sexual identity categories, queer theory takes as its project the task of exposing the operations of *heteronormativity* in order to work the hetero/homosexual opposition to the point of critical collapse. This represents an attempt to further Foucault's project of challenging the association of sexuality with subjectivity, that is, of challenging the notion that there exist distinct hetero- and homosexual species of being.

Diana Fuss's introduction to the anthology *Inside/Out: Lesbian Theories, Gay Theories* provides an exemplary illustration of this queer theoreticopolitical strategy. She argues that the hetero/homosexual binary is the effect of a "metaphysics of identity" that functions through the related opposition of inside/outside. Reframing earlier liberationist and constructionist models through the lens of poststructuralism, Fuss highlights the unavoidable interdependence of each term of the binary. Identifying this metaphysical logic as heteronormative, she goes on to argue that "the homo in relation to the hetero, much like the feminine in relation to the masculine, operates as an indispensable interior exclusion—an outside which is inside interiority making the articulation of the latter possible, a transgression of the border which is necessary to constitute the border as such."[22]

In grasping the utopian naïveté of Foucault's call for a "radical break" with the regime of sexuality, Fuss instead calls for us to rework, use up and exhaust its categories in an effort to contest their putative coherence. "Change may well happen," she suggests, "by working on the insides of our inherited sexual vocabularies and turning them inside out, giving them a new face" (7). Fuss draws on Jane Gallop's influential argument that "identity must be continually assumed and immediately called into question."[23] Judith Butler echoes something similar in her suggestion that identity may be "a necessary error"; that through reverse affirmations, for example, "homophobic deployments" of the categories of gay and lesbian in "law, public policy, on the street, in 'private' life" must be refuted and resisted.[24] It is for these reasons that Lee Edelman "embraces" gay identity in his work *Homographesis*. His intention is to "endorse the deployment of 'gay identity'" not as "a predetermined category of human experience" but as a multiply inflected "signifier of resistance" to a rigid binary "*logic* of 'identity'."[25] In other words, each theorist recognizes the for now inescapable nature of the economy of (hetero)sexuality, suggesting a more realistic and complicated negotiation of its identity categories than a Foucauldian anti-identitarian strategy would allow. Here the multidimensions of queer have been identified by many theorists as a potent political force in the quest to complicate and challenge the binarization of sexual identity.

Within queer theory 'sexuality' has become the primary and overarching analytical axis for probing cultural discourses powered by procedures of (hetero)normalization. Warner suggests this to be a theoretical leap, perhaps not unlike the feminist development of gender as an analytic paradigm.[26] In addition to this perspective, however, a partial disarticulation of sexuality from gender has become a defining feature of much queer theory. This move is predicated on the observation that although the two axes are "definitionally intertwined," they are not, as Sedgwick points out, coextensive.[27] Here Sedgwick is drawing on the influential work of Gayle Rubin. In "Thinking Sex," first published in 1984, Rubin called for the analytic separation of gender and sexuality in order "to reflect more accurately their separate social existence."[28] This suggestion was couched in terms of a critique of radical feminist antipornography discourses of the early 1980s. Rubin was attempting to demonstrate, against such claims as those of Catharine MacKinnon, that sexual oppression cannot always or only be explained in terms of gender oppression. It was also crucially influenced by Foucault's work in *The History of Sexuality*, which, for Rubin, suggested that "there were systems other than kinship which had assumed [historically] some kind of relative autonomy."[29] Sedgwick reframes this suggestion of Rubin's in order to posit her infamous "axiom 2": "The study of sexuality is not coextensive with the study of gender; correspondingly, antihomophobic inquiry is not coextensive with feminist inquiry. But we can't know in advance how they will be different."[30] Sedgwick supports this axiom by reminding us that there are numerous dimensions of sexual choice that are not simply reducible to gender. Autoeroticism, intergenerational and interspecies sexuality, sexual choice based on similarities or differences of class, race, and ethnicity are among those modalities of sexuality that lead her to question the prevailing analytic connection of sexuality and gender proffered by much contemporary feminism (30–31).

Sedgwick's analysis is opening up new frontiers for queer theory and the theorization of sexualities. It would also appear to provide fertile ground for the theorization of a particular form of bisexuality: namely, that in which gender is not the determinant of object choice in the last instance.[31] For gender and sexuality are not isomorphic structures. However, the fact that they are treated as such, suggests Sedgwick, leads to a privileging of gender, a category that may well produce a "damaging bias toward heterosocial or heterosexist assumptions."[32] This kind of conceptual move is at the core of queer theory, divesting gender of its analytical primacy in the realm of sexuality. Warner welcomes this disarticulating impulse proposed by Rubin and Sedgwick and reinforces the conceptual incommensurability of the analytic axes of race, class, and gender. He argues that queer is unlike and irreducible to any of these: "Unlike any other identity movements, for example, queerness has always been defined centrally by discourses of morality. There have always been moral prescriptions about how to be a woman or a worker or an Anglo-Saxon; but not about whether to be one."[33]

It seems to me that the centrality and importance of Sedgwick's work for the amplifying field of queer theory extends beyond the recognition of the need for "an analytic distance between gender and sexuality."[34] I suggest that there is a productive theoreticopolitical connection between the primary assumption of *Epistemology of the Closet* and the recent conceptual enactment of queer as a cogent new nomination for cultural radicalism. The phrase "epistemology of the closet" is meant to highlight the way in which ignorance(s) function in Western regimes of knowledge. That is, while "ignorance is ignorance *of* a knowledge," Sedgwick demonstrates that so-called ignorances are far from "pieces of the originary dark," but are "produced by and correspond to particular regimes of truth" (8). Furthermore, "epistemology of the closet" foregrounds the notion that hetero/homosexual definition has been a "presiding master term of the past century" and has thoroughly permeated and inflected "many of the major nodes of thought and knowledge in twentieth-century Western culture as a whole" (11, 1). Sedgwick's task is not only to situate her analysis at some deconstructive site that exposes the contradictions inherent to the hetero/homosexual binary. It is also to propose that struggles of discourse/power are themselves attempts to dictate and benefit from the play of contradiction (11). The connection I am pointing to relates to the definitional ambiguity of the very term queer. As I noted earlier, many queer theorists and activists are stimulated by this sense of ambiguity, or absence of boundaries. Queer appears to potentially escape definition, in its occupancy of the realm of the mysterious, the shady, the *unknown*. Ellis Hanson provides one such example:

> By 'queer', I mean the odd, the uncanny, the undecidable. But, more importantly, I refer to 'queer' sexuality, that no-man's land beyond the heterosexual norm, that categorical domain virtually synonymous with homosexuality and yet wonderfully suggestive of a whole range of sexual possibilities ... that challenge the familiar distinctions between normal and pathological, straight and gay, masculine men and feminine women.[35]

Sedgwick implores us to acknowledge the centrality of the processes of unknowing, or the determinative function of ignorances in Western regimes of truth. Herein lies the connection I am attempting to establish. The invocation of queer theory initiates a double movement. First, it forces a radical encounter between ignorance and knowledge, hetero- and homosexual definition. The implication is that each term of the binaries is therefore central to the structure of discursive formations.[36] It is on these grounds that many queer theorists (and indeed activists) reject the trope of marginality in favor of centrality.[37] Second, queer theory aims to compete for discursive power by activating the contradictions and ambiguities that currently structure sexual definition; that is, to dictate the "operations of such an incoherence of [queer] definition."[38] The queer locale, in this context, could be seen as the enactment, via Sedgwick, of a kind of deconstructive praxis. The ground beneath any articulation of hetero- or homosexual identity is thus unearthed, leaving the epistemological reiteration of the hetero/homosexual structure profoundly destabilized. At least that appears to be the assumption behind queer theory's deconstruction of sexual identity.

But how well has queer theory executed some of these crucial deconstructive moves? How unstable is the hetero/homosexual structure after the queer intervention? And, more important for this study, how does the category of bisexuality figure in this deconstructive scenario?

QUEERING QUEER THEORY

> Any discourse that is based on the questioning of boundary lines must never stop questioning its own.
> —Barbara Johnson 1987

In its role as an umbrella category for the sexually marginalized, queer has been successful in initiating a new and powerful form of political organization. Notwithstanding massive debate regarding its effectiveness,[39] queer has provided a new discursive space through which to foster political alliances across class, gender, racial, and sexual borders. Here the category of bisexuality in the present tense has for the first time found a welcoming space for the articulation of its identity. At the organizational and activist level, this queer impulse is discernible not only in the way bisexuality is being appended to many 'lesbian and gay' groups, but in the way it is being incorporated into 'queer' groups as a part of the very category of queer.[40] In the domain of the academy, however, the situation is markedly different. In the canonical deconstructive texts of queer theory a palpable marginalization at best, and erasure at worst, surrounds the theoretical question of bisexuality.[41] This seems to me rather odd given that the central finding of this book is that the category of bisexuality has been pivotal to the epistemic *construction* of the hetero/homosexual opposition. That this is indeed the case, ought not the category of bisexuality also figure in the *deconstruction* of hetero- and homosexuality? What is the relationship between social constructionism and deconstruction, between history and theory? It is with these questions in mind that I would like now to return to some of these canonical texts in order to interrogate the erasure of bisexuality.

I suggested earlier that the impetus for much queer theory has been Sedgwick's claim that any analysis of "modern Western culture" requires a "critical analysis of modern homo/heterosexual definition."[42] That bisexuality has been pivotal to the discursive construction of this opposition, however, has been completely overlooked by Sedgwick. This is in large part a structural effect of the central organizing principle of her work: the trope of the closet. For Sedgwick this trope is a useful metaphor for interrogating the "relations of the known and the unknown, the explicit and the inexplicit" (3) as they have served to structure modern hetero/homosexual definition. Sexual definition and, indeed, meaning in Western culture itself, she quite rightly argues, have been themselves structured around, among others, the oppositions secrecy/disclosure, knowledge/ignorance, masculine/feminine, natural/artificial, same/different, active/passive, in/out. However, what Sedgwick does not consider is the fact that in the history of discourses of sexuality it is the force of these very oppositions that has served to elide bisexuality from the present tense.

As I have demonstrated in part 1 of this book, bisexuality has been rendered an artifact of our evolutionary prehistory, a state outside or prior to culture or civilization, a myth, a catachresis, and a (utopian) sexual impossibility. This is precisely because bisexuality cannot be represented through these binary formulations, blurring as it does any easy distinction of their terms (by in fact partaking of each of the polar terms). In order to secure its binary structure, one of the primary moves of the epistemology of the closet is to repudiate bisexuality, or else render it consonant with its binary logic. In the former, bisexuality is set up as an interior exclusion; in the latter, it is subsumed either by hetero- or homosexuality. By failing to interrogate the interior exclusions and binary appropriations instantiated and performed by the epistemology of the closet, Sedgwick's analysis thus falls short of analyzing its terms. And as Maria Pramaggiore argues, "closets are not definitive: they continuously dissolve and reproduce themselves. Nor are they comprehensive: the logic of the closet does not define all sexualities."[43]

Sedgwick does usefully expose the way the hetero/homosexual opposition inheres in and structures—through its "ineffaceable marking" of fundamental binarisms—modern Western thought. She also brilliantly traces the conceptual contradictions responsible for the (continuing) "modern crisis of homo/heterosexual definition" since the turn of the century. By crisis Sedgwick is not celebrating the "self-corrosive efficacy of the contradictions inherent to these definitional binarisms." In other words, discourses concerned with securing sexual definition are not about to disappear as a result of an "incoherence of definition." Rather, what she is attempting to highlight is the way these contradictions drive discourses of sexuality. In the history of sexuality, therefore, "contests for discursive power" can be seen as "competitions" to "set the terms of, and profit in some way from, the operations of such an incoherence of definition."[44] An analysis of the centrality of this definitional incoherence thus comprises the primary undertaking of *Epistemology of the Closet*. Yet despite her deconstructive labors, Sedgwick does not inquire into precisely *how* discourses of sexuality vie for "rhetorical leverage" (11), that is, *how* modern homo/heterosexual definition is (in)coherently instantiated. As I have demonstrated throughout this discussion, bisexuality is the third term in the hetero/homosexual binary that has absorbed and regulated the contradictions inherent to the reproduction of modern sexual definition. In ignoring bisexuality and, indeed, the metonymical association of bisexuality with binary contradiction, Sedgwick's deconstructive framework does not go far enough in *critically analyzing* modern hetero/homosexual definition. Doing this more effectively would require sustained attention, as I have suggested, to the interior exclusions constitutive of the epistemology of the closet. As it stands, therefore, Sedgwick, perhaps like Foucault, appears content with a description rather than explanation of the production of hetero/homosexual definition. For theorists of bisexuality, however, such a rhetorical analysis only repeats the problematic erasure of bisexuality that is the closet's point of departure.

Diana Fuss's edited collection *Inside/Out: Lesbian Theories, Gay Theories* is another of the canonical texts of queer theory that effects a similar marginalization and erasure of bisexuality. In her introduction to this collection, Fuss follows Sedgwick's lead in analyzing the discursive mechanics of modern hetero/homosexual definition. In a brief theoretical analysis she argues that it is "another related opposition"—that of inside/outside—that provides the structural foundations for the opposition of hetero- and homosexuality. Fuss raises a series of questions in order to foreground her analysis: "How do outsides and insides come about? What philosophical and critical operations or modes produce the specious distinction between a pure and natural heterosexual inside and an impure and unnatural homosexual outside? Where exactly, in this borderline sexual economy, does one identity leave off and the other begin?" (2).

Drawing more explicitly from Derridean deconstruction, Fuss appears to be asking questions from a position that cannot fail to explore the location of bisexuality in this binary economy. First, she is alluding to the fallacy of a pure inside and a pure outside through which to distinguish hetero- from homosexuality. Second, she appears to be setting herself the task of inquiring into precisely *how* these homogeneous fallacies are epistemologically ("philosophical and critical operations") created. And third, she is directly addressing the question of the very threshold between these two sexual identities, that is, the spatial, temporal, and discursive points where the boundaries between hetero- and homosexuality are blurred. Bisexuality is unmistakably implicated in every one of these questions. Yet Fuss is confusing on this point, as is evidenced by the problematic parenthetical appearance of bisexuality in the following fourth question. She asks, "And what gets left out of the inside/outside, heterosexual/homosexual opposition, an opposition which could at least plausibly be said to secure its seemingly inviolable dialectical structure only by assimilating and internalizing other sexualities (bisexuality, transvestism, transsexualism . . .) to its own rigid polar logic?" (2).

There are a number of problems with this account. Michael du Plessis argues that the identities Fuss "lists as somehow in excess of 'homosexuality' and 'heterosexuality' are cordoned off by those parentheses from the body of her own text, taken into consideration only in order to be more insidiously expelled."[45] What I argue, though, is that this rendering of bisexuality as excessive or Other to hetero- and homosexuality implies, rather problematically, the existence of a mode of bisexuality outside the economy of (hetero)sexuality and its binary logic. As I have demonstrated throughout this discussion, however, bisexuality *as a concept of sexuality* is historically and epistemologically implicated in this binarized economy, unthinkable outside its terms. Additionally, and concomitantly, Fuss seems to come close to suggesting that the appropriation of bisexuality by the inside/outside, heterosexual/homosexual binaries works *only*, therefore, to *secure* their "seemingly dialectical structure." She overlooks the fact that not only is bisexuality internal to the dialectical structure of hetero- and homosexuality, but that bisexuality, in a different yet related definitional guise, preceded and conditioned its historical invention. That is, before its appearance in the economy of (hetero)sexuality—indeed, before the construction of this economy—bisexuality was a mythological and evolutionary concept constructed to explain the origins of male and female sex difference. Fuss is not referring to this sense of bisexuality, however. Instead, she is referring to bisexuality as a mode of sexuality. Had she historicized the dialectical structure of hetero- and homosexuality, therefore, she might have recognized that bisexuality has served *both* to secure and, simultaneously, to disrupt its boundaries. For instance, within discourses of sexology, Freudian psychoanalysis, and gay liberation, bisexuality has been invoked as an explanatory causal principle in the production of hetero- and homosexuality. Yet within the very same discourses bisexuality has been obscured from the present tense and even repudiated at the very point when it threatens to blur the boundaries between the two.[46]

In fairness to Fuss, however, it is possible that I have misread the thrust of her claim that the hetero/homosexual opposition secures "its seemingly inviolable dialectical structure only by assimilating and internalizing other sexualities (bisexuality, transvestism, transsexualism . . .) to its own rigid polar logic." A more 'faithful' reading might be that, with respect to bisexuality at least, it can *only* be accommodated by the hetero/homosexual opposition if it is to conform to the inherent binary logic. In this way, some of the claims of this book with regard to the logical functioning of this opposition may appear to be in agreement with Fuss. On one hand I believe this is the case, and that my first reading interpreted this sentence by ignoring the term "only." On the other hand, however, Fuss appears to diverge from my reading of bisexuality in a way that I think justifies my original critique. To say that bisexuality is *assimilated* and *internalized* by the hetero/homosexual opposition is, as I noted above, to impute a kind of distinctness to bisexuality. This suggests that bisexuality undergoes a kind of 'conversion' by binary logic and that it can exist as a mode of sexuality outside this oppositional framework. My argument, on the contrary, is that bisexuality is an epistemological part of this framework, *unthinkable outside of binary logic*.

An obvious riposte might well be that Fuss is in fact implicitly referring to a notion of bisexuality that our binary logic refuses to acknowledge and that this idea is scarcely different from what I refer to as the disavowal of bisexuality in the present tense. Even if this is the case, however, the notion of bisexuality in the present tense is also, as I have repeatedly shown, produced through the workings of binary logic. Any concept of bisexuality can only ever be one of the binary logic's *effects*. By thus situating some version of bisexuality *outside* the hetero/homosexual binary, Fuss is in fact implying precisely what my original interpretation suggests: that all versions of bisexuality *inside* the hetero/homosexual binary *only* reinforce or "secure" its "dialectical structure." Yet as we have seen, in the history of sexuality this is only part of the story. Another part is that bisexuality simultaneously *disrupts*, at every turn, and within the very terms of binary logic, the dialectical structure of hetero/homosexuality.

Fuss's figuring of bisexuality highlights a deeper problem with her invocation of the inside/outside binary. Inscribed as Other to the hetero/homosexual opposition, bisexuality is situated *outside* the monogamic and monosexual figuring of the very 'couple' inside and outside. It is therefore only possible for Fuss to secure the dialectical structure of this binary *as an explanatory principle* by in turn deploying its self-constituting binary logic. The law of this logic is the law of noncontradiction. Each term in a binary, therefore, is either A or not-A. Any term that is both A and not-A, or, neither A nor not-A, is excluded. Fuss relies on this law, however, by failing to consider what it excludes: the logics of both/and, neither/nor. This effectively repudiates the Möbius-like figure that is both inside and outside simultaneously, yet reducible to neither. In reading sexuality through this structure, Fuss aims to turn the categories of hetero- and homosexuality *inside/out*. However, this only demonstrates their logical interdependence. In order to go one step further in deconstructing the hetero/homosexual structure, Fuss would need to mobilize the repudiated logics and explore the undecidable within the terms of this dialectical structure. An analysis of bisexuality as undecidable, as both inside and outside, heterosexual and homosexual (yet at the same time none of these), is one crucial way of doing this. However, for Fuss, bisexuality is not identified as the third term in this epistemological configuration, but is bracketed out of the analysis. So rather than fully expose the workings of binary logic and the exclusions it attempts to hide, Fuss in fact takes this logic at its word and reinforces its modus operandi.[47]

Yet another startling example of this tendency to render bisexuality parenthetical to queer analysis is Lee Edelman's recent book *Homographesis*. It exhibits a striking similarity to the case of Fuss. One of the primary objectives of the book is to "explore the determining relation between 'homosexuality' and 'identity' as both have been constructed in modern Euro-American societies."[48] Following Sedgwick's lead, therefore, he also locates homosexuality as central to any cultural "enterprise of . . . identity-determination" (xv). In yet another self-avowedly Derridean mode, this entails and aspires to a deconstruction of the heterosexual logic of identity. Edelman performs this analysis by tracing the rhetorical and contradictory operations of sameness and difference through which (homosexual) identity is instantiated. He suggests that homosexuality is constructed as an *anxious* effect of the very crisis of representation itself. Indeed, and more specifically, "'homosexuality'," he argues, "is constructed to bear the cultural burden of the rhetoricity inherent in 'sexuality' itself" (xiv). Homosexuality thereby stands in for and serves "to contain . . . the unknowability of the sexual" (xv).

Interestingly, Edelman affirms his project as a "work of *gay* theory" (xvi). Despite this invocation, however, the nomination 'gay' is not premised on the stability of a fixed referent. Instead, it is deployed as a "signifier of resistance," a deconstructive tool used to challenge the logic of identity. In other words, homosexuality becomes the privileged deconstructive site for this project because it is "'gay sexuality' [that] functions in the modern West as the very agency of sexual meaningfulness, the construct without which sexual meaning, and therefore, in a larger sense, meaning itself, becomes virtually unthinkable" (xv). Scrutinizing a wide range of cultural productions, *Homographesis* is indicative of the queer deconstructive impulse determined to work the opposition of hetero/homosexuality to the point of epistemological frustration.

What is most startling about Edelman's work is not the almost complete absence of any discussion of bisexuality, although this is in itself rather astonishing (bisexuality does not even make it into the book's index). Rather, it is the fact that bisexuality is called forth in the preface by way of parenthetical reference only to be dismissed as antithetical to the theoretical project of deconstruction. Curiously, however, this reference occurs in the context of Edelman locating his work under the rubric of gay theory. Like Fuss's parenthesizing of bisexuality, Edelman's takes place in one rather complex, ambiguous, and perhaps even contradictory sentence:

> By retaining the signifier of a specific sexuality within the hetero/homo binarism (a binarism more effectively reinforced than disrupted by the "third term" of bisexuality) even as it challenges the ideology of that categorical dispensation, this enterprise intends to mark its avowal of the multiple sexualities, the various modes of interaction and relation, that the hierarchizing imperative of the hetero/homo binarism attempts to discredit. (xvi)

Why does bisexuality simultaneously appear and disappear in this context despite Edelman's claim to *avow* that which the "hetero/homo binarism attempts to discredit"? It seems that Edelman is attempting to reassure readers that the theoretical entity of 'gay' need not be seen as simply reiterative of the logic of identity and the hetero/homosexual opposition. Is he here attempting to respond to or to reject in advance the claim that the epistemic category of bisexuality might be equally or better positioned to expose the rhetorical operations of sameness and difference in the construction of sexual identity? If this were the case, Edelman's move would scarcely be different from an *anxious* gesture of containment. Is homosexuality the only category in the hetero/homosexual binary that provides deconstructive leverage for challenging and exposing the stability and fixity of sexual identity? What kind of reductive and essentializing labor is performed on the category of bisexuality in order to render it mere reinforcement to this binary?

Edelman appears to be undertaking, perhaps in Foucauldian fashion, an *observation* of "how 'homo' and 'hetero', 'same' and 'different', switch places" (xviii–xix) in the rhetorical operations of hegemonic discourse. Yet nowhere does he consider how the category of bisexuality might be implicated in this economy. In fact, such an analysis appears to be wittingly foreclosed in advance by unknowingly performing a "metaphorizing totalization" (11) on bisexuality. Yet in the history of discourses of sexuality, as I have demonstrated in part 1, bisexuality is *both* the stabilizing *and* destabilizing element in the epistemic construction of sexual identity. Indeed, it has been the category through and against which sexual identity has been discursively constructed. Edelman's claim that bisexuality only reinforces the hetero/homosexual binary thus ignores the historical and epistemological figuring of bisexuality. Like 'homosexuality', it cannot be represented as a fixed and stable category.

In addition to this, Edelman fails to interrogate the way in which the (absent) presence of bisexuality marks the play of sameness and difference. He quite rightly suggests that "homosexuality marks the otherness, the difference internal to 'sexuality' and sexual discourse itself" (xix). What he means is that the logic of identity has installed homosexuality in order to contain the internal crisis of meaning engendered by the "rhetoricity inherent in 'sexuality' itself" (xiv). However, he does not ask what the logic of identity must exclude or disavow in order to perform this operation. That is, how does the discourse of sexual identity ensure the mutual exclusivity of sameness and difference, hetero- and homosexuality? Clearly, bisexuality must be disavowed for these operations. For in relation to hetero- and homosexuality, bisexuality is both same and different. Edelman ignores the fact that it is the repudiation of bisexuality that makes possible, indeed makes coherent, the very switching of places between hetero and homo. His project of "locat[ing] the critical force of homosexuality at the very point of discrimination between sameness and difference" (20) therefore repeats the gesture of bisexual disavowal that sustains the logic of (sexual) identity.

In *Making Things Perfectly Queer* Alexander Doty provides one of the few self-critical comments regarding his neglect in theorizing bisexuality as a position for reading mass cultural texts: "Looking through this book, I realize I have given rather cursory attention to specifically bisexual positions. Since examining bisexuality seems crucial in many ways to theorizing nongay and nonlesbian queerness—indeed, some see bisexuality *as* queerness—I consider the absence in this book of any extended discussion of bisexuality and mass culture a major omission."[49] This realization was not enough or came too late to force a conceptual rethinking of his project, however. Even more problematically, this assertion was bracketed out from his text, marginalized to an endnote. Ruth Goldman has suggested that despite Doty's marginalization of bisexuality, his willingness to "broaden his own discourse on queerness to include bisexuality can serve as an example/foundation for other queer theorists to build upon."[50] Instead of identifying "specifically bisexual positions" or "bisexual texts,"[51] however, I would suggest that bisexuality might also be deployed as a means of troubling the opposition of identification/desire that has worked to construct as distinct the spectator positions of gay, lesbian, and heterosexual. In this way, bisexuality would represent more than a mere additive to the list of discrete categories of sexual identity. Rather, bisexuality might potentially disrupt, indeed queer, theories of spectatorship that reproduce these viewing/reading positions by reifying gender in the theorization of spectator identifications. In this context, bisexuality might better function, then, to challenge the concept of sexuality or sexual identity itself.

I noted at the beginning of this chapter that one of the foundational principles of poststructuralist-inspired queer theory is the belief in the relationality of identity. Yet it is clear from the foregoing analysis that many of the canonized works of this body of knowledge have fallen short in their examination and application of this principle. Far from being identified as a pivotal logical and relational component of hetero/homosexuality, bisexuality has instead been parenthesized or cast outside the constitutive terms of this binarism. Bisexuality has, in other words, once again been erased from the present tense.

GENDER TROUBLE IN QUEER THEORY

> Queer means to fuck with gender.
> —Cherry Smyth 1991

So how are we to understand the erasure of bisexuality in some of the fundamental works of the queer canon? Earlier I suggested that for queer theory the category of sexuality has opened up a promising discursive space for interrogating and deconstructing Western discourses constituted through the hetero/homosexual binarism. As the editors of *The Lesbian and Gay Studies Reader* point out, "Lesbian/gay[/queer] studies does for *sex* and *sexuality* approximately what women's studies does for gender."[52] To say that the work of Foucault has been enormously influential in this development is to understate the case. His genealogical account of the emergence of sexuality as coextensive with modern subjectivity has been absorbed as axiomatic to the field of queer theory.[53] It appears, however, that this productive deployment of Foucault's work has also brought with it a constraining limitation: namely, a problematic relationship to gender.

Increasingly, there is a distinct concern, particularly among feminist theorists, that the category of sexuality has become reified to the point of exclusion in discourses of queer theory. Feminism and the category of gender, so the argument goes, are being cast as redundant explanatory principles as a result of queer theory's attempt to disarticulate gender and sexuality. In this section I will begin by tracing and extending these arguments in order to put forward an argument of my own in relation to bisexuality. I will argue that despite its productive potential, the disarticulation of gender and sexuality, and the Foucauldian-inflected reification of the latter, has proceeded in such a way as to occlude bisexuality from analytic view.

Judith Butler has recently problematized the above claim made by the editors of *The Lesbian and Gay Studies Reader*. She argues that it represents an unwitting, yet *aggressive* and *violent*, discursive appropriation of sexuality as the "proper object" of gay/lesbian/queer studies over and against a feminism whose proper object is gender.[54] This creates, Butler suggests, more than a tendentious methodological distinction between feminism and gay/lesbian/queer studies. It serves as well to make feminist inquiry into sexuality obsolete. In interrogating the terms of the analogy between feminism and gay/lesbian/queer in her essay "Against Proper Objects," Butler claims that the analogy falls down around the editors' invocation of a Foucauldian-inflected category of 'sex': "The editors lead us through analogy from a feminism in which gender and sex are conflated to a notion of lesbian and gay studies in which 'sex' encompasses and exceeds the purview of feminism: 'sex' in this second instance would include not only questions of identity and attribute (female or male), but discourses of sensation, acts, and sexual practice as well" (2). Butler argues that the category of 'sex' is common both to feminism and gay/lesbian/queer studies, yet this "commonality must be denied" (2). The "implicit argument," she suggests, "is that lesbian and gay studies does precisely what feminism is said to do, but does it in a more expansive and complex way" (4).

Butler identifies the appropriation of Gayle Rubin's essay "Thinking Sex" as the gesture serving to authorize the methodological founding of lesbian/gay/queer studies. However, she argues that a decontextualized appropriation of Rubin's call for an analytic separation of gender and sexuality effects not only a significant "restriction of the scope of feminist scholarship" (8, 21), but breaks the long-standing coalition between feminism and lesbian/gay studies. While I remain unconvinced of the mechanics of Butler's argument as it pivots on and is extrapolated from the editors' introduction to *The Lesbian and Gay Studies Reader*—an argument made, I should add, with almost no reference to the canonical texts of queer theory[55]—she has identified an emergent tendency that is perhaps more usefully explored through a grounded analysis of specific queer texts.[56]

Biddy Martin takes a first step in this direction in her essay "Sexualities without Genders and Other Queer Utopias."[57] She provides the basis for a more productive and grounded analysis of some of the issues raised by Butler. Despite welcoming the possibilities opened up by disarticulating gender and sexuality, like Butler, Martin is concerned also that this is taking place at the expense of feminism and important feminist destabilizations of the category of gender. Sexuality, she argues, is too often being cast as that which "exceeds, transgresses, or supersedes gender."[58] Gender, and indeed feminism, on the other hand, are increasingly being framed as fixed and constraining, hampering the celebration of queerity.[59]

Martin argues that Sedgwick's work is indicative of this tendency. In "axiom 2" of *Epistemology of the Closet*, Sedgwick attempts to keep analytically distinct the two senses of the category of sex: chromosomal sex and sex as sexuality/act/fantasy/pleasure. She goes on to suggest that the latter is "virtually impossible to situate on a map delimited by the feminist-defined sex/gender distinction."[60] Instead, Sedgwick stresses that the development of an antihomophobic discourse more suited to an analysis of sexuality "as an alternative analytic axis" is not just required, but "a particularly urgent project" (32). In collapsing sex and gender "more simply under the rubric 'gender'," Sedgwick puts forward the claim that sexuality is inflected by a form of conceptual ambiguity in a way unknown to the category of gender. Rendered the more fixed, gender is considered the *proper object* of feminist discourse and is less suited to deconstructive analysis. Sexuality, on other hand, is the more apt object of deconstruction, exceeding "the bare choreographies of procreation," perhaps even situated as "the very opposite" to chromosomal sex, to gender (29).

Martin argues that it is one thing to posit the irreducibility of sexuality and gender, but quite another to react to this, as does Sedgwick, "by making them more distinct, even opposed to one another."[61] She also objects to the way Sedgwick privileges sexuality and defines antihomophobic analysis not just against but over and above monolithic and fixed notions of both feminism and gender. For example, sexuality, argues Sedgwick, "could occupy . . . even more than 'gender' the polar position of the relational, the social/symbolic, the constructed, the variable, the representational."[62] Moreover, sex (an "array of acts, expectations, narratives, pleasures," etc.) and sexuality, unlike gender, "tend to represent the full spectrum of positions between the most intimate and the most social, the most predetermined and the most aleatory, the most physically rooted and the most symbolically infused, the most innate and the most learned, the most autonomous and the most relational traits of being" (29). Sedgwick perhaps anticipates the kind of feminist objection raised by Martin with the reassurance that she is not calling for "any epistemological or ontological privileging of an axis of sexuality over an axis of gender" (34). However, in reifying sexuality as the analytically autonomous and "apter deconstructive object" (34), Sedgwick is thus able to install the hetero/homosexual opposition as *the* pivotal organizing principle of Western thought over and above that of male/female. Sexuality thereby becomes the *proper object* not of feminist but of antihomophobic inquiry (as though the two are not overlapping).[63]

The problems encountered with this reified account of sexuality and its disarticulation from gender are made even more palpable when we examine the figure of bisexuality. As I discussed earlier, Sedgwick's epistemological mapping of the logic of the closet rests on a repudiation and erasure of bisexuality. Moreover, it has been my argument that bisexuality has in fact regulated the axes of gender and sexuality. Yet despite Sedgwick's acknowledgment that these axes are "inextricable from one another,"[64] her analysis of modern hetero/homosexual definition ignores this very crucial space of overlap between gender and sexuality. Take, for example, her attempt to map the "models" of "gay/straight definition" through which homosexuality has been articulated historically. Sedgwick offers a table with two separate horizontal rows for sexuality and gender. Each row is then vertically divided by two columns, one representing "separatist" models, the other "integrative" or "transitive" ones. On the one hand, homosexuality has been defined *sexually*: as an essentialist minority (separatist) *and* as a universal and cultural potential (integrative). On the other hand, it has been defined in terms of *gender identification*: male and female homosexual desire as a natural effect of male and female gender identification respectively (separatist) *and* as a result of cross-gender identification (integrative).[65]

While this model captures some of the contradictions and cross-identifications made possible within and between the separatist and integrative axes of homosexual definition, it remains in the end only a model, as Sedgwick herself calls it, of "gay/straight definition" (88). Bisexuality is incorporated at best only as a universalizing potential; at worst it is implicitly collapsed into hetero- and homosexualities. Sedgwick's reliance on hegemonic constructions of sexual identity thereby repeats the exclusionary gesture necessary to sustain the workings of binary logic. Moreover, her unraveling of gender and sexuality as distinct axes has left her unable to accommodate, as du Plessis points out, "people for whom sexuality and gender may match up differently." This does "damage," argues du Plessis, "to the realities of transgender sexualities and bisexual genders."[66] I would argue also that this kind of exclusionary mapping of sexuality serves to sustain the analytic distance Sedgwick has installed between feminism and gay/lesbian/queer studies. That is, bisexuality (and indeed transgenderism) is the pawn that is forced out in an act of methodological and disciplinary secessionism.

A similar tendency to privilege and reify sexuality over and against gender is apparent in Fuss's work in "Inside/Out." Fuss takes the hetero/homosexual binarism as her prioritized point of deconstructive departure. Her primary task is to expose only the interdependence of the hetero on the homo; that is, the homo as always already inside the hetero. However, rather than examine the inextricable enmeshment of the hetero/homo, inside/outside oppositions with that of male/female, Fuss follows a path similar to Sedgwick's by separating too radically gender and sexuality. This move takes place in her discussion of what is "most urgently" needed in current "gay and lesbian theory": that is, a "theory of sexual borders" that can take into account and promote organizational strategies required to address "the new cultural and sexual arrangements occasioned by the movements and transmutations of pleasure in the social field."[67] This new theory, it would seem, is a queer theory of sexuality. In the next sentence Fuss does invoke the opposition of gender, but only to dethrone it as the primary paradigm through which to read sexuality: "Recent and past work on the question of sexual difference has yet to meet this pressing need, largely because, as Stephen Heath accurately targets the problem, our notion of sexual difference all too often subsumes sexual differences, upholding 'a defining difference of man/woman at the expense of gay, lesbian, bisexual, and indeed *hetero* heterosexual reality'" (5). This quote of Heath's is also part of an argument that gender and sexuality "can and should be separated from one another."[68] However, like Rubin and Sedgwick, Heath is formulating such a claim against Catharine MacKinnon's radical feminist collapsing of sexuality as a mere expression of gender.[69] So by drawing on Heath in order to fault recent and past feminist work on sexual difference, Fuss has not exactly remained faithful to the quote's original context. She is also suggesting that the vanguard position for this new *theory of sexual borders* is not feminism but gay/lesbian/queer studies. "Gay and lesbian readers of culture," she suggests, have a "responsibility . . . to reshape and to reorient the field of sexual difference to include sexual differences."[70] Curiously, this responsibility is conferred primarily, or perhaps only, on "gay and lesbian readers." Where are antihomophobic heterosexual, feminist, bisexual, or transgendered readers of culture situated in relation to this urgent political task?

I suggest that Fuss's failure to incorporate these 'others' within the vanguard of this new sexual theory is the complex product of the problematic reification of sexuality over and above gender. Let us recall the opening statement of her introduction to *Inside/Out:* "The philosophical opposition between 'heterosexual' and 'homosexual' . . . has always been constructed on the foundations of . . . the couple 'inside' and 'outside'" (1). Here Fuss has immediately elided or at the very least suspended a discussion of gender as an opposition that also fundamentally undergirds the hetero/homosexual opposition. She does invoke gender, but only in order to foreground her deconstructive analysis of the hetero/homosexual, inside/outside binaries. Homosexuality, she quite rightly points out, "is produced inside the dominant discourse of sexual difference as its necessary outside, but this is not to say that the homo exerts no pressure on the hetero nor that this outside stands in any simple relation of exteriority to the inside" (5). Fuss indeed seems to be acknowledging the inexplicable interlacing of gender (sexual difference) and sexuality, the latter seen as the expurgated inside of the former. However, she appears to effect a curious analytic slippage whereby gender, or sexual difference, is invoked only to be immediately subsumed or displaced by heterosexuality.[71] Homosexuality is then called forth as the internally erected border that works "to define and defend" the heterosexual inside. It is identified as the subversive element "occupying the frontier position of inside out" in the "discourse of sexual difference," "neither completely outside" it "nor wholly inside it either."[72]

In representing (homo)sexuality as transgressive or excessive of sexual difference, Fuss is attempting to gesture toward a theory of sexuality not beholden to an analysis of gender. The axis of sexuality appears to be superimposed on the axis of gender, subsuming gender as a subsidiary component. Lee Edelman appears to perform a similar move. He suggests that "where heterosexuality . . . seeks to assure the sameness or purity internal to the categorical 'opposites' of anatomical 'sex' . . . homosexuality would multiply the differences that desire can apprehend in ways that menace the internal coherence of the sexed identities that the order of heterosexuality demands."[73] Again, it is homosexuality that is identified as the subversive agent. I would argue, however, that this maneuver performed by Fuss and Edelman reads as an allegory of the relationship being instantiated between feminism and queer theory. Feminism is metonymically associated with gender, queer theory with (homo)sexuality, the latter in a relationship of subversive excess to the former. In other words, queer theory is that through which Fuss's new theory of sexual borders and Edelman's project of *Homographesis* can be advanced over a redundant feminism. As Butler puts it so well:

> If gender is said to belong to feminism, and sexuality in the hands of lesbian and gay [and queer] studies is conceived as liberated from gender, then the sexuality that is "liberated" from feminism will be one which suspends the reference to masculine and feminine, reenforcing the refusal to mark that difference, which is the conventional way in which the masculine has achieved the status of the "sex" which is one.[74]

Fuss's new theory of sexual borders, I would add, appears to be the exclusive domain not of antihomophobic feminists, bisexuals, and transgenders, but of 'gays and lesbians'. For it is they who are seen to occupy the subversive "frontier position" of homosexuality. If this is in fact the case, this move of Fuss's sits uncomfortably within a deconstructive framework concerned with challenging the identity paradigm. It would also seem at odds with a deconstructive psychoanalysis that would problematize the specious conflation of identity or subject-position and subjectivity.

Despite acknowledging the fact that homosexuality is constituted inside the discourse of gender or sexual difference, Fuss and Edelman tend to construct sexuality as synonymous with the hetero/homosexual opposition, distinct from and superimposed over the top of this discourse. Partially displacing gender, sexuality (or the hetero/homosexual opposition), is then identified as the privileged upper layer of deconstructive analysis. In other words, there is a sense in both Fuss's and Edelman's work that sexuality must first be deconstructed in order to prize it away from, and thus render it autonomous of gender. However, this reification of a sexuality disarticulated from and epistemologically privileged over gender obfuscates an analysis of their mutual interrelation. As a result, an analysis of bisexuality as the figure shoring up binary sexual identity is occluded. For it is bisexuality that has not just traversed but historically and epistemologically regulated the axes of sexuality *and* gender in the continuing production of hetero- and homosexual identities.

CONCLUSION: "ALWAYS HISTORICIZE!"

Like Foucault, and perhaps partly as a result of his enduring legacy, some of the prominent queer theorists have rendered gender "historically subordinate to sexuality."[75] As I have argued, however, sexuality was constituted as an effect of a difference internal to phallocentric gender. That is to say, that sexuality was produced around crises or deviations of normative gender. So the axis of sexuality was never entirely, or even nearly, separate from that of gender in the modern economy of (hetero)sexuality. Sexuality was produced in and through gender.

Queer theorists are certainly cognizant of this historical fact. Indeed, it is upon this knowledge that the call to separate sexuality from gender is predicated. In other words, it is because of this historical reduction of sexuality to gender dynamics that such a future-oriented project to disarticulate the two is undertaken. However, this future-oriented project of the present appears to have distorted the terms of a deconstructive project oriented to dismantling figurations of sexuality inherited from the past. That is, it is perhaps a presentist tendency in queer theory that has undermined more properly historicized deconstructive analyses. In subordinating gender to sexuality and insisting on a degree of analytic autonomy for the latter, queer theorists have thought the two axes vertically or hierarchically rather than relationally and obliquely. As a result, bisexuality, an important historical and epistemological regulator of the axes of gender and sexuality, has been elided in the present tense and, indeed, in almost any sense at all.

Here it is perhaps pertinent to offer as a reminder Fredric Jameson's infamous slogan: "Always historicize!"[76] Clearly, deconstructive critique of all kinds presupposes the historicity of identity categories. However, in the case of the queer deconstructive theory I have examined, a reliance on this presumption has meant the evacuation of a significant part of the very history at the heart of sexuality's historicity. As I argued at the beginning of this book, *any* deconstruction of historically overdetermined identity concepts and categories must engage the history on whose behalf it speaks. In this way, historicization and deconstruction might be seen in a more productive light as part of the same process.

Part of the problem also lies, as I have mentioned, in what appears to be a tension, or, as Lisa Duggan puts it, a strained relationship, between the fields of gay/lesbian history and queer theory.[77] The lack of critical and self-reflexive dialogue between the two fields has restricted the potential of constructionist and deconstructive analyses of sexuality alike. With regard to the latter, though, the failure to acknowledge a debt to gay/lesbian history has left queer theorists uncritically reliant upon a historiography of sexuality built squarely around the identity paradigm. Recall that within this paradigm, constructionist historians have been concerned primarily with tracing the emergence of homosexual identities, less often with tracing the epistemological processes informing their production. Figured as a nonidentity, however, as the Other to sexual identity itself, the category of bisexuality has been occluded in this historical field of vision. This has meant that, for queer theory, the identity paradigm, and thus the hetero/homosexual opposition, has been unwittingly reproduced in a presentist deconstructive theory derivative of such historical accounts. So despite the assault on essentializing notions of identity, queer theory has neglected to address important aspects of the relationality of identity within the very history of (bi)sexuality.

What I have been trying to do in this book is go some way toward initiating a productive exchange between the respective fields of queer theory and constructionist gay/lesbian history. Despite the focus of this chapter being the terrain of queer deconstructive theories and not specific lesbian and gay history texts, it is a queer deconstructive rereading of the historiography of sexuality *produced in large part by these texts* that has enabled me to mount a historical critique of queer theory itself.

However, queer theory's uncritical reliance on an identity-based historiography is not the only factor contributing to the erasure of bisexuality. As I have also shown, in betraying the foundational principle of the relationality of identity, the *theoretical* terms of queer theory's own discourse have impeded an analysis of the epistemological function of bisexuality within the hetero/homosexual structure. Efforts to unpack the workings of binary logic in representations of sexuality have concentrated on the dialectical relationship between the polar terms hetero- and homosexuality. Each term has thus been shown to rely on the other for its definition. This suggests, in other words, that the oppositional terms are not in fact distinct and exclusive. However, in order for binary logic to succeed in positing these binary terms as distinct and exclusive there must be a simultaneous process of repressing, disavowing, or excluding those elements of the Other; elements each term has relied upon to posit its identity but that would undermine its fallacious homogeneity. Each term must be seen in its totality, therefore, to be *either* one *or* the Other (the logic of either/or). I have been arguing that this reveals only one (extremely important) aspect of binary logic's mode of functioning. Another interrelated aspect of the law of noncontradiction is the prohibition of binary logic's Other, the logic of both/and, and this is an area queer theorists have been less thorough in examining. In order for something to be only one or the other, it is therefore necessary to prohibit a term being both one *and* the other. Anything that is both one and the other contradicts the logic of either/or and must be repressed, disavowed, or excluded. As we have seen, in the hetero/homosexual structure the position of both/and is occupied by bisexuality; hence its contradictory presence must be erased. By focusing primarily on the dialectical interrelation of polar terms, at the expense of examining the prohibited logic of both/and, queer theorists have worked in concert with binary logic's either/or model and the accompanying erasure of bisexuality.[78]

[|]

To conclude this chapter I return to the issue of bisexuality's relationship to the interlocking axes of gender and sexuality. The fact that the queer deconstructive analyses I have discussed have problematically subordinated gender to sexuality does not mean that the move to disarticulate the two is therefore flawed. Rather, it is a matter of method—the *way* such disarticulations have been carried out—that is the problem. For such a move is as necessary as ever, it seems to me. Installing an analytical distance between gender and sexuality enables the two to be cast in a more productive *relation* to one another. This does not mean that they are always autonomous and that they do not overlap and mutually constitute one another in many cases. What it does mean, however, is that such a distance between gender and sexuality opens up other discursive spaces for thinking certain forms of identity, sexuality, desire, and pleasure rather differently. It is here that bisexuality *as a polymorphic analytic category* has much to offer feminism and queer theory. Among its many meanings, forms, and uses, bisexuality can, on the one hand, *foreground* gender in analyses of identity, sexuality, desire, and pleasure—and thereby highlight the interconnections of gender and sexuality. On the other hand, it can also *displace* gender as the primary means for understanding certain forms of identity, sexuality, desire, and pleasure. For as queer and bisexual theorists have made all too clear, some routes of identification, desire and pleasure have little if anything to do with gender. It would seem that bisexuality thus speaks well to the queer impulse to disarticulate gender and sexuality.[79]

Michael du Plessis has suggested recently that "bisexuals may gain something by keeping our [sic] distance from the thriving scene of queer theory."[80] I suggest, on the contrary, that bisexuality is already implicated, and importantly so, within the field of queer theory. While queer has not fared very well so far in theorizing bisexuality, this is certainly no reason to abandon it. In fact, it is reason to deploy queer all the more, to keep queer(ing). As I have tried to demonstrate in this book, by employing bisexuality as an analytic category *within a framework informed by queer theory*, I have been able to turn queer back on itself, to turn queer inside/out, to queer *queer*. And it is this kind of self-reflexivity, this ability to incorporate a critique of its own discursive operations and boundaries, this ability to think identity categories *relationally*, that is so exciting about queer. And this is also, it seems to me, to think bisexuality most productively in relation to sexuality, to gender, and to queer theory. In this way, therefore, the theorization of bisexuality has served as a *rejoinder* for feminism and queer theory, and can, as I have shown, facilitate more sophisticated and better historicized deconstructive accounts of the relationship between the registers of (among others) gender and sexuality. After all, what are queer theory and feminism if not mutually constituting and mutually implicating domains?[81]

8

BEYOND SEXUALITY

The departure point for this book was a concern with bisexuality as a contemporary political, theoretical, and historical problematic. Why is bisexuality the object of such consistent and intense skepticism? Why does bisexuality continue to represent an absence or blind spot in research on sexuality? Why has bisexuality, in stark contrast to homosexuality, only recently emerged as a nascent and palpable political and cultural identity? In short, why has bisexuality been rendered, for the most part, incidental and even irrelevant to the history, theory, and politics of sexuality? I suggested in chapter 1 that in order to address these questions it would be necessary to trace the broader history of bisexuality as an epistemological category. I suggested also that questions of bisexuality are inextricable from the history and epistemology of *sexuality* in general; that in order to understand representations of bisexuality it would be necessary to undertake a genealogical analysis of their relational construction to both hetero- and homosexuality. As a form of deconstructive history, I have in this discussion examined not the ontological questions of what bisexuality *is* and what bisexuality *means*, but the performative questions of what bisexuality *does* and *how* bisexuality *means*. In other words, I have questioned bisexuality's historical, political, and theoretical *function* in the production of knowledge about sexuality.

When Eve Sedgwick intervened in the discussion over bisexuality on the QStudy internet list in 1994, she was attempting to shift the terms of current political debate in precisely this manner: away from questions of ontology, and thus, from authenticity and ownership, to questions of performativity, and thus, toward function and utility. Recall Sedgwick's preferred line of questioning: "'What does it *do?*—What does it make happen?—What (in the ways it is being or *could be* used) does it make easier or harder for people of various kinds to accomplish and think?'"[1] As I sug-

[190]

gested at the outset of this book, the question of history is central to questions of politics and theory. In contemporary discourses of sexuality, therefore, what bisexuality does and what bisexuality might do are in large measure conditioned by what it *has done* and *has made happen* within discourses inherited from the past. Yet up until now an adequate account of the history of sexuality and bisexuality's place in it has been largely absent from the entire interdisciplinary field of sexuality studies. Having taken some important first steps in rectifying this omission in our historical archive, I would like in this concluding chapter to turn to the question proposed by Sedgwick of possible uses for the category of bisexuality. There are, no doubt, many ways of approaching this question. I will limit my discussion primarily to the question of how bisexuality *could* be used to enhance queer deconstructive theory in general and queer deconstructions of the science of sexuality in particular. Let us first take a moment to revisit the history of (bi)sexuality.

In part 1 I began by tracing the emergence and consolidation of the hetero/homosexual opposition in sexology and Freudian psychoanalysis and articulating how the evolutionary category of bisexuality was central to this development. For instance, for sexologists such as Krafft-Ebing and Havelock Ellis, the notion that primordial bisexuality occupied a significant place in our evolutionary heritage helped explain differences of both sex and sexuality. However, the very same concept of bisexuality profoundly undermined these evolutionary taxonomies. My argument was that 'full bisexuality' had to be erased from the present tense in order to avert a crisis of meaning for the binary categories of man, woman, heterosexual, and homosexual. I then demonstrated how Freud took over the concept of evolutionary bisexuality and installed it as the biological foundation of his psychoanalytic theory of gender and sexuality. Despite his attempts to elucidate the psychical reflections of this biological foundation, the concept of bisexuality remained a mystery, "embarrass[ing] all our enquiries into the subject and mak[ing] them harder to describe."[2] I argued that within the Freudian schema bisexuality had to remain a mystery in order to avoid contradicting the binarized structure of the Oedipus complex. Like the sexologists, then, Freud erased bisexuality from the present tense. This served as a kind of payoff for situating bisexuality as central to the formation of all sexualities, 'normal' or otherwise.

However, the category of bisexuality proved far too problematic for post-Freudian psychoanalytic discourse, particularly in light of the implications opened up by Freud's radical rereading of sexuality. In a climate of Cold War paranoia and homophobia, the Freudian idea that "all human beings are capable of making a homosexual object-choice and have in fact made one in their unconscious" was anathema.³ The subversive threat of homosexuality, like communism, had to be extirpated from the social and individual body. Intent on pathologizing homosexuality and proffering a psychotherapeutic cure, psychoanalysts found it expedient to repudiate bisexuality as an explanatory concept. It was erased not just in the present tense but in all temporal modes. This broad temporal erasure effectively precluded homosexuality from infiltrating the sphere of normative sexuality and served to reinforce the arbitrary and precarious boundaries of the hetero/homosexual opposition.

Judith Butler's poststructuralist work on performativity and identity provides a useful theoretical model for thinking about the historical production and reproduction of binary notions of sexuality within sexology and psychoanalysis. Performativity is that "reiterative and citational practice by which discourse produces the effects it names."⁴ For Butler, all identity categories are normative signifying practices, performatively produced within discourse as the effect of power and a *compulsive* process of repetition.⁵ To use Butler's terms, identity functions as a norm, and the materialization of identity takes place through a "forcible reiteration of those norms."⁶ In other words, in order for identity to enjoy some degree of durability, the regulatory norms responsible for its production must be continually cited and repeated in discourse. With regard to sexual identity, the norms with which I have been concerned in this book are those pertaining to the logic of binary oppositions. According to this logic, hetero- and homosexuality are nonoverlapping and mutually defining terms, with the latter subordinate to the former, and with no possibility of a term that is neither one nor the other or is both one and the other. Thus to even traffic in the concept of sexual identity, sexology and psychoanalysis were compelled, with each and every articulation, to cite and thus reiterate the norms (re)productive of the binarism of hetero/homosexuality. As pointed out in part 1, the persistent refusal to accept bisexuality as a sexual identity encompassing both hetero- and homosexuality was the effect of these very norms that functioned performatively to reproduce hetero- and homosexuality as exclusive identities.

That sexual identities require reiteration to sustain an image (however illusory) of permanence and fixity is in fact evidence, as Butler puts it in *Bodies That Matter*, "that materialization is never quite complete" (2), that an identity never quite corresponds to its epistemological ideal. As deconstruction has revealed, oppositional identities are constituted through a structure of exclusion and externalization, whereby each category contains its oppositional Other as its own founding and internal exclusion. Never self-identical, identity, as Diana Fuss notes, "always contains the specter of non-identity within it."[7] Each term is thus constituted as simultaneously internal and external to the other. Such is the radical instability at the heart of identity, and this instability is unfailingly exacerbated by the continual shifting of the very boundaries, and norms, designed to secure the idealized mutual exclusivity of binary pairs. The history of modern sexuality is a case in point. As cultural norms, practices, and political and theoretical models change, so too do the meanings we ascribe to our categories of sexuality. Thus, since its invention in the late nineteenth century, the binarism of hetero- and homosexuality has been subject to a process of perpetual contestation and redefinition, its boundaries never to be fixed once and for all.[8] Sexual identity, indeed all identity, is therefore in a state of perpetual crisis: an inability to complete, and the compulsion to repeat, the forever unstable and shifting norms and boundaries of identity. This is *the crisis of identity which is identity itself.*[9]

In part 2 I traced some of the prominent politicotheoretical attempts to engage this crisis of identity in an effort to deconstruct our binary categories of sexuality. By the early 1970s the psychomedical monopoly on questions of 'deviant' sexuality was coming under increasing attack. I began by examining gay liberation's attempt to contest what they saw as the artificiality of hetero- and homosexuality. In order to do this gay and lesbian activists revivified a concept of universal bisexuality. Framed as an inherent potential or capacity to respond erotically to either sex, bisexuality was constructed as both the original foundation *and* utopian future of human sexuality and society. This theoretical move represents what Butler might call a strategy of "subversive repetition": an intervention "*within* the practices of repetitive signifying" and made possible by the very identity constructions being contested.[10] Due to practical and political exigencies, however, gay liberation abandoned the reinscription of bisexuality, maintaining that not until society had abolished the distinctions between masculinity and femininity, heterosexuality and homosexuality, could human bisexual potential become a reality. Once again, bisexuality, as a sexual practice and a sexual identity, was refused in the present tense. Contrary to gay liberation aims, therefore, the hetero/homosexual opposition remained inviolate.

The primary finding of this study is that within the prevailing discourse of sexuality from sexology to gay liberation, bisexuality has functioned as the structural Other to sexual identity itself, that against and through which the identities of hetero- and homosexuality are constituted. At this point I would like to return for a moment to Sedgwick's question of what bisexuality *could do* in contemporary antihomophobic and anti-heteronormative discourses of sexuality.

Sedgwick's own response to this question is a rather pessimistic one. She argues that articulations of bisexuality would most likely consolidate and complete the gendered and dichotomized framework of hetero/homosexuality.[11] In fact, in what is in some ways reminiscent of the gay liberationist position, Sedgwick consigns bisexuality's political utility to the distant future. "I should add," she notes in parentheses in her 1994 QStudy posting, "that in a discursive context that *wasn't* so radically structured already around gender-of-object-choice, the concept of bisexuality could work very differently: instead of seeming to add the finishing touch to a totalizing vision of human sexuality/gender, it could function as one sexually dissident self-description among many others." Many bisexual and queer theorists agree, as we have seen, with this 'impotence' model of bisexuality. For instance, Donald Hall claims that bisexuality "inescapably encodes binarism";[12] while for Lee Edelman the hetero/homosexual binarism is "more effectively reinforced than disrupted by the 'third term' of bisexuality."[13] It is assumptions such as these that lead Sedgwick and others to conclude that it is the category of 'queer' *and not bisexuality* that holds the key to challenges to our prevailing idiom of sexuality.[14]

In view of the historical findings of this study, however, I would argue that such claims are premature, based as they are upon a somewhat inadequate understanding of bisexuality's place in the history of sexuality. Rather than identifying a univocal category of bisexuality as somehow recuperative of the hetero/homosexual binarism, it would be more accurate and less totalizing to define the historically specific formulations of bisexuality and their *relation* to this binarism. For as I have demonstrated, it is a particular *relationship* between the multiple definitions of bisexuality and the notion of sexual identity itself that has worked to (re)produce the hetero/homosexual binarism. This relationship has been structured, as I have argued, by a curious *dis/avowal* of bisexuality, where only some of its possible meanings have been authorized. A particular temporal framing of sexuality has thus cast bisexuality in the past or future, but never in the *present tense*. In other words, bisexuality has been identified only as a prehistoric, precultural, infantile, or utopian state, and not as a distinct identity. This means that it is *not* bisexuality *per se* that reinforces our binary categories of sexuality. Rather, it is the temporal framing of bisexuality—*the persistent epistemological refusal to recognize bisexuality in the present tense*—that has functioned to reinforce the hetero/homosexual binarism.

Concomitant with an understanding of this all-important distinction is a necessary reconsideration of the way we think about bisexuality's current and future politicotheoretical possibilities. I have demonstrated that in the history of sexuality, the notion of bisexuality as a sexual identity in the present tense has threatened to subvert the boundaries of the hetero/homosexual opposition. It follows, then, that if bisexuality's rearticulation is taken seriously, it might at the very least make difficult any attempt to resignify this opposition as a fixed and exclusive one. This possibility would indicate that the politicization of bisexuality in the 1990s and beyond represents more than an extremely useful countermove for its historical erasure. It might also effectively induce a radical encounter between the binary logic of sexual identity and one of its fundamental structuring absences. No longer possible to elide its existence, bisexuality's irruption into the politicodiscursive field would oblige a recognition of its very existence by discourses of sexuality. And perhaps such a development might indeed engender—as it had threatened to do in sexological and psychoanalytic discourse—a state of epistemological fatigue or identity crisis, profoundly weakening or even twisting and distorting the framework of sexual identity itself.[15]

I will return to this point in more detail shortly; particularly insofar as deconstructive theory might be deployed to help procure this encounter between sexuality and its Other(s). First, though, I would like to propose that in order to bring about this encounter, an analysis of bisexuality must be taken seriously by queer or any other antihomophobic and anti-heteronormative discourses. With steadily expanding bisexual activism, conferences, and publications throughout the United States and other parts of the Western world, this crucial first step of politicizing bisexuality is well under way. Bisexual theorists and activists have formulated critiques of dominant theories of bisexuality, of cultural 'biphobia', of gay and lesbian identity politics, and of gay and lesbian and queer theories. They have also begun to produce their own bisexual narratives, politics, and theory. What does it mean to be bisexual? How can we make bisexuality visible in a culture that has sanctioned its marginalization? What are the most effective means of organizing politically? How might we formulate bisexual political theory? What might a bisexual perspective look like? How are images and meanings of bisexuality produced and distributed? What are the cultural effects of representations of bisexuality? How might we most effectively represent bisexualities? What might a bisexual imaginary look like? These are only some of a number of questions being addressed by bisexual activists and theorists. Despite a multiplicity of political and theoretical positions, this growing 'bisexual movement' exemplifies a common concern with issues of visibility and representation. More important, however, this concern is with improving our theoretical tools for thinking about the visibility and representation *of* bisexuals and bisexualities. These are certainly critical issues that need to be considered if we are to redress the presiding cultural ignorance regarding bisexuality.[16]

The question of bisexuality is not only relevant to self-identified bisexuals, however. It is a question that must be addressed in any study of modern sexuality in the West. Having said this, I should perhaps point out that while the concerns of this book intersect in various ways with questions of the visibility and representation *of* bisexuality, it has not been undertaken *in the name of bisexuality*. That is to say that my genealogy is less a representation of bisexuality or bisexualities in history, politics, or theory than it is an interpretation of dominant historical representations of (bi)sexuality. It is certainly the case that an interpretation also functions as a representation. Although, notably, there is a difference between metaphysical representations of something (What is bisexuality? What does bisexuality mean?) and analyzing modes of representation, or the techniques through which something has been represented. In the case of the former, the representation is marked by a particular positivity or presence of qualities with regard to that which is represented; it is a question of referentiality. Whereas in the case of the latter there is no such instantiation; instead, it is a question of the conditions of possibility of such representations and of referentiality itself. So it is neither my aim nor my interest to produce 'bisexual' history or 'bisexual' theory or to provide a critique from a 'bisexual' perspective. Just as it is neither my aim nor my interest to produce metaphysical representations of bisexuality ("subjects and cultures of fluid desire"), or "the bisexual imaginary."[17] Far from a social history of bisexuality, this book is a history of the political production of truth about (bi)sexuality. This study may prove useful for social history, bisexual theory, and bisexual politics. But I am suggesting that, as important and empowering as these projects are, they are best left to, and indeed are currently being carried out by, those more suitably qualified.

My intervention lies elsewhere. This deconstructive genealogy is intended, to quote Foucault, "not to discover the roots of our identity, but to commit itself to its dissipation."[18] Tracking the epistemic path of bisexuality has been for me one way of bringing into clearer view the *failure* of our epistemology of sexuality; that is, the impossibility of *any* attempt to posit this thing called 'sexuality', and its component identity-parts of hetero-, homo-, and bisexual.[19] It might well be argued that the last thing we need is yet another deconstructive reading of sexuality. Is deconstruction not dead? Are we not beyond deconstruction? Engaging these questions, I would suggest, is to misunderstand the point of deconstruction altogether. As a strategy of destabilization, displacement, and subversion, deconstruction is forever incomplete and interminable. We cannot go *beyond* binary oppositions. Inevitably hierarchical oppositions reestablish themselves.[20] The lesson of deconstruction is that any notion of identity is "*inherently* repressive of internal differences,"[21] that the epistemic violence of the binary logic of identity enables only some things to become intelligible while rendering others marginal or meaningless. In so doing, it is a logic bent on falsely homogenizing and universalizing, on reducing difference to a univocal identity, and on misrepresenting difference.[22] Deconstruction remains useful precisely because it sheds light on the workings of binary logic, the distortions of social relations and meaning, and the oppressive relations of power that such logic frequently produces and supports. With regard to sexuality, for instance, it is depressingly clear that, despite years of deconstructive work, the opposition of hetero/homosexuality is as sturdy as ever. One of the reasons for this (among others) is that this opposition serves all too well to obfuscate the irreducibly heterogeneous and contradictory character, not to mention the complicated material and discursive history, of those taken-for-granted realms—of knowledge, emotion, desire, fantasy, pleasure, and so on—designated as 'heterosexuality' and 'homosexuality'. Moreover, in most Western countries gays, lesbians, and bisexuals (among others) continue to be excluded from dominant institutions and power structures. These and myriad other identities (not to mention expressions of desire, fantasy, and pleasure) are far too often subordinated, silenced, erased, and frequently even vilified and terrorized, all *in the name of (hetero)normative identity*. This only makes the project of deconstruction as indispensable as ever.[23]

But deconstruction is incompatible with the bisexual movement's goal of visibility and representation, is it not? In deconstructing (bisexual) identity, will we not remove the very ground beneath the bisexual movement? Will deconstruction thus render invisible and inaudible the very identity and voice that bisexuals have only just begun to claim? First, as Merl Storr has pointed out, the nascent bisexual identity has emerged under the conditions of postmodernity and in the context of postmodern theory.[24] Many bisexual theorists and activists have in fact politicized bisexuality under the rubric of postmodern, poststructuralist, and deconstructive theories. However, even without an association between postmodern theory and bisexuality, one of the significant features of bisexual politics and theory is its attention to difference. Of all the bisexual movement's publications in the last decade or so, I have found few that appear to contain rigid exclusionary gestures regarding bisexual identity or politics. What I *have* found is a commitment to coalition building and political organizing, an overwhelming resistance to hard and fast definitions of bisexuality, and a desire to leave the category of bisexuality, or of bisexual identity, open-ended, and incomplete.[25] Although the overarching desire is for bisexuality to 'mean' something and to represent an individual or group—a desire I do not share—in my view all of these factors are compatible with deconstruction.

Second, deconstruction does not herald the end of identity, but, as I noted, an incomplete and interminable analysis of the very conditions of possibility for its (re)production. Because binary relations of sameness and difference are an inevitable feature of signification, we cannot transcend binary classifications. We cannot *do* without identity. Besides, in discourses of sexuality, as we have seen, binary oppositions tend to reestablish themselves as hierarchies.[26] What we *can* do is learn how to manage identity more productively. Deconstruction is extremely effective in this regard. Its theoretical strategies enliven our *analyses* of the procedures, exclusions, power relations, and effects of identity formation, just as they facilitate a self-reflexive attention to these very dynamics in the *(re)articulation* of our own identificatory categories.

Third, because deconstruction views identity categories as both inevitable and as inevitably produced through hierarchical relations, it understands deconstructive strategy as a "double gesture." This means that for an opposition to be deconstructed there must be not just a displacement, but a simultaneous "overturning" or reversal, of the violent hierarchy in question. The overturning phase is, as Derrida points out, "structural" and "interminable." "Unlike those authors whose death does not await their demise," he says, "the time for overturning is never a dead letter."[27] In our case, this suggests that precisely because bisexuality has been figured as the Other to sexual identity (and so long as this is the case), this oppositional relation needs to be constantly overturned. Gay liberation attempted this move. So too does Marjorie Garber, as I noted in the opening chapter of this book. To use Derrida's terms, it is a move "which brings low what was high" (42). That is, to continue the example, gay liberation and Garber both demote the category of hetero/homosexual identity to the position of inferior Other to the 'real truth', which is bisexuality. A similar maneuver has been the basis of many forms of homosexual politics. Although claims that homosexuality is more 'natural' than heterosexuality are rare, claims that homosexuality is *as natural* as heterosexuality are common. This constitutes a kind of overturning of the hierarchical ordering of the pair. So it might be argued that a bisexual identity, or rather, bisexual identities, are *required* in the very act of overturning. In order to counter the persistent figuration of bisexual Otherness, therefore, we actually need to insist constantly on *bringing low what was high*, on (re)figuring bisexuality as sexual identity.

Although this book details the psychomedical construction of sexuality from the late nineteenth century until only the 1970s, it is obvious this does not represent the final effort to 'discover' (i.e., invent) the origins and 'truth' of binary notions of sexual identity. Scientific studies of this kind continue apace with constructionist and deconstructionist attempts to discredit their very terms.[28] Even more disconcerting is the fact that most of this scientific research remains completely oblivious even to the intervention, let alone content, of deconstructive critique. Hence we need continuous deconstructions of the oxymoronic, or catachrestic, signifier of binarized, and indeed univocal, sexual identity as much as we need the continuous articulation of bisexuality and of bisexual identities.[29] Both are important in the deconstruction of sexuality. The question then is not why more deconstruction but how to make deconstruction more effective.[30] So what insights might we gain from this genealogy of (bi)sexuality to further this project? What challenge is produced by a confrontation between 'sexuality' and its Other, bisexuality?

This deconstructive history has demonstrated that no analysis of sexuality can afford to ignore the category of bisexuality, which mandates a critical rethinking of some of the central terms and strategies of Foucauldian and queer theories. While these theories have provided, and continue to provide, cogent political and theoretical tools for antihomophobic and anti-heteronormative inquiry, it is important to attend to their own structuring exclusions in order to strengthen their political and theoretical promise. For as I demonstrated in chapters 6 and 7, despite the important antiessentialist shift wrought by social constructionist, poststructuralist, and queer theories, dominant deconstructive analyses have remained too heavily reliant upon the very logic of (heterosexual) identity they aim to contest. They have also had little or no impact on dominant scientific theories of sexuality. This has weakened the effectiveness of such interventions in dislodging the hetero/homosexual binarism. Indeed, to date Foucauldian and queer analyses have obfuscated rather than elucidated the complex historical relationship between the interlocking registers of gender and sexuality. These factors have rendered them largely complicit in the theoretical erasure and depoliticization of bisexuality, and thus, as well, in the reinscription of the dichotomy of hetero- and homosexuality.

What this discussion has revealed is that where there is hetero- and homosexuality so too must there be bisexuality. So if we are to take seriously the poststructuralist insight, as I think we should, that identity is only ever relational, then the relationship between (at least) these three categories of sexuality must be continually interrogated rather than ignored. Bisexuality is thus not simply a pivotal player, but the third term in the (re)production of the hetero/homosexual opposition. In each and every instantiation of homo- or heterosexuality, then, the figure of bisexuality, as repudiated Other to binarized notions of sexual identity, forever lurks. This is a far cry from liberationist suggestions that everyone is inherently bisexual. Nor is it an attempt to accord some kind of ontological status to homo-, hetero-, and bisexuality. (In fact, I consider these to be empty signifiers, catachreses, tropes without referents.) Instead I am positing a rather simple epistemological argument or formula: whether in terms of identification and identity formation or social and scientific research, whenever the categories of homo- or heterosexuality are invoked, epistemological assumptions and definitions are being made also *through* as well as *about* bisexuality. In other words, as I have stated, where queer theory posits the mutually constituting nature of hetero- and homosexuality (each term requiring the other for its self-definition), my reading, worth reiterating, posits in its place a trinary relationship: Within our modern epistemology of sexuality, any figuration of homo- or heterosexuality necessarily entails—wittingly or unwittingly—a figuration of bisexuality. In other words, to invoke and define any one of the terms hetero-, homo-, or bisexuality is to invoke and define the others by default. Each requires the other two for its self-definition. The effect of this logical structure is such that shifts in any one of the terms hetero-, bi-, or homosexuality require and engender shifts in the others.[31]

One of the implications of this trinary relationship is that a rethinking is required not only of the methodological foundation of queer theory and gay and lesbian history, *but of any research into modern sexuality in the West*. Thanks to a constantly expanding archive of poststructuralist and constructionist research into sexuality we now know that identity categories in general and the hetero/homosexual structure in particular are far from self-evident. They are not universal or natural, but instead historically and culturally specific. Neither are they self-identical unities. All categories of identity are normative closures founded on a repudiation of internal and irreducible differences. In order to stay faithful to, and build upon, this knowledge, it is therefore crucial that as researchers we remember not to presume uncritically the existence of 'sexuality' or the hetero/homosexual dyad (or indeed any identity categories) as our point of departure.[32] For to state this somewhat differently, the history of sexuality represents more than just the discursive construction of 'sexuality' as an epistemological category. The history of the discourse of sexuality also, as I mentioned above, represents the failure or impossibility of securing the very meaning of 'sexuality' itself.[33] So instead of presuming the meaning and existence of 'sexuality' we ought to inquire into the discursive conditions of possibility of what Kaja Silverman might call the "dominant fiction" of 'sexuality' and its counterpart the hetero/homosexual dyad.[34] Otherwise we risk both marginalizing and erasing the very differences we seek to historicize, and we risk reinscribing the very heteronormative logic of identity we seek to challenge. Neither can we neglect to examine the mutually constitutive relationship between the binarized axes of (among others) sexuality and gender.[35] As we have seen throughout this study, the analysis of bisexuality has proved eminently useful for this task.

As deconstructive readers and cultural critics we need continually to monitor the sites through which the reiteration of sexuality, and its accompanying hierarchy of hetero- and homosexuality, is taking place. Currently, one of the most authoritative of these sites is the field of science. The last couple of decades have witnessed a revolution in science and a return of biologism. Psychiatry and psychoanalysis no longer dominate discussions of the etiology of sexuality. Now the fields of genetics and molecular biology have gained cultural ascendancy in the popular imagination. Advances in mapping and sequencing the human genome have led geneticists and molecular biologists to extend their explanatory reach to all forms of human behavior. I have made my objections about this research into behavior, in general, and sexuality, in particular, known elsewhere.[36] Nonetheless, it is imperative that we intervene above and beyond the level of social science discourse. We need to transport our deconstructive analyses to the very sites where this research is being produced and disseminated. This means lobbying and writing to scientific journals, newspapers, and magazines with our critiques and analyses, for instance. It means getting ourselves heard, pursuing interdisciplinary dialogue as best we can. It means becoming public intellectuals and commentators. It means disseminating the vast knowledge of the humanities and social sciences into broader networks. It means educating the broader public and media on deconstructive reading practices. It means exercising our expertise in sexuality research. With human genetic screening and cloning an ever-present reality, the need for such social scientific interventions is ever more urgent.[37] Although I have argued elsewhere that there can never be such a thing as a 'gay gene', and thus a 'cure' for homosexuality, the fact that much folk wisdom would argue the contrary is enough for me to imagine efforts, *precisely in the name of this hypothetical gene*, to abort fetuses or to attempt potentially damaging gene 'therapy' (a euphemism for genetic manipulation).[38]

The deconstructive method I have been proposing is far from irrelevant to this burgeoning body of research. For instance, one barely has to scratch the surface of Dean Hamer's frenetic 'search' for the 'gay gene' to confront the glaring erasure of bisexuality at its core. Bisexuality was deliberately overlooked, Hamer noted, "because our first goal was to determine whether genes had any influence on sexual orientation, which meant it was important to study only those individuals whose orientation was unambiguous."[39] This, he declared unproblematically, was necessary in order to guard against "diagnostic uncertainty."[40] In other words, bisexuality is once again rendered the Other to "sexual orientation." In this respect Hamer's thought is little different from that of Havelock Ellis a century ago. And he is certainly not alone in his unwillingness and inability to incorporate bisexuality into his rigid binary model. Simon LeVay's work on homosexuality and the size of the anterior region of the hypothalamus exhibits similar problems.[41] Instead of erasing bisexuality from the study, however, LeVay chose to collapse it into that of homosexuality. In fact, as Edward Stein notes, after a comprehensive investigation into scientific theories of sexuality, "scientists interested in developing a theory of the origins of sexual orientation . . . seem to appreciate that there are 'genuine' bisexuals but go on to ignore them for the purpose of developing their theories."[42] Replicating the century-long scientific and psychomedical tradition of erasing bisexuality from the present tense, biological researchers appear to have added next to nothing to etiological theories of sexuality. The terms of analysis have remained almost the same, the only difference is that the explanatory notion of a 'bisexual embryo' or an 'overbearing mother' has been replaced by 'the gene' or 'the hypothalamus'.

Far from taking up a preordained position that would 'complete' the binary structure of hetero/homosexuality within Hamer's genetic or LeVay's neuroanatomical model, it would seem to me that the incorporation of bisexuality, in the first instance at least, might destabilize the very terms of these models. For it is precisely the repudiation of ambiguity, uncertainty, indeed bisexuality, that sustains the operative distinction between hetero- and homosexuality. As Judith Butler notes of the logic of sexual identity formation, "The more rigid the position, the greater the ghost, and the more threatening it is in some way."[43] Bisexuality has always been sexual identity's most fearful ghost. While it is certainly conceivable that, in attempting to include bisexuality in this model, Hamer or LeVay might very well assign it a definition as a category altogether distinct from hetero- and homosexuality, it is far less clear that such a move would, as Sedgwick speculates, "add the finishing touch to a totalizing vision of human sexuality/gender."[44] Given the variables associated with sexuality—fantasy, desire, pleasure, behavior, identity, temporality, and so on—it would be theoretically impossible for any researcher to delimit exactly and universally where the category of heterosexuality leaves off and the categories of bi- and homosexuality begin; at least impossible without unmistakable and multiple exclusions. Even if we are to base our definitions on only one variable, let us say fantasy, precisely how much same-sex sexual fantasizing by a self-identified heterosexual and how much different-sex sexual fantasizing by a self-identified homosexual qualifies as an instance of a 'bisexual' fantasy structure, or of 'bisexuality'? The question of *degree* always confounds our classifications. In his 1980 study, *Straight Women/Gay Men*, John Malone confronted this very dilemma. The concept of bisexuality has always had various, vague, indeterminate, and confused meanings, he noted: "A word that is used defensively by one person in order to avoid admitting the real nature of his sexuality and boastfully by another person to proclaim his liberation," Malone argued, "is in danger of losing all meaning."[45] I am arguing that this crisis of meaning is not confined only to bisexuality. Bisexuality is a relational element of the structure of hetero- and homosexuality. As such, the crisis of meaning is a crisis for this entire epistemological structure. In thus having to account not just for two terms (hetero- and homosexuality) but also a third term (bisexuality), *which itself partakes in many and varied ways of the other two terms*, science would have an infinitely more unstable basis for grounding a theory of sexuality. It is in this way that I envisage the category of bisexuality as potentially outgrowing its cause, to quote Žižek, becoming a force whose excess our binary epistemology is "no longer able to master and which thus detonates its unity, its capacity to reproduce itself."[46] This is a crisis to which I hope this study might contribute.

Of course, in order to destabilize the terms of scientific discourse, it is not enough to deconstruct the binarism of hetero- and homosexuality in isolation. Its mutually defining relationship with the axis of gender must be constantly interrogated.[47] As I have shown, in this respect queer theory has too radically disarticulated the axes of gender and sexuality. An abiding presentism has meant much queer deconstructive work has been blind to the place of bisexuality in shaping the relationship of gender and sexuality in psychomedical theory. Yet we have seen that bisexuality has been nothing but trouble for theories predicated on a causal relationship between gender and sexuality. In view of this, I would expect that the illumination of the category of bisexuality has much to offer in the deconstruction of this scenario in science. In the theories of Hamer and LeVay, gender is installed as prior to sexuality, as sexuality's essential and originary force. Our desire, in other words, is first and foremost construed as a desire *for* a particular gender. For instance, the subjects of Hamer's study were defined as 'homosexual' on account of their response to which gender they desire, fantasize about, and have sex with.[48] But what of those individuals, such as bisexuals, for whom sexual object choice is determined by factors other than gender? Certain modes of sexuality reflect not a desire for either a man or a woman, but a desire for a particular race, age, object, species, personality, body type, authority figure, or practice, to name a few. How would Hamer's or LeVay's model accommodate such variations of sexuality? What would the recognition of such dissident 'sexualities' do to the epistemological framework of this type of scientific research? With respect to bisexuality alone, I would think that the disarticulation of gender and sexuality, which bisexuality in some forms represents, might very well engender a radical shake-up of the structuring assumptions and the endemic heteronormativity of such scientific frameworks. Bisexuality (among other Others) is one particularly crucial concept that must be brought to bear on scientific practice and theory in order to undermine the fallacy of the universal connection between gender and sexuality.[49]

Sedgwick herself claims that in the discursive field of sexuality—which, as we saw in her QStudy posting, is "structured almost exclusively around the issue of gender-of-object-choice"—the recognition of bisexuality, empowering as it might be for bisexuals, is primarily incompatible with the goals of queer deconstructive theory. This is because by insisting on occupying a space within a field where sexuality is reducible to gender, bisexuality is thought only to reinforce this association. Sedgwick's conclusion is that the concept of bisexuality is not an effective means through which to "launch a meaningful challenge" to the gendered division of hetero/homosexuality. That certain forms of bisexuality falsify the causal link between gender and sexuality, however, signals a more complicated picture than the one depicted by Sedgwick's seemingly inevitable teleology. Unfortunately, without an appreciation of (bi)sexuality's history, Sedgwick's well-intentioned intervention is more regulatory than it is productive. I would argue strongly, therefore, that scientists must be made to account in their studies for the complexities of (bi)sexuality. In my view this would indeed represent a meaningful challenge to the structure of hetero/homosexuality.

Even if we could accurately predict that the incorporation of bisexuality would engender a totalizing vision of sexuality within science, what would this mean? Would the category of bisexuality be rendered useless? Might we be better off to continue the tradition of ignoring or denying bisexuality? I argue that as long as the binary epistemology of sexuality holds sway—with or without a substantive recognition of bisexuality—an analysis of the figuration of bisexuality will always prove useful for deconstructing the relational construction of hetero- and homosexuality. At the very least, the fact that our binary epistemology has been characterized by a steadfast erasure of bisexuality in the present tense means that to reverse this situation would be to transform *inevitably*—however much or however little—the internal mechanics of this epistemology.[50] We cannot know in advance what the effects of this, or any, transformation might be. *Nor will we ever know, as long as bisexuality continues to be erased in the present tense.* Whatever the outcome, a deconstructionist's work is never done.

I have been proposing, then, that we begin by inciting an encounter between the abiding binary epistemology and its founding repudiations, or ghostly Others. It scarcely warrants repeating that, while there are perhaps many such structuring Others that other scholars will reveal in due course, obviously the one that concerns this book is bisexuality. To reiterate, we must insist vehemently and incessantly that the category of bisexuality be acknowledged, defined, and incorporated in any scientific study and theory of sexuality. This is *not*, I should repeat, in order to ascertain some supposed ontological truth of bisexuality; on the contrary, it is in order to demonstrate the error or the impossibility of ascribing ontological meaning to the categories of homo-, hetero-, and bisexuality. One way of performing a more damaging deconstruction than those heretofore performed is, as this study has repeatedly shown, *to ask the question of bisexuality*. If bisexuality is in fact defined in the scientific account under examination, a deconstructive analysis of its relational construction to hetero- and homosexuality must be executed; if it is not explicitly addressed, we must uncover the implicit figuration of bisexuality that we now know inevitably sustains all binary models of sexuality. One way of doing this is to locate *precisely where the definition of heterosexuality leaves off and homosexuality begins*—that is, *at which point heterosexuality becomes homosexuality*, and vice versa. For it is this liminal point that will lead us to those internal differences whose disavowal was necessary for the (re)creation of the supposedly seamless and univocal categories of hetero- and homosexuality. Significantly, this is also the point at which we will find bisexuality; a point that, when brought to the surface, will cause nothing but trouble for any definition of hetero- or homosexuality.

[|]

To deconstruct the science of sexuality is not to imply that scientists abandon entirely research into those things that go under the rubric of 'sexuality', although it *is* to imply that scientists relinquish the futile biologically reductionist search for 'sexuality's' supposed origins. For if a century of sex research has revealed anything, it is that the category of 'sexuality' far exceeds a narrow biological definition. That which we refer to as 'sexuality' can never be understood in ontological terms only, as *what a body is*, which is inextricable from *what a body does*; and what a body is and does is thus indissociable from discourse, history, and change. Just as the human genome is a *potentiality*, where the form it takes is dependent on a range of biological, environmental, cultural, and behavioral functions, relations, and changes, so too is 'sexuality'. If 'it' is anything, 'sexuality' is a *potentiality*, or in Deleuzian terms, a becoming, whose ever-shifting contours depend also on these things.[51] Scientific funding and effort would be much better spent not on questions that are impossible for *any* discourse to answer. Science clearly cannot find the answer to the origins of something it can never define and that will forever exceed its epistemic scope. And, as we have seen, 'sexuality', and the identities that it is seen to encapsulate, are prime examples of 'objects' that scientists have been, and continue to be, unable to define or to reduce to the reductionist terms of scientistic inquiry. The story so far has been one of circular reasoning: the elusive quest for the origins of homosexuality has been none other than the quest for the meaning of homosexuality itself.[52] Ill-defined and unproven notions of 'sexuality' and 'identity' ought to be at the very least problematized, better still eliminated, from within the scientific mode of inquiry. Hail the 'death of man', I say, a no less relevant exhortation to scientistic than it is to social scientific practice. Neither 'sexuality' nor the hetero/homosexual opposition ought to be assumed as a methodological axiom by any research in the field of human behavior.[53]

This suggests to me not that science ought to abandon questions relevant to those things assigned to the category of 'sexuality', but that scientists ought to pursue a different set of questions altogether. One possible way to reformulate scientific inquiry might be to ask not What is the nature of someone with a homosexual 'orientation'? or What are the origins of homosexuality? but What are the biological functions involved in desire, fantasy, pleasure, and (object) choice? and How might these interact at the level of individual mental and physical functioning?[54] Few fresh questions, perspectives, or insights have been raised in the 'search for origins' mode of inquiry in well over a century now. Something along the lines of the latter approach, in contrast, might better enable scientists to raise infinitely more productive questions and thus avenues of inquiry for examining the complex biological processes behind some of our most intimate endowments. The breadth of possible positions for viewing these kinds of questions would also be matched by the breadth of scientific subfields required to examine them.[55] Scientific research is pivotal to the evolution of human knowledge. Deconstruction neither closes down possibilities for the production of knowledge nor renders the search for this knowledge meaningless. On the contrary, it effectively opens up the field of knowledge, making knowledge infinitely *more meaningful.*

This caution applies also to my deconstructive history of (bi)sexuality. My aim has not been to resolve and de*limit* the meaning of our concepts of sexuality. What I have tried to do is to open them up, analyze their function, their various and contested meanings, and the exclusionary operations of their production. I have found bisexuality to be eminently valuable for this deconstructive task. Bisexuality's value, moreover, might go well beyond the boundaries of this study. We have seen how the category of bisexuality has repeatedly functioned as the epistemic sorting house for a wide range of contradictions and differences incompatible with hetero- and homosexuality. In fact, bisexuality has represented the very uncertainty of the hetero/homosexual division itself. This suggests to me that the epistemological site of bisexuality may prove fertile ground for exploring, and thus releasing, other differences whose repudiation serves to fortify the enduring hetero/homosexual structure. Perhaps this is yet another way the category of bisexuality might assist, even further, the deconstruction of sexuality.

NOTES

CHAPTER 1

1 It is not necessary at this point to provide a list of references regarding such characterizations of bisexuality. Apart from the fact that they are the rule rather than the exception and, thus, are part of a rather large corpus, these kinds of representations of bisexuality will be covered extensively throughout the book. However, the notion of bisexuality as a superficial fashion trend and marketing tool is not discussed any further. See Sue Wilkinson, "Bisexuality 'A La Mode'," *Women's Studies International Forum* 19, no. 3 (1996): 293–301.

2 The medicalization of sexuality has been well documented. For a useful comparison of sexological definitions in the nineteenth and twentieth centuries, compare the pioneering nineteenth-century sexologist Richard von Krafft-Ebing, *Psychopathia Sexualis, With Especial Reference to the Antipathic Instinct: A Medico Forensic Study* (New York: Arcade Publishing, 1965), and the current leading sexologist, John Money, *Gay, Straight, and In-Between: The Sexology of Erotic Orientation* (New York: Oxford University Press, 1988).

3 Michel Foucault, *The History of Sexuality*. Vol. 1: *An Introduction* (New York: Vintage Books, 1980), 77.

4 Martin S. Weinberg et al., *Dual Attraction: Understanding Bisexuality* (Oxford: Oxford University Press, 1994), 4. The advent of HIV/AIDS has certainly led to the incorporation of bisexuality into social science and epidemiological research. See, e.g., Peter Aggleton, ed., *Bisexualities and AIDS: International Perspectives* (London: Taylor and Francis, 1996). However, with respect to analyzing bisexuality in relation to theoretical models of sexual identity production and formation, a paucity of research exists.

5 Marjorie Garber, *Vice Versa: Bisexuality and the Eroticism of Everyday Life* (New York: Simon and Schuster, 1995).

6 I agree with Michael du Plessis ("Blatantly Bisexual; or, Unthinking Queer Theory," in *RePresenting Bisexualities: Subjects and Cultures of Fluid Desire*, edited by Donald E. Hall and Maria Pramaggiore [New York: New York University Press, 1996], 43 n. 2), who argues that the "assumption that sexuality *has* a nature, albeit a fluid one, seems tendentious, just as the belief that sexuality somehow involves 'growth' seems open to question." Of course, imputing a 'nature' to sexuality contradicts Garber's claim that sexuality is not a "knowable state of being."

7 Although this quote is taken from a question Garber introduces at the beginning of her book, it is in fact a rhetorical question whose answer Garber has already presupposed and which she explicitly states (65).

8 She actually says of the Möbius model: "That this is closer to a diagram of bisexuality—that is to say, *sexuality* . . . will be an important part of my argument here" (30).

9 Foucault, *History of Sexuality*, 58.

10 See Jacques Derrida, *Positions*, translated by Alan Bass (Chicago: University of Chicago Press, 1981), 40–46; Harold Beaver, "Homosexual Signs," *Critical Inquiry* 8 (Autumn 1981): 115.

11 Eve Kosofsky Sedgwick, "Bi," at QSTUDY-L@UBVM.cc.buffalo.edu, 17 August 1994.

12 BiAcademic Intervention, ed., *The Bisexual Imaginary: Representation, Identity and Desire* (London: Cassell, 1997), esp. chap. 11.

13 Elizabeth D. Däumer, "Queer Ethics; or, The Challenge of Bisexuality to Lesbian Ethics," *Hypatia* 7, no. 4 (1992): 98, 96.

14 Amanda Udis-Kessler, "Present Tense: Biphobia as a Crisis of Meaning," in *Bi Any Other Name: Bisexual People Speak Out*, edited by Loraine Hutchins and Lani Kaahumanu (Boston: Alyson Publications, 1991), 356, 357.

15 Other authors who have represented bisexuality as subversive are Rebecca Shuster, "Sexuality as a Continuum: The Bisexual Identity," in *Lesbian Psychologies: Explorations and Challenges*, edited by the Boston Lesbian Psychologies Collective (Urbana: University of Illinois Press, 1987); Clare Hemmings, "From Lesbian Nation to Transgender Liberation: A Bisexual Feminist Perspective," *critical inQueeries* 1, no. 2 (1996): 60–61, "Resituating the Bisexual Body," in *Activating Theory*, edited by Joseph Bristow and Angelia R. Wilson (London: Lawrence and Wishart, 1993), 118–38; Jo Eadie, "Activating Bisexuality: Towards a Bi/sexual Politics," in *Activating Theory*, 139–70; Ruth Goldman, "Who Is That Queer Queer? Exploring Norms around Sexuality, Race, and Class in Queer Theory," in *Queer Studies: A Lesbian, Gay, Bisexual, and Transgender Anthology*, edited by Brett Beemyn and Mickey Eliason (New York: New York University Press, 1996), 178; Lucy Friedland and Liz A. Highleyman, "The Fine Art of Labeling: The Convergence of Anarchism, Feminism, and Bisexuality," in *Bi Any Other Name*, 285–98; Kathleen Bennett, "Feminist Bisexuality: A Both/And Option for an Either/Or World," in *Closer to Home: Bisexuality and Feminism*, edited by Elizabeth Reba Weise (Seattle: Seal Press, 1992), 215, 225–77; Karin Baker, "Bisexual Feminist Politics: Because Bisexuality Is Not Enough," in *Closer to Home*, 266; Paula C. Rust, "Who Are We and Where Do We Go from Here? Conceptualizing Bisexuality," in *Closer to Home*, 284.

16 Jonathan Dollimore suggests that some of these theoretical celebrations of bisexuality as subversive are instances of "wishful theory." For Dollimore this kind of theory "tends to erase the psychic, social and historical complexities of the cultural life it addresses." Additionally, it is "a theoretical narrative whose plausibility is often in inverse proportion to the degree to which it makes its proponents feel better. To that extent, wishful theory is also feel-good theory." See Jonathan Dollimore, "Bisexuality, Heterosexuality, and Wishful Theory," *Textual Practice* 10, no. 3 (1996): 531, 532–33.

17 As Henry Abelove points out, "One of the key elements in the production of a progressive political outlook is a sound historical perspective. Without such a perspective to guide and inform us, we'd be hard put to make cogent political analysis." See "Critically Queer: Interview with Henry Abelove," *critical inQueeries* 1, no. 1 (1995): 14.

18 Michael du Plessis, "Blatantly Bisexual; or, Unthinking Queer Theory," 21.

19 Jeffrey Weeks, *Coming Out: Homosexual Politics in Britain from the Nineteenth Century to the Present* (London: Quartet Books, 1990), 3. Robert Padgug says something similar in "Sexual Matters: Rethinking Sexuality in History," in *Hidden from History: Reclaiming the Gay and Lesbian Past*, edited by Martin Duberman et al. (New York: Meridian, 1990), 60.

20 Chris Cagle, "Rough Trade: Sexual Taxonomy in Postwar America," in *RePresenting Bisexualities*, 236.

21 George Chauncey, *Gay New York: Gender, Urban Culture, and the Making of the Gay Male World, 1890–1940* (New York: Basic Books, 1994), 13; my emphasis.

22 Erwin J. Haeberle, "Bisexuality: History and Dimensions of a Modern Scientific Problem," in *Bisexualities: The Ideology and Practice of Sexual Contact with Both Men and Women*, edited by Edwin J. Haeberle and Rolf Gindorf (New York: Continuum, 1998), 14. By "modern bisexuality" Haeberle is referring to the notion of an "erotic interest in both sexes." Recall that Garber's book serves to reverse this notion. It should be noted, however, that she does not historicize bisexuality, nor does she discuss the ways historians have dealt with bisexuality. So her move is not framed as a reversal of a dominant historical assumption among gay and lesbian historians, but as a reversal of a dominant theoretical assumption.

23 Diana Fuss, "Inside/Out," in *Inside/Out: Lesbian Theories, Gay Theories*, edited by Diana Fuss (New York: Routledge, 1991), 1.

24 Lee Edelman, *Homographesis: Essays in Gay Literary and Cultural Theory* (New York: Routledge, 1993), xvi. Diana Fuss says something similar in "Inside/Out," 2.

25 Lisa Duggan, "The Discipline Problem: Queer Theory Meets Lesbian and Gay History," in Lisa Duggan and Nan Hunter, *Sex Wars: Sexual Dissent and Political Culture* (New York: Routledge, 1995), 197. See also Steven Maynard, "'Respect Your Elders, Know Your Past': History and the Queer Theorists," *Radical History Review* 75 (1999): 56–78.

26 Jeffrey Escoffier, Regina Kunzel, Molly McGarry, "The Queer Issue: New Visions of America's Lesbian and Gay Past," *Radical History Review* 62 (Spring 1995): 3.

27 This argument will be elaborated upon in chap. 7 below. I have borrowed the phrase "proper object" from Judith Butler, "Introduction: Against Proper Objects," *differences* 6, nos. 2 and 3 (1994): 1–26.

28 See Henry Abelove, "The Queering of Lesbian/Gay History," *Radical History Review* 62 (1995): esp. 47–48, for a useful discussion of queer's use of the tropes of 'presence' and 'centrality' in preference to that of 'marginalization'.

29 Ian Hacking might describe my work as a form of "rebellious" social constructionism, according to which I would hold that: (1) the categories of sexuality, homosexuality, heterosexuality, and bisexuality need not have existed, or need not be at all as they are, that they are not determined by the nature of things, that they are not inevitable; (2) that these categories are quite bad as they are; and (3) we would be much better off if these categories were done away with, or at least radically transformed. I would probably conflate 2 and 3, and describe them quite differently; e.g., I would say that these categories are unnecessary and often harmful (though often empowering), and that they are not truthful representations of some ontological reality. See Ian Hacking, *The*

Social Construction of What? (Cambridge, Mass.: Harvard University Press, 1999), esp. 6–7.

30 Sedgwick, "Bi," see n. 11 above. I should point out that in this post Sedgwick is actually referring to bisexuality. On the 'performative turn', see Judith Butler, *Gender Trouble: Feminism and the Subversion of Identity* (New York: Routledge, 1990); Diana Fuss, ed., *Inside/Out*; Judith Butler, *Bodies That Matter: On the Discursive Limits of 'Sex'* (New York: Routledge, 1993), *Excitable Speech: A Politics of the Performative* (New York: Routledge, 1997); Eve Kosofsky Sedgwick, *Epistemology*, and *Tendencies* (Durham, N.C.: Duke University Press, 1993), "Queer Performativity: Henry James's *The Art of the Novel*," *GLQ: A Journal of Lesbian and Gay Studies* 1, no. 1 (1993): 1–16; Eve Kosofsky Sedgwick and Andrew Parker, eds., *Performativity and Performance* (New York: Routledge, 1994); Jeffrey T. Nealon, *Alterity Politics: Ethics and Performative Subjectivity* (Durham, N.C.: Duke University Press, 1998).

31 Mary Poovey, "Feminism and Deconstruction," *Feminist Studies* 14, no. 1 (1988): 52.

32 Michel Foucault quoted in Robert Castel, "'Problematization' as a Mode of Reading History," in *Foucault and the Writing of History*, edited by Jan Goldstein (Cambridge, Mass.: Blackwell Publishers, 1994), 237–38.

33 Quoted in "Bisexuality. Not Gay. Not Straight. A New Sexual Identity Emerges," *Newsweek*, 17 July 1995, 46.

34 "History of the present" is Foucault's phrase taken from Michel Foucault, *Discipline and Punish: The Birth of the Prison*, translated by Alan Sheridan (New York: Pantheon, 1977), 31. See also "Critical Theory/Intellectual History," 1983 interview with Gérard Raulet, in *Michel Foucault. Politics, Philosophy, Culture: Interviews and Other Writings, 1977–1984*, edited by Lawrence D. Kritzman (New York: Routledge, 1988), 35–77.

35 See Jennifer Terry, "Theorizing Deviant Historiography," *differences* 3, no. 2 (1991): 57.

36 Jo Eadie, "Activating Bisexuality,"139; see n. 15 above.

37 Clare Hemmings, "Editors' Roundtable Discussion: The Bisexual Imaginary," in *The Bisexual Imaginary*, 199; see n. 12 above.

38 Eva Cantarella, *Bisexuality in the Ancient World*, translated by Cormac Ó'Cuilleanáin (New Haven, Conn.: Yale University Press, 1992).

39 Amanda Udis-Kessler, "Identity/Politics: Historical Sources of the Bisexual Movement," in *Queer Studies: A Lesbian, Gay, Bisexual, and Transgender Anthology*, edited by Brett Beemyn and Mickey Eliason (New York: New York University Press, 1996), 53.

40 Michel Foucault, *The Archaeology of Knowledge*, translated by A. M. Sheridan Smith (New York: Routledge, 1991), 14.

41 Merl Storr, "The Sexual Reproduction of 'Race': Bisexuality, History and Racialization," in *The Bisexual Imaginary*, 73–88; see n. 12 above.

42 Jonathan Dollimore, *Sexual Dissidence: Augustine to Wilde, Freud to Foucault* (Oxford: Clarendon Press, 1991), 24–25.

43 Val Plumwood, *Feminism and the Mastery of Nature* (New York: Routledge, 1993), 42.

44 Joan W. Scott, "The Evidence of Experience," *Critical Inquiry* 17 (1991): 792.

45 Diana Fuss, *Essentially Speaking: Feminism, Nature and Difference* (New York: Routledge, 1989), 103.

46 For a discussion of the hetero/homosexual opposition as methodological assumption of gay and lesbian studies, see Donna Penn, "Queer: Theorizing Politics and History," *Radical History Review* 62 (1995): 32.

47 See Jonathan Ned Katz, *The Invention of Heterosexuality* (New York: Dutton, 1995).

48 According to Jonathan Ned Katz ("The Invention of Heterosexuality," *Socialist Review* 21, no. 1 [1990]: 12), homosexuality was first articulated in public discourse in German by Karl Maria Kertbeny in 1869, with his concept of heterosexuality appearing in 1880. In 1889 Krafft-Ebing used the term heterosexual "where it was distinguished from homosexual." Interestingly, however, the concept of bisexuality in fact predates—albeit in a different epistemological register, as we will see in chap. 2—those of homo- and heterosexuality. In chaps. 7 and 8 I will touch on the theoretical issue of bisexuality as neither/nor.

49 I should also point out that I am in no way suggesting that this binary structure exhausts or straightforwardly defines all sexualities constructed within psychomedical discourse. But what I am suggesting is that it must be taken into account in any analysis of the construction of sexuality in general (as does its mutually constitutive relation to the axis of gender, as we will see). Of course, as well as this we must attend to the mutually constituting nature of other interrelated axes of analysis, such as class, race, gender, etc., and the ways that shifts in the nature of each of these and their components work to redefine sexuality, and vice versa.

50 Du Plessis, "Blatantly Bisexual," 26; my emphasis.

51 In relation to bisexuality, this phrase was first used by Amanda Udis-Kessler, "Present Tense," 350–58. While my usage of this phrase might overlap with Udis-Kessler's—and I am therefore indebted to her for applying it to bisexuality—it is also very different. Udis-Kessler is using it in a contemporary context to refer to the crisis of meaning bisexuals and bisexuality pose to essentialist understandings of sexuality. She argues that bisexuals and bisexuality bring home the constructionist understanding of sexuality as fluid and amenable to choice, thereby challenging the fixity of both hetero- and homosexualities. I am using the phrase as a way of interrogating and describing the specific historical and epistemological processes by which bisexuality has been erased as a legitimate identity in discourses of sexuality in the modern West.

CHAPTER 2

1 Eve Kosofsky Sedgwick, *Epistemology of the Closet* (Berkeley and Los Angeles: University of California Press, 1990), 1; my emphasis.

2 The literature is voluminous. For particularly influential and useful examples see the many works of Jeffrey Weeks, including, *Coming Out: Homosexual Politics in Britain from the Nineteenth Century to the Present* (London: Quartet, 1977), *Sex, Politics and Society: The Regulation of Sexuality since 1880* (London: Longman, 1981), *Sexuality and Its Discontents: Meanings, Myths and Modern Sexualities* (London: Routledge, 1985); see also Randolph Trumbach, "Gender and the Homosexual Role in Modern Western Culture:

The 18th and 19th Centuries Compared," in *Homosexuality, Which Homosexuality? Essays from the International Scientific Conference on Lesbian and Gay Studies*, edited by Dennis Altman et al. (London: GMP Publishers, 1989), 149–69; George Chauncey, "From Sexual Inversion to Homosexuality: Medicine and the Changing Conceptualization of Female Deviance," *Salmagundi*, nos. 58–59 (Fall 1982–Winter 1983): 114–46, *Gay New York: Gender, Urban Culture, and the Making of the Gay Male World 1890–1940* (New York: Basic Books, 1994); David F. Greenberg, *The Construction of Homosexuality* (Chicago: University of Chicago Press, 1988); Vern L. Bullough, *Science in the Bedroom: A History of Sex Research* (New York: Basic Books, 1994); Jonathan Ned Katz, *The Invention of Heterosexuality* (New York: Dutton, 1995).

3 Gayle Rubin, "Thinking Sex: Notes for a Radical Theory of the Politics of Sexuality," in *The Gay and Lesbian Studies Reader*, edited by Henry Abelove et al. (New York: Routledge, 1993), 16.

4 For a useful discussion of the emergence of a distinction between sex and sexuality, see Arnold I. Davidson, "Sex and the Emergence of Sexuality," *Critical Inquiry* 14 (Autumn 1987): 16–48.

5 See Henry Abelove's remarks in "Critically Queer: Interview with Henry Abelove," *critical inQueeries* 1, no. 1 (September 1995): 13–14.

6 Elizabeth Grosz, *Sexual Subversions: Three French Feminists* (Sydney: Allen & Unwin, 1989), xx.

7 Luce Irigaray, *This Sex Which Is Not One*, translated by Catherine Porter (Ithaca, N.Y.: Cornell University Press, 1985), 74.

8 Luce Irigaray, "Women's Exile," *Ideology and Consciousness*, no. 1 (1977): 64.

9 Of course, I am not here suggesting that the categories 'woman' and 'man' actually represent the varying referents occupying the material and discursive positions 'women' and 'men', only that the logic of phallogocentric discourse would have us think not just that there are indeed only two genders, but that they are adequately represented by the homogeneous categories of 'woman' and 'man'.

10 For one of the most incisive feminist analyses along these lines, see Joan Scott, "Gender: A Useful Category of Historical Analysis," *American Historical Review* 91 (1986): 1053–75.

11 Elizabeth Grosz, "The Hetero and the Homo: The Sexual Ethics of Luce Irigaray," *Gay Information*, nos. 17–18 (1988): 40.

12 Thomas Laqueur, *Making Sex: Body and Gender from the Greeks to Freud* (Cambridge, Mass.: Harvard University Press, 1990), 4, 6.

13 For critiques of Irigaray's notion of "hom(m)osexuality," see Diana Fuss, *Essentially Speaking: Feminism, Nature and Difference* (New York: Routledge, 1989), esp. 49; and Craig Owens, "Outlaws: Gay Men in Feminism," in *Men in Feminism*, edited by Alice Jardine and Paul Smith (New York: Methuen, 1987), 219–32.

14 Through a historical survey of the scientific construction of hermaphroditism, Alice Domurat Dreger suggests a similar critique of Laqueur. See Alice Domurat Dreger, *Hermaphrodites and the Medical Invention of Sex* (Cambridge, Mass.: Harvard University Press, 1998).

15 Homi K. Bhabha, "Are You a Man or a Mouse?" in *Constructing Masculinity*, edited by Maurice Berger et al. (New York: Routledge, 1995), 58.

16 See Kaja Silverman, *Male Subjectivity at the Margins* (New York: Routledge, 1992).

17 See J. Tosh and M. Roper, *Manful Assertions: Masculinities in Britain since 1800* (London: Routledge, 1991).

18 Cynthia Eagle Russett, *Sexual Science: The Victorian Construction of Womanhood* (Cambridge, Mass.: Harvard University Press, 1989), 3.

19 See Nancy Stepan, *The Idea of Race in Science: Great Britain 1800–1960* (London: Macmillan, 1982), "Biology and Degeneration: Races and Proper Places," in *Degeneration: The Dark Side of Progress*, edited by J. Edward Chamberlin and Sander Gilman (New York: Columbia University Press, 1985), 97–120; George M. Fredrickson, *The Black Image in the White Mind: The Debate on Afro-American Character and Destiny, 1817–1914* (Middletown, Conn.: Wesleyan University Press, 1971); Russett, *Sexual Science*; Susan Sleeth Mosedale, "Science Corrupted: Victorian Biologists Consider 'the Woman Question'," *Journal of the History of Biology* 11, no. 1 (Spring 1978): 1–55.

20 See Olive Banks, *Faces of Feminism: A Study of Feminism as a Social Movement* (Oxford: Martin Robertson, 1981); Jane Rendall, *The Origins of Modern Feminism: Women in Britain, France and the United States 1780–1860* (London: Macmillan, 1985); Jane Rendall, ed., *Equal or Different: Women's Politics 1800–1914* (London: Basil Blackwell, 1987); Mary Maynard, "Privilege and Patriarchy: Feminist Thought in the Nineteenth Century," in *Sexuality and Subordination: Interdisciplinary Studies of Gender in the Nineteenth Century*, edited by Susan Mendus and Jane Rendall (New York: Routledge, 1989), 221–47.

21 Quoted in Maynard, "Privilege and Patriarchy," 228.

22 See Evelleen Richards, "Darwin and the Descent of Woman," in *The Wider Domain of Evolutionary Thought*, edited by D. Oldroyd and I. Langham (Boston: D. Reidel, 1983), 57–111, who argues against the idea put forward by Ruth Hubbard that Charles Darwin was motivated by antifeminism. Richards suggests instead that Darwin's ideas "were as much constrained by his commitment to a naturalistic or scientific explanation of human mental and moral characteristics as they were by his socially derived assumptions of the innate inferiority and domesticity of women" (60).

23 For a historical account of the male-domination of science and medicine, see Ludmilla Jordanova, *Sexual Visions: Images of Gender in Science and Medicine between the Eighteenth and Twentieth Centuries* (Madison: University of Wisconsin Press, 1989).

24 Prior to the canonization of evolutionary theory, the debate over the creation of human races took two forms: monogenism, the idea that the various races derived from Adam and Eve, with changes due to environment and degeneration; and polygenism, whereby races were distinct biological species descending from different sources. Despite the fact that a monogenic framework prevailed within evolutionary Darwinism, the polygenic argument was merely shaped to fit the evolutionary model. The polygenists simply conceded the common ancestral source but argued that races had diverged into separate species through differential inheritance. See Stephen Jay Gould, *The Mismeasure of Man* (Middlesex: Penguin, 1981), chaps. 2 and 3.

25 Quoted in Russett, *Sexual Science*, 2.

26 Charles Darwin, *The Descent of Man, and Selection in Relation to Sex* (New York: Modern Library, 1927).
27 Quoted in Mosedale, "Science Corrupted," 6–7.
28 Quoted in Stepan, *The Idea of Race in Science*, 60.
29 Quoted in Mosedale, "Science Corrupted," 14.
30 Quoted in Russett, *Sexual Science*, 43.
31 Quoted in Russett, *Sexual Science*, 74.
32 See Russett, *Sexual Science*, esp. chap. 1; Gould, *Mismeasure of Man*, chap. 3, esp. 103–7.
33 Quoted in Gould, *Mismeasure of Man*, 103.
34 Quoted in Darwin, *Descent of Man*, 875.
35 Quoted in Gould, *Mismeasure of Man*, 103.
36 Russett, *Sexual Science*, 28.
37 Mosedale, "Science Corrupted," 9 n. 21.
38 Sander Gilman, *Difference and Pathology: Race and Madness* (Ithaca, N.Y.: Cornell University Press, 1985), 112.
39 See Sander Gilman, "Black Bodies, White Bodies: Toward an Iconography of Female Sexuality in Late Nineteenth-Century Art, Medicine, and Literature," *Critical Inquiry* 12 (Autumn 1985): 204–42.
40 Siobhan Somerville, "Scientific Racism and the Emergence of the Homosexual Body," *Journal of the History of Sexuality* 5, no. 2 (1994): 252.
41 The notion of a bipotentiality of sexual differentiation (which is related to but not the same thing as hermaphroditism) had been in some ways anticipated some years before this. John Money notes that the idea of sexual differentiation being bipotential was speculated on as early as 1813 by Tiedemann; in Money, "Homosexuality: Bipotentiality, Terminology, and History," in *Bisexualities: The Ideology and Practice of Sexual Contact with Both Men and Women*, edited by Erwin J. Haeberle and Rolf Gindorf (New York: Continuum, 1998), 118.
42 Waldeyer quoted in Darwin, *Descent of Man*, 525.
43 With respect to the developing embryo, the categories of hermaphroditism and bisexuality were for the most part conceptually interchangeable. However, for people born of 'doubtful' or ambiguous sex, the term 'hermaphrodite' was the most common medical designation. See Dreger, *Hermaphrodites*, n. 14 above.
44 Cope and Hall, respectively, quoted in Russett, *Sexual Science*, 55.
45 In this model, then, hermaphrodites were constructed as the lowest of the low.
46 Lawson Tait, *Diseases of Women* (New York: William Wood & Co., 1879), 123.
47 Gilbert Herdt, "Introduction: Third Sexes and Third Genders," in *Third Sex, Third Gender: Beyond Sexual Dimorphism in Culture and History*, edited by Gilbert Herdt (New York: Zone Books, 1994), 21–81, esp. 25–33.
48 See, e.g., Mary Poovey, "In Parenthesis: Immaculate Conception and Feminine Desire," in *Body/Politics: Women and the Discourses of Science*, edited by Mary Jacobus et al. (London: Routledge, 1990), 11–28.

49 In the nineteenth century, sex was predominantly conceived of as a limited-energy system, too much semen expenditure effecting an overall energy loss. See, e.g., Carroll Smith-Rosenberg, "Sex as Symbol in Victorian Purity: An Ethnohistorical Analysis of Jacksonian America," in *Turning Points: Historical and Sociological Essays on the Family*, edited by John Demos and Sarane Spruce Boocock (Chicago: University of Chicago Press, 1978), 212–47; see also G. J. Barker-Benfield, "The Spermatic Economy: A Nineteenth-Century View of Sexuality," in *The American Family in Social-Historical Perspective*, 2d ed., edited by Michael Gordon (New York: St. Martin's Press, 1978), 374–402, for a discussion of sexual excess (particularly masturbation) and its metaphorical link to industrializing discourses of economics and potential for chaos and decay.

50 See Frank J. Sulloway, *Freud, Biologist of the Mind* (London: Burnett Books, 1979), 252–57.

51 For useful essays on degeneration in the nineteenth century, see Chamberlin and Gilman, n. 19 above.

52 For a comprehensive discussion of the social and economic context in the second half of the nineteenth century in America and Western Europe, see Greenberg, *Construction of Homosexuality*, chaps. 8 and 9.

53 See Carroll Smith-Rosenberg, "Discourses of Sexuality and Subjectivity: The New Woman, 1870–1936," in *Hidden from History: Reclaiming the Gay and Lesbian Past*, edited by Martin Duberman et al. (New York: Meridian, 1990), 264–80.

54 For useful discussions of the challenge of subordinate masculinities in the Victorian period, see Ed Cohen, *Talk on the Wilde Side: Toward a Genealogy of a Discourse on Male Sexualities* (New York: Routledge, 1993); Angus McLaren, *The Trials of Masculinity: Policing Sexual Boundaries, 1870–1930* (Chicago: University of Chicago Press, 1997); James Eli Adams, *Dandies and Desert Saints: Styles of Victorian Masculinity* (Ithaca, N.Y.: Cornell University Press, 1995); Rhonda K. Garelick, *Rising Star: Dandyism, Gender, and Performance in the Fin-de-Siècle* (Princeton, N.J.: Princeton University Press, 1998).

55 Sexual anarchy is Elaine Showalter's description for this period. She also discusses the crisis of masculinity at this time. See her *Sexual Anarchy: Gender and Culture at the Fin-de-Siècle* (New York: Viking, 1990), esp. 9–15. See also Joe L. Dubbert, "Progressivism and the Masculinity Crisis," *Psychoanalytic Review* 61 (1974): 443–55; Peter Filene, *Him/Her/Self: Sex Roles in Modern America* (New York: Harcourt Brace Jovanovich, 1975); Michael S. Kimmel, "Men's Responses to Feminism at the Turn of the Century," *Gender and Society* 1 (1987): 517–30; E. A. Rotundo, "Body and Soul: Changing Ideals of American Middle Class Manhood, 1770–1920," *Journal of Social History* 16 (1983): 23–38.

56 Clearly, the problem of miscegenation is relevant here. However, it is at this point that I must, due to problems of space, narrow my analysis to the 'problem of homosexuality' in its relation to bisexuality. For useful discussions of miscegenation, see Joel Williamson, *New People: Miscegenation and Mulattos in the United States* (New York: Free Press, 1980). There is at this time a representational intersection and overlap among discourses of miscegenation and homosexuality. See Somerville, "Scientific Racism," 256–60; Andrew Koppelman, "The Miscegenation Analogy: Sodomy Law as Sex Discrimination," *Yale Law Journal* 98 (November 1988): 145–64.

57   Trumbach, "Gender and the Homosexual Role," 155; see n. 2 above.

58   Michel Foucault, *The History of Sexuality*, vol. 1: *An Introduction* (New York: Vintage Books, 1980), 123.

59   Sexologist Iwan Bloch conferred this title on Krafft-Ebing at the turn of the century. See Sulloway, *Freud*, 279.

60   See Karl Heinrich Ulrichs, *The Riddle of "Man-Manly" Love: The Pioneering Work on Male Homosexuality*, vol. 1, translated by Michael A. Lombardi-Nash (New York: Prometheus Books, 1994). See Hubert C. Kennedy, "The 'Third Sex' Theory of Karl Heinrich Ulrichs," *Journal of Homosexuality* 6, nos. 1/2 (Fall/Winter 1980/81): 107–8, where Krafft-Ebing is quoted in a letter to Ulrichs in 1879 acknowledging the latter's influence: "The study of your writings on love between men interested me in the highest degree . . . since you for the first time openly spoke about these matters. From that day on, when—I believe it was in 1866—you sent me your writings, I have devoted my full attention to this phenomenon, which at the time was as puzzling to me as it was interesting; it was the knowledge of your writings alone which led to my studies in this highly important field."

61   Richard von Krafft-Ebing, *Psychopathia Sexualis: A Medico-Forensic Study*, translated by Harry E. Wedeck (New York: G. P. Putnam's Sons, 1965), 357–58; my emphasis.

62   The physician Carl Westphal was also influenced by Ulrich's writings, the first writer to scientifically articulate the notion of a third sex. The inversion of the normal sexual instinct he called "contrary sexual feeling." See Bullough, *Science in the Bedroom*, 38, n. 2 above.

63   Chauncey, "From Sexual Inversion to Homosexuality," esp. 121.

64   Krafft-Ebing, *Psychopathia Sexualis*, 364.

65   Quoted in Chauncey, "From Sexual Inversion to Homosexuality," 119.

66   Gert Hekma, "'A Female Soul in a Male Body': Sexual Inversion as Gender Inversion in Nineteenth-Century Sexology," in *Third Sex, Third Gender: Beyond Sexual Dimorphism in Culture and History*, edited by Gilbert Herdt (New York: Zone Books, 1994), 234. See Smith-Rosenberg, "Discourses of Sexuality and Subjectivity," 264–80; and Esther Newton, "The Mythic Mannish Lesbian: Radclyffe Hall and the New Woman," in *Hidden from History*, edited by Duberman et al. (New York: Meridian, 1990), 281–93, for discussions of the creation of the mannish lesbian.

67   Smith-Rosenberg, "Discourses of Sexuality," 270; see also Lillian Faderman, *Surpassing the Love of Men* (New York: Morrow, 1981), chap. 2.

68   Davidson, "Sex and the Emergence of Sexuality," 41; see n. 4 above.

69   The effects of this inscription for later theorizing on sexuality will become all too apparent in the ensuing chapters.

70   Chauncey, "From Sexual Inversion to Homosexuality," 143.

71   Havelock Ellis, *Studies in the Psychology of Sex*, 3d ed., rev. and enlarged, vol. 2: *Sexual Inversion* (hereafter abbreviated to *Studies 2*) (1901; reprint, Philadelphia: F. A. Davis Co., 1928), 285.

72   Havelock Ellis and John Addington Symonds, *Sexual Inversion* (London: Wilson & Macmillan, 1897), 63.

73 See Smith-Rosenberg, "Discourses of Sexuality"; Newton, "The Mythic Mannish Lesbian"; and Chauncey, "From Sexual Inversion to Homosexuality."
74 Ellis, *Sexual Inversion*, 96–97.
75 Alice Jardine, *Gynesis: Configurations of Woman and Modernity* (Ithaca, N.Y.: Cornell University Press, 1985), 68.
76 Chauncey, "From Sexual Inversion to Homosexuality," esp. 128–32; Sulloway, *Freud*, 290–96.
77 Havelock Ellis, *Psychology of Sex: A Manual for Students* (New York: Emerson, 1933), 105.
78 Chauncey, "From Sexual Inversion to Homosexuality," 130–31.
79 Sulloway, *Freud*, 300.
80 For a brief account of anthropological studies during this time, see Sulloway, *Freud*, 315–18.
81 James G. Kiernan, "Sexual Perversion and the Whitechapel Murders," *Medical Standard* 4 (1888): 129–30.
82 G. Frank Lydston, "Sexual Perversion, Satyriasis and Nymphomania," *Medical and Surgical Reporter* 61 (1889): 255. For a fuller treatment, see Lydston's *The Diseases of Society* (Philadelphia: Lippincott, 1904).
83 Havelock Ellis makes this latter point in *Sexual Inversion*, 133 n. 2.
84 Lydston, "Sexual Perversion," 255.
85 Quoted in Sulloway, *Freud*, 293.
86 Sulloway, *Freud*, 295.
87 *Studies 2*, 314.
88 There were, of course, other sexologists, but in this brief sketch I can only mention the most significant. For more comprehensive discussions, see Bullough, *Science in the Bedroom*, chaps. 2 and 3; and Sulloway, *Freud*, chap. 8.
89 This is a summary of Max Dessoir by Bullough, *Science in the Bedroom*, 47.
90 Sulloway, *Freud*, 295–96.
91 Havelock Ellis, *Man and Woman: A Study of Human Secondary Sexual Characters* (1904; reprint, London: Walter Scott, 1914), 23.
92 Quoted in Russett, *Sexual Science*, 72.
93 Ellis, *Man and Woman*, chap. 6.
94 Ellis, *Sexual Inversion*, x.
95 *Studies 2*, 79–80.
96 *Studies 2*, 312.
97 For a discussion of miscegenation, or the mixed racial body, see Somerville, "Scientific Racism," 256–62.
98 Ellis, *Sexual Inversion*, 133; my emphasis.
99 See Kennedy, "The 'Third Sex' Theory," 107 (see n. 60 above); Ulrichs, *The Riddle*, 161.
100 Krafft-Ebing, *Psychopathia Sexualis*, 373–85.

101 "Pseudo-homosexuality" was a term to describe homosexual activity as an effect of female scarcity. The usual examples relate homosexual sex in same-sex institutions such as prisons. See Ellis, *Studies* 2, 4.

102 *Studies* 2, 88.

103 Quoted in Dreger, *Hermaphrodites*, 30, n. 14 above.

104 *Studies* 2, 311.

105 This is a quote by a physiologist that Ellis endorses; Ellis, *Studies* 2, 313.

106 *Studies* 2, 88.

107 The term "'full bisexuality'" is used by Jonathan Dollimore, *Sexual Dissidence: Augustine to Wilde, Freud to Foucault* (Oxford: Clarendon Press, 1991), 217, in a discussion of Freud. See also Michael du Plessis, "Blatantly Bisexual; or, Unthinking Queer Theory," in *RePresenting Bisexualities: Subjects and Cultures of Fluid Desire*, edited by Donald E. Hall and Maria Pramaggiore (New York: New York University Press, 1996), 29.

CHAPTER 3

1 It is interesting that Sigmund Freud, prior to 1927, in "Some Psychical Consequences of the Anatomical Distinction between the Sexes" (1925) (*The Standard Edition of the Complete Psychological Works of Sigmund Freud*, 24 vols., edited by James Strachey [London: Hogarth Press, 1953–1974], vol. 19, 253), suggests "disavowal" (or denial) to be the opposite of repression, "a process which in the mental life of children seems neither uncommon nor very dangerous but which in an adult would mean the beginning of a psychosis." I will leave the reader to ponder the implications of this. (Hereafter, *The Standard Edition* is cited as *SE*, followed immediately by the volume number and, if applicable, the page.)

2 In a letter to Fliess in 1901, Freud, upon realizing the enormity of the concept of bisexuality, wrote: "And now the main thing! As far as I can see, my next work will be called 'Human Bisexuality.' It will go to the root of the problem and say the last word." See Jeffrey Moussaieff Masson, ed., *Complete Letters of Sigmund Freud to Wilhelm Fliess, 1887–1904* (Cambridge, Mass.: Harvard University Press, 1985), 448.

3 Lance Spurr, "When Straight Boys Stray," *Melbourne Star Observer*, 11 August 1995, 8.

4 See Marjorie Garber, *Vice Versa: Bisexuality and the Eroticism of Everyday Life* (New York: Simon and Schuster, 1995), chaps. 7 and 8; Frank J. Sulloway, *Freud, Biologist of the Mind: Beyond the Psychoanalytic Legend* (London: Burnett Books, 1979), 158–60; and Sigmund Freud, *Three Essays on the Theory of Sexuality*, *SE* 7:141. Freud posited a distinction between "hermaphroditism" (one of his obscure and varying definitions of bisexuality) and "true hermaphroditism." The former "occurs normally" such that in "every normal male or female individual, traces are found of the apparatus of the opposite sex." As regards the latter, in "rare cases both kinds of sexual apparatus are found side by side fully developed."

5 In suggesting his usage to be a neo-Freudian form of fantasy, I am merely pointing to the fact that Freud was the first theorist of sexuality to introduce a psychological concept of fantasy as central to the theory of human sexuality.

6 John Fletcher, "Freud and His Uses: Psychoanalysis and Gay Theory," in *Coming On*

Strong: Gay Politics and Culture, edited by Simon Shepherd and Mick Wallis (London: Unwin Hyman, 1989), 101.

7 Sulloway, *Freud*, 3–22, 238–76.

8 Sigmund Freud, *An Autobiographical Study* (1925), SE 20:14.

9 Sandor Rado, *Psychoanalysis of Behavior: Collected Papers* (New York: Grune and Stratton, 1956), 139–40, argues that "bisexuality far antedates the scientific era and owes its origin to primeval, emotional needs of animistic man. It is important to bear this in mind in our examination of the part played by the same concept in modern science." He goes further to suggest that myths of hermaphroditism far predate Greek mythology.

10 Charles Darwin quoted in Sulloway, *Freud*, 159.

11 Sulloway, *Freud*, 159. Darwin considered this missing link to be the ascidian organisms discovered by Aleksandr Kovalevsky. They were thought to contain a rudimentary spinal chord.

12 See Sigmund Freud, letter to Fliess, 7 August 1901, in Masson, *Complete Letters*, 448.

13 Sulloway, *Freud*, 158–60, 292–96.

14 Freud, letter to Fliess, 1 August 1899, in Sigmund Freud, *The Origins of Psycho-Analysis: Letters to Wilhelm Fliess, Drafts and Notes: 1887–1902* (London: Imago, 1954), 289.

15 Freud, *Three Essays*, 141. Fliess suggested in *Origins of Psycho-Analysis*, 7, that "consideration of these two groups of biological phenomena points to the conclusion that they have a solid inner connection with both male and female sexual characteristics. And if both—only with different emphasis—are present in both man and woman, that is only consistent with our bisexual constitution."

16 Freud quoted in Sulloway, *Freud*, 275.

17 Freud quoted in Sulloway, *Freud*, 275.

18 It is worth noting here that bisexuality is central to Freud's notion of repression, the cornerstone of the unconscious. Repression, he suggested to Fliess in confirmation of Fliess's notion of bisexuality, "is possible only through reaction between two sexual currents." See letter to Fliess, 7 August 1901, in Masson, *Complete Letters*, 448–50; see also Sulloway, *Freud*, chaps. 5–7, for a painstaking account of Freud's use of Fliessian and evolutionary biological concepts.

19 Freud, letter to Fliess, 12 June 1897, *The Origins of Psycho-Analysis*, 211.

20 It seems that even by 1898 the aspirations of psychoanalytic independence must have been concerning Fliess. In a letter of response to Fliess, 22 September 1898, Freud stated: "I am not in the least in disagreement with you, and have no desire at all to leave the psychology hanging in the air with no organic basis. But, beyond a feeling of conviction, I have nothing, either theoretical or therapeutic, to work on, and so I must behave as if I were confronted by psychological factors only" (*The Origins of Psycho-Analysis*, 264).

21 Freud, letter to Fliess, 19 September 1901, in Masson, *Complete Letters*, 450; my emphasis.

22 Ernest Jones quoted in Sulloway, *Freud*, 223.

23 Sigmund Freud, *The Psychopathology of Everyday Life* (1901), SE 6:143–44.

24 For the most comprehensive account of the Freud-Fliess split, see Sulloway, *Freud*, 213–37; see also Garber, *Vice Versa*, chap. 7.

25 Freud, letter to Fliess, 23 July 1904, in Masson, *Complete Letters*, 464.

26 Garber, *Vice Versa*, 194, suggests something similar: "Freud never came to write a book called 'Human Bisexuality' [a book he said to Fliess that he intended to write], but it is arguable that the entire corpus of his work could be regarded under that title."

27 See Diana Fuss, "Freud's Fallen Woman: Identification, Desire, and 'A Case of Homosexuality in a Woman'," in *Fear of a Queer Planet: Queer Politics and Social Theory*, edited by Michael Warner (Minneapolis: University of Minnesota Press, 1993), 46, where she uses these terms in relation to female homosexuality. I have borrowed them to refer to bisexuality, which is itself inextricably bound to Freud's 'enigma of woman'. For an interesting discussion of bisexuality and 'the woman question', see Sarah Kofman, *The Enigma of Woman: Woman in Freud's Writing*, translated by Catherine Porter (Ithaca, N.Y.: Cornell University Press, 1985).

28 Freud, *Three Essays*, 220.

29 For an interesting reading, and a brief summary of psychoanalytic readings, of Freud himself regarding the separation from Fliess and its continuing influence on his life and work, see Russell H. Davis, *Freud's Concept of Passivity* (Madison, Wisc.: International Universities Press, 1993), chaps. 5, 6.

30 Sulloway, *Freud*, 183, notes that "what is not perhaps sufficiently appreciated by most historians of psychoanalysis is just how extensively this notion of bisexuality served to link Freud's psychoanalytic conception of human development to the biological theory championed by Fliess."

31 Freud, letter to Fliess, 22 September 1898, *The Origins of Psycho-Analysis*, 264.

32 Sigmund Freud, "The Psychogenesis of a Case of Homosexuality in a Woman" (1920), SE 18:171.

33 See Garber, *Vice Versa*, chaps. 6–7, where she traces Freud's use of "mythological tropes of bisexuality." Freud was aware of the tenuous borders between science and mythology. See Sigmund Freud, "Why War?" (1933), SE 22:211, where, in writing to Albert Einstein he says: "It may perhaps seem to you as though our theories are a kind of mythology and, in the present case, not even an agreeable one. But does not every science come in the end to a kind of mythology like this?"

34 See Sigmund Freud, *Civilization and Its Discontents* (1930), SE 21:42–43 n. 3, where he alludes to this conflation of mythology and biology, based it seems, on Aristophanes' fable of Hermaphroditus. The epigraph that opens this section is quoted in Garber, *Vice Versa*, 170.

35 Freud, letter to Fliess, 22 September 1898, *The Origins of Psycho-Analysis*, 264.

36 Freud, *Civilization and Its Discontents*, 43 n. 3.

37 Sigmund Freud, *An Outline of Psycho-Analysis* (1940), SE 23:188.

38 Freud, letters to Fliess, 7 August 1901 and 19 September 1901, *The Origins of Psycho-Analysis*, 334–35, 337.

39 Sigmund Freud, "The Claims of Psycho-Analysis to Scientific Interest" (1913), SE 13:182.

40 Sigmund Freud, "From the History of an Infantile Neurosis" (1918), SE 17:110.

41 Sigmund Freud, "Analysis Terminable and Interminable" (1937), SE 23:251.

42 See Freud, "Analysis Terminable," for Freud's discussion on his desire not to "sexualise repression in this way—that is, to explain it on biological grounds instead of on psychological ones."

43 Sigmund Freud, "Two Encyclopaedia Articles" (1923), SE 18:247.

44 Freud, letter to Fliess, 15 October 1897, in Masson, *Complete Letters*, 272.

45 Sigmund Freud, *The Interpretation of Dreams* (1900), SE 4:257.

46 Sigmund Freud, "Female Sexuality" (1931), SE 21:228.

47 This idea was first developed in Sigmund Freud, "A Child Is Being Beaten" (1919), SE 17:175–204.

48 Sigmund Freud, *The Ego and the Id* (1923), SE 19:31.

49 Freud, *The Ego and the Id*, 33.

50 Freud, "Female Sexuality," 229.

51 Sigmund Freud, "Some Psychical Consequences of the Anatomical Distinction between the Sexes" (1925), SE 19:257.

52 Sigmund Freud, "The Dissolution of the Oedipus Complex" (1924), SE 19:176.

53 Freud, "The Dissolution of the Oedipus Complex," 176–77.

54 Freud, *Three Essays*, 144–45. For accounts of Freud's theories on male homosexuality, see Kenneth Lewes, *The Psychoanalytic Theory of Male Homosexuality* (New York: Simon and Schuster, 1988), chap. 2; and Michael Warner, "Homo-Narcissism; or Heterosexuality," in *Engendering Men: The Question of Male Feminist Criticism*, edited by Joseph A. Boone and Michael Cadden (New York: Routledge, 1990), 190–206.

55 Freud, "Dissolution," 178.

56 Freud, "Female Sexuality," 226.

57 See Sigmund Freud, postscript to *An Autobiographical Study* (1925), SE 20:36; and "Female Sexuality," 228.

58 Luce Irigaray, *This Sex Which Is Not One*, translated by Catherine Porter (Ithaca, N.Y.: Cornell University Press, 1985), 74.

59 Freud, "Some Psychical Consequences," 256.

60 Freud, "Some Psychical Consequences," 252.

61 Sigmund Freud, "Femininity" (1933), SE 22:124.

62 Freud, "Femininity," 128.

63 Freud, "Female Sexuality," 230.

64 For excellent discussions on Freud and female homosexuality, see Teresa de Lauretis, *The Practice of Love: Lesbian Sexuality and Perverse Desire* (Bloomington: Indiana University Press, 1994), chap. 1; and Judith Roof, *A Lure of Knowledge: Lesbian Sexuality and Theory* (New York: Columbia University Press, 1991), chap. 4.

65 Freud, "A Child Is Being Beaten," 202. This innate constitution is, as Freud himself

reveals, a biomyth: "The theory of the instincts is, as it were, our mythology. The instincts are mythical beings, superb in their indefiniteness." Freud quoted in Rado, *Psychoanalysis of Behavior*, 131–32; see n. 9 above.

66 Freud, *The Ego and the Id*, 34.

67 Mikkel Borch-Jacobsen, *The Freudian Subject*, translated by Catherine Porter (Stanford, Calif.: Stanford University Press, 1988), 47.

68 Freud, *The Ego and the Id*, 34.

69 Freud quoted in Rado, *Psychoanalysis of Behavior*, 186.

70 Freud, *Three Essays*, 239–40; my emphasis.

71 Freud, "Psychogenesis," 169; see n. 32 above.

72 Freud, "Some Psychical Consequences," 257.

73 Freud, "From the History of an Infantile Neurosis," 86.

74 Sigmund Freud, *Introductory Lectures on Psycho-Analysis* (1916–17), SE 15–16:370–71.

75 Freud, *Three Essays*, 125–243, esp. 243.

76 Freud, "Psychogenesis," 171; my emphasis.

77 Freud, "Analysis Terminable and Interminable," 252–53.

78 Freud, "Femininity," 132.

79 Freud, *Three Essays*, 241.

80 In a paper delivered to the British Psycho-Analytical Society, January 1929, Douglas Bryan ("Bisexuality," *International Journal of Psycho-Analysis* 11 [1930]: 150–66), called for greater attention to Freud's notion of bisexuality. He lamented, however, that little attention was paid, even by Freud himself, to bisexuality as it relates to adult sexuality. Bryan alluded, perhaps unwittingly, to the implication in Freudian thought that sexuality is constructed as an evolutionary movement from child to adult. "Are we to suppose that the infant gradually loses its bisexuality as it progresses to the adult normal sexuality, or is it retained and only manifested in the fore-pleasure as has also been suggested?" (152). It is important to point out that the Freudian heteronormative teleological account is thoroughly racialized. In addition to the irredeemable 'loss' of bisexuality identified by Bryan, there is the concomitant 'loss' (or rather, elision) of racial markers formative of Western (constructions of) subjectivity. The unexplained association of primitive culture with (the non-Western) race was indicative of early (Western) psychoanalytic theorizing. A state of primitivity against which Western 'civilization' is founded becomes a space of 'blackness'. In the Freudian account of psychosexual development then, the 'mature' child emerges as the unmarked figure of normality, both white and heterosexual. For a very useful discussion of the interimplicating axes of sexuality, gender, and race constitutive of the early Eurocentric psychoanalytic theorization of subjectivity (and the residual inattention to race in contemporary psychoanalytic feminism), see Jean Walton, "Re-Placing Race in (White) Psychoanalytic Discourse: Founding Narratives of Feminism," *Critical Inquiry* 21 (Summer 1995): 775–804.

81 For an excellent discussion and critique of the assumptions within Freud's representation of homosexuality as narcissism, see Warner, "Homo-Narcissism"; see n. 54 above.

82 Freud, *Three Essays*, 144–45.

83 For a discussion of bisexuality and hysteria, see Sigmund Freud, "Hysterical Phantasies and Their Relation to Bisexuality" (1908), SE 9:155–66.

84 Sigmund Freud, Preface to Reik's *Ritual: Psycho-Analytic Studies* (1919), SE 17:262.

85 See Garber, *Vice Versa*, 204–6, for a discussion on civilization and the repression of bisexuality.

86 Fuss, "Freud's Fallen Woman," 53; see n. 27 above.

87 Sigmund Freud, *New Introductory Lectures on Psychoanalysis* (1933), SE 22:21.

88 For an excellent discussion of Freud's desire to establish psychoanalysis as disciplinary counterpart to biology, see Sulloway, *Freud*, chaps. 1, 12.

89 Freud, Letter to Fliess, 22 September 1898, *The Origins of Psycho-Analysis*, 264.

90 Freud, "Psychogenesis," 169; Freud, *Three Essays*, 135–48.

91 Freud, "Psychogenesis," 171; see n. 32 above.

92 See Juliet Mitchell, *Psychoanalysis and Feminism* (New York: Vintage Press, 1974), esp. the introduction. My chapter title, "The Unsolved Figure in the Carpet," is taken from Mitchell's study, 50.

93 Sigmund Freud, "On the Universal Tendency to Debasement in the Sphere of Love" (1912), SE 11:189.

94 Mitchell, *Psychoanalysis and Feminism*, 47–48.

95 See Freud, *Outline of Psycho-Analysis*, 45; and Freud, *Civilization and Its Discontents*, 43.

96 Freud, "The Claims of Psycho-Analysis," 182.

97 Freud, *Civilization and Its Discontents*, 43.

98 Freud, "Two Encyclopaedia Articles," 258; see n. 43 above.

99 Garber, *Vice Versa*, 203–4, 182.

100 Freud, "Analysis Terminable and Interminable," 243–44.

101 Judith Butler, *Gender Trouble: Feminism and the Subversion of Identity* (New York: Routledge, 1990), 61.

102 Butler, *Gender Trouble*, 61; original emphasis.

103 Freud, "Hysterical Phantasies"; see n. 83 above.

104 See Jacqueline Rose, "Introduction-II," in *Feminine Sexuality: Jacques Lacan and the école Freudienne*, edited by Juliet Mitchell and Jacqueline Rose (New York: W. W. Norton, 1982), 49.

105 See Rado, *Psychoanalysis of Behavior*, 141–42, where he suggests in relation to Freud that "if the hypothesis were abandoned in the field of biology from which it had been taken, the data accumulated by psychoanalysis would have to be reinterpreted."

106 Mitchell, *Psychoanalysis and Feminism*, 49 n. 14.

107 Freud, *Outline of Psycho-Analysis*, 188; see n. 37 above.

108 Butler, *Gender Trouble*, 60.

109 I have taken the term "psychophysiology" from Simone de Beauvoir, *The Second Sex* (Harmondsworth: Penguin, 1972), 69.

110 Guy Hocquenghem, *Homosexual Desire*, translated by Daniella Dangoor (London: Allison and Busby, 1978), 61.

111 Freud, *Three Essays*, 145 n. 1. This footnote was added in 1915.

CHAPTER 4

1 Sigmund Freud, *Three Essays on the Theory of Sexuality* (1905), SE 7:220.

2 Freud, "Hysterical Phantasies and Their Relation to Bisexuality" (1908), SE 9:165–66.

3 Lynne Segal, *Slow Motion: Changing Masculinities, Changing Men* (London: Virago Press, 1990), 141. See also John D'Emilio, "The Homosexual Menace: The Politics of Sexuality in Cold War America," in *Passion and Power: Sexuality and History*, edited by Kathy Peiss et al. (Philadelphia: Temple University Press, 1989), 226–40.

4 Henry Abelove, "Freud, Male Homosexuality, and the Americans," in *The Lesbian and Gay Studies Reader*, edited by Henry Abelove et al. (New York: Routledge, 1993), 391.

5 Peter Gay, ed., *The Freud Reader* (London: Vintage, 1995), xlvii.

6 Maryse Choisy, *Sigmund Freud: A New Appraisal* (London: Peter Owen, 1963), 5.

7 See Sigmund Freud, *Civilization and Its Discontents* (1930), SE 22:41, for a concise summary of these revolutionary views.

8 Freud, *Three Essays*, 144–45.

9 See Abelove, "Freud, Male Homosexuality," 381–93, for a useful discussion of Freud's attitude to male homosexuality. While Freud dealt almost entirely with male homosexuality, his single study of female homosexuality did not seem to consider it a pathological variation. See Sigmund Freud, "The Psychogenesis of a Case of Homosexuality in a Woman" (1920), SE 18:155–72.

10 Freud quoted in Abelove, "Freud, Male Homosexuality," 382; original emphasis.

11 Abelove, "Freud, Male Homosexuality," 383.

12 Freud quoted in Ernest Jones, *The Life and Work of Sigmund Freud*, vol. 3, *The Last Phase: 1919 to 1939* (New York: Basic Books, 1957), 195–96.

13 Abelove, "Freud, Male Homosexuality," 383.

14 See Sigmund Freud, the section entitled "The Ego and the Super-Ego (Ego Ideal)," in *The Ego and the Id* (1923), SE 19:28–39.

15 See Kenneth Lewes, *The Psychoanalytic Theory of Male Homosexuality* (New York: Simon and Schuster, 1988), 69–94, for a discussion of oedipal resolutions.

16 I am borrowing, and will be later elaborating on Judith Butler's phrase "proper object." See her "Introduction: Against Proper Objects," *differences* 6, nos. 2 and 3 (1994): 1–26.

17 This is not to suggest that aspects of his thinking were not structured by the logic of noncontradiction; rather, Freud attempted a more sophisticated approach that often, in fact, incorporated contradiction.

18 Freud, *Three Essays*, 239.

19 Sigmund Freud, "The Psychogenesis of a Case of Homosexuality in a Woman" (1920), SE 18:151.

20 Butler, "Against Proper Objects," 6.

21 D'Emilio, "The Homosexual Menace," 226–40, esp. 233.

22 Michel Foucault, "Truth and Power," Interview with Alessandro Fontana and Pasquale Pasquino in *Power/Knowledge: Selected Interviews and Other Writings, 1972–1977*, edited by Colin Gordon (New York: Pantheon Books, 1980), 131–32. Foucault sees this economy as being characterized by five important traits: "'Truth' is centered on the form of scientific discourse and the institutions which produce it; it is subject to constant economic and political incitement (the demand for truth, as much for economic production as for political power); it is the object, under diverse forms, of immense diffusion and consumption (circulating through apparatuses of education and information whose extent is relatively broad in the social body, notwithstanding certain strict limitations); it is produced and transmitted under the control, dominant if not exclusive, of a few great political and economic apparatuses (university, army, writing, media); lastly, it is the issue of a whole political debate and social confrontation ('ideological' struggles)."

23 I say only *some* because despite the fact that Wilhelm Stekel declared in *Bi-Sexual Love* (translated by James S. Van Teslaar [New York: Emerson Books, 1950], 43) that "nature has created us bisexual beings and requires us to act as bisexual beings," later he suggested that "the human race requires the frequent suppression of certain instincts and every step in ethical and cultural progress involves giving up some portion of instinctive cravings."

24 Lewes, *Psychoanalytic Theory*, 102; see n. 15 above. Rado first read his work on bisexuality at the ninety-sixth annual meeting of the American Psychiatric Association, Cincinnati, Ohio, 20–24 May 1940, before the joint session with the American Psychoanalytic Association.

25 For an overview of this period, see Lewes, *Psychoanalytic Theory*, 95–121.

26 Melanie Klein, *The Psycho-Analysis of Children* (New York: Delacorte, 1932).

27 Freud alluded in some way to the possibility of oral determinants in the case of homosexuality. In his study of Leonardo da Vinci he stated: "We will for a moment leave aside the question as to what connection there is between homosexuality and sucking at the mother's breast." Freud is here quoted in Edmund Bergler, "The Myth of a New National Disease: Homosexuality and the Kinsey Report," *Psychiatric Quarterly* 22 (1948): 70. See also Freud, *Three Essays*, 181–83, where he says: "No one who has seen a baby sinking back satiated from the breast and falling asleep with flushed cheeks and a blissful smile can escape the reflection that this picture persists as a prototype of the expression of sexual satisfaction in later life."

28 Freud, "Psychogenesis," 171.

29 Sandor Rado, "A Critical Examination of the Concept of Bisexuality," *Psychosomatic Medicine* 2 (1940): 459–67; reprinted in *Psychoanalysis of Behavior: Collected Papers* (New York: Grune & Stratton, 1956). Quotes from this essay are taken from the version printed in this collection.

30 Rado argued that the evolution of the sexes and sexual behavior "followed a push and pull principle." In short, intercourse is designed as a complementary procedure whereby the penis 'pushes' into the vagina, and the vagina 'pulls', or 'milks' the penis. This produces a "generalized 'push and pull' toward the union of sperm and egg" (188).

31 Despite the fact that his discussion in this article is about female castration fear, the phrase that I have quoted is applicable to both male and female homosexuality. Heterosexuality is the natural 'inner orientation', but it can remain hidden due to certain social relationships.

32 For a discussion of the "pleasure organization," see Rado, "A Critical Examination of the Concept of Bisexuality," 145–49.

33 See Freud, *Three Essays*, 181–83; see n. 1 above.

34 In *Psychoanalysis of Behavior*, 119, Rado suggested that the "inner orientation" of neurotic women was thrown off course by an "untrue compass." I am using this metaphor of Rado's somewhat differently to his usage, but I suggest it to be an accurate reflection with widespread application to the rest of his heteronormative sexual theory.

35 Lionel Ovesey ("The Homosexual Conflict: An Adaptational Analysis," *Psychiatry* 17 [1954]: 243–50), popularized the term "pseudohomosexuality," which was the articulation of the dominant view during this period of anything other than heterosexuality.

36 Rado, "A Critical Examination of the Concept of Bisexuality," 209–10.

37 Lewes, *Psychoanalytic Theory*, 102.

38 Ironically, of course, this antiessentialism was not extended to the realm of normative sexuality, as we will see shortly. In fact, this antiessentialism was itself grounded in heterosexual essentialism.

39 Bernard Robbins, "Psychological Implications of the Male Homosexual 'Marriage'," *Psychoanalytic Review* 10 (1943): 436.

40 Charles Hulbeck, "Emotional Conflicts in Homosexuality," *American Journal of Psychoanalysis* 8 (1948): 72; my emphasis.

41 Harry Gershman, "Some Aspects of Compulsive Homosexuality," *American Journal of Psychoanalysis* 12 (1952): 100, "Considerations of Some Aspects of Homosexuality," *American Journal of Psychoanalysis* 13 (1953): 82–83.

42 John Poe, "The Successful Treatment of a 40-Year-Old Passive Homosexual Based on an Adaptational View of Sexual Behavior," *Psychoanalytic Review* 39 (1952): 23–33, quote on p. 23.

43 Apart from an obvious skepticism that is required when reading accounts of "successful treatment" and gauging what this in fact means, Poe's generalizations—like most psychoanalytic theories of homosexuality for sixty or so years—were based on the account of one patient. I scarcely need to point out the theoretical problems with this approach.

44 Ovesey, "The Homosexual Conflict," 244; my emphasis.

45 Alfred Kinsey and his Institute for Sex Research were criticized for contributing to the moral degeneration of American society, thus further exposing it to the threat of communism. See Paul H. Gebhard, "The Institute," in *Sex Research: Studies from the Kinsey Institute*, edited by Martin S. Weinberg (New York: Oxford University Press, 1976), 10–22.

46 Cleland S. Ford and Frank A. Beach, *Patterns of Sexual Behavior* (New York: Harper and Brothers, 1951), 143.

47 For a concise yet comprehensive summary of this period, see D'Emilio, "The Homosexual Menace"; see n. 3 above. See also John D'Emilio, *Sexual Politics, Sexual Communities: The Making of a Homosexual Minority in the United States 1940–1970* (Chicago: University of Chicago Press, 1983), 40–125.

48 Segal, *Slow Motion*, 10. See also Shari L. Thurer, *The Myths of Motherhood: How Culture Reinvents the Good Mother* (New York: Houghton Mifflin, 1994), chap. 7.

49 Melitta Sperling paraphrased by J. Arlow, "Report: Panel on Perversion: Theoretical and Therapeutic Aspects," *Journal of the American Psychoanalytic Association* 2 (1954): 342–43.

50 See, e.g., D'Emilio, "The Homosexual Menace."

51 Sigmund Freud, "The Sexual Aberrations (Three Contributions to the Theory of Sex)," in *The Basic Writings of Sigmund Freud*, edited and translated by A. A. Brill (New York: Modern Library, 1938), 574–75.

52 Klein, *Psycho-Analysis of Children*, 342–50; see n. 26 above.

53 Ludwig Eidelberg and Edmund Bergler, "Der Mammakomplex des Mannes," *Internationale Zeitschrift fuer Psychoanalyse* 19 (1933): 547–83.

54 Edmund Bergler, *Homosexuality: Disease or Way of Life?* (New York: Collier Books, 1962), 9. This book was originally published in 1956 by Hill and Wang.

55 Lewes, *Psychoanalytic Theory*, 122–23.

56 Alfred Kinsey et al., *Sexual Behavior in the Human Male* (Philadelphia: Saunders, 1948), esp. 199–203. Kinsey's 'findings' led him and his researchers to raise "a question as to whether the terms 'normal' and 'abnormal' belong in a scientific vocabulary" (199).

57 Lewes, *Psychoanalytic Theory*, 122, 124.

58 See Lewes, *Psychoanalytic Theory*, chap. 6, for a survey of the various analytic responses to the Kinsey report. For a discussion of North American social reactions, see Janice M. Irvine, *Disorders of Desire: Sex and Gender in Modern American Sexology* (Philadelphia: Temple University Press, 1990), 31–66.

59 Arlow, "Report," 338.

60 Bergler, "Myth of a New National Disease," 66–88; see n. 27 above.

61 See also Bergler, *Homosexuality*, 174, where he was vehement in his rejection of Kinsey's study, going as far as arguing that the report would in fact *harm* homosexuals, by obscuring "the only means of coping with the problem: medical treatment."

62 Bergler, *Homosexuality*, 140.

63 Edmund Bergler, "Differential Diagnosis between Spurious Homosexuality and Perversion Homosexuality," *Psychiatric Quarterly* 31 (1947): 405.

64 Bergler, *Homosexuality*, 8. Bergler is here referring to the discipline of psychoanalysis as a whole; for as early as 1933 with the publication of "The Breast Complex" he claimed, along with Eidelberg, to have cured a case of male homosexuality. See Edmund Bergler, "Eight Prerequisites for the Psychoanalytic Treatment of Homosexuality," *Psychoanalytic Review* 31 (1944): 260. In addition to this he had already developed the theory of homosexuality in his 1944 paper.

65 Bergler, *Homosexuality*, 64.

66 Bergler, *Homosexuality*, 102. Bergler actually uses the word "unknown," but he is also arguing that it was 'undiscovered'.

67 Bergler, *Homosexuality*, 27.

68 Bergler, *Homosexuality*, 42–43.

69 Bergler, "Differential Diagnosis," 400.

70 Bergler, *Homosexuality*, 145.

71 Bergler, "Differential Diagnosis," 402–3.

72 Bergler, *Homosexuality*, 245, 246.

73 Lewes, *Psychoanalytic Theory*, 153; see n. 15 above.

74 Luce Irigaray, *This Sex Which Is Not One*, translated by Catherine Porter (Ithaca, N.Y.: Cornell University Press, 1985), 74.

75 See Bergler, "Differential Diagnosis," 399–409.

76 Bergler, *Homosexuality*, 8. I am not suggesting that any other trope has a literal referent, for of course in the world of poststructuralism, all names are improper. I am merely highlighting the fact that in Bergler's framework most names refer to 'true' objects, yet bisexuality does not.

77 Bergler, *Homosexuality*, 80.

78 For a succinct account of the common themes of the oral thesis, see Charles Berg, "Editorial Survey," in *The Problem of Homosexuality*, edited by Charles Berg and C. Allen (New York: Citadel Press, 1958), 37–41.

79 Abram Kardiner et al., "A Methodological Study of Freudian Theory III: Narcissism, Bisexuality and the Dual Instinct Theory," *Journal of Nervous and Mental Disease* 129, no. 3 (September 1959): 212.

80 To be sure, there were counterhegemonic theories of homosexuality within the psychoanalytic field during this period. Their voices were, however, marginal to the psychoanalytic consensus. I will deal briefly with some of these in the next chapter. See Ronald Bayer, *Homosexuality and American Psychiatry: The Politics of Diagnosis* (Princeton, N.J.: Princeton University Press, 1987), chap. 2; and Lewes, *Psychoanalytic Theory*, for a discussion of these dissenting views.

81 Karen Horney, *The Neurotic Personality of Our Time* (New York: Norton, 1937).

82 Clara Thompson, "Changing Concepts in Psychoanalysis," in *Homosexuality: A Subjective and Objective Investigation*, edited by Charles Berg and A. M. Krich (London: George Allen and Unwin, 1958), 313.

83 American Psychiatric Association, *Diagnostic and Statistical Manual, Mental Disorders* (Washington, D.C.: APA, 1952), 34.

84 Harry Gershman, "Psychopathology of Compulsive Homosexuality," *American Journal of Psychoanalysis* 17 (1957): 62.

85 Irving Bieber et al., *Homosexuality: A Psychoanalytic Study of Male Homosexuals* (New York: Basic Books, 1962).

86 Lewes, *Psychoanalytic Theory*, 184, 207.

87 Kinsey, *Sexual Behavior*, 8, 199.

88 Bieber worked hard to maintain an objectivist tone, which makes difficult any pre-

cise claims as to the influence of the Kinsey report. However, he clearly rejected Kinsey's statistical approach. "The statistical norm," he argued, "cannot by itself be taken as a criterion of the presence or absence of pathology." See Irving Bieber, "Sexual Deviations. I: Introduction," in *Comprehensive Textbook of Psychiatry*, edited by Alfred Freedman and Harold Kaplan (Baltimore: Williams and Wilkins, 1967), 959; see also Irving Bieber, "Sexual Deviations. II: Homosexuality," in *Comprehensive Textbook of Psychiatry*, 966.

89 Bieber, "Sexual Deviations. II," 968.
90 Bieber, *Homosexuality*, 319.
91 Bieber, "Sexual Deviations. II," 972.
92 Bieber, "Sexual Deviations. II," 970. This move could also be seen to harken back to the nineteenth-century denial of preoedipal sexuality.
93 Bieber, *Homosexuality*, 173.
94 Bieber, "Sexual Deviations. II," 970–71.
95 One wonders whether for Bieber heterosexuality in women is ensured by way of sexual seduction. He implies that sexual feelings for daughters are natural for the father, as long as they are expressed "affectionately" and not "in a conspiratorial way" (975).
96 Charles Socarides, "Homosexuality and Medicine," *Journal of the American Medical Association* 212, no. 7 (18 May 1970): 1202.
97 Charles Socarides, "Homosexuality—Basic Concepts and Psychodynamics," *International Journal of Psychiatry* 10 (1972): 120.
98 Socarides, "Homosexuality and Medicine," 1199; my emphasis.
99 Charles Socarides, "A Provisional Theory of Aetiology in Male Homosexuality," *International Journal of Psycho-Analysis* 49 (1968): 9.
100 Socarides, "Homosexuality and Medicine," 1201.
101 L. Hornstra, "Homosexuality," *International Journal of Psycho-Analysis* 48 (1966): 400.
102 Harry Gershman, "Psychopathology," 72.
103 Frederick A. Weiss, "Discussion," *American Journal of Psychoanalysis* 17 (1957): 74.
104 Bieber, "Sexual Deviations. II," 968.
105 Although ironically it could be argued that all homosexuals within this theoretical model are more aptly described as 'bisexuals'. After all, they are all really latent heterosexuals.
106 Bergler, *Homosexuality*, 81.
107 George Wiedeman, "Symposium on Homosexuality," *International Journal of Psycho-Analysis* 45 (1964): 215.
108 Ovesey, "The Homosexual Conflict," 243; see n. 35 above.
109 Stekel, *Bi-Sexual Love*, 69; my emphasis.
110 Douglas Bryan, "Bisexuality," *International Journal of Psycho-Analysis* 11 (1930): 150.
111 For an interesting historical discussion of a psychoanalytic use of the concept "identity crisis," see Cushing Strout, "Ego Psychology and the Historian," *History and*

Theory 7 (1968): 281–97. In fact, Strout's analysis provides an interesting perspective through which to view not so much the kind of generalized epistemic identity crisis of which I am predominantly speaking, but a kind of individual identity crisis that I have alluded to, particularly in the case of Bergler. See esp. 284–86, where, using a combination of Freudian psychoanalysis and Eriksonian ego psychology, Strout suggests that in certain crises "the subject's conflicts reanimate earlier tensions of his psychic growth" (284), tensions that functioned to redefine identifications at moments of a threatened sense of identity. However, this perhaps comes too close to the crude psychoanalytic reading that I am trying to avoid, one that might suggest that Bergler's extreme reaction to the issue of homosexuality is but a reactively formed screen against his own repressed homosexual desires.

112 Sigmund Freud, *Three Essays*, 145; see n. 1 above.

113 Kinsey, *Sexual Behavior*, 660, see n. 56 above; Ford and Beach, *Patterns*, 258–59, see n. 46 above.

114 Marjorie Garber, *Vice Versa: Bisexuality and the Eroticism of Everyday Life* (New York: Simon and Schuster, 1995), 253.

115 At most, bisexuality was deployed in a statistical or behavioral sense in terms of an individual taking part in both homosexual and heterosexual practices throughout a lifetime. So despite the fact that Bieber and others describe some of their subjects as bisexuals, in terms of the structures of individual identity they seem to be either homosexual or heterosexual. There was no such thing as a bisexual at the level of ego structure.

CHAPTER 5

1 See Sohnya Sayres et al., eds., *The 60s without Apology* (Minneapolis: University of Minnesota Press, 1984), 4.

2 Sayres, *The 60s without Apology*, 4.

3 Steven V. Roberts, "Homosexuals in Revolt," *New York Times*, 24 August 1970, 1.

4 On the historical development of a homophile movement in the United States, see John D'Emilio, *Sexual Politics, Sexual Communities: The Making of a Homosexual Minority in the United States 1940–1970* (Chicago: University of Chicago Press, 1983), 57–222; and Ronald Bayer, *Homosexuality and American Psychiatry: The Politics of Diagnosis* (Princeton, N.J.: Princeton University Press, 1987), 67–88; in Britain, see Jeffrey Weeks, *Coming Out: Homosexual Politics in Britain from the Nineteenth Century to the Present*, rev. ed. (London: Quartet Books, 1990), esp. 168–82.

5 D'Emilio, *Sexual Politics*, 223.

6 Peter Sedgwick, *Psycho Politics: Laing, Foucault, Goffman, Szasz and the Future of Mass Psychiatry* (New York: Harper and Row, 1982), 4.

7 Weeks, *Coming Out*, 186.

8 On this theme of self-determination, see D'Emilio, *Sexual Politics*, 224–27.

9 Dennis Altman, *Homosexual: Oppression and Liberation* (Ringwood, Vic.: Penguin Books, 1973), 155.

10 Quoted in Roberts, "Homosexuals in Revolt," 28.

11 Quoted in Roberts, "Homosexuals in Revolt," 28.

12 Bob Milne quoted in Roberts, "Homosexuals in Revolt," 28.

13 This is Theodore Roszak's phrase, which is, in fact, the title of his widely cited book *The Making of a Counter Culture: Reflections on the Technocratic Society and Its Youthful Opposition* (London: Faber and Faber, 1970).

14 Alfred C. Kinsey et al., *Sexual Behavior in the Human Male* (Philadelphia: W. B. Saunders Co., 1948), 203, 199.

15 Clellan S. Ford and Frank A. Beach, *Patterns of Sexual Behavior* (New York: Harper and Row, 1951), 236.

16 Bayer, *Homosexuality and American Psychiatry*, 49.

17 Evelyn Hooker, "The Adjustment of the Male Overt Homosexual," in *The Problem of Homosexuality in Modern Society*, edited by Hendrik M. Ruitenbeek (New York: E. P. Dutton and Co., 1963), 159.

18 See Paul Chance, "Tolerance Is Condescending: Facts That Liberated the Gay Community," Interview with Evelyn Hooker, *Psychology Today*, December 1975, 52.

19 Ford and Beach, *Patterns*, 258–59.

20 Hooker, "The Adjustment of the Male Overt Homosexual," 160.

21 Quoted in Chance, "Tolerance Is Condescending," 55.

22 For Kinsey, e.g., there is no such thing as a homosexual person, only a homosexual practice; and for Hooker ("The Adjustment of the Male Overt Homosexual," 160) "homosexuality as a clinical entity does not exist." On the issue of choice, see Kinsey, *Sexual Behavior*, 661.

23 Kinsey, *Sexual Behavior*, 657.

24 Kinsey went on to point out that because of its "wide currency" the term will continue to be used, but that it should be used cognizant of this problem and "with the understanding that it is patterned on the words heterosexual and homosexual and, like them . . . proves nothing about the constitution of the person who is labeled bisexual."

25 On the antipsychiatry movement, see Sedgwick, *Psycho Politics*; n. 6 above.

26 Even the traditionally conservative homophile groups such as the Mattachine Society had begun to more militantly contest psychiatric opinion on homosexuality. For the most part the Mattachine Society and other homophile groups were more concerned with securing social approval in order to counter discrimination of homosexuals in society, often seeking the support of psychiatrists. However, by the mid-1960s many in the groups began to oppose explicitly the institution of psychiatry. See Frank E. Kameny, "Homosexuals as a Minority Group," in *The Other Minorities*, edited by Edward Sagarin (Waltham, Mass.: Xerox College Publishing, 1971), 50–65; and Bayer, *Homosexuality and American Psychiatry*, 67–100.

27 Sedgwick, *Psycho Politics*, 4.

28 Bayer, *Homosexuality and American Psychiatry*, 58.

29 Thomas S. Szasz, "The Myth of Mental Illness," in *Ideology and Insanity: Essays on the Psychiatric Dehumanization of Man* (London: Calder and Boyars, 1973), 12.

30 Thomas S. Szasz, *The Manufacture of Madness* (New York: Delta Books, 1970), 170–71.

31 Roberts, "Homosexuals in Revolt," 28.

32 Annamarie Jagose, *Queer Theory* (Melbourne: Melbourne University Press, 1996), 36.

33 See Weeks, *Coming Out*, 189; see n. 4 above.

34 Lynne Segal, *Straight Sex: The Politics of Pleasure* (London: Virago, 1994), 168.

35 Bayer, *Homosexuality and American Psychiatry*, 99; see n. 4 above.

36 The Counter Psychiatry Group of the Melbourne Gay Liberation Front (hereafter, Melbourne Gay Liberation Front), undated leaflet, "Why Its Name . . . Why It Exists," Gay Liberation Ephemera File, Australian Lesbian and Gay Archives.

37 Dennis Altman, "Forum on Sexual Liberation," *Coming Out in the Seventies* (Sydney: Wild and Woolley, 1979), 17.

38 Chicago Gay Liberation Front, "A Leaflet for the American Medical Association" in *Out of the Closets: Voices of Gay Liberation*, edited by Karla Jay and Allen Young (New York: Douglas Book Corporation, 1972), 146.

39 Quoted in Roberts, "Homosexuals in Revolt," 1, 28.

40 Chicago Gay Liberation Front, "Leaflet for the American Medical Association," 146.

41 Chicago Gay Liberation Front, "Leaflet for the American Medical Association," 146–47.

42 Melbourne Gay Liberation Front, "Why Its Name."

43 Quoted in Paul Foss, "Gay Liberation in Australia," *William and John* 1, no. 8 (1972): 8.

44 Martha Shelley, "Gay Is Good," in *Out of the Closets: Voices of Gay Liberation*, edited by Karla Jay and Allen Young (New York: Douglas Book Corporation, 1972), 33.

45 Carl Wittman, "A Gay Manifesto" in *Out of the Closets: Voices of Gay Liberation*, edited by Karla Jay and Allen Young (New York: Douglas Book Corporation, 1972), 331.

46 Robert Hugh Reynolds, *Sexuality, Citizenship and Subjectivity: A Textual History of the Australian Gay Movement 1970–1974*, Ph.D. thesis, University of Melbourne, 1996, 186–94.

47 Reynolds, *Sexuality, Citizenship and Subjectivity*, 190.

48 Steven Seidman, "Identity Politics in a 'Postmodern' Gay Culture: Some Historical and Conceptual Notes," in *Fear of a Queer Planet: Queer Politics and Social Theory*, edited by Michael Warner (Minneapolis: University of Minnesota Press, 1993), 110.

49 Denise Thompson, *Flaws in the Social Fabric: Homosexuals and Society in Sydney* (Sydney: Allen and Unwin, 1985), 42.

50 Altman, *Homosexual*, 72.

51 See, e.g., Altman, *Homosexual*, 94–96. Altman did caution against Norman O. Brown's argument for the "total relaxation of repression," and argued that at "the very least I suspect one has to accept the need for some form of postponed gratification" (94).

52 Another example of the simplification of the bisexuality within gay liberation is Steven Epstein, "Gay Politics, Ethnic Identity: The Limits of Social Constructionism," in *Unfinished Business: Twenty Years of Socialist Review*, edited by the *Socialist Review* Collective (New York: Verso, 1991), 74–75.

53 Dennis Altman, "Pro Homo," *Outrage*, June 1992, 30. See also Jeffrey Weeks's introduction to the 1993 printing of Altman, *Homosexual: Oppression and Liberation* (New York: New York University Press, 1993), 12.

54 Reynolds's account is somewhat of an exception, although he does not mention Kinsey, Ford and Beach, and Hooker and seems at times to privilege the notion of Freudian bisexuality as representative of gay liberation ideology. He does, however, discuss the emergence within Australian gay liberation of a notion of sexuality as social conditioning. As I will discuss shortly, this notion captures the meaning of sexuality opened up by Kinsey, Ford and Beach, and Hooker.

55 "The New Bisexuals," *Time*, 13 May 1974, 55.

56 Margaret Mead quoted in Stephen Donaldson, "The Bisexual Movement's Beginnings in the 1970s: A Personal Retrospective," in *Bisexual Politics: Theories, Queries, and Visions*, edited by Naomi Tucker (New York: Harrington Park Press, 1995), 41.

57 Quoted in Donaldson, "The Bisexual Movement's Beginnings," 41.

58 Charles Socarides quoted in "Bisexuality in Bloom," 63.

59 Natalie Shainess quoted in "The New Bisexuals," 56.

60 This is especially so in the case of Millett who was radically anti-Freudian (see Kate Millett, *Sexual Politics* [London: Rupert-Hart Davis, 1971]). Millett's formulation was clearly influenced by the theory of social conditioning premised on a sexually neutral subject, a formulation similar to Kinsey, Ford and Beach, and Hooker.

61 Kinsey, *Sexual Behavior*, 650, 656; see n. 14 above.

62 David Lourea quoted in "Bay Area Bisexual History: An Interview with David Lourea," in *Bisexual Politics: Theories, Queries, and Visions*, edited by Naomi Tucker (New York: Harrington Park Press, 1995), 49.

63 Tucker, *Bisexual Politics*, 48.

64 Radical Freudianism was particularly popular within French gay liberation thought. This is evidenced in the work of Guy Hocquenghem and, as Jeffrey Weeks suggests in the preface to the 1978 edition of Hocquenghem's *Homosexual Desire*, reflects the different intellectual background of the French movement. This background was grounded in a strong tradition of psychoanalysis. See Guy Hocquenghem, *Homosexual Desire*, translated by Daniella Dangoon (London: Allison and Busby, 1978), 27–28.

65 Wittman, "A Gay Manifesto," 331.

66 It is also worth pointing out that the conception of music through which Wittman is analogizing sexuality is "infinite and varied, depending on the *capabilities* of the players"; my emphasis.

67 In "A Leaflet for the American Medical Association," 146, Chicago Gay Liberation Front cited Ford as alternative scientific evidence contesting psychomedical claims.

68 Reynolds, *Sexuality, Citizenship and Subjectivity*, 246–58.

69 Reynolds, *Sexuality, Citizenship and Subjectivity*, 190.

70 Reynolds, *Sexuality, Citizenship and Subjectivity*, 191.

71 Quoted in *William and John* 1, no. 4 (1972): 23.

72 Tony Diamond, "The Search for the Total Man," *Come Out* 1, no. 7 (1970): 17.

73 Quoted in Reynolds, *Sexuality, Citizenship and Subjectivity*, 191.
74 Don Clark, *Loving Someone Gay* (Millbrae, Calif.: Celestial Arts, 1977), 103–6.
75 Clark, *Loving Someone Gay*, 103–6.
76 Allen Young, "Out of the Closets, Into the Streets," in *Out of the Closets: Voices of Gay Liberation*, edited by Karla Jay and Allen Young (New York: Douglas Book Corporation, 1972), 29.
77 Kerryn, "Feminist Consciousness and Sexuality," undated leaflet, Radicalesbian File, Australian Lesbian and Gay Archives. See also Laurie Bebbington and Jocelyn Clarke, "Lesbian Oppression and Liberation," 2–3, Radicalesbian File, Australian Lesbian and Gay Archives.
78 Altman, *Homosexual*, 107; see n. 9 above.
79 Altman, *Homosexual*, 233.
80 Melbourne Gay Liberation Front, "Melbourne Gay Liberation: What Is Gay???" undated pamphlet, Gay Liberation Ephemera File, Australian Lesbian and Gay Archives. This notion of the artificiality of all sexual labels was common to all gay liberation groups.
81 Altman, *Homosexual*, 107.
82 Gore Vidal similarly refused the ontological categories of sexuality, suggesting in "Bisexual Politics" (in *The New Gay Liberation Book*, edited by Len Richmond and Gary Noguera [San Francisco: Ramparts Press, 1979], 41) that "there is no such thing as a homosexual. Despite current usage, the word is an adjective describing a sexual action, not a noun describing a recognizable type. All beings are bisexual."
83 Altman, *Homosexual*, 107.
84 Simon Watney, "The Ideology of GLF," in *Homosexuality: Power and Politics*, edited by the Gay Left Collective (London: Allison and Busby, 1980), 72.
85 Altman, *Homosexual*, 134.
86 The catchcry "the personal is political" was coined by Carol Hanisch. See Hester Eisenstein, *Contemporary Feminist Thought* (London: Unwin, 1984), 12.
87 Hocquenghem, *Homosexual Desire*, 122.
88 Katz, "Smashing Phallic Imperialism," in *Out of the Closets: Voices of Gay Liberation*, edited by Karla Jay and Allen Young (New York: Douglas Book Corporation, 1972), 260–61.
89 Reynolds, *Sexuality, Citizenship and Subjectivity*, 244.
90 Altman, *Homosexual*, 147.
91 See Lex Watson, "Looking Back over Five Gay Years," *Gay Liberation Newsletter*, Melbourne, September 1975. Watson noted that the rhetoric was "identical" to that deployed by lesbians at the First National Homosexual conference in Melbourne in 1975.
92 Melbourne Gay Liberation Front, "Queens and Dykes Want Gay Lib Back," October 1972, Gay Liberation Ephemera File, Australian Lesbian and Gay Archives.
93 Steve Gavin, "Consciousness Raising Exposes the Orwellian Lies of Sexist Amerika," *Come Out*, 2, no. 7b (1971): 19.
94 Melbourne Gay Liberation Front, "Melbourne Gay Liberation."

95 Young, "Out of the Closets," 28.
96 Altman, *Homosexual*, 148.
97 Young, "Out of the Closets," 24.
98 *Gay Power* 1 (1969): 16.
99 Reynolds, *Sexuality, Citizenship and Subjectivity*, 254–55.
100 Quoted in Reynolds, *Sexuality, Citizenship and Subjectivity*, 255–56.
101 Quoted in Thompson, *Flaws*, 40. See also Altman, *Homosexual*, 80–81.
102 Watney, "The Ideology of GLF," 65.
103 Wittman, "A Gay Manifesto," 332.
104 Melbourne Gay Liberation Front, "Gay Liberation Manifesto," 1972, Gay Liberation Ephemera File, Australian Lesbian and Gay Archives. This was reprinted from the London gay liberation manifesto.
105 Young, "Out of the Closets," 29.
106 Hocquenghem, *Homosexual Desire*, 125.
107 Ralph Hall, "Gay Liberation Front" column, *Gay Power* 1, no. 7 (1969): 8.
108 Melbourne Gay Liberation Front, "Gay Liberation Manifesto," 7.
109 Hocquenghem, *Homosexual Desire*, 125.
110 Wittman, "A Gay Manifesto," 331.
111 Shelley, "Gay Is Good," 34.
112 Foss, "Gay Liberation in Australia," 9.
113 Gay Revolution Party Women's Caucus, "Realesbians and Politicalesbians," in *Out of the Closets: Voices of Gay Liberation*, edited by Karla Jay and Allen Young (New York: Douglas Book Corporation, 1972), 179–80.
114 Bob Martin, "Gay Power: An Evolutionary Step," *Gay Power* 1, no. 5 (1969): 23.
115 Quoted in *Woroni*, 8 September 1972.
116 Larry S, "S and M and the Revolution," *Come Out* 2, no. 8 (1972): 14.
117 Quoted in Jagose, *Queer Theory*, 38.
118 Quoted in *Melbourne Gay Liberation Newsletter*, January 1975.
119 Brenda Marie Blasingame, "The Roots of Biphobia: Racism and Internalized Heterosexism," in *Closer to Home: Bisexuality and Feminism*, edited by Elizabeth Reba Weise (Seattle: Seal Press, 1992), 53.
120 Donaldson, "The Bisexual Movement's Beginnings," 38.
121 Verity Burgmann, *Power and Protest: Movements for Social Change in Australian Society* (Sydney: Allen and Unwin, 1993), 159–60.
122 Quoted in Reynolds, *Sexuality, Citizenship and Subjectivity*, 253.
123 On lesbian dissension in the United States see, e.g., Del Whan, "Elitism," and New York City Radicalesbians, "Leaving the Gay Men Behind," in *Out of the Closets: Voices of Gay Liberation*, edited by Karla Jay and Allen Young (New York: Douglas Book Corporation, 1972), 318–23 and 290–93, respectively; in the case of Australia, see Melbourne Radicalesbian File, Australian Lesbian and Gay Archives; Reynolds, *Sexuality, Citizenship and Subjectivity*, 258–80; and Steven Angelides, *A Will to Truth: (Homo)sex-*

uality and Authenticity in 1970s Melbourne, honors thesis, Department of History, University of Melbourne, 1992, 31–47.

124 See Altman, *Homosexual*, 138–39. Despite it being male only, see also A Gay Male Group, "Notes on Gay Male Consciousness-Raising," in *Out of the Closets*, 293–301, for an example of the gay liberation theory and practice of consciousness-raising.

125 Jocelyn Clarke, "Life as a Lesbian," in *The Other Half: Women in Australian Society*, edited by Jan Mercer (Melbourne: Penguin, 1975), 336.

126 This was a slogan of the New York Radicalesbian group, which was reproduced by the Melbourne chapter. See *Radicalesbian Conference*, Sorrento, Australia, 6–8 July 1973, Radicalesbian File, Australian Lesbian and Gay Archives.

127 *Gay Liberation Newsletter*, Melbourne, no. 4, September 1973.

128 *Gay Liberation Newsletter*, Melbourne, no. 4, September 1973.

129 *Gay Liberation Newsletter*, Melbourne, no. 4, September 1973.

130 See *The Radical Manifesto*, Melbourne, undated, Radicalesbian File, Australian Lesbian and Gay Archives, 1–2.

131 See Chris Sitka, "Feminist Culture," and "Lesbianism and Its Relationship to Feminism," in Radicalesbian File, Australian Lesbian and Gay Archives.

132 See Chris Sitka, "Feminist Culture," and "Lesbianism and Its Relationship to Feminism," in Radicalesbian File, Australian Lesbian and Gay Archives.

133 Barbara Creed, "Turning the Fan Around," *Radicalesbian Conference*, 2.

134 "Editorial," *Refractory Girl* 5 (Summer 1974): 2.

135 Quoted in Burgmann, *Power and Protest*, 160.

136 Again, I am using the terms of Luce Irigaray, *This Sex Which Is Not One*, translated by Catherine Porter (Ithaca, N.Y.: Cornell University Press, 1985).

CHAPTER 6

1 Steven Epstein, "Gay Politics, Ethnic Identity: The Limits of Social Constructionism," in *Unfinished Business: Twenty Years of Socialist Review*, edited by the Socialist Review Collective (New York: Verso, 1991), 71.

2 Dennis Altman, *The Homosexualization of America, The Americanization of the Homosexual* (Boston: Beacon Press, 1983), 21. See also Epstein, "Gay Politics."

3 See Stephen O. Murray, "The Institutional Elaboration of a Quasi-Ethnic Community," *International Review of Modern Sociology* 9 (July–December 1979); see also Epstein, "Gay Politics."

4 Steven Seidman, "Identity Politics in a 'Postmodern' Gay Culture: Some Historical and Conceptual Notes," in *Fear of a Queer Planet: Queer Politics and Social Theory*, edited by Michael Warner (Minneapolis: University of Minnesota Press, 1993), 117.

5 Adrienne Rich, "Compulsory Heterosexuality and Lesbian Existence," first published in 1980 and reprinted in *The Lesbian and Gay Studies Reader*, edited by Henry Abelove et al. (New York: Routledge, 1993), 239.

6 Marilyn Frye, *The Politics of Reality: Essays in Feminist Theory* (New York: Crossing Press, 1983), 145.

7 According to Frye one of the primary values gay men have learned in our phallocratic society is "woman-hating" (140).

8 Altman, *Homosexualization*, 85, 81.

9 The phrase "aestheticization of everyday life" is Sharon Zukin's. See John Frow, "What Was Post-Modernism?" in *Past the Last Post: Theorizing Post-Colonialism and Post-Modernism*, edited by Ian Adam and Helen Tiffin (New York: Harvester Wheatsheaf, 1991), 147–49.

10 Guy Hocquenghem, *Homosexual Desire*, translated by Daniella Dangoon (London: Allison and Busby, 1978).

11 Quotes cited in Altman, *Homosexualization*, 20, 18.

12 See Edward Stein, ed., *Forms of Desire: Sexual Orientation and the Social Construction Controversy* (New York: Routledge, 1990), 5; and Carole Vance, "Social Construction Theory: Problems in the History of Sexuality," in *Which Homosexuality? Essays from the International Scientific Conference on Lesbian and Gay Studies*, edited by Dennis Altman et al. (London: GMP Publishers, 1989), 20.

13 Vance, "Social Construction Theory," 20.

14 Judith Butler, "Introduction: Against Proper Objects," *differences* 6, nos. 2 and 3 (1994): 6. Vance suggests that anthropologists of the 1960s were precursors to constructionism. "However, these anthropologists," she argues, "accepted without question the existence of universal categories like heterosexual and homosexual, male and female sexuality, and sex drive" (19). Here she is attempting to distinguish some kind of 'true' social constructionism of the 1970s from earlier theorists exhibiting only early constructionist tendencies. She argues that while this work is "a precursor to social construction theory, it clearly contains many essentialist elements" (20). While she is in some sense correct in this observation, it seems to me that she is not only ignoring some of the work in the sociology of deviance and cross-cultural anthropology (Ford and Beach), which clearly rejected the hetero/homosexual opposition, but also overstating the antiessentialism of much 1970s social construction theory. This, despite her own acknowledgment of the "different degrees of social construction" (18). Even constructionist theorists such as Kenneth Plummer and Dennis Altman accepted some notion of a biological sexual capacity. See Kenneth Plummer, *Sexual Stigma: An Interactionist Account* (London: Routledge and Kegan Paul, 1975), esp. 37; and Altman, *Homosexualization*, 41. Stein, *Forms of Desire*, 5, also argues that the "debate about sexual orientation between the social constructionists and the essentialists started fairly recently." In the next sentence he immediately cites Mary McIntosh's 1968 article. In relation to interactionism and deviance, Plummer suggests something similar to my analysis: "To talk of interactionism as a new approach to deviancy is to be blind to history" (*Sexual Stigma*, 20).

15 Plummer, *Sexual Stigma*, chap. 2, esp. 20.

16 M. H. Kuhn, "Kinsey's View on Human Behaviour," *Social Problems* 1 (1954): 123.

17 John H. Gagnon, "Sexuality and Sexual Learning in the Child," in *Sexual Deviance*, edited by John H. Gagnon and William Simon (New York: Harper and Row, 1967), 21–22.

18 John H. Gagnon and William Simon, *Sexual Conduct* (Chicago: Aldine, 1973), 19.

19 Gagnon and Simon, *Sexual Conduct*, 22–23.
20 Jeffrey Weeks, *Against Nature: Essays on History, Sexuality and Identity* (London: Rivers Oram Press, 1991), 25.
21 Plummer, *Sexual Stigma*, 30.
22 All quotes cited in Plummer, *Sexual Stigma*, 5.
23 Gagnon and Simon, *Sexual Deviance*, 2–3.
24 Mary McIntosh, "The Homosexual Role," in *The Making of the Modern Homosexual*, edited by Kenneth Plummer (London: Hutchinson, 1981), 31–32. This article was first published in *Social Problems* 16, no. 3 (Fall 1968).
25 Gagnon and Simon, *Sexual Deviance*, 2–3.
26 McIntosh, "The Homosexual Role," 32.
27 Plummer, *Sexual Stigma*, 96–101.
28 Epstein, "Gay Politics," 75–76.
29 Despite the increasing visibility of bisexuality as a 'swinging' sexual practice or category of sexuality during the late 1960s and early 1970s, within sociological and psychoanalytical discourses, it was scarcely analyzed at all.
30 Steven Seidman (Introduction to *Queer Theory/Sociology*, edited by Steven Seidman [Cambridge, Mass.: Blackwell Publishers, 1996], 7) has also argued along these lines.
31 Seidman, in *Queer Theory/Sociology*, has also suggested that these constructionist sociologists "did not critically investigate the categories of sexuality, heterosexuality, and homosexuality. They did not question the social functioning of the hetero/homosexual binary as the master category of a modern regime of sexuality. Moreover, many sociologists lacked an historical perspective while perpetuating an approach that isolated the question of homosexuality from dynamics of social modernization and politics" (7–8).
32 McIntosh, "The Homosexual Role," 46.
33 Jeffrey Weeks, *Coming Out: Homosexual Politics in Britain from the Nineteenth Century to the Present* (London: Quartet Books, 1977); Jonathan Katz, *Gay American History: Lesbians and Gay Men in the USA* (New York: Thomas and Crowell, 1976); John D'Emilio, *Sexual Politics, Sexual Communities: The Making of a Homosexual Minority in the United States, 1940–1970* (Chicago: University of Chicago Press, 1983); Randolph Trumbach, "London's Sodomites: Homosexual Behavior and Western Culture in the 18th Century," *Journal of Social History* 11 (Fall 1977): 1–33; Carroll Smith-Rosenberg, "The Female World of Love and Ritual: Relations between Women in Nineteenth-Century America," *Signs* 1, no. 1 (1975): 1–29; Lillian Faderman, *Surpassing the Love of Men: Romantic Friendship and Love between Women from the Renaissance to the Present* (London: Junction Books, 1981).
34 Seidman, Introduction to *Queer Theory/Sociology*, 9.
35 Jonathan Katz acknowledges this in retrospect. In "The Invention of Heterosexuality" (*Socialist Review* 20, no. 1 [1990]: 8), he states: "Considering the popularity of the heterosexual idea, one imagines that tracing the notion's history would have tempted many eager scholar-beavers. The importance of analyzing the dominant term of the

dominant sexual ideology seems obvious. But heterosexuality has been the idea whose time has not come. The role of the universal heterosexual hypothesis as prop to the dominant mode of sexual organization has determined its not-so-benign scholarly neglect." See also Ki Namaste, "The Politics of Inside/Out: Queer Theory, Poststructuralism, and a Sociological Approach to Sexuality," in *Queer Theory/Sociology*, edited by Stephen Seidman (Cambridge, Mass.: Blackwell Publishers, 1996), 202–6.

36 Stein, *Forms of Desire*, 6, calls Foucault's *History of Sexuality*, vol. 1, the *locus classicus* of social constructionism.

37 Foucault, of course, rejected all labels to describe him and his work, including that of 'poststructuralist'. However, when analyzed in its historical and theoretical context, Foucault is clearly part of the shift to poststructuralism that took place in France after 1968.

38 Stein, *Forms of Desire*, 5–6.

39 Michel Foucault, *The History of Sexuality*, vol. 1: *An Introduction*, translated by Robert Hurley (New York: Vintage Books, 1980), 105.

40 Michel Foucault, *The History of Sexuality*, vol. 2: *The Use of Pleasure*, translated by Robert Hurley (Harmondsworth: Penguin Books, 1987), 4. Hereafter, vol. 2 of Foucault's History will be referred to as *Use of Pleasure*; when I refer to *History of Sexuality* I will be citing Foucault's first volume only.

41 Foucault, *History of Sexuality*, 103.

42 See also Judith Butler, "Sexual Inversions," in *Discourses of Sexuality: From Aristotle to AIDS*, edited by Domna C. Stanton (Ann Arbor: University of Michigan Press, 1992), 349–50. Butler has provided an excellent critique of Foucault's historical account of this shift in power through an analysis of the discursive regulation of HIV/AIDS in contemporary society. She argues that "there is no historical shift from juridical to productive power from the start and that the shift . . . is within power, not between two historically or logically distinct forms of power."

43 Foucault, *History of Sexuality*, 141, 140.

44 Michel Foucault, "The Subject and Power," Afterword to *Michel Foucault: Beyond Structuralism and Hermeneutics*, edited by Hubert L. Dreyfus and Paul Rabinow (Chicago: University of Chicago Press, 1983), 212.

45 Foucault, *History of Sexuality*, 42, 43.

46 Rosi Braidotti, "Embodiment, Sexual Difference, and the Nomadic Subject," *Hypatia* 8, no. 1 (1993): 4.

47 See Foucault, *History of Sexuality*, 3–13; quote on 10.

48 Foucault, *History of Sexuality*, 10.

49 Michel Foucault, "The Confession of the Flesh," in *Power/Knowledge: Selected Interviews and Other Writings 1972–1977*, edited by Colin Gordon (New York: Pantheon Books, 1980), 219.

50 Foucault, *History of Sexuality*, 10.

51 Foucault, *History of Sexuality*, 110.

52 Quoted in David M. Halperin, *Saint Foucault: Towards a Gay Hagiography* (New York: Oxford University Press, 1995), 58–59.

53 Quoted in Bob Gallagher and Alexander Wilson, "Michel Foucault. An Interview: Sex, Power and the Politics of Identity," *The Advocate*, no. 400 (7 August 1984): 27.

54 Quoted in Halperin, *Saint Foucault*, 96.

55 Michel Foucault, "On Power," Interview with Pierre Boncenne in *Michel Foucault, Politics, Philosophy, Culture: Interviews and Other Writings, 1977–1984*, edited by L. D. Kritzman (New York: Routledge, 1988), 106.

56 Foucault, *History of Sexuality*, 92–96; my emphasis.

57 Foucault, "Subject and Power," 212.

58 Foucault, *Use of Pleasure*, 6.

59 Foucault, *History of Sexuality*, 157.

60 Quoted in Gallagher and Wilson, "Michel Foucault," 27.

61 Michel Foucault, "Power and Sex," Interview with Bernard-Henri Lévy in *Michel Foucault. Politics, Philosophy, Culture: Interviews and Other Writings, 1977–1984*, edited by L. D. Kritzman (New York: Routledge, 1988), 116.

62 Quoted in Gallagher and Wilson, "Michel Foucault," 28.

63 Halperin, *Saint Foucault*, 78.

64 While Foucault is speaking specifically in relation to the gay movement, clearly this holds for everyone.

65 This is how Foucault describes his own stance as an intellectual, a position clearly reflecting the political and ethical agenda he invites us to take up. See Michel Foucault, "How Do We Behave?" Interview by Paul Rabinow and Hubert L. Dreyfus, *Vanity Fair*, November 1983, 62.

66 Quoted in Gallagher and Wilson, "Michel Foucault," 28.

67 In a review essay on Michel Foucault (*History and Theory* 27 [1988]), Michael S. Roth describes the practical and political consequences of Foucault's approach as a form of "freedom as revolt" (73). As I argued earlier, however, for Foucault the exercise of power and resistance is made possible by virtue of the fact that we are free. This is a very different notion of freedom from one constructed through the repressive hypothesis. I disagree with Roth's formulation, therefore, which does not seem to capture this sense of the relationship of power, resistance, and freedom. I should point out, however, that Foucault's language in interviews at times implies this kind of formulation. For example, in Gallagher and Wilson, "Michel Foucault," he responds in the affirmative to the interviewers' suggestion that sexual identity has been politically useful: "It has been *very* useful, but it limits us and I think we have (and can have) a right to be free" (28). While I would like to avoid ascribing any authorial coherence to Foucault's oeuvre (which might seem to be a rather *un*-Foucauldian gesture; but would not the claim of *un*-Foucauldianness itself rely on an assumption of authorial coherence?) I would suggest that Foucault might more usefully be read as describing a kind of general freedom *from* the apparatus of sexuality rather than a notion of freedom as the basis for individual action.

68 In *The Ticklish Subject: The Absent Centre of Political Ontology* (London: Verso, 2000), Slavoj Žižek argues that Foucault's pessimism regarding the idea that resistance is co-opted in advance "precludes the possibility that the system itself, on account of its inherent inconsistency, may give birth to a force whose excess it is no longer able to master and which thus detonates its unity, its capacity to reproduced itself. In short, Foucault does not consider the possibility of an effect escaping, outgrowing its cause, so that although it emerges as a form of resistance to power and is as such absolutely inherent to it, it can outgrow and explode it" (256).

69 Allan Megill, "The Reception of Foucault by Historians," *Journal of the History of Ideas* 48 (1987): 117.

70 Foucault, *Use of Pleasure*, 9.

71 Quoted in Megill, "The Reception of Foucault," 117.

72 See Michel Foucault, "Nietzsche, Genealogy, History," in *The Foucault Reader*, edited by Paul Rabinow (London: Penguin, 1991), 76–100.

73 Foucault, "Nietzsche, Genealogy, History," 88.

74 Foucault, *Use of Pleasure*, 4; my emphasis.

75 Here I am reworking a phrase taken from Carolyne J. Dean, "The Productive Hypothesis: Foucault, Gender, and the History of Sexuality," *History and Theory* 33 (1994), who uses it to describe Foucault's "neglect of gender" (277). I am suggesting instead that this neglect was in fact the effect of his complicity in the deployment of sexuality.

76 Foucault, *Use of Pleasure*, 3.

77 Quoted in Gallagher and Wilson, "Michel Foucault," 29.

78 Foucault, "Subject and Power," 212; my emphasis.

79 The list of feminist critiques of this kind is endless. For good examples, see Irene Diamond and Lee Quinby, eds., *Feminism and Foucault: Reflections on Resistance* (Boston: Northeastern University Press, 1988); and Nancy Hartsock, "Foucault on Power: A Theory for Women?" in *Feminism/Postmodernism*, edited by Linda Nicholson (New York: Routledge, 1990), 157–75.

80 Quoted in Gallagher and Wilson, "Michel Foucault," 29.

81 Frances Bartkowski, "Epistemic Drift in Foucault," in *Feminism and Foucault: Reflections on Resistance*, edited by Irene Diamond and Lee Quinby (Boston: Northeastern University Press, 1988), 48. Of course, to this must be added the category of 'non-Western people'.

82 Quoted in Lynne Segal, *Slow Motion: Changing Masculinities, Changing Men* (London: Virago, 1990), 136. See also Randolph Trumbach, "Gender and the Homosexual Role in Modern Western Culture: The 18th and 19th Centuries Compared," in *Which Homosexuality? Essays from the International Scientific Conference on Lesbian and Gay Studies*, edited by Dennis Altman et al. (London: GMP Publishers, 1989), esp. 159–60, where he argues that indicting the nineteenth-century medical model "makes for a splendid melodrama but is somewhat unconvincing history." In his *Three Essays on the Theory of Sexuality* (1905), SE 7:7–9, Sigmund Freud provides an example of this reaction of which Silverstolpe speaks. Referring to Ulrichs, Freud attempts to discredit his "lay" theory of bisexuality, which, he says, "has been expressed in its crudest form by a spokesperson of the male inverts" (8).

83 Bartkowski, "Epistemic Drift," 47.

84 Abdul JanMohamed, "Sexuality on/of the Racial Border: Foucault, Wright, and the

Articulation of 'Racialized Sexuality'," in *Discourses of Sexuality: From Aristotle to AIDS*, edited by Domna C. Stanton (Ann Arbor: University of Michigan Press, 1992), 116.

85 Foucault, *History of Sexuality*, 86.

86 Lynn Hunt, "Foucault's Subject in *The History of Sexuality*," in *Discourses of Sexuality: From Aristotle to AIDS*, edited by Domna C. Stanton (Ann Arbor: University of Michigan Press, 1992), 86.

87 See also Carole Pateman, *The Sexual Contract* (Cambridge: Polity Press, 1991). She has argued that this notion of the self-possessing individual is "the fulcrum on which modern patriarchy turns" (14).

88 Hunt, "Foucault's Subject," 85.

89 It is this kind of microanalysis that I have performed in this book. Such an analysis is not proffered as a substitute for Foucault's brilliant history of sexuality. Instead, it is intended as an extension of Foucault's macroanalysis.

90 Foucault's use of the term "sex" encompasses not just sexual practice, pleasure, etc., but sex difference, or, gender. My use of the term 'gender' similarly incorporates each of these meanings (with the exception of sexual practice). However, I would argue that the meaning of sexual practices and pleasures, as well as the notion of male-female sex difference, are only ever discursively produced, to use Judith Butler's phraseology, through a matrix of gender. Thus, I consider such a matrix to precede and condition Foucault's understanding of "sex."

91 Foucault, *History of Sexuality*, 154.

92 Judith Butler ("Revisiting Bodies and Pleasures," *Theory, Culture and Society* 16, no. 2 [1999]) argues that "the very 'sex-desire' that bodies and pleasures are said to refute is precisely what bodies and pleasures must *presuppose*. And 'sex-desire' must be presupposed in order for 'bodies and pleasures' to become the name for an historical time of sexuality that is decisively beyond sexuality in its regulatory sense; is this anti-regulatory deployment of bodies and pleasures one whose very status as an opposition is dependent upon reinstating what it seeks to encounter" (17).

93 In "Revisiting Bodies and Pleasures," Butler argues the Foucault's insistence on bodies and pleasures unwittingly "constricts our vocabulary through a move that appears to prioritize bodies and pleasures over sex-desire, and which makes sexual difference and homosexuality strangely unspeakable within this frame" (12).

94 Judith Butler, *Gender Trouble: Feminism and the Subversion of Identity* (New York: Routledge, 1990), 94.

95 Butler, *Gender Trouble*, 96–97.

96 Michel Foucault, Introduction to *Herculine Barbin: Being the Recently Discovered Memoirs of a Nineteenth-Century Hermaphrodite*, translated by Richard McDougall (Brighton: Harvester Press, 1980), xiii.

97 Butler, *Gender Trouble*, 96.

98 I have used the indefinite article *a* rather than the definite article *the* to describe this construction of the modern self. I do this in order to problematize any universalizing notion of subjectivity and to allude to the need to historicize the multiplicity of forms of modern subjectivity. See Dean, "The Productive Hypothesis" (n. 75 above) for just such a critique of Hunt.

99 Luce Irigaray, *This Sex Which Is Not One*, translated by Catherine Porter (Ithaca, N.Y.: Cornell University Press, 1985), 74; my emphasis. While I find Irigaray's analysis of phallogocentric logic useful as a critical tool for deconstructing representations of sexuality, I would suggest that this theoretical approach itself needs to be grounded and historicized. This is important in order to appreciate the different and shifting historical constructions of male sexuality/subjectivity. For to reinscribe problematic ahistorical and universal categories of male subjectivity is to remain conditioned by a phallogocentric economy of the same.

100 Christopher Lane, *The Burdens of Intimacy: Psychoanalysis and Victorian Masculinity* (Chicago: University of Chicago Press, 1999), 17–18.

101 Foucault, "Subject and Power," 212.

102 Hunt, "Foucault's Subject," 85.

103 Foucault, *History of Sexuality*, 155.

104 Diana Fuss, "Inside/Out," in *Inside/Out: Lesbian Theories, Gay Theories*, edited by Diana Fuss (New York: Routledge, 1991), 7.

105 Quoted in Halperin, *Saint Foucault*, 78. Again while Foucault is speaking specifically in relation to the gay movement, clearly this holds for everyone.

106 This is, of course, true of race as well. In "Revisiting," Butler notes that "if we think we might say no to sex and desire in the rush to embrace bodies and pleasures . . . then I think we miss the chance to understand how the analysis of sexuality is pervasively structured by sexual difference" (20).

107 Foucault, *History of Sexuality*, 157.

108 Fuss, "Inside/Out," 1.

109 In chap. 7 I will take up the issue of how well queer theory has theorized this relationship.

110 Foucault, *History of Sexuality*, 157.

111 For an excellent deconstruction of the essentialist/constructionist opposition see Diana Fuss, *Essentially Speaking: Feminism, Nature and Difference* (New York: Routledge, 1989).

112 At least within post-Freudian psychoanalysis, bisexuality was clearly a structuring absence.

113 Clearly, this is also the case with the category of race. My focus on bisexuality (and the limitations of space) prevents me from doing more than gesturing toward the theoretical deconstruction of sexuality through the category of race. This would require another, differently oriented, project.

114 Žižek, *The Ticklish Subject*, 256.

CHAPTER 7

1 This is not to suggest that certain formulations of queer theory are not replicating the Foucauldian anti-identity approach. Indeed, several critics have lamented the anti-identitarian rejection of gay and lesbian identity/politics that they see as structuring much queer theory. See, e.g., Steven Seidman, "Identity and Politics in a 'Postmodern' Gay Culture: Some Historical and Conceptual Notes," in *Fear of a Queer Planet: Queer*

Politics and Social Theory, edited by Michael Warner (Minneapolis: University of Minnesota Press, 1993), 132–33; Sally O'Driscoll, "Outlaw Readings: Beyond Queer Theory," *Signs* 22, no. 1 (1996): 30–51.

2 Diana Fuss, "Inside/Out," in *Inside/Out: Lesbian Theories, Gay Theories*, edited by Diana Fuss (New York: Routledge, 1991), 1.

3 Jo Eadie, "Activating Bisexuality: Towards a Bi/Sexual Politics," in *Activating Theory: Lesbian, Gay, Bisexual Politics*, edited by Joseph Bristow and Angela R. Wilson (London: Lawrence and Wishart, 1993), 139–70; Clare Hemmings, "Resituating the Bisexual Body," in *Activating Theory*, 118–38; Christopher James, "Denying Complexity: Dismissal and Appropriation of Bisexuality in Queer, Lesbian, and Gay Theory," in *Queer Studies: A Lesbian, Gay, Bisexual, and Transgender Anthology*, edited by Brett Beemyn and Mickey Eliason (New York: New York University Press, 1996), 217–40; Stacey Young, "Dichotomies and Displacement: Bisexuality in Queer Theory and Politics," in *Playing with Fire: Queer Politics, Queer Theories*, edited by Shane Phelan (New York: Routledge, 1997), 51–74. Ki Namaste's useful analysis is an exception, although he is concerned primarily with theorizing the erasure of bisexuality at the level of semiotic theory. To this must be added a historical analysis. See Ki Namaste, "From Performativity to Interpretation: Toward a Social Semiotic Account of Bisexuality," in *RePresenting Bisexualities: Subjects and Cultures of Fluid Desires*, edited by Donald E. Hall and Maria Pramaggiore (New York: New York University Press, 1996), 70–95.

4 *The Concise Oxford Dictionary*, 6th ed., edited by H. W. Fowler and F. G. Fowler (Oxford: Clarendon Press, 1976). It is important to note that little has changed in the definition of queer. In the Australian edition of the 1990 *Collins Concise English Dictionary*, 2d ed., queer denotes something strange, odd, dubious, and shady.

5 *The Shorter Oxford English Dictionary on Historical Principles*, 3d ed., vol. 2, edited by C. T. Onions (Oxford: Clarendon Press, 1991).

6 Lisa Duggan, "Making It Perfectly Queer," *Socialist Review* 22, no. 1 (January–March 1992): 27; Annamarie Jagose, *Queer Theory* (Melbourne: Melbourne University Press, 1996), 93–96.

7 Duggan, "Making it Perfectly Queer," 20.

8 See Amber Hollibaugh and Cherríe Moraga, "What We're Rollin Around in Bed With: Sexual Silences in Feminism," in *Desire: The Politics of Sexuality*, edited by Ann Snitow et al. (London: Virago, 1984), esp. 409, 412; Cherry Smyth, *Lesbians Talk Queer Notions* (London: Scarlet Press, 1991), esp. 26–27.

9 In "The Politics of Queer Theory in the (Post)Modern Moment" (*Genders*, no. 17 [Fall 1993], 121), Donald Morton has suggested that queer theory calls for the articulation of an "'erotics'—a (post)conceptual, (post)discursive recognition of sexualities as the 'sublime' (in the Kantian sense) of the social." I disagree with Morton's homogenizing representation of queer theory, which, he argues, is ludicly grounded in the sensory (139). Queer assumes myriad positions, and in setting up a *straw queer person* for the purposes of his critique, Morton is erasing any discussion of queer as a destabilizing identity category.

10 See Duggan, "Making it Perfectly Queer," for a range of these constructions of queer in the United States. For examples of queer in Britain, see Smyth, *Lesbians Talk*, and es-

says in Joseph Bristow and Angelia R. Wilson, eds., *Activating Theory: Lesbian, Gay, Bisexual Politics* (London: Lawrence and Wishart, 1993). In Australia, see Angelides, "The Queer Intervention: Sexuality, Identity, and Cultural Politics," *Melbourne Journal of Politics* 22 (1994): 66–88; Robert Reynolds, "Postmodernism and Gay/Queer Identities," in *Gay Perspectives II: More Essays in Australian Gay Culture*, edited by Robert Aldrich (Sydney: University of Sydney: Department of Economic History, 1993), 245–74.

11 Michael Warner, "Introduction: Fear of a Queer Planet," *Social Text* 29 (1991): 16.

12 Duggan, "Making It Perfectly Queer," 25.

13 Angelides, "The Queer Intervention."

14 For a concise summary of the historical and intellectual context of queer theory, see Jagose, *Queer Theory*, 75–83.

15 An assumption of this book is that the modernism/postmodernism distinction is a problematic one that implies a fiction of periodization, and that such linearity ignores the mutual interdependence of the two terms. I agree with Ernesto Laclau that in many ways postmodernism is a reformulation of modernism. However, it is important to note that there are a multiplicity of differences within, and between, each category; such differences are elided when the categories are invoked in the singular. I am not claiming that queer marks a total break with what is usually associated with *modernism*; rather, queer is attempting to utilize some of the critical practices opened up by poststructuralism (as it is enmeshed with postmodernism) in order to carve out a discursive space for the articulation of difference. For a useful discussion on postmodernism, see Ernesto Laclau, "Politics and the Limits of Modernity," in *Universal Abandon? The Politics of Postmodernism*, edited by Andrew Ross (Minneapolis: University of Minnesota Press, 1989), 63–82.

16 See Henry Abelove, "The Queering of Lesbian/Gay History," *Radical History Review* 62 (1995): 50.

17 Jagose, *Queer Theory*, 4.

18 Jonathan Dollimore, *Sexual Dissidence: Augustine to Wilde, Freud to Foucault* (Oxford: Clarendon Press, 1991), esp. chaps. 19–20 and 21–23 for an explication of his use of the term 'post/modernism'.

19 Judith Butler, *Gender Trouble: Feminism and the Subversion of Identity* (New York: Routledge, 1990), x.

20 Eve Kosofsky Sedgwick, *Epistemology of the Closet* (Berkeley: University of California Press, 1990), 1.

21 Steven Seidman, Introduction to *Queer Theory/Sociology*, edited by Steven Seidman (Cambridge, Mass.: Blackwell Publishers, 1996), 9.

22 Fuss, "Inside/Out," 3.

23 Jane Gallop quoted in Diana Fuss, *Essentially Speaking: Feminism, Nature and Difference* (New York: Routledge, 1989), 104.

24 Judith Butler, *Bodies That Matter: On the Discursive Limits of 'Sex'* (New York: Routledge, 1993), 229, 230.

25 Lee Edelman, *Homographesis: Essays in Gay Literary and Cultural Theory* (New York: Routledge, 1994), xvi.

26 Warner, "Introduction: Fear of a Queer Planet," 8.
27 Sedgwick, *Epistemology*, 31.
28 Gayle Rubin, "Thinking Sex: Notes for a Radical Theory of the Politics of Sexuality," in *The Lesbian and Gay Studies Reader*, edited by Henry Abelove et al. (New York: Routledge, 1993), 33.
29 Gayle Rubin, "Sexual Traffic," Interview with Judith Butler, *differences* 6, nos. 2 and 3 (1994): 84.
30 Sedgwick, *Epistemology*, 27–35; quote on 27.
31 As we will see, however, Sedgwick does not think this to be the case. This will be explored in the second part of this chapter and also in chap. 8.
32 Sedgwick, *Epistemology*, 30–32; quote on 31.
33 Warner, "Introduction: Fear of a Queer Planet," 13–14.
34 Sedgwick, *Epistemology*, 30.
35 Ellis Hanson, "Technology, Paranoia and the Queer Voice," *Screen* 34, no. 2 (Summer 1993): 137–38; see also Alexander Doty, *Making Things Perfectly Queer: Interpreting Mass Culture* (Minneapolis: University of Minnesota Press, 1993), 2.
36 Sedgwick, *Epistemology*, esp. 11.
37 See Abelove, "Queering of Lesbian/Gay History," 48.
38 Sedgwick, *Epistemology*, 11.
39 There is a growing body of work critiquing queer theory. Among these are Sally O'Driscoll, "Outlaw Readings: Beyond Queer Theory," *Signs* 22, no. 1 (1996): 30–51; Morton, "The Politics of Queer Theory"; Harriet Malinowitz, "Queer Theory: Whose Theory?" *Frontiers* 13, no. 2 (1992): 168–84; Rosemary Hennessey, "Queer Visibility in Commodity Culture," *Cultural Critique* 29 (Winter 1994–95): 31–76; Elizabeth Grosz, "Theorising Corporeality: Bodies, Sexuality and the Feminist Academy," Interview with Wei Leng Kwok and Kaz Ross, *Melbourne Journal of Politics* 22 (1994): 3–29; Michael du Plessis, "Blatantly Bisexual; or, Unthinking Queer Theory," in *RePresenting Bisexualities: Subjects and Cultures of Fluid Desire*, edited by Donald E. Hall and Maria Pramaggiore (New York: New York University Press, 1996), 19–54; Biddy Martin, "Sexualities without Genders and Other Queer Utopias," *diacritics* 24, nos. 2 and 3 (1994): 104–21; Judith Butler, "Introduction: Against Proper Objects," *differences* 6, nos. 2 and 3 (1994): 1–26.
40 To be sure, there have been heated debates surrounding the inclusion of bisexuality in group and conference titles working under the rubric of 'lesbian and gay'. See, e.g., Stacey Young, "Dichotomies and Displacement: Bisexuality in Queer Theory and Politics," in *Playing With Fire: Queer Politics, Queer Theories*, edited by Shane Phelan (New York: Routledge, 1997), 63–65.
41 Michael du Plessis ("Blatantly Bisexual; or, Unthinking Queer Theory," 23), discusses the infamous 1991 Rutgers Lesbian and Gay Conference that dropped "bisexual" from its title. One rumor to have circulated was that one of the reasons for this decision was that *"bisexuals have not produced good theory."* Many more theorists of bisexuality and bisexual theorists have identified this erasure. For some examples, see Clare Hemmings, "Resituating the Bisexual Body," in *Activating Theory*, 118–38; Jo Eadie, "Activating Bi-

sexuality: Towards a Bi/Sexual Politics," in *Activating Theory*, 139–70; Christopher James, "Denying Complexity: Dismissal and Appropriation of Bisexuality in Queer, Lesbian, and Gay Theory," in *Queer Studies*, 217–40; Young, "Dichotomies and Displacement," in *Playing with Fire*, 51–74.

42 Sedgwick, *Epistemology*, 1.

43 Maria Pramaggiore, "BI-ntroduction I: Epistemologies of the Fence," in *RePresenting Bisexualities: Subjects and Cultures of Fluid Desires*, edited by Donald E. Hall and Maria Pramaggiore (New York: New York University Press, 1996), 3.

44 Sedgwick, *Epistemology*, 11.

45 Du Plessis, "Blatantly Bisexual," 37.

46 Of course, in post-Freudian psychoanalysis this threat was contained by the outright repudiation of bisexuality's existence.

47 Ironically, Fuss ("Inside/Out," 5) points out that "the problem, of course, with the inside/outside rhetoric, if it remains deconstructed, is that such polemics disguise the fact that most of us are both inside and outside at the same time."

48 Edelman, *Homographesis*, xiv; see n. 25 above.

49 Doty, *Making Things Perfectly Queer*, 105–6; see n. 35 above.

50 Ruth Goldman, "Who Is That Queer Queer? Exploring Norms around Sexuality, Race, and Class in Queer Theory," in *Queer Studies: A Lesbian, Gay, Bisexual, and Transgender Anthology*, edited by Brett Beemyn and Mickey Eliason (New York: New York University Press, 1996), 117. At a conference Goldman questioned Doty on bisexuality and says he responded by suggesting that "he wasn't quite sure how to theorize about it in relation to popular culture." Maria Pramaggiore ("Straddling the Screen: Bisexual Spectatorship and Contemporary Narrative Film," in *RePresenting Bisexualities: Subjects and Cultures of Fluid Desires*, edited by Donald E. Hall and Maria Pramaggiore [New York: New York University Press, 1996]) also considers Doty's suggestion "a useful starting point from which to examine contemporary films . . . and to ask whether they invite specifically bisexual readings" (273).

51 Doty, *Making Things Perfectly Queer*, 106 n. 13. Perhaps it is this kind of construction of bisexuality that Edelman thinks simply reinforces the hetero/homosexual binary.

52 Henry Abelove et al., eds., *The Lesbian and Gay Studies Reader*, xv. The reason I have put queer in parentheses is because the editors to this reader consider 'queer' a structuring part of lesbian and gay studies. "Our choice of 'lesbian/gay'," they point out, "indicates no wish on our part to make lesbian/gay studies look less assertive, less unsettling, and less queer than it already does" (xvii).

53 See, e.g., Sedgwick, *Epistemology*, 3.

54 Judith Butler, "Against Proper Objects," *differences* 6, nos. 2 and 3 (1994): 5, 6. Butler suggests that it was an unintentional move, "given that all three have made strong contributions to feminist scholarship" (5).

55 Butler, "Against Proper Objects," 23–24 n. 8, refers to Sedgwick, but only in a footnote.

56 I would argue that there is nothing problematic, per se, about insisting on the partial analytic separability of gender and sexuality, feminism and lesbian/gay studies. Such a

move does not translate into a clean methodological distinction. It seems to me that the editors are fully cognizant of the fact that not only is queer *both* feminism *and* lesbian/gay studies, but that it is also, simultaneously, the force that subjects both to a critique of their founding and structuring assumptions. In this way queer is more usefully seen as a continual movement within, through, and across both feminism and lesbian/gay studies. I think the editors' choice of authors and articles in the *Reader*, and their suggestion that gay/lesbian studies is already queer, reflects this productive contradiction in a way Butler downplays. I would argue, therefore, that the editors are neither intentionally nor unintentionally ascribing *proper objects* to distinct methodologies of feminism versus lesbian/gay studies. Rather, they are attempting to flag the benefits to be gained from a partial analytic separation of gender and sexuality in order to free up the relations between the two and blur the already artificial boundaries between feminism and gay/lesbian studies. It would also seem to me that their insistence on *sex* and *sexuality* as launching points for gay/lesbian/queer studies is a means of foregrounding certain kinds of analyses that may be obscured or even foreclosed by foregrounding gender not only in 'feminism' but *also* in 'gay and lesbian' studies. This aids the queer project of analyzing sexuality in relation (not subordination) to gender and has the potential to bring into the field of vision those sexualities of which gender is not the most, or even *a*, salient feature. Finally, Butler claims that the editors have deployed a Foucauldian notion of sex but repudiated one of the two meanings associated with the term: that is, sex in the sense of gender. I would suggest that Butler overinterprets the Foucauldianness of the editors' use of the category of 'sex'. While they may have conflated 'sex' and 'gender', I would suggest that they are using sex to mean sexual practices, pleasures etc. Sex in the sense of gender is, I suggest, not so much repudiated as it is perhaps suspended. It is that which is the point of commonality between feminism and gay/lesbian studies but which must be suspended in order to analyze *sex* (acts, pleasures, etc.) and *sexuality* as not only or always containable by heteronormative gender. In other words, gender is momentarily suspended in order to set them into productive *relation* with sexuality.

57 Martin, "Sexualities without Genders"; see n. 39 above.

58 Biddy Martin, "Extraordinary Homosexuals and the Fear of Being Ordinary," *differences* 6, nos. 2 and 3 (1994): 101.

59 Martin, "Sexualities without Genders," 106–7.

60 Sedgwick, *Epistemology*, 29.

61 Martin, "Sexualities," 107.

62 Sedgwick, *Epistemology*, 29.

63 Morton ("The Politics of Queer Theory") has also argued that queer theorists have displaced gender with sexuality: "Today, under the pressure of the experiential and pleasure-oriented ludicism of the 1980s and 1990s, the concept of gender has become too 'serious' for the bourgeois subject: in other words, because it smacks too much of *concepts* such as 'the social'/'the economic'/ . . . gender has to be displaced by sexuality" (141). He says this about "Queer Theory in *all* its variants" (my emphasis). While this appears to be true of Sedgwick's analysis, it is certainly problematic to generalize on behalf of all queer theorists. The work of Butler and Teresa de Lauretis, e.g., has always been calibrated by a sophisticated analysis of gender.

64 Sedgwick, *Epistemology*, 30.

65 Sedgwick, *Epistemology*, 86–90, esp. 88.

66 Du Plessis, "Blatantly Bisexual," 33. Butler, in "Against Proper Objects" (24 n. 8), argues along lines similar to du Plessis's.

67 Fuss, "Inside/Out," 5.

68 Stephen Heath, "The Ethics of Sexual Difference," *Discourse* 12, no. 2 (Spring–Summer 1990): 140–41.

69 See, e.g., Catharine MacKinnon, "Marxism, Feminism, Method and the State: An Agenda for Theory," *Signs* 7, no. 3 (1982): 515–44.

70 Fuss, "Inside/Out," 6.

71 While Lacanian influenced theorists such as Fuss might distinguish sexual difference from a more sociological category of gender, I am using gender along lines similar to Judith Butler, whereby she has attempted to construct a theory of gender which retains some of the insights of Lacanian sexual difference whilst also incorporating a transformative notion of gender. See Butler, "Against Proper Objects," 18, 24–25 n. 13. In this way, following Butler, I see the notion of sexual difference as already constituted through a matrix of gender. When I discuss the separation of gender and sexuality in the work of theorists such as Fuss, therefore, I use gender interchangeably with sexual difference.

72 Fuss, "Inside/Out," 5–6.

73 Edelman, *Homographesis*, 10.

74 Butler, "Against Proper Objects," 20. Despite the fact that Butler uses the conjunction "lesbian and gay" in this quote, she does in fact use queer and lesbian and gay interchangeably throughout the essay. In addition to this, the issue of *differences* within which the essay appears is a special issue called "More Gender Trouble: Feminism Meets Queer Theory."

75 Michel Foucault, *The History of Sexuality*, vol. 1: *An Introduction*, translated by Robert Hurley (New York: Vintage Books, 1980), 157. Foucault actually uses the term "sex," however this term encompasses not just sexual practice, pleasure, etc., but also gender. In "Revisiting Bodies and Pleasures" (*Theory, Culture and Society* 16, no. 2 [1999]: 17–18), Judith Butler suggests that because much queer theory has embraced Foucault's call for a break from 'sex-desire' and a rallying instead around the trope of 'bodies and pleasures', what might effectively be installed is the regime of 'sex-desire' as "the 'unconscious' of the time of bodies and pleasures." Not only would this compel "the return of what is repressed," she argues, but it would problematically deprive us "of the critical tools we need in order to read the trace and phantom of heteronormativity in the midst of our imagined transcendence." As I have demonstrated, this indeed seems to be the case with regard to queer deconstructions of sexuality that have disarticulated gender and sexuality seemingly in the name of 'bodies and pleasures'.

76 Fredric Jameson, *The Political Unconscious: Narrative as a Socially Symbolic Act* (Ithaca, N.Y.: Cornell University Press, 1981), 9.

77 Lisa Duggan, "The Discipline Problem: Queer Theory Meets Lesbian and Gay History," in Lisa Duggan and Nan Hunter, *Sex Wars: Sexual Dissent and Political Culture* (New York: Routledge, 1995), 197.

78 The logic of neither/nor also requires analysis, but unfortunately this is beyond the scope of the present study.

79 Clearly, a notion of sexuality not beholden to gender is very different from one that bears the unmistakable and constituting mark of gender. In my view, a notion of sexuality not enmeshed with gender is in fact not sexuality at all (if I am even to accept the terms of our abiding apparatus of sexuality that is), but rather something else entirely different (although of course I would argue that any notion of sexuality is different from that which is designated as 'sexuality'; sexuality in my view is a catachresis). For me, this brings into relief the irresolvable problems associated with any attempt to define a concept of 'sexuality', just as it underlines queer theory's dilemma regarding the analytic subordination of gender to sexuality. In the following chapter I will touch on the catachrestic nature of 'sexuality' and the shortcomings of it as a category of analysis.

80 Du Plessis, "Blatantly Bisexual," 24.

81 In *Bodies*, Judith Butler argues that the distinction of gender and sexuality "needs to be rethought in order to muddle the lines between queer theory and feminism," and to "establish their constitutive interrelationship" (239, 240).

CHAPTER 8

1 Eve Kosofsky Sedgwick, "Bi," at QSTUDY-L@UBVM.cc.buffalo.edu, 17 August 1994.

2 Sigmund Freud, *An Outline of Psycho-Analysis* (1940), in *The Standard Edition of the Complete Psychological Works of Sigmund Freud*, 24 vols., edited by James Strachey (London: Hogarth Press, 1953–1974), 23:188.

3 Sigmund Freud, *Three Essays on the Theory of Sexuality*, SE 7:145.

4 Judith Butler, *Bodies That Matter: On the Discursive Limits of 'Sex'* (New York: Routledge, 1993), 2.

5 She says that "all signification takes place within the orbit of the compulsion to repeat." Judith Butler, *Gender Trouble: Feminism and the Subversion of Identity* (New York: Routledge, 1990), 145.

6 Butler, *Bodies*, 2.

7 Diana Fuss, *Essentially Speaking: Feminism, Nature and Difference* (New York: Routledge, 1989), 103; See also Eve Kosofsky Sedgwick, *Epistemology of the Closet* (Berkeley: University of California Press, 1990), 10; Diana Fuss, "Inside/Out," in *Inside/Out: Lesbian Theories, Gay Theories*, edited by Diana Fuss (New York: Routledge, 1991), 1–10; Butler, *Bodies*, esp. 3.

8 Although part 1 of my genealogy details the construction of sexual identity within psychomedical discourse up until the 1970s, the redefinition of hetero/homosexual structure continues today (as it will, I maintain, as long as we have the categories of hetero- and homosexuality).

9 For Jacqueline Rose (*Sexuality in the Field of Vision* [London: Verso, 1986]), the "unconscious constantly reveals the 'failure' of identity. Because there is no continuity of psychic life, so there is no stability of sexual identity, no position for women (or for men) which is ever simply achieved" (91). This failure, she argues, is interminably reiterated precisely because "there is a resistance to identity at the very heart of psychic life." See also Diana Fuss, *Identification Papers* (New York: Routledge, 1995), chaps. 1, 2.

10 Butler, *Gender Trouble*, 145, 147.

11 Sedgwick, "Bi."

12 Donald E. Hall, "BI-ntroduction II: Epistemologies of the Fence," in *RePresenting Bisexualities: Subjects and Cultures of Fluid Desire*, edited by Donald E. Hall and Maria Pramaggiore (New York: New York University Press, 1996), 11.

13 Lee Edelman, *Homographesis: Essays in Gay Literary and Cultural Theory* (NewYork: Routledge, 1994), xvi.

14 Sedgwick says that "a challenge to the *decisiveness* of gender-of-object-choice as a way of understanding sexuality . . . is well under way, and . . . the rubric most often associated with it is 'queer' not 'bisexual'."

15 It would seem to me that we need more not fewer ways of intervening within this epistemology of sexuality. To thus deny bisexuality any politicotheoretical utility is to close off potential avenues of intervention. Moreover, it must be remembered that no identity is inherently and only subversive or inherently and only oppressive. All sexual identities can therefore function in myriad ways, both oppressively and subversively. It is thus a question not of which identities to use, but how to use (and use up) the identities we have in a manner which suits our various political and theoretical concerns.

16 Despite fifteen years or so of activism, bisexuality is still seriously undertheorized. The cultural ignorance on matters of bisexuality is still an abiding presence. Given this, issues of visibility and representation are crucial.

17 The first phrase is the subtitle of Hall and Pramaggiore's *RePresenting Bisexualities*; the second is the title of a recent collection of essays on bisexuality: *The Bisexual Imaginary: Representation, Identity and Desire*, edited by the BiAcademic Intervention (London: Cassell, 1997).

18 Michel Foucault, "Nietzsche, Genealogy, History," in *The Foucault Reader: An Introduction to Foucault's Thought*, edited by Paul Rabinow (London: Penguin, 1991), 95.

19 In *The Burdens of Intimacy: Psychoanalysis and Victorian Masculinity* (Chicago: University of Chicago Press, 1999), Christopher Lane underscores the important but generally neglected point that history represents not just the construction of sexual meaning but also its failure (225).

20 Jacques Derrida, *Positions*, translated by Alan Bass (Chicago: University of Chicago Press, 1981), 42.

21 Barbara Johnson, *The Wake of Deconstruction* (Cambridge, Mass.: Blackwell, 1994), 29.

22 Of course, as Joan Copjec points out, "closure and totality" are also simultaneously the condition of difference's possibility. See Copjec, *Read My Desire: Lacan against the Historicists* (Cambridge, Mass.: MIT Press, 1994), 60.

23 I am not here making a naive anti-identity argument, as though all identity categories ought to be resisted (as if this is even possible!). I am merely foregrounding the usefulness of deconstruction in attending to the epistemic construction of identity categories, the effects of which are sometimes violent and oppressive. Having said this, however, I *am* implicitly suggesting perhaps that the notion of *sexual* identity is far from necessary in an idealized nonhomophobic and non-heteronormative Western culture in a way that something like a gendered identity might not be. I agree with Allison Weir's suggestion that deconstructive critiques of identity might be sharpened by specifying

normative criteria for distinguishing useful from useless (she says "acceptable" and "unacceptable") forms of identity. See Allison Weir, *Sacrificial Logics: Feminist Theory and the Critique of Identity* (New York: Routledge, 1996), 128–29.

24 Merl Storr, "Postmodern Bisexuality," *Sexualities* 2, no. 3 (1999): 309–25.

25 In part, the reason for this heightened self-reflexivity might be the knowledge of bisexuality's historical (and present) erasure from hegemonic discourses and institutions, and the first-hand experience of many bisexuals of exclusion from gay liberationism and lesbian and gay identity politics. As well as this, as I have mentioned, is the often strong association of bisexuality with postmodern theorizing.

26 Earlier I said that oppositions always reestablish themselves. There I was referring more generally to the idea that because identity is necessarily figured through a repudiation of difference, we will always have binary oppositions. In the case of historically specific oppositions, in this instance the hetero/homosexual opposition, this is not *necessarily* the case. Given that we have not always had the hetero/homosexual opposition, it is more than feasible that there may come a time when it outlives its usefulness.

27 Derrida, *Positions*, 41–42.

28 For a comprehensive overview of recent scientific research into sexuality, see Edward Stein, *The Mismeasure of Desire* (New York: Oxford University Press, 1999). I should also point out that my account of sexology and psychoanalysis is not meant as a comprehensive examination of discourses of sexuality in the twentieth century; only, as I have said, the most dominant discourses. However, alongside these discourses were those of endocrinology, which attempted to provide explanations of sexuality through the action of hormones. My argument about the erasure of bisexuality in the present tense is also relevant to these discourses. See Stephanie H. Kenen, "Who Counts When You're Counting Homosexuals? Hormones and Homosexuality in Mid-Twentieth-Century America," in *Science and Homosexualities*, edited by Vernon A. Rosario (New York: Routledge, 1997), 197–218.

29 In *The Burdens of Intimacy* Christopher Lane indeed suggests that the phrase 'sexual identity' is oxymoronic (229). From a psychoanalytic perspective, he argues that "the desires, acts, and relationships we invoke as elements of our *sexual identity* are never quite the same as the contradictory psychic impulses of which this identity consists. Indeed, the discrepancy between psychic drives and sexuality's social representation undermines the idea that there is a sexual *consistency* across historical periods, cultures, and—perhaps above all—between different subjects" (228).

30 I am aware that textual deconstructions are not in themselves enough necessarily to engender wholesale social and discursive change. Analyses of subjectivity, of the *reception* of discourses of sexuality at the level of individuals and groups, are also essential for transforming ourselves and our epistemological heritage. In other words, the relationship between text and subjectivity must also be taken into account if we are to understand, and thus intervene more fully, in the social effects of discourse, if we are to understand individual and group investments in certain discursive formations. It is here that psychoanalysis has proved indispensable. Having said that, however, I would not suggest that specific deconstructive analyses without psychoanalysis do not produce transformative effects, both individual and social. I think they most certainly can and

do. There is no reason to assume that the transformation of discourse through deconstructive intervention might not alter the relationship between text and subjectivity, although it would be up to psychoanalysis to analyze how this occurs. For an excellent argument of the importance of (Lacanian) psychoanalysis for analyzing the relationship between text and subjectivity and from making criticism socially significant, see Mark Bracher, *Lacan, Discourse, and Social Change: A Psychoanalytic Cultural Criticism* (Ithaca, N.Y.: Cornell University Press, 1993).

31 I am not suggesting that there are not other categories of sexuality that are appropriated by this logical structure of hetero/homosexuality. I am simply suggesting that the (classical) logical structure of this binarism is built in large measure around these three terms. Whether or not these terms themselves exclude others (and they surely do) is another question, and one which is beyond the scope of the present book.

32 Carole Vance cautioned against the uncritical use of the category of sexuality in "Social Construction Theory: Problems in the History of Sexuality," in *Homosexuality, Which Homosexuality? International Conference on Gay and Lesbian Studies*, edited by Dennis Altman et al. (London: GMP, 1989), 21–23.

33 Lane suggests something similar in *Burdens of Intimacy*, 225.

34 Kaja Silverman, *Male Subjectivity at the Margins* (New York: Routledge, 1992), esp. 15–51.

35 Clearly, the task for further research is to open up avenues of analysis for delineating the interrelationships of these 'other' axes.

36 See Steven Angelides, "Queering the Gay Gene Genie," in *History on the Edge: Essays in Memory of John Foster*, edited by Mark Baker (Melbourne: University of Melbourne History Department, 1997), 303–17.

37 Steven Brint argues that "intellectuals appear to have withdrawn from public life." See *In an Age of Experts: The Changing Role of Professionals in Politics and Public Life* (Princeton, N.J.: Princeton University Press, 1994), 210. After the turn of the twentieth century it would seem that this is still the case, if not increasingly so. See also Richard Rorty, *Achieving Our Country: Leftist Thought in Twentieth-Century America* (Cambridge, Mass.: Harvard University Press, 1998). In classical liberal style, Rorty says that "intellectuals are supposed to be aware of, and speak to, issues of social justice" (82). While I am not sure intellectuals "are supposed to . . . speak to . . . issues of social justice," I think it would be highly beneficial if they did.

38 See Angelides, "Queering the Gay Gene Genie." If, as Hamer himself admits, homosexually identified men may not have the purported 'gay gene' while heterosexually identified men may, then quite clearly the 'gay gene' is not 'gay' at all. What is perhaps the greatest irony in all of this is that, in Hamer's terms, the sought after gene would appear, if anything, to be 'bisexual'! Of course, I am not suggesting that the supposed gene is really bisexual, I am just turning Hamer's own terms back on himself. The comment that homosexual men may not have the gene and heterosexual men may have it was made in a television interview screened on the Australian Broadcasting Commission's "Four Corners," March 1994.

39 Dean Hamer and Peter Copeland, *The Science of Desire: The Search for the Gay Gene and the Biology of Human Behavior* (New York: Simon and Schuster, 1994), 146.

40 Dean Hamer et al., "Linkage between Sexual Orientation and Chromosome Xq28 in Males but Not in Females," *Nature Genetics* 11 (November 1995): 249.

41 Simon LeVay, "A Difference in Hypothalamic Structure between Heterosexual and Homosexual Men," *Science* 253 (1991): 1034–37.

42 Stein, *Mismeasure*, 50.

43 Judith Butler, "Gender as Performance: An Interview with Judith Butler," *Radical Philosophy* 67 (Summer 1994): 34.

44 Sedgwick, "Bi"; see n. 1 above.

45 John Malone, *Straight Women/Gay Men: A Special Relationship* (New York: Dial Press, 1980), 165, 167.

46 Slavoj Žižek, *The Ticklish Subject: The Absent Centre of Political Ontology* (London: Verso, 2000), 256.

47 Again, as we know, there are other axes which intersect and give meaning to the hetero/homosexual opposition as this opposition is (re)produced *relationally* in discourse. However, these other axes, take those of race and class, for instance, are not themselves, strictly speaking, defined by gender in the first instance. On another note, deconstructing the hetero/homosexual opposition, as I mentioned earlier, might also be supplemented by psychoanalytic analyses and interventions regarding the relationship of discourse and subjectivity.

48 Hamer, *Science of Desire*, 52–73. The assigning of (homo)sexuality to the subjects of LeVay's study is even more problematic. Examining the brains of the dead, LeVay was not even able to ask his subjects about sexual fantasy, desire, and behavior. Edward Stein, *Mismeasure*, 139, provides a summary of LeVay's 'scientific' technique for presuming and thus assigning the 'sexual orientation' of his subjects: "for women, subjects were all presumed heterosexual; for men with AIDS, subjects were grouped according to membership in risk group for HIV infection as indicated on their medical records; if the patient indicated he had engaged in same-sex activity, then he was presumed to be homosexual; otherwise, he was presumed to be heterosexual. All men who died of causes not related to AIDS were presumed to be heterosexual (as part of their medical records, two of these explicitly denied homosexual activity)"!

49 More important, I think, bisexuality can problematize the association of gender and sexuality without the latter erasing the former, as is often the case in queer theory. This is because the 'bi' in bisexuality both invokes and undermines gender as constitutive of sexual desire. I should also note that the other modes of sexuality I mentioned would also represent significant challenges, but frankly it might be a bit easier for the likes of Hamer or LeVay to digest and thus incorporate bisexuality first; especially given they acknowledge bisexuality's existence.

50 Sedgwick, "Bi." Nan Hunter's legal arguments in relation to the concept of gay marriage in my view provide a useful analogy to my argument about the necessary and destablizing effects of an incorporation of bisexuality within our epistemology of sexuality. In contrast to particular feminist and gay liberation arguments for the total overthrow of the institution of marriage, or the argument that gay marriage is only to buy into oppression, Hunter suggests, and I think correctly, that expanding the definition of marriage to incorporate gay men and lesbians is not merely a victory for advocates of equality. Indeed, to legalize gay marriages "will be to dismantle the legal structure of gender in every marriage." See Lisa Duggan and Nan Hunter, *Sex Wars: Sexual Dissent and Political Culture* (New York: Routledge, 1995), 114.

51 See Angelides, "Queering the Gay Gene Genie"; Gilles Deleuze, *The Deleuze Reader*, edited by Constantin V. Boundas (New York: Columbia University Press, 1993), 39–41, 122–26.

52 It goes without saying of course that typically normative (hetero)sexuality has been represented through negation, as that which it is not; and that which it is not is more often than not homosexuality. The search for normative (hetero)sexuality is thus usually the search for homosexuality.

53 For an excellent Lacanian analysis of how to disarticulate notions of desire, sexuality, and identity, see Tim Dean, *Beyond Sexuality* (Chicago: University of Chicago Press, 2000). Dean wants to depersonalize understandings of sexuality in order to "theorize sexuality outside the realm of individuals—indeed outside the realm of persons" (17). Although Dean writes from a theoretical perspective very different from my own, I share his objective to depersonalize desire. I hope that my approach might also provide a useful (albeit very different) and in some way complementary angle from which to tackle this problem.

54 No doubt many scholars may have problems with such a formulation. I am not so much trying to suggest what the right questions are, just that the wrong questions are being asked. For instance, if, as noted above, supposedly homosexual men may not have the hypothetical gay gene and supposedly heterosexual may have it, then clearly it makes sense to eliminate these identity categories from the equation. It might even be more productive and less problematic (not problem free) to ask, as some researchers have begun asking, for instance, what gives an individual the strength to identify as homosexual in the face of likely social hostility and denigration? Additionally, I would argue that any attempt to account for *sexuality* and *desire* must engage (with) psychoanalysis, and thus with an analysis of fantasy and the unconscious. On this issue, see Tim Dean, "On the Eve of a Queer Future" (*Raritan* 15, no. 1 [1995]: 116–34) and *Beyond Sexuality*; and Lane, *Burdens of Intimacy*.

55 For instance, it is not just genes that are responsible for biological functioning, despite the barrage of media hype that would suggest their omnipotence. Genes are but one relational element in a vast and interacting network of biological elements and functions. So just as genes inevitably interact with these other elements and functions, genetics must also interact with the respective branches of science devoted to particular areas of biological functioning.

BIBLIOGRAPHY

Abelove, Henry. "Critically Queer: Interview with Henry Abelove." *critical inQueeries* 1, no. 1 (1995).

———. "Freud, Male Homosexuality, and the Americans." In *The Lesbian and Gay Studies Reader*, edited by H. Abelove et al. New York: Routledge, 1993.

———. "The Queering of Lesbian/Gay History." *Radical History Review* 62 (1995): 44–57.

Abelove, Henry, et al., eds. *The Lesbian and Gay Studies Reader*. New York: Routledge, 1993.

Adam, Barry D. *The Rise of a Gay and Lesbian Liberation Movement*. Boston: Twayne Publishers, 1987.

Adams, James Eli. *Dandies and Desert Saints: Styles of Victorian Masculinity*. Ithaca, N.Y.: Cornell University Press, 1995.

Aggleton, Peter, ed. *Bisexualities and AIDS: International Perspectives*. London: Taylor & Francis, 1996.

Altman, Dennis. "Forum on Sexual Liberation." *Coming Out in the Seventies*. Sydney: Wild & Woolley, 1979.

———. *Homosexual: Oppression and Liberation*. Ringwood, Vic.: Penguin Books, 1973.

———. *The Homosexualization of America, The Americanization of the Homosexual*. Boston: Beacon Press, 1983.

Angelides, Steven. "Queering the Gay Gene Genie." In *History on the Edge: Essays in Memory of John Foster*, edited by Mark Baker, 303–17. Melbourne: University of Melbourne History Department, 1997.

———. "The Queer Intervention: Sexuality, Identity, and Cultural Politics." *Melbourne Journal of Politics* 22, no. 4 (1994): 66–88.

Arlow, J. "Report: Panel on Perversion: Theoretical and Therapeutic Aspects." *Journal of the American Psychoanalytic Association* 2 (1954): 342–43.

Baker, Karin. "Bisexual Feminist Politics: Because Bisexuality Is Not Enough." In *Closer to Home: Bisexuality and Feminism*, edited by Elizabeth Reba Weise. Seattle: Seal Press, 1992.

Banks, Olive. *Faces of Feminism: A Study of Feminism as a Social Movement*. Oxford: Martin Robertson, 1981.

Barker-Benfield, G. J. "The Spermatic Economy: A Nineteenth-Century View of Sexuality." In *The American Family in Social-Historical Perspective*, 2d ed. Edited by Michael Gordon. New York: St. Martin's Press, 1978.

Bartkowski, Frances. "Epistemic Drift in Foucault." In *Feminism and Foucault*, edited by Irene Diamond and Lee Quinby. Boston: Northeastern University Press, 1988.

Bayer, Ronald. *Homosexuality and American Psychiatry: The Politics of Diagnosis.* Princeton, N.J.: Princeton University Press, 1987.

Beauvoir, Simone de. *The Second Sex.* Harmondsworth: Penguin, 1972.

Beaver, Harold. "Homosexual Signs." *Critical Inquiry* 8 (Autumn 1981): 99–119.

Bennett, Kathleen. "Feminist Bisexuality: A Both/And Option for an Either/Or World." In *Closer to Home: Bisexuality and Feminism*, edited by Elizabeth Reba Weise. Seattle: Seal Press, 1992.

Berg, Charles. "Editorial Survey." In *The Problem of Homosexuality*, edited by Charles Berg and C. Allen. New York: Citadel Press, 1958.

Bergler, Edmund. "Differential Diagnosis between Spurious Homosexuality and Perversion Homosexuality." *Psychiatric Quarterly* 31 (1947): 399–409.

———. "Eight Prerequisites for the Psychoanalytic Treatment of Homosexuality." *Psychoanalytic Review* 31 (1944): 253–86.

———. *Homosexuality: Disease or Way of Life?* New York: Collier Books, 1962.

———. "The Myth of a New National Disease: Homosexuality and the Kinsey Report." *Psychiatric Quarterly* 22 (1948): 66–88.

Bhabha, Homi K. "Are You a Man or a Mouse?" In *Constructing Masculinity*, edited by Maurice Berger et al. New York: Routledge, 1995.

BiAcademic Intervention, ed. *The Bisexual Imaginary: Representation, Identity and Desire.* London: Cassell, 1997.

Bieber, Irving. "Sexual Deviations. I: Introduction." *Comprehensive Textbook of Psychiatry*, edited by A. Freedman and H. Kaplan. Baltimore: Williams & Wilkins, 1967.

———. "Sexual Deviations. II: Homosexuality." *Comprehensive Textbook of Psychiatry*, edited by A. Freedman and H. Kaplan. Baltimore: Williams & Wilkins, 1967.

Bieber, Irving, et al. *Homosexuality: A Psychoanalytic Study of Male Homosexuals.* New York: Basic Books, 1962.

Blasingame, Brenda Marie. "The Roots of Biphobia: Racism and Internalized Heterosexism." In *Closer to Home: Bisexuality and Feminism*, edited by Elizabeth Reba Weise. Seattle: Seal Press, 1992.

Borch-Jacobsen, Mikkel. *The Freudian Subject*, translated by Catherine Porter. Stanford, Calif.: Stanford University Press, 1988.

Bracher, Mark. *Lacan, Discourse, and Social Change: A Psychoanalytic Cultural Criticism.* Ithaca, N.Y.: Cornell University Press, 1993.

Braidotti, Rosi. "Embodiment, Sexual Difference, and the Nomadic Subject." *Hypatia* 8, no. 1 (1993): 1–13.

Brint, Steven. *In an Age of Experts: The Changing Role of Professionals in Politics and Public Life.* Princeton, N.J.: Princeton University Press, 1994.

Bristow, Joseph, and Angelia R. Wilson, eds. *Activating Theory: Lesbian, Gay, Bisexual Politics.* London: Lawrence & Wishart, 1993.

Bryan, Douglas. "Bisexuality." *International Journal of Psycho-Analysis* 11 (1930): 150–66.

Bullough, Vern L. *Science in the Bedroom: A History of Sex Research*. New York: Basic Books, 1994.

Burgmann, Verity. *Power and Protest: Movements for Social Change in Australian Society*. Sydney: Allen & Unwin, 1993.

Butler, Judith. *Bodies That Matter: On the Discursive Limits of 'Sex'*. New York: Routledge, 1993.

———. *Excitable Speech: A Politics of the Performative*. New York: Routledge, 1997.

———. "Gender as Performance: An Interview with Judith Butler." *Radical Philosophy* 67 (Summer 1994): 32–39.

———. *Gender Trouble: Feminism and the Subversion of Identity*. New York: Routledge, 1990.

———. "Introduction: Against Proper Objects." *differences* 6, nos. 2 and 3 (1994): 1–26.

———. "Revisiting Bodies and Pleasures." *Theory, Culture and Society* 16, no. 2 (1999): 17–18.

———. "Sexual Inversions." In *Discourses of Sexuality: From Aristotle to AIDS*, edited by Domna C. Stanton. Ann Arbor: University of Michigan Press, 1992.

Cagle, Chris. "Rough Trade: Sexual Taxonomy in Postwar America." In *RePresenting Bisexualities: Subjects and Cultures of Fluid Desire*, edited by Donald E. Hall and Maria Pramaggiore. New York: New York University Press, 1996.

Cantarella, Eva. *Bisexuality in the Ancient World*, translated by Cormac Ó'Cuilleanáin. New Haven, Conn.: Yale University Press, 1992.

Castel, Robert. "'Problematization' as a Mode of Reading History." In *Foucault and the Writing of History*, edited by Jan Goldstein. Cambridge, Mass.: Blackwell Publishers, 1994.

Chauncey, George. "From Sexual Inversion to Homosexuality: Medicine and the Changing Conceptualization of Female Deviance." *Salmagundi*, nos. 58–59 (Fall 1992–Winter 1983): 114–46.

———. *Gay New York: Gender, Urban Culture, and the Making of the Gay Male World, 1890–1940*. New York: Basic Books, 1994.

Choisy, Maryse. *Sigmund Freud: A New Appraisal*. London: Peter Owen, 1963.

Clark, Don. *Loving Someone Gay*. Millbrae, Calif.: Celestial Arts, 1977.

Clarke, Jocelyn. "Life as a Lesbian." In *The Other Half: Women in Australian Society*, edited by Jan Mercer. Melbourne: Penguin, 1975.

Cohen, Ed. *Talk on the Wilde Side: Toward a Genealogy of a Discourse on Male Sexualities*. New York: Routledge, 1993.

Copjec, Joan. *Read My Desire: Lacan against the Historicists*. Cambridge, Mass.: MIT Press, 1994.

Darwin, Charles. *The Descent of Man, and Selection in Relation to Sex*. New York: Modern Library, 1927.

Däumer, Elizabeth D. "Queer Ethics; or, The Challenge of Bisexuality to Lesbian Ethics." *Hypatia* 7, no. 4 (1992): 91–105.

Davidson, Arnold I. "Sex and the Emergence of Sexuality." *Critical Inquiry* 14 (Autumn 1987): 16–48.

Davis, Russell H. *Freud's Concept of Passivity*. Madison, Wisc: International Universities Press, 1993.

Dean, Carolyne J. "The Productive Hypothesis: Foucault, Gender, and the History of Sexuality." *History and Theory* 33 (1994): 271–96.

Dean, Tim. *Beyond Sexuality*. Chicago: University of Chicago Press, 2000.

———. "On the Eve of a Queer Future." *Raritan* 15, no. 1 (1995): 116–34.

De Lauretis, Teresa. *The Practice of Love: Lesbian Sexuality and Perverse Desire*. Bloomington: Indiana University Press, 1994.

Deleuze, Gilles. *The Deleuze Reader*, edited by Constantin V. Boundas. New York: Columbia University Press, 1993.

D'Emilio, John. "The Homosexual Menace: The Politics of Sexuality in Cold War America." In *Passion and Power: Sexuality and History*, edited by Kathy Peiss et al. Philadelphia: Temple University Press, 1989.

———. *Sexual Politics, Sexual Communities: The Making of a Homosexual Minority in the United States, 1940–1970*. Chicago: University of Chicago Press, 1983.

Derrida, Jacques. *Positions*, translated by Alan Bass. Chicago: University of Chicago Press, 1981.

Diamond, Irene, and Lee Quinby, eds. *Feminism and Foucault: Reflections on Resistance*. Boston: Northeastern University Press, 1988.

Diamond, Tony. "The Search for the Total Man." *Come Out* 1, no. 7 (1970): 17.

Dollimore, Jonathan. "Bisexuality, Heterosexuality, and Wishful Theory." *Textual Practice* 10, no. 3 (1996): 523–39.

———. *Sexual Dissidence: Augustine to Wilde, Freud to Foucault*. Oxford: Clarendon Press, 1991.

Donaldson, Stephen. "The Bisexual Movement's Beginnings in the 1970s: A Personal Retrospective." In *Bisexual Politics: Theories, Queries, and Visions*, edited by Naomi Tucker. New York: Harrington Park Press, 1995.

Doty, Alexander. *Making Things Perfectly Queer: Interpreting Mass Culture*. Minneapolis: University of Minnesota Press, 1993.

Dreger, Alice Domurat. *Hermaphrodites and the Medical Invention of Sex*. Cambridge, Mass.: Harvard University Press, 1988.

Dubbert, Joe L. "Progressivism and the Masculinity Crisis." *Psychoanalytic Review* 61 (1974): 443–55.

Duggan, Lisa. "The Discipline Problem: Queer Theory Meets Lesbian and Gay History." In *Sex Wars: Sexual Dissent and Political Culture*, by Lisa Duggan and Nan Hunter. New York: Routledge, 1995.

———. "Making It Perfectly Queer." *Socialist Review* 22, no. 1 (January–March 1992): 11–31.

Duggan, Lisa, and Nan Hunter. *Sex Wars: Sexual Dissent and Political Culture*. New York: Routledge, 1995.

Du Plessis, Michael. "Blatantly Bisexual; or, Unthinking Queer Theory." In *RePresenting Bisexualities: Subjects and Cultures of Fluid Desire*, edited by Donald E. Hall and Maria Pramaggiore. New York: New York University Press, 1996.

Eadie, Jo. "Activating Bisexuality: Towards a Bi/Sexual Politics." In *Activating Theory: Lesbian, Gay, Bisexual Politics*, edited by Joseph Bristow and Angelia R. Wilson. London: Lawrence & Wishart, 1993.

Edelman, Lee. *Homographesis: Essays in Gay Literary and Cultural Theory*. New York: Routledge, 1993.

Eidelberg, Ludwig, and Edmund Bergler. "Der Mammakomplex des Mannes." *Internationale Zeitschrift fuer Psychoanalyse* 19 (1933): 547–83.

Eisenstein, Hester. *Contemporary Feminist Thought*. London: Allan & Unwin, 1984.

Ellis, Havelock. *Man and Woman: A Study of Human Secondary Sexual Characters*. London: Walter Scott, 1914.

———. *Psychology of Sex: A Manual for Students*. New York: Emerson, 1933.

———. *Studies in the Psychology of Sex*. Vol. 2: *Sexual Inversion*, 3d rev. and enlarged ed. Philadelphia: F. A. Davis Co., 1928.

Ellis, Havelock, and John Addington Symonds. *Sexual Inversion*. London: Wilson & Macmillan, 1897.

Epstein, Steven. "Gay Politics, Ethnic Identity: The Limits of Social Constructionism." In *Unfinished Business: Twenty Years of Socialist Review*, edited by Socialist Review Collectives. New York: Verso, 1991.

Escoffier, Jeffrey, Regina Kunzel, and Molly McGarry. "The Queer Issue: New Visions of America's Lesbian and Gay Past." *Radical History Review* 62 (Spring 1995): 1–6.

Faderman, Lillian. *Surpassing the Love of Men: Romantic Friendship and Love between Women from the Renaissance to the Present*. New York: Morrow, 1981.

Filene, Peter. *Him/Her/Self: Sex Roles in Modern America*. New York: Harcourt Brace Jovanovich, 1975.

Fletcher, John. "Freud and His Uses: Psychoanalysis and Gay Theory." In *Coming On Strong: Gay Politics and Culture*, edited by Simon Shepherd and Mick Wallis. London: Unwin Hyman, 1989.

Ford, Clellan S., and Frank A. Beach. *Patterns of Sexual Behavior*. New York: Harper & Row, 1951.

Foss, Paul. "Gay Liberation in Australia." *William and John* 1, no. 8 (1972): 5–9, 72.

Foucault, Michel. *The Archaeology of Knowledge*, translated by A. M. Sheridan Smith. New York: Routledge, 1991.

———. "The Confession of the Flesh." In *Power/Knowledge: Selected Interviews and Other Writings, 1972–1977*, edited by Colin Gordon. New York: Pantheon Books, 1980.

———. "Critical Theory/Intellectual History." 1983 interview with Gérard Raulet. In *Michel Foucault. Politics, Philosophy, Culture: Interviews and Other Writings, 1977–1984*, edited by Lawrence D. Kritzman. New York: Routledge, 1988.

———. *Discipline and Punish: The Birth of the Prison*, translated by Alan Sheridan. New York: Pantheon, 1977.

———. *The History of Sexuality*. Vol. 1: *An Introduction*, translated by Robert Hurley. New York: Vintage Books, 1980.

———. *The History of Sexuality*. Vol. 2: *The Use of Pleasure*, translated by Robert Hurley. Harmondsworth: Penguin Books, 1987.

———. Introduction to *Herculine Barbin: Being the Recently Discovered Memoirs of a Nineteenth-Century Hermaphrodite*, translated by Richard McDougall. Brighton: Harvester Press, 1980.

———. "Nietzsche, Genealogy, History." *The Foucault Reader*, edited by Paul Rabinow. London: Penguin, 1991.

———. "On Power." Interview with Pierre Boncenne. In *Michel Foucault. Politics, Philosophy, Culture: Interviews and Other Writings, 1977–1984*, edited by L. D. Kritzman. New York: Routledge, 1988.

———. "Power and Sex." Interview with Bernard-Henri Lévy. In *Michel Foucault. Politics, Philosophy, Culture: Interviews and Other Writings, 1977–1984*, edited by L. D. Kritzman. New York: Routledge, 1988.

———. "The Subject and Power." Afterword to *Michel Foucault: Beyond Structuralism and Hermeneutics*, edited by Hubert L. Dreyfus and Paul Rabinow. Chicago: University of Chicago Press, 1983.

———. "Truth and Power." Interview with Alessandro Fontana and Pasquale Pasquino. In *Power/Knowledge: Selected Interviews and Other Writings, 1972–1977*, edited by Colin Gordon. New York: Pantheon Books, 1980.

Fredrickson, George M. *The Black Image in the White Mind: The Debate on Afro-American Character and Destiny, 1817–1914*. Middletown, Conn.: Wesleyan University Press, 1971.

Freud, Sigmund. "Analysis Terminable and Interminable" (1937). In vol. 23 of *The Standard Edition of the Complete Psychological Works of Sigmund Freud*, 24 vols. Edited by James Strachey. London: Hogarth Press, 1953–74. (Hereafter SE).

———. *An Autobiographical Study* (1925). In vol. 21 of SE.

———. "A Child Is Being Beaten" (1919). In vol. 17 of SE.

———. *Civilization and Its Discontents* (1930), translated by Joan Riviere. In vol. 21 of SE.

———. "The Claims of Psycho-Analysis to Scientific Interest" (1913). In vol. 13 of SE.

———. "The Dissolution of the Oedipus Complex" (1924). In vol. 19 of SE.

———. *The Ego and the Id* (1923). In vol. 19 of SE.

———. "Female Sexuality" (1931). In vol. 21 of SE.

———. "Femininity" (1933). In vol. 22 of SE.

———. "From the History of an Infantile Neurosis" (1918). In vol. 17 of SE.

———. "Hysterical Phantasies and Their Relation to Bisexuality" (1908). In vol. 9 of SE.

———. *The Interpretation of Dreams* (1900). In vol. 4 of SE.

———. *Introductory Lectures on Psycho-Analysis* (1916–17). In vols. 15–16 of SE.

———. *New Introductory Lectures on Psycho-Analysis* (1933). In vol. 22 of SE.

———. "On the Universal Tendency to Debasement in the Sphere of Love" (1912). In vol. 11 of SE.

———. *The Origins of Psycho-Analysis: Letters to Wilhelm Fliess, Drafts and Notes: 1887–1902*. London: Imago, 1954.

———. *An Outline of Psycho-Analysis* (1940). In vol. 23 of SE.

———. Preface to Reik's *Ritual: Psycho-Analytic Studies* (1919). In vol. 22 of SE.

———. "The Psychogenesis of a Case of Homosexuality in a Woman" (1920). In vol. 18 of SE.

———. *The Psychopathology of Everyday Life* (1902). In vol. 6 of SE.

———. "The Sexual Aberrations (Three Contributions to the Theory of Sex)." In *The Basic Writings of Sigmund Freud*, edited and translated by A. A. Brill. New York: Modern Library, 1938.

———. "Some Psychical Consequences of the Anatomical Distinction between the Sexes" (1925). In vol. 19 of SE.

———. *Three Essays on the Theory of Sexuality* (1905). In vol. 7 of SE.

———. "Two Encyclopaedia Articles" (1923). In vol. 18 of SE.

———. "Why War?" (1933). In vol. 22 of SE.

Friedland, Lucy, and Liz A. Highleyman. "The Fine Art of Labeling: The Convergence of Anarchism, Feminism, and Bisexuality." In *Bi Any Other Name: Bisexual People Speak Out*, edited by Loraine Hutchins and Lani Kaahumanu. Boston: Alyson Publications, 1991.

Frow, John. "What Was Post-Modernism?" In *Past the Last Post: Theorizing Post-Colonialism and Post-Modernism*, edited by Ian Adam and Helen Tiffin. New York: Harvester Wheatsheaf, 1991.

Frye, Marilyn. *The Politics of Reality: Essays in Feminist Theory*. New York: Crossing Press, 1983.

Fuss, Diana. *Essentially Speaking: Feminism, Nature and Difference*. New York: Routledge, 1989.

———. "Freud's Fallen Woman: Identification, Desire, and 'A Case of Homosexuality in a Woman.'" In *Fear of a Queer Planet: Queer Politics and Social Theory*, edited by Michael Warner. Minneapolis: University of Minnesota Press, 1993.

———. *Identification Papers*. New York: Routledge, 1995.

———. "Inside/Out." In *Inside/Out: Lesbian Theories, Gay Theories*, edited by Diana Fuss. New York: Routledge, 1991.

Gagnon, John H. "Sexuality and Sexual Learning in the Child." In *Sexual Deviance*, edited by John H. Gagnon and William Simon. New York: Harper & Row, 1967.

Gagnon, John H., and William Simon. *Sexual Conduct*. Chicago: Aldine, 1973.

Gallagher, Bob, and Alexander Wilson. "Michel Foucault. An Interview: Sex, Power and the Politics of Identity." *The Advocate*, no. 400, 7 August 1984.

Garber, Marjorie. *Vice Versa: Bisexuality and the Eroticism of Everyday Life*. New York: Simon & Schuster, 1995.

Garelick, Rhonda K. *Rising Star: Dandyism, Gender, and Performance in the Fin-de-Siècle*. Princeton, N.J.: Princeton University Press, 1998.

Gavin, Steve. "Consciousness-Raising Exposes the Orwellian Lies of Sexist Amerika." *Come Out* 2, no.7 (1971): 19.

Gay, Peter, ed. *The Freud Reader*. London: Vintage, 1995.

Gebhard, Paul H. "The Institute." In *Sex Research: Studies from the Kinsey Institute*, edited by Martin S. Weinberg. New York: Oxford University Press, 1976.

Gershman, Harry. "Considerations of Some Aspects of Homosexuality." *American Journal of Psychoanalysis* 13 (1953): 82–83.

———. "Psychopathology of Compulsive Homosexuality." *American Journal of Psychoanalysis* 17 (1957): 58–77.

———. "Some Aspects of Compulsive Homosexuality." *American Journal of Psychoanalysis* 12 (1952): 100–101.

Gilman, Sander. "Black Bodies, White Bodies: Toward an Iconography of Female Sexuality in Late Nineteenth-Century Art, Medicine, and Literature." *Critical Inquiry* 12 (Autumn 1985): 204–42.

———. *Difference and Pathology: Race and Madness*. Ithaca, N.Y.: Cornell University Press, 1985.

Goldman, Ruth. "Who Is That Queer Queer? Exploring Norms around Sexuality, Race, and Class in Queer Theory." In *Queer Studies: A Lesbian, Gay, Bisexual, and Transgender Anthology*, edited by Brett Beemyn and Mickey Eliason. New York: New York University Press, 1996.

Gould, Stephen Jay. *The Mismeasure of Man*. Middlesex: Penguin, 1981.

Greenberg, David F. *The Construction of Homosexuality*. Chicago: University of Chicago Press, 1988.

Grosz, Elizabeth. "The Hetero and the Homo: The Sexual Ethics of Luce Irigaray." *Gay Information*, nos. 17–18 (1988).

———. *Sexual Subversions: Three French Feminists*. Sydney: Allen & Unwin, 1989.

———. "Theorising Corporeality: Bodies, Sexuality and the Feminist Academy." Interview with Wei Leng Kwok and Kaz Ross. *Melbourne Journal of Politics* 22 (1994): 3–29.

Hacking, Ian. *The Social Construction of What?* Cambridge, Mass.: Harvard University Press, 1999.

Haeberle, Erwin J. "Bisexuality: History and Dimensions of a Modern Scientific Problem." In *Bisexualities: The Ideology and Practice of Sexual Contact with Both Men and Women*, edited by Edwin J. Haeberle and Rolf Gindorf. New York: Continuum, 1998.

Hall, Donald E. "BI-ntroduction II: Epistemologies of the Fence." In *RePresenting Bisexualities: Subjects and Cultures of Fluid Desire*, edited by Donald E. Hall and Maria Pramaggiore. New York: New York University Press, 1996.

Halperin, David M. *Saint Foucault: Towards a Gay Hagiography*. New York: Oxford University Press, 1995.

Hamer, Dean, et al. "Linkage between Sexual Orientation and Chromosome Xq28 in Males but Not in Females." *Nature Genetics* 11 (November 1995): 248–56.

Hamer, Dean, and Peter Copeland. *The Science of Desire: The Search for the Gay Gene and the Biology of Human Behavior*. New York: Simon & Schuster, 1994.

Hanson, Ellis. "Technology, Paranoia and the Queer Voice." *Screen* 34, no. 2 (Summer 1993): 137–38.

Hartsock, Nancy. "Foucault on Power: A Theory for Women?" In *Feminism/Postmodernism*, edited by Linda Nicholson. New York: Routledge, 1990.

Heath, Stephen. "The Ethics of Sexual Difference." *Discourse* 12, no. 2 (Spring–Summer 1990): 140–41.

Hekma, Gert. "'A Female Soul in a Male Body': Sexual Inversion as Gender Inversion in Nineteenth-Century Sexology." In *Third Sex, Third Gender: Beyond Sexual Dimorphism in Culture and History*, edited by Gilbert Herdt. New York: Zone Books, 1994.

Hemmings, Clare. "Editors' Roundtable Discussion: The Bisexual Imaginary." In *The Bisexual Imaginary: Representation, Identity and Desire*, edited by BiAcademic Intervention. London: Cassell, 1997.

———. "From Lesbian Nation to Transgender Liberation: A Bisexual Feminist Perspective." *critical inQueeries* 1, no. 2 (1996): 59–82.

———. "Resituating the Bisexual Body." In *Activating Theory: Lesbian, Gay, Bisexual Politics*, edited by Joseph Bristow and Angelia R. Wilson. London: Lawrence & Wishart, 1993.

Hennessey, Rosemary. "Queer Visibility in Commodity Culture." *Cultural Critique*, no. 29 (Winter 1994–95): 31–76.

Herdt, Gilbert. "Introduction: Third Sexes and Third Genders." In *Third Sex, Third Gender: Beyond Sexual Dimorphism in Culture and History*, edited by Gilbert Herdt. New York: Zone Books, 1994.

Hocquenghem, Guy. *Homosexual Desire*, translated by Daniella Dangoon. London: Allison & Busby, 1978.

Hollibaugh, Amber, and Cherrée Moraga. "What We're Rollin Around in Bed With: Sexual Silences in Feminism." In *Desire: The Politics of Sexuality*, edited by Ann Snitow et al. London: Virago, 1984.

Hooker, Evelyn. "The Adjustment of the Male Overt Homosexual." In *The Problem of Homosexuality in Modern Society*, edited by Hendrik M. Ruitenbeek. New York: E. P. Dutton, 1963.

Horney, Karen. *The Neurotic Personality of Our Time*. New York: Norton, 1937.

Hornstra, L. "Homosexuality." *International Journal of Psycho-Analysis* 48 (1966).

Hulbeck, Charles. "Emotional Conflicts in Homosexuality." *American Journal of Psychoanalysis* 8 (1948).

Hunt, Lynn. "Foucault's Subject in *The History of Sexuality*." In *Discourses of Sexuality:*

From Aristotle to AIDS, edited by Domna Stanton. Ann Arbor: University of Michigan Press, 1992.

Irigaray, Luce. *This Sex Which Is Not One*, translated by Catherine Porter. Ithaca, N.Y.: Cornell University Press, 1985.

———. "Women's Exile." *Ideology and Consciousness*, no. 1 (1977).

Irvine, Janice M. *Disorders of Desire: Sex and Gender in Modern American Sexology*. Philadelphia: Temple University Press, 1990.

Jagose, Annamarie. *Queer Theory*. Melbourne: Melbourne University Press, 1996.

James, Christopher. "Denying Complexity: Dismissal and Appropriation of Bisexuality in Queer, Lesbian, and Gay Theory." In *Queer Studies: A Lesbian, Gay, Bisexual, and Transgender Anthology*, edited by Brett Beemyn and Mickey Eliason. New York: New York University Press, 1996.

Jameson, Fredric. *The Political Unconscious: Narrative as a Socially Symbolic Act*. Ithaca, N.Y.: Cornell University Press, 1981.

JanMohamed, Abdul. "Sexuality on/of the Racial Border: Foucault, Wright, and the Articulation of 'Racialized Sexuality'." In *Discourses of Sexuality: From Aristotle to AIDS*, edited by Domna C. Stanton. Ann Arbor: University of Michigan Press, 1992.

Jardine, Alice. *Gynesis: Configurations of Woman and Modernity*. Ithaca, N.Y.: Cornell University Press, 1985.

Jay, Karla, and Allen Young, eds. *Out of the Closets: Voices of Gay Liberation*. New York: Douglas Book Corporation, 1972.

Johnson, Barbara. *The Wake of Deconstruction*. Cambridge, Mass.: Blackwell, 1994.

———. *A World of Difference*. Baltimore: Johns Hopkins University Press, 1987.

Jones, Ernest. *The Life and Work of Sigmund Freud*. Vol. 3: *The Last Phase: 1919 to 1939*. New York: Basic Books, 1957.

Jordanova, Ludmilla. *Sexual Visions: Images of Gender in Science and Medicine between the Eighteenth and Twentieth Centuries*. Madison: University of Wisconsin Press, 1989.

Kameny, Frank E. "Homosexuals as a Minority Group." In *The Other Minorities*, edited by Edward Sagarin. Waltham, Mass.: Xerox College Publishing, 1971.

Kardiner, Abram, et al. "A Methodological Study of Freudian Theory III: Narcissism, Bisexuality and the Dual Instinct Theory." *Journal of Nervous and Mental Disease* 129, no. 3 (September 1959).

Katz. "Smashing Phallic Imperialism." In *Out of the Closets: Voices of Gay Liberation*, edited by Karla Jay and Allen Young. New York: Douglas Book Corporation, 1972.

Katz, Jonathan Ned. *Gay American History: Lesbians and Gay Men in the USA*. New York: Thomas & Crowell, 1976.

———. "The Invention of Heterosexuality." *Socialist Review* 21, no. 1 (1990): 12.

———. *The Invention of Heterosexuality*. New York: Dutton, 1995.

Kenen, Stephanie H. "Who Counts When You're Counting Homosexuals? Hormones and Homosexuality in Mid-Twentieth-Century America." In *Science and Homosexualities*, edited by Vernon A. Rosario. New York: Routledge, 1997.

Kennedy, Hubert C. "The 'Third Sex' Theory of Karl Heinrich Ulrichs." *Journal of Homosexuality* 6, nos. 1/2 (Fall 1980/Winter 1981): 107–8.

Kiernan, James G. "Sexual Perversion and the Whitechapel Murders." *Medical Standard* 4 (1888): 129–30.

Kimmel, Michael S. "Men's Responses to Feminism at the Turn of the Century." *Gender and Society* 1 (1987): 517–30.

Kinsey, Alfred C., et al. *Sexual Behavior in the Human Male*. Philadelphia: Saunders, 1948.

Klein, Melanie. *The Psycho-Analysis of Children*. New York: Delacorte, 1932.

Kofman, Sarah. *The Enigma of Woman: Woman in Freud's Writing*, translated by Catherine Porter. Ithaca, N.Y.: Cornell University Press, 1985.

Koppelman, Andrew. "The Miscegenation Analogy: Sodomy Law as Sex Discrimination." *Yale Law Journal* 98 (November 1988): 145–64.

Krafft-Ebing, Richard von. *Psychopathia Sexualis: A Medico Forensic Study*, translated by Harry E. Wedeck. New York: G. P. Putnam's Sons, 1965.

Kuhn, M. H. "Kinsey's View on Human Behaviour." *Social Problems* 1 (1954): 123.

Laclau, Ernesto. "Politics and the Limits of Modernity." In *Universal Abandon? The Politics of Postmodernism*, edited by Andrew Ross. Minneapolis: University of Minnesota Press, 1989.

Lacquer, Thomas. *Making Sex: Body and Gender from the Greeks to Freud*. Cambridge, Mass.: Harvard University Press, 1990.

Lane, Christopher. *The Burdens of Intimacy: Psychoanalysis and Victorian Masculinity*. Chicago: University of Chicago Press, 1999.

LeVay, Simon. "A Difference in Hypothalamic Structure between Heterosexual and Homosexual Men." *Science* 253 (1991): 1034–37.

Lewes, Kenneth. *The Psychoanalytic Theory of Male Homosexuality*. New York: Simon & Schuster, 1988.

Lydston, G. Frank. *The Diseases of Society*. Philadelphia: Lippincott, 1904.

———. "Sexual Perversion, Satyriasis and Nymphomania." *Medical and Surgical Reporter* 61 (1889).

Mackinnon, Catharine. "Marxism, Feminism, Method and the State: An Agenda for Theory." *Signs* 7, no. 3 (1982): 515–44.

Malinowitz, Harriet. "Queer Theory: Whose Theory?" *Frontiers* 13, no. 2 (1992): 168–84.

Malone, John. *Straight Women/Gay Men: A Special Relationship*. New York: Dial Press, 1980.

Martin, Biddy. "Extraordinary Homosexuals and the Fear of Being Ordinary." *differences* 6, nos. 2 and 3 (1994): 100–125.

———. "Sexualities without Genders and Other Queer Utopias." *diacritics* 24, nos. 2 and 3 (1994): 104–21.

Masson, Jeffrey Moussaieff, ed. *Complete Letters of Sigmund Freud to Wilhelm Fliess, 1887–1904.* Cambridge, Mass.: Harvard University Press, 1985.

Maynard, Mary. "Privilege and Patriarchy: Feminist Thought in the Nineteenth Century." In *Sexuality and Subordination: Interdisciplinary Studies of Gender in the Nineteenth Century*, edited by Susan Mendus and Jane Rendall. New York: Routledge, 1989.

Maynard, Steven. "'Respect Your Elders, Know Your Past': History and the Queer Theorists." *Radical History Review* 75 (1999): 56–78.

McIntosh, Mary. "The Homosexual Role." *Social Problems* 16, no. 3 (Fall 1968); reprinted in *The Making of the Modern Homosexual*, edited by Kenneth Plummer. London: Hutchinson, 1981.

McLaren, Angus. *The Trials of Masculinity: Policing Sexual Boundaries, 1870–1930.* Chicago: University of Chicago Press, 1997.

Megill, Allan. "The Reception of Foucault by Historians." *Journal of the History of Ideas* 48 (1987).

Millett, Kate. *Sexual Politics.* London: Rupert-Hart Davis, 1971.

Mitchell, Juliet. *Psychoanalysis and Feminism.* New York: Vintage Books, 1974.

Money, John. *Gay, Straight, and In-Between: The Sexology of Erotic Orientation.* New York: Oxford University Press, 1988.

———. "Homosexuality: Bipotentiality, Terminology, and History." In *Bisexualities: The Ideology and Practice of Sexual Contact with Both Men and Women*, edited by Erwin J. Haeberle and Rolf Gindorf. New York: Continuum, 1998.

Morton, Donald. "The Politics of Queer Theory in the (Post)Modern Moment." *Genders* 17 (Fall 1993): 121–50.

Mosedale, Susan Sleeth. "Science Corrupted: Victorian Biologists Consider 'the Woman Question.'" *Journal of the History of Biology* 11, no. 1 (Spring 1978): 1–55.

Murray, Stephen O. "The Institutional Elaboration of a Quasi-Ethnic Community." *International Review of Modern Sociology* 9 (July–December 1979): 165–78.

Namaste, Ki. "From Performativity to Interpretation: Toward a Social Semiotic Account of Bisexuality." In *RePresenting Bisexualities: Subjects and Cultures of Fluid Desires*, edited by Donald E. Hall and Maria Pramaggiore. New York: New York University Press, 1996.

———. "The Politics of Inside/Out: Queer Theory, Poststructuralism, and a Sociological Approach to Sexuality." In *Queer Theory/Sociology*, edited by Steven Seidman. Cambridge, Mass.: Blackwell, 1996.

Nealon, Jeffrey T. *Alterity Politics: Ethics and Performative Subjectivity.* Durham, N.C.: Duke University Press, 1998.

Newton, Esther. "The Mythic Mannish Lesbian: Radclyffe Hall and the New Woman." In *Hidden from History: Reclaiming the Gay and Lesbian Past*, edited by Martin Duberman et al. New York: Meridian, 1990.

O'Driscoll, Sally. "Outlaw Readings: Beyond Queer Theory." *Signs* 22, no. 1 (1996): 30–51.

Ovesey, Lionel. "The Homosexual Conflict: An Adaptational Analysis." *Psychiatry* 17 (1954): 243-50.
Owens, Craig. "Outlaws: Gay Men in Feminism." In *Men in Feminism*, edited by Alice Jardine and Paul Smith. New York: Methuen, 1987.
Padgug, Robert. "Sexual Matters: Rethinking Sexuality in History." In *Hidden from History: Reclaiming the Gay and Lesbian Past*, edited by Martin Duberman et al. New York: Meridian, 1990.
Pateman, Carole. *The Sexual Contract*. Cambridge: Polity Press, 1991.
Penn, Donna. "Queer: Theorizing Politics and History." *Radical History Review* 62 (1995): 24-42.
Plummer, Kenneth. *Sexual Stigma: An Interactionist Account*. London: Routledge & Kegan Paul, 1975.
Plumwood, Val. *Feminism and the Mastery of Nature*. New York: Routledge, 1993.
Poe, John. "The Successful Treatment of a 40-Year-Old Passive Homosexual Based on an Adaptational View of Sexual Behavior." *Psychoanalytic Review* 39 (1952): 23-33.
Poovey, Mary. "Feminism and Deconstruction." *Feminist Studies* 14, no. 1 (1988): 52.
———. "In Parenthesis: Immaculate Conception and Feminine Desire." In *Body/Politics: Women and the Discourses of Science*, edited by Mary Jacobus et al. London: Routledge, 1990.
Pramaggiore, Maria. "BI-ntroduction I: Epistemologies of the Fence." In *RePresenting Bisexualities: Subjects and Cultures of Fluid Desire*, edited by Donald E. Hall and Maria Pramaggiore. New York: New York University Press, 1996.
———. "Straddling the Screen: Bisexual Spectatorship and Contemporary Narrative Film." In *RePresenting Bisexualities: Subjects and Cultures of Fluid Desire*, edited by Donald E. Hall and Maria Pramaggiore. New York: New York University Press, 1996.
Rado, Sandor. "A Critical Examination of the Concept of Bisexuality." *Psychosomatic Medicine* 2 (1940): 459-67.
———. *Psychoanalysis of Behavior: Collected Papers*. New York: Grune & Stratton, 1956.
Rendall, Jane, ed. *Equal or Different: Women's Politics, 1800-1914*. London: Basil Blackwell, 1987.
———. *The Origins of Modern Feminism: Women in Britain, France and the United States, 1780-1860*. London: Macmillan, 1985.
Reynolds, Robert. "Postmodernism and Gay/Queer Identities." In *Gay Perspectives II: More Essays in Australian Gay Culture*, edited by Robert Aldrich. Sydney: University of Sydney, Department of Economic History, 1993.
Reynolds, Robert Hugh. *Sexuality, Citizenship and Subjectivity: A Textual History of the Australian Gay Movement, 1970-1974*. Ph.D. thesis, University of Melbourne, 1996.
Rich, Adrienne. "Compulsory Heterosexuality and Lesbian Existence" (1980); reprinted in *The Lesbian and Gay Studies Reader*, edited by Henry Abelove et al. New York: Routledge, 1993.

Richards, Evelleen. "Darwin and the Descent of Woman." In *The Wider Domain of Evolutionary Thought*, edited by D. Oldroyd and I. Langham. Boston: D. Reidel, 1983.

Robbins, Bernard. "Psychological Implications of the Male Homosexual 'Marriage'." *Psychoanalytic Review* 10 (1943): 428–37.

Roof, Judith. *A Lure of Knowledge: Lesbian Sexuality and Theory*. New York: Columbia University Press, 1991.

Rorty, Richard. *Achieving Our Country: Leftist Thought in Twentieth-Century America*. Cambridge, Mass.: Harvard University Press, 1998.

Rose, Jacqueline. "Introduction-II." In *Feminine Sexuality: Jacques Lacan and the école Freudienne*, edited by Juliet Mitchell and Jacqueline Rose. Norton: W. W. Norton, 1982.

———. *Sexuality in the Field of Vision*. London: Verso, 1986.

Roszak, Theodore. *The Making of a Counter Culture: Reflections on the Technocratic Society and Its Youthful Opposition*. London: Faber & Faber, 1970.

Roth, Michael S. Review essay on Michel Foucault. *History and Theory* 27 (1988): 70–80.

Rotundo, E. A. "Body and Soul: Changing Ideals of American Middle Class Manhood, 1770–1920." *Journal of Social History* 16 (1983): 23–38.

Rubin, Gayle. "Sexual Traffic." Interview with Judith Butler, *differences* 6, nos. 2 and 3 (1994): 62–99.

———. "Thinking Sex: Notes for a Radical Theory of the Politics of Sexuality." In *The Lesbian and Gay Studies Reader*, edited by Henry Abelove et al. New York: Routledge, 1993.

Russett, Cynthia Eagle. *Sexual Science: The Victorian Construction of Womanhood*. Cambridge, Mass.: Harvard University Press, 1989.

Rust, Paula C. "Who Are We and Where Do We Go from Here? Conceptualizing Bisexuality." In *Closer to Home: Bisexuality and Feminism*, edited by Elizabeth Reba Weise. Seattle: Seal Press, 1992.

Sayres, Sohnya, et al., eds. *The 60s without Apology*. Minneapolis: University of Minnesota Press, 1984.

Scott, Joan W. "The Evidence of Experience." *Critical Inquiry* 17 (1991): 773–97.

———. "Gender: A Useful Category of Historical Analysis." *American Historical Review* 91 (1986): 1053–75.

Sedgwick, Eve Kosofsky. *Epistemology of the Closet*. Berkeley and Los Angeles: University of California Press, 1990.

———. "Queer Performativity: Henry James's *The Art of the Novel*." *GLQ: A Journal of Lesbian and Gay Studies* 1, no.1 (1993): 1–16.

———. *Tendencies*. Durham, N.C.: Duke University Press, 1993.

Sedgwick, Eve Kosofsky, and Andrew Parker, eds. *Performativity and Performance*. New York: Routledge, 1994.

Sedgwick, Peter. *Psycho Politics: Laing, Foucault, Goffman, Szasz and the Future of Mass Psychiatry*. New York: Harper & Row, 1982.

Segal, Lynne. *Slow Motion: Changing Masculinities, Changing Men*. London: Virago Press, 1990.
———. *Straight Sex: The Politics of Pleasure*. London: Virago Press, 1994.
Seidman, Steven. "Identity Politics in a 'Postmodern' Gay Culture: Some Historical and Conceptual Notes." In *Fear of a Queer Planet: Queer Politics and Social Theory*, edited by Michael Warner. Minneapolis: University of Minnesota Press, 1993.
———, ed. *Queer Theory/Sociology*. Cambridge, Mass.: Blackwell Publishers, 1996.
Shelley, Martha. "Gay Is Good." In *Out of the Closets: Voices of Gay Liberation*, edited by Karla Jay and Allen Young. New York: Douglas Book Corporation, 1972.
Showalter, Elaine. *Sexual Anarchy: Gender and Culture at the Fin de Siècle*. New York: Viking, 1990.
Shuster, Rebecca. "Sexuality as a Continuum: The Bisexual Identity." In *Lesbian Psychologies: Explorations and Challenges*, edited by the Boston Lesbian Psychologies Collective. Urbana: University of Illinois Press, 1987.
Silverman, Kaja. *Male Subjectivity at the Margins*. New York: Routledge, 1992.
Smith-Rosenberg, Carroll. "Discourses of Sexuality and Subjectivity: The New Woman, 1870–1936." In *Hidden from History: Reclaiming the Gay and Lesbian Past*, edited by Martin Duberman et al. New York: Meridian, 1990.
———. "The Female World of Love and Ritual: Relations between Women in Nineteenth-Century America." *Signs* 1 (1975): 1–29.
———. "Sex as Symbol in Victorian Purity: An Ethnohistorical Analysis of Jacksonian America." In *Turning Points: Historical and Sociological Essays on the Family*, edited by John Demos and Sarane Spence Boocock. Chicago: University of Chicago Press, 1978.
Smyth, Cherry. *Lesbians Talk Queer Notions*. London: Scarlet Press, 1991.
Socarides, Charles. "Homosexuality and Medicine." *Journal of the American Medical Association* 212, no. 7 (18 May 1970): 1202.
———. "Homosexuality—Basic Concepts and Psychodynamics." *International Journal of Psychiatry* 10 (1972): 118–25.
———. "A Provisional Theory of Aetiology in Male Homosexuality." *International Journal of Psycho-Analysis* 49 (1968): 27–37.
Somerville, Siobhan. "Scientific Racism and the Emergence of the Homosexual Body." *Journal of the History of Sexuality* 5, no. 2 (1994).
Spurr, Lance. "When Straight Boys Stray." *Melbourne Star Observer*, 11 August 1995.
Stein, Edward. *The Mismeasure of Desire*. New York: Oxford University Press, 1999.
———, ed. *Forms of Desire: Sexual Orientation and the Social Construction Controversy*. New York: Routledge, 1990.
Stekel, Wilhelm. *Bi-Sexual Love*, translated by James S. Van Teslaar. New York: Emerson Books, 1950.
Stepan, Nancy. "Biology and Degeneration: Races and Proper Places." In *Degeneration: The Dark Side of Progress*, edited by J. Edward Chamberlin and Sander Gilman. New York: Columbia University Press, 1985.

———. *The Idea of Race in Science: Great Britain, 1800–1900.* London: Macmillan, 1982.

Storr, Merl. "Postmodern Bisexuality." *Sexualities* 2, no. 3 (1999): 309–25.

———. "The Sexual Reproduction of 'Race': Bisexuality, History and Racialization." In *The Bisexual Imaginary: Representation, Identity and Desire*, edited by BiAcademic Intervention. London: Cassell, 1997.

———, ed. *Bisexuality: A Critical Reader.* New York: Routledge, 1999.

Strout, Cushing. "Ego Psychology and the Historian." *History and Theory* 7 (1968): 281–97.

Sulloway, Frank J. *Freud, Biologist of the Mind: Beyond the Psychoanalytic Legend.* London: Burnett Books, 1979.

Szasz, Thomas S. *The Manufacture of Madness.* New York: Delta Books, 1970.

———. "The Myth of Mental Illness." In *Ideology and Insanity: Essays on the Psychiatric Dehumanization of Man.* London: Calder and Boyars, 1973.

Tait, Lawson. *Diseases of Women.* New York: William Wood & Co., 1879.

Terry, Jennifer. "Theorizing Deviant Historiography." *differences* 3, no. 2 (1991): 55–74.

Thompson, Clara. "Changing Concepts in Psychoanalysis." In *Homosexuality: A Subjective and Objective Investigation*, edited by Charles Berg and A. M. Krich. London: George Allen & Unwin, 1958.

Thompson, Denise. *Flaws in the Social Fabric: Homosexuals and Society in Sydney.* Sydney: Allen & Unwin, 1985.

Thurer, Shari L. *The Myths of Motherhood: How Culture Reinvents the Good Mother.* New York: Houghton Mifflin, 1994.

Tosh, J., and M. Roper. *Manful Assertions: Masculinities in Britain since 1800.* London: Routledge, 1991.

Trumbach, Randolph. "Gender and the Homosexual Role in Modern Western Culture: The 18th and 19th Centuries Compared." In *Homosexuality, Which Homosexuality? Essays from the International Scientific Conference on Lesbian and Gay Studies*, edited by Dennis Altman et al. London: GMP Publishers, 1989.

———. "London's Sodomites: Homosexual Behavior and Western Culture in the 18th Century." *Journal of Social History* 11 (Fall 1977): 1–33.

Tucker, Naomi. "Bay Area Bisexual History: An Interview with David Lourea." In *Bisexual Politics: Theories, Queries, and Visions*, edited by Naomi Tucker. New York: Haworth Press, 1995.

Udis-Kessler, Amanda. "Identity/Politics: Historical Sources of the Bisexual Movement." In *Queer Studies: A Lesbian, Gay, Bisexual, and Transgender Anthology*, edited by Brett Beemyn and Mickey Eliason. New York: New York University Press, 1996.

———. "Present Tense: Biphobia as a Crisis of Meaning." In *Bi Any Other Name: Bisexual People Speak Out*, edited by Loraine Hutchins and Lani Kaahumanu. Boston: Alyson Publications, 1991.

Ulrichs, Karl Heinrich. *The Riddle of "Man-Manly" Love: The Pioneering Work on Male Homosexuality*, vol. 1. Translated by Michael A. Lombardi-Nash. New York: Prometheus Books, 1994.

Vance, Carole. "Social Construction Theory: Problems in the History of Sexuality." In *Homosexuality, Which Homosexuality? International Conference on Gay and Lesbian Studies*, edited by Dennis Altman et al. London: GMP, 1989.

Vidal, Gore. "Bisexual Politics." In *The New Gay Liberation Book*, edited by Len Richmond and Gary Noguera. San Francisco: Ramparts Press, 1979.

Walton, Jean. "Re-Placing Race in (White) Psychoanalytic Discourse: Founding Narratives of Feminism." *Critical Inquiry* 21 (Summer 1995): 775–804.

Warner, Michael. "Homo-Narcissism; or Heterosexuality." In *Engendering Men: The Question of Male Feminist Criticism*, edited by Joseph A. Boone and Michael Cadden. New York: Routledge, 1990.

———. "Introduction: Fear of a Queer Planet." *Social Text* 29 (1991): 3–17.

———, ed. *Fear of a Queer Planet: Queer Politics and Social Theory*. Minneapolis: University of Minnesota Press, 1993.

Watney, Simon. "The Ideology of GLF." *Homosexuality: Power and Politics*, edited by the Gay Left Collective. London: Allison & Busby, 1980.

Watson, Lex. "Looking Back over Five Gay Years." *Gay Liberation Newsletter*, Melbourne. September 1975.

Weeks, Jeffrey. *Against Nature: Essays on History, Sexuality and Identity*. London: Rivers Oram Press, 1991.

———. *Coming Out: Homosexual Politics in Britain from the Nineteenth Century to the Present*. London: Quartet Books, 1990.

———. Introduction to the 1993 printing of *Homosexual: Oppression and Liberation*, edited by Dennis Altman. New York: New York University Press, 1993.

———. *Sex, Politics and Society: The Regulation of Sexuality since 1880*. London: Longman, 1981.

———. *Sexuality and Its Discontents: Meanings, Myths and Modern Sexualities*. London: Routledge, 1985.

Weinberg, Martin S., et al. *Dual Attraction: Understanding Bisexuality*. Oxford: Oxford University Press, 1994.

Weir, Allison. *Sacrificial Logics: Feminist Theory and the Critique of Identity*. New York: Routledge, 1996.

Weiss, Frederick A. "Discussion." *American Journal of Psychoanalysis* 17 (1957).

Wiedeman, George. "Symposium on Homosexuality." *International Journal of Psycho-Analysis* 45 (1964): 215.

Wilkinson, Sue. "Bisexuality 'A La Mode'." *Women's Studies International Forum* 19, no. 3 (1996): 293–301.

Williamson, Joel. *New People: Miscegenation and Mulattos in the United States*. New York: Free Press, 1980.

Young, Stacey. "Dichotomies and Displacement: Bisexuality in Queer Theory and Politics." In *Playing with Fire: Queer Politics, Queer Theories*, edited by Shane Phelan. New York: Routledge, 1997.

Žižek, Slavoj. *The Ticklish Subject: The Absent Centre of Political Ontology*. London: Verso, 2000.

INDEX

Abelove, Henry, 75, 210 n. 17
Allen, Grant, 31
Altman, Dennis: on bisexuality, 122–23, 127; on gay liberation, 109, 124, 125, 127; on homosexual minority, 133; on liberationist politics, 123, 234 n. 51; on psychiatry and homosexuality, 116; radical Freudianism and, 118; on sexualization of society, 134
American Psychiatric Association, 94
Anderson, Jim, 121
antipsychiatry, 108–15

Bartkowski, Frances, 152
Bayer, Ronald, 111, 114
Beach, F. A., 85, 111, 112–13
Beard, George, 37
Bergler, Edmund: on bisexuality, 93, 101; on bisexuality as psychology, 86–88, 101; on homosexual cure, 95, 97; on Kinsey, 87–89, 229 n. 61; theory of female homosexuality, 92; theory of male homosexuality, 89–92
Bhabha, Homi, 27
Bieber, Irving: on bisexuality, 95, 101; on heterosexuality, 231 n. 95; on homosexual cure, 95; on Kinsey, 230 n. 88; theory of female homosexuality, 97; theory of male homosexuality, 94–98
binary logic of identity, 192, 197, 213 n. 49; bisexuality and, 15–16; deconstruction and, 14. *See also* hetero/homosexual binary
bisexuality: as bipotentiality, 112–13, 216 n. 41; as chic, 119, 120; deconstruction and, 160–61; endocrinology and, 254 n. 28; erasure of, 16–17, 125–28, 194, 209 n. 4, 213 n. 51, 254 n. 28; and gender and sexuality, 188–89, 256 n. 49; impotence model of, 4–5, 253 n. 15; performativity and, 10, 13; political uses of, 195–96, 200, 201–6, 253 n. 15; psychoanalytic rejection of, 79–80, 83–84, 232 n. 115; as psychology, 82; sexology and, 32–35, 38, 40–43, 71; as third term, 15–16, 102, 161, 187–88, 191–92, 193, 194, 198–99, 200
Blasingame, Brenda Marie, 128
Borch-Jacobsen, Mikkel, 58
Braidotti, Rosi, 145
Brint, Steven, 255 n. 37
Brown, Michael, 109
Bryan, Douglas, 102, 224 n. 80
Burgmann, Verity, 128
Butler, Judith: on Foucault, 156–57, 241 n. 42, 244 n. 92, 245 n. 106; on Freud, 66, 68; on gender parody, 167–68; on identity, 169, 202; on performativity, 192; on proper objects, 76, 136; on queer theory and feminism, 181, 185, 249 nn. 54, 56, 251 n. 75, 252 n. 81; on subversive repetition, 193

Cagle, Chris, 7
Campbell, Harry, 31
Cantarella, Eva, 12
Chauncey, George, 7, 37, 40
Chevalier, Julien, 41–42
Clark, Don, 121
Clarke, Jocelyn, 129
Cope, Edward Drinker, 30, 33
Copjec, Joan, 253 n. 22
crisis of identity, 193

Darwin, Charles, 29–30, 31, 32, 34, 51
Daümer, Elizabeth, 4–5
Davidson, Arnold, 38
Dean, Carolyne J., 243 n. 75
Dean, Tim, 257 n. 53
deconstruction, 3–4, 11, 253 n. 23, 254 n. 30; and bisexuality, 15–16, 197–206; and hetero/homosexual binary, 196–97; and psychoanalysis, 254 n. 30; and queer theory, 7–9. *See also* binary logic of identity
deconstructive history. *See* queer history
D'Emilio, John, 109
Derrida, Jacques, 198

[277]

Dessoir, Max, 42
Diamond, Tony, 121
Dollimore, Jonathan, 14, 210 n. 16
Doty, Alexander, 179, 249 n. 50
Duggan, Lisa, 8, 165, 187
du Plessis, Michael, 5, 16–17, 175, 183, 189, 209 n. 6, 248 n. 41

Eadie, Jo, 12
economy of (hetero)sexuality, 23–24, 41, 68, 102, 131, 160–61, 186–87, 188–89
Edelman, Lee: and bisexual erasure, 178–79; on gay identity, 169; on gender and sexuality, 185–86; and hetero/homosexual binary, 177–79, 194
Eidelberg, Ludwig, 87
Ellis, Havelock: and bisexuality, 42, 45, 46–48, 71; and evolutionary theory, 44–46; on female homosexuality, 39; on homosexuality, 39; on race, 44–46; on sex and gender, 43–46; on sexology, 40
Epstein, Stephen, 132, 139
evolutionary theory: and bisexuality, 32–35, 38, 40–43. *See also* sexual science

feminism: nineteenth-century, 28–29, 35; science on, 29–31
Fletcher, John, 50
Fliess, Wilhelm, 51, 52, 53, 221 n. 15
Ford, C. S., 85, 111, 112–13
Foss, Paul, 127
Foucault, Michel, 36, 77, 132–61, 227 n. 22; activism and anti-identity and, 146–50, 156–59, 196, 241 n. 37, 242 n. 65; on biopower, 143–45, 146, 153; on bodies and pleasures, 149, 157; critique of, 151–61; on deployment of sexuality, 142, 146, 153–54, 156, 160; on freedom and liberation, 146–50, 242 n. 67; on history and genealogy, 11, 12, 150, 196; on power and resistance, 147–48, 151–52, 158, 242 nn. 67, 68; on problematization, 11, 145; on the repressive hypothesis, 145; on *scientia sexualis*, 142–44, 146; on sex and selfhood, 2, 3, 132, 141–42, 155–56, 244 n. 90; on sexuality as an object of discourse, 142–44; on subjectification, 144, 147–48
Freud, Sigmund, 49–70; on biology and evolutionary theory, 51–54, 61–62, 224 n. 80; on biology vs. psychoanalysis, 52–54, 60–61, 63–64, 65, 221 n. 20; on bisexuality, 51–54, 58, 60–63, 66–68, 71–72, 191, 220 n. 4, 222 n. 30, 243 n. 82; on castration and penis envy, 55–57, 61; on etiology of sexuality, 59, 76, 227 n. 27; on female sexuality, 55; on heterosexuality, 61–62; on homosexuality, 56–57, 61–62, 74–75, 76, 103, 191; on identification and desire, 58–68; on masculine and feminine dispositions, 57–59, 62; on neurosis vs. perversion, 86; on Oedipus complex, 54–58, 60–62, 75; on phylogeny, 59–60; on repression, 54–55, 221 n. 18
Fromm, Erich, 83
Frow, John, 134
Frye, Marilyn, 134
Fuss, Diana: and bisexual erasure, 174–77; and gender and sexuality, 184–86; and hetero/homosexual binary, 7, 163, 168, 174–77, 249 n. 47; on identity, 14, 158–59, 168, 193, 249 n. 47

Gagnon, John H., 136–38
Gallagher, Bob, 149
Gallop, Jane, 169
Garber, Marjorie: on bisexuality, 2, 11, 12, 210 n. 8, 211 n. 22; on bisexuality as deconstructive, 3–4, 198, 209 n. 7; on Freudian bisexuality, 53, 66–67; on Kinsey and bisexuality, 103
Gavin, Steve, 125
gay and lesbian history, 15; bisexuality and, 6–8; and hetero/homosexual binary, 15; and queer theory, 8–10
gay gene, 202, 255 n. 38, 257 nn. 54, 55. *See also* Hamer, Dean
gay liberation, 108–31; and antipsychiatry, 116; and bisexual erasure, 125–28, 130; and bisexuality/bipotentiality, 112–13, 117–18, 119–24; and coming out, 115, 127–28; and consciousness-raising, 115, 125, 129; elitism in, 126, 130; on gay identity, 125; and gay pride, 115; globalization and, 115–19; on human nature, 117–18; on humansexual, 121–22; radical Freudianism and, 120, 235 n. 64; sexism and, 124, 126, 129–30
Gershman, Harry, 83, 94, 100
Gilman, Sander, 31
Goldman, Ruth, 179, 249 n. 50
Grosz, Elizabeth, 25

Hacking, Ian, 211 n. 29
Haeberle, Erwin, 7, 211 n. 22
Hall, Donald, 4, 194
Hall, Ralph, 126

Hall, Stanley, 33
Halperin, David, 149
Hamer, Dean, 202, 203, 204, 255 n. 38
Hanisch, Carol, 236 n. 86
Hanson, Ellis, 171
Harvey, David, 134
Heath, Stephen, 184
Herculine Barbin, 157
Herdt, Gilbert, 34
hermaphroditism, 32–33, 216 n. 43. *See also* bisexuality
hetero/homosexual binary, 10–11, 194–95, 200–201, 204–5, 256 n. 47; and bisexuality, 11, 15–16, 24, 160–61, 194; constructionism and, 7; queer theory and, 7, 9. *See also* binary logic of identity
heterosexuality. *See* economy of (hetero)sexuality; sexuality
Hocquenghem, Guy, 69, 123–24, 127, 134–35
homophile groups, 233 n. 26
homosexuality: adaptational theory of, 77–82; childrearing and motherhood and, 85–86, 96; Cold War and, 72–73; crisis of, 87, 89; cure for, 84, 90, 95, 97; as ethnic identity, 133–35; neurotic theory of, 83–84, 86, 94, 96, 100; pathologization of, 72; preoedipal theories of sexuality, 75, 78, 81, 84, 90; as proper object, 75, 76–77, 81–82, 89, 97; sexological theory of, 41–43; as third sex, 36–40
Hooker, Evelyn, 111–13, 233 n. 22
Horney, Karen, 94
Hulbeck, Charles, 83
Hunt, Lynn, 153–54
Hunter, Nan, 256 n. 50
Huschke, E., 31

Irigaray, Luce, 25–28, 92, 245 n. 99

Jagose, Annamarie, 115, 167
Jameson, Fredric, 187
JanMohamed, Abdul, 153
Jardine, Alice, 39
Jones, Ernest, 74

Kardiner, Abram, 94
Karush, Aaron, 94
Katz, Jonathan Ned, 213 n. 48, 240 n. 35
Kiernan, James G., 41
Kinsey, Alfred, 95; on bipotentiality, 112–13; on bisexuality, 112–13, 233 n. 24; on hetero- and homosexuality, 110–11; on the normal vs. the pathological, 107–8, 110; *Sexual Behavior in the Human Male* (the Kinsey report), 84–85, 88–89, 95, 119, 228 n. 45
Klein, Melanie, 78, 86–87
Kovalevsky, Aleksandr, 32
Krafft-Ebing, Richard von, 36–37, 42, 46–47, 218 n. 60
Kuhn, M. H., 136

labeling theory. *See* social constructionism
Laclau, Ernesto, 247
Lane, Christopher, 158, 253 n. 19, 254 n. 29
Laqueur, Thomas, 26–27
Lesbian and Gay Studies Reader, The, 180–81, 249 n. 52
lesbian separatism, 133–34
LeVay, Simon, 202, 203, 204, 256 n. 48
Lewes, Kenneth, 78, 82, 88, 92, 95
Lourea, David, 120
Lydston, G. Frank, 41

Malone, John, 203
Martin, Biddy, 181–83
Martin, Bob, 127
masculine identity: crisis of, 23, 25, 35–36, 37, 39–40; theorization of, 25–28
McIntosh, Mary, 135–36, 138–39, 140
Mead, Margaret, 119
Megill, Allan, 150
Millett, Kate, 119, 235 n. 60
Milne, Bob, 109
Mitchell, Juliet, 64–65, 67
Moll, Albert, 40, 42
monogenism, 215 n. 24
Morton, Donald, 246 n. 9, 250 n. 63

Namaste, Ki, 246 n. 3
New Women, 35

oral theories of sexuality. *See* homosexuality; psychoanalysis
Ovesey, Lionel, 84, 94, 102, 117

Pateman, Carole, 244 n. 87
phallogocentrism, 25–28, 214 n. 9, 245 n. 99
Plummer, Kenneth, 137
Plumwood, Val, 14
Poe, John, 83–84
polygenism, 215 n. 24
Poovey, Mary, 11
postmodernism, 166–67, 247 n. 15

poststructuralism, 166–67, 200. *See also* deconstruction
Pramaggiore, Maria, 173
psychiatry. *See* psychoanalysis
psychoanalysis: and homophobia, 73; post-Freudian, 72–103; preoedipal theories of sexuality, 75, 78, 81, 84, 90, 94; sexuality and, 257 n. 54. *See also* Freud, Sigmund
public intellectuals, 201, 255 n. 37

queer history, 6–12, 24–25
queer identity: definitions of, 163–65, 246 n. 4; history of, 164–65
queer theory, 162–89; and binary logic, 175–77, 188; and critique of identity, 165–66, 167–68, 245 n. 1; deconstruction and bisexual erasure in, 7–9, 171–80, 186–88; and feminism, 180–86; and Foucault, 180, 186; and gay and lesbian history, 187–88; and hetero/homosexual binary, 15, 163, 168, 171–80; separating gender and sexuality, 180–86, 188–89, 249 n. 56; and sexuality, 169–70

race, 31–32. *See also* sexual science
radicalesbians, 122, 129
radical Freudianism, 116, 118. *See also* gay liberation
Rado, Sandor, 77–82; on bisexuality, 78–80, 221 n. 9; on evolution and sexuality, 227 n. 30; on Freud, 81, 225 n. 105; on homosexuality, 80–81
Rank, Otto, 74
Reynolds, Robert H., 117–18, 121, 124, 125–26, 128, 235 n. 54
Rich, Adrienne, 133–34
Richards, Evelleen, 215 n. 22
Robbins, Bernard, 83
Roberts, Steven, 108
Romanes, George J., 30
Rorty, Richard, 255 n. 37
Rose, Jacqueline, 67, 252 n. 9
Roth, Michael S., 242 n. 67
Rubin, Gayle, 24, 169, 181
Russett, Cynthia, 28, 29, 31

Scott, Joan, 14
Sedgwick, Eve Kosofsky: and bisexual erasure, 172–74; on bisexuality, 4, 193–94, 203, 204; on epistemology of the closet, 23, 24, 170–71, 173–74; on gender and sexuality, 169–70, 182–83; and hetero/homosexual binary, 23, 24, 168, 172–74; on performativity and bisexuality, 10, 11, 190
Sedgwick, Peter, 113
Segal, Lynne, 72, 85, 116
Seidman, Steven, 118, 140, 168, 240 n. 31
sexology, 38–43, 71
sexual dimorphism, 26–27, 34–35
sexual identity: crisis of, 77, 82, 102–3. *See also* deconstruction; hetero/homosexual binary
sexuality: as catachresis, 196, 199, 200, 206, 252 n. 79; Cold War and, 72–73; genetics and molecular biology on, 201–7; invention of, 37–43; psychoanalytic theories of, 72–103; as trinary structure, 15–16, 73, 102, 160–61. *See also* hetero/homosexual binary; homosexuality
sexual science, 29–34, 44–46
Shainess, Natalie, 119
Shelley, Martha, 117, 127
Silverman, Kaja, 201
Silverstolpe, Frederick, 152
Simon, William, 136–38
Sitka, Chris, 130
Smith-Rosenberg, Carroll, 37
Socarides, Charles, 98–100, 119
social constructionism, 135–41; and bisexual erasure, 6–9, 139–41; and hetero/homosexual binary, 139–40, 240 n. 31; history of, 136–41, 239 n. 14; and history writing, 6–10; on homosexuality, 138–39; and theory of sexuality, 137–38. *See also* Foucault, Michel; gay and lesbian history
Somerville, Siobhan, 32
Spencer, Herbert, 30, 31
Sperling, Melitta, 85–86
Spurr, Lance, 50, 69
Stein, Edward, 141, 202
Stekel, Wilhelm, 77–78, 102, 227 n. 23
Storr, Merl, 13, 197
Strout, Cushing, 231 n. 111
Sulloway, Frank, 43, 51, 222 n. 30
symbolic interactionism. *See* social constructionism
Szasz, Thomas, 113–14

Tait, Lawson, 33
Thompson, Clara, 94
Thompson, Denise, 118
Trumbach, Randolph, 36, 152, 243 n. 82

Udis-Kessler, Amanda, 5, 12, 213 n. 51
Ulrichs, Karl Heinrich, 36, 46